AF539596

INTERVIEWS WITH ARTISTS

1966-2012

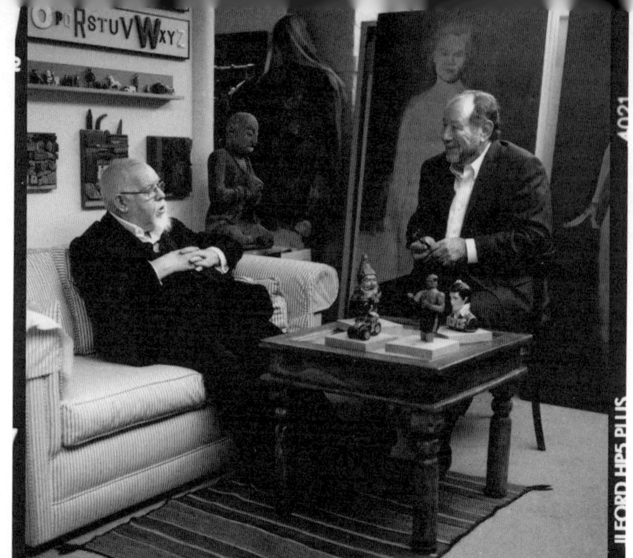
4021
ILFORD HP5 PLUS

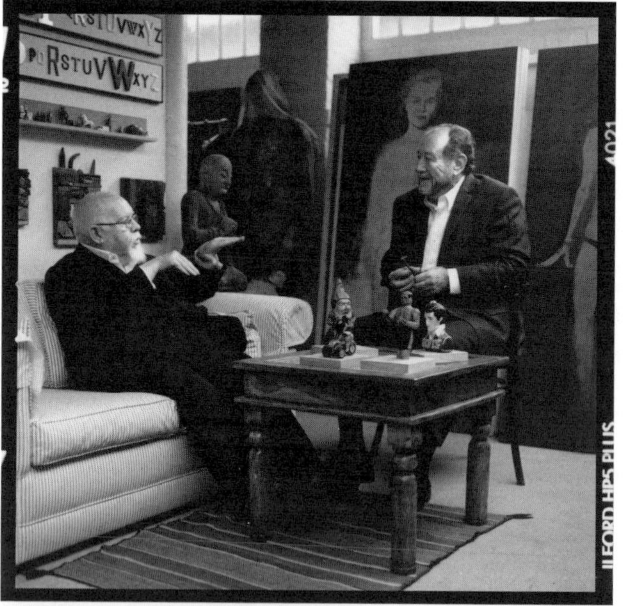
4021
ILFORD HP5 PLUS

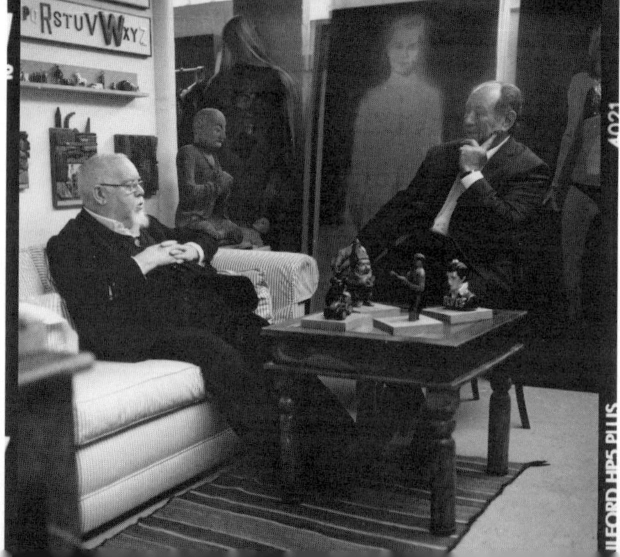
4021
ILFORD HP5 PLUS

INTERVIEWS WITH ARTISTS

1966–2012

MICHAEL PEPPIATT

YALE UNIVERSITY PRESS NEW HAVEN AND LONDON

CONTENTS

THREE PHOTOGRAPHERS

EUROPEAN ARTISTS

INTRODUCTION

I have always thought that if you can get the artist to talk directly about his or her work, you are likely to find out more, more rapidly and more memorably, than if you try to write about it yourself or read the opinions of other critics and commentators. In this particular domain, the artists are of course the horse's mouth: they and they alone know out of what strange brew of thought and fantasy their images have risen and how they have been cajoled and crafted into existence. If not the most objective judges of their own achievement, they are the greatest experts on what happened, both imaginatively and technically, in the studio.

No sooner has this been said than alarm bells ring and caveats resound. 'Never believe what artists say, only what they do', David Hockney once cautioned, apparently quoting Sickert (though I suspect he may have been quoting himself). As an unusually articulate, prolific apologist, Hockney clearly knows whereof he speaks; and to an extent he is demonstrably right here. Artists have always used interviews and statements to shape the way the public views them and their work, even if they are barely conscious of wishing to project a certain 'image'. Thus some tend to obfuscate obvious influences on their creative development: Francis Bacon was past master at this,[1] and several other artists interviewed in the following pages are at pains to hide or gloss over their sources and even their motives as they work. Others make barely disguised, self-aggrandizing claims. Henry Moore regularly suggested kinship with Michelangelo and Rodin by comparing his views and working methods with theirs ('We all know Michelangelo had studio assistants, we all know Rodin had studio assistants'[2]), thus implicitly positioning himself as their direct heir. Others still allude to arcane knowledge – of esoteric religions, Byzantine perspective, quantum physics – informing their imagery, which subsequently assumes all manner of beguiling, but not necessarily valid, implications. When a *peintre savant* such as Antoni Tàpies talked, the range of reference that came into play, from the Veda to Pythagoras or medieval Catalan poetry, subtly infused his every calligraphic swirl of paint with hidden meaning.

Some artists are especially gifted at talking about what they do, sometimes to the extent that their verbal prowess acts in counterpoint to what they create. Jean Dubuffet comes to mind here. As Dubuffet spoke about his art and about creativity in general, it is as though he were testing and refining his own pictorial inventiveness as well as the coherence of the extreme, combative positions he had taken up. When Peter Blake gives an interview, his replies are to the point and not particularly discursive, yet there is a strain of humour throughout his conversation that constantly illuminates his pictures, like a witty, extended caption.

But as one talks one's way more and more widely around the art world Hockney's warning against taking artists at their word becomes increasingly worth heeding. Certain artists promote themselves and their work so plausibly, providing seamless explanations to questions that have not even been asked, that one quickly ends up admiring their presentational skills more than their art. (There will be no naming of names here; suffice it to say they have not met the criteria for inclusion in the present anthology.) One should add in all fairness that if the artist is occasionally as volubly overwhelming as a PR pro, the interviewer is sometimes dismally underprepared, with scant knowledge of the artist's work and a tell-tale tendency to fall back on lame, one-size-fits-all questions like 'Do you always do preparatory drawings – or do you sometimes go "straight in"?' and 'Have you got several works on the go at the moment?'.

At the other extreme, in my experience of doing interviews, there are equally gifted and sincere artists for whom talking about their work is a torture or an impossibility, and often both. For them, all the meaning and the explanation has already been transmitted through the paint and the plaster, through chisel and pencil point. Even Bacon, a notably suave expositor of artistic praxis, insisted that painting was its own, tightly sealed language; and that if a picture could be explained, there would be no point in making it. Balthus completely agreed and refused, more out of dandyish disdain than any specific conviction, to be drawn into a genuine discussion of his work. However, the artist who found talking about painting most difficult – almost physically painful – was a man who had survived far more life-threatening torture in Dachau. Out of innate courtesy, Zoran Music accepted interviews even though he knew he would suffer in the process, not because he lacked things to say but because painting was the only medium through which he could express the near-inexpressible horror of the concentration camp.

So while we should indeed be on our guard as to what artists say, comparing it (as with politicians) with what they actually do, interviews – what artsts say and the way they say it – remain the best introduction to their world. Thereafter an especially perceptive critic might deepen or expand the insights an artist has already given by placing the work, say, in a comparative or historical context. But the artist's words – however big the pinch of salt that should accompany them – retain a gospel-like authority. One has only to think of how influential Delacroix's 'Diary' or Van Gogh's 'Letters' remain as sources of information and opinion about those artists' respective work, lives and times. Of all the texts that exist on Giacometti's art, from writers as brilliant and diverse as Sartre and Genet, Dupin and Bonnefoy, none has the insight and power of the interviews that Giacometti gave in abundance in the latter part of his career. The artist not the commentator takes us to the heart of the matter. Who would not, to put it in a nutshell, give all Vasari for a short, searching conversation with Michelangelo?

*

The earliest interview in the selection that follows dates from 1966, the latest from 2012, and they bracket my own career as an art critic to date. That first interview, with Balthus, took place in the splendidly vaulted, frescoed rooms that he occupied at that time as director of the Villa Medici in Rome; the two most recent, with Claes Oldenburg, in the faded grandeur of the Ritz hotel in Madrid, and with Bill Jacklin, in a friend's apartment in Greenwich Village. Many of those that intervene took place in Paris, for the simple reason that I lived and worked there from 1966 onwards for nearly three decades. As a result, there is a pronounced Gallic or certainly European slant to the artists included here. Had I not lived in Paris, I would probably never have talked to Brassaï or Dubuffet, Sonia Delaunay or Cartier-Bresson, Diego Giacometti or Pierre Soulages. On the other hand, since I was commissioned by both French and international publications,[3] many of the interviews took place outside France, from places as different as Copenhagen and Copacabana beach, a Venetian palazzo on the Grand Canal and a studio overlooking the southernmost tip of Sicily.

Since I had already made my connection with the School of London artists – notably with Bacon, Freud, Auerbach and Kitaj – before leaving London for Paris, there is also a marked English or at least 'London' bias. A number of these interviews have been grouped accordingly under the 'School of London' banner here; and in the opening two, Auerbach and Kitaj, actually discuss their reactions to the whole notion of this 'school', with Auerbach commenting that he thought a certain 'rivalry' had united them for a time – a notion that had not occurred to me when I was curating exhibitions of their work and which I now find very credible and revealing.[4]

Under the 'School of London' rubric come several younger artists, all of whom I interviewed to provide a catalogue preface to a show of their work. The two other main categories in the texts that follow are 'Studio Visits' – descriptive vignettes with substantial quotes – and 'European Artists', which are either straight question-and-answer pieces or interviews that I turned into 'monologues' or direct statements from the artists. Finally, since I was lucky enough to interview some of the great architects and photographers of our time, two shorter sections have been devoted to them.

The most successful interviews in this book all share a good dollop of luck. As in many encounters, there is only a degree to which both people, interviewer and interviewee, can prepare. The rest depends on timing (a good or bad day at home or in the studio) and a flow of sympathy which cannot be rehearsed. Often, I found, a particular interview would begin in a matter-of-fact, fairly unpromising way, then suddenly accelerate if both parties seemed on their toes and a definition of an image or a technique seemed within reach. At that point the interview became not only part of the artist's critical arsenal; it actually helped settle some pertinent questions about the whys and wherefores of his daily battle in the studio – or helped open up a new line of inquiry. With Auerbach, with whom I have done half a dozen interviews over the years, talking is an art that runs parallel to his painting; and each time we finished a long session, he pruned his vivid, elegant responses down so radically I suspected that, left alone, he would have scraped all the words off the paper and begun again; yet what remains seems to me to illuminate his paintings and his daily working methods brilliantly.

With Bacon, all my interviews were fairly epic, usually accompanied by quantities of fine wine, yet the results were surprisingly cogent, and apart from the odd repetition there was very little to change or edit between the recording and the transcript. Although he became more and more loquacious in drink, Bacon could switch effortlessly into interview mode and make every word count. For him, in any case, talking was a means of exploring the nature of painting and what he himself sought to achieve, and the lure of dissecting and defining every shift of meaning never dimmed. Not all artists responded positively to being interviewed. Bacon himself would affect ignorance or dismay that we were 'doing something' rather than just being out on the town. Balthus and Diego Giacometti both played cat and mouse with me, repeatedly complaining there was nothing to say about themselves or their art; I slipped easily enough into the role of mouse thirty or forty years ago and eventually I got their interest. César proved perfectly willing to talk, but he also talked to everybody else in sight, as though he were perpetually at the bar of a café, and before I'd got my 'story' he had given me the slip a dozen times and disappeared into other chance conversations. Kitaj was very professional but his well-argued points of view never sounded as spontaneous as I should have liked. I did manage to capture the spontaneity of Soulages, a big, cordial man from Rodez with a voice to match, but our exchange was edited down to sound more like an artist's statement and – since everyone reading such interviews instinctively conjures up the artist's physical presence – I think it remains poorer as a result. However, re-reading it today I find it has stood the test of time (over three decades) remarkably well, which the earlier, more colourful version with the 'voice' might not have done.

*

Very roughly, these interviews reflect my personal interests and tastes in art, at least to the extent that I avoided interviewing an artist whose work antagonized me or left me cold (and there have been, over the years, a fair number of those). On the other hand, I cannot pretend that they reflect an absolute ideal, since with some of the artists I should have liked most to interview the opportunity never for one reason or another arose. So there is, as in most things in life, a certain haphazardness in the result. Similarly, most of the interviews were done to order for a wide range of newspapers and magazines, so that the spirit, the tone and the length often changed radically according to the publication that commissioned them. On gathering them together and rereading them I have found some – notably certain 'Studio Visits' – a good deal more breezy or impressionistic than I should have liked, and others now come across as too overtly linked to specific events, such as retrospectives at home or significant first shows abroad, that no doubt had their importance then but have now shrunk into a sobering insignificance. Tempting though it sometimes was, I have avoided cutting or editing such shortcomings and excrescences in the belief that it was better to keep them *dans leur jus*, as the French say, or as we might put it more brutally, with 'warts 'n' all'. Each interview belongs to its own period, after all, and none of them was ever conducted with the idea that it would one day be hauled out of the past and republished in book form.

At the same time, many of these interviews represented a milestone in my life, to the extent that together they constitute a kind of weird, patchy but exalting autobiography. I remember vividly the circumstances and the atmosphere in which they took place, and even the oddities that characterized them. Thus, while I sat in state with Balthus in the Villa Medici's domed dining room, served by attendants in livery and white gloves, I ate fish with my fingers in the port at Sète with Soulages, then went back to the translucent summer house he and his wife had designed overlooking the Mediterranean. To get to Henry Moore, I remember plunging down tiny leaf-covered lanes, like dark green tunnels, with my mother, who lived in the nearby village of Stocking Pelham, nervously negotiating the overhanging branches that threatened to decapitate our old family car. The interviews with Tàpies began solemnly in an august private library (now part of the Tàpies Foundation) in a discreet residential area of Barcelona then ended uproariously with much wine and strange-looking shellfish in a Galician bistro downtown. My talks with Sean Scully got under way in New York, London and Munich, but they did not come into focus and get recorded until we were cut off by snow in a Bavarian farmhouse that he and his girlfriend had taken as their principal hideout. I can't dissociate my conversations with Ida Barbarigo from her magnificent marble halls, filled with her and her forebears' paintings, on the first floor of a palazzo overlooking the Grand Canal in Venice. She and her husband, Zoran Music, became close friends of mine, so our interviews were enriched by scores of evenings spent in their Paris or Venetian homes. With Brassaï I walked through the night streets of Paris that he had photographed so memorably between the wars, and with Cartier-Bresson, who also became a good friend, I first travelled by train from Paris to Mannheim for an exhibition opening, and we chatted and laughed together like two overage schoolboys on a trip abroad.

I could go on and describe how I played highly competitive games of ping-pong with Sean Scully between interviews, or had to wade through waist-high waters in Venice to talk to Ida Barbarigo and Zoran Music; or how Hans Hartung, with whom I was immediately in tune, slapped me so hard on the back while he was telling a joke that I fell to the floor. Oscar Niemeyer drew flowing dream buildings across huge sheets of paper while we talked, then made me a present of them all, just as Arikha, Mason and Dado did portraits of me that I still have today. Talking of Dado, It would be tempting to go on and describe how he lived perpetually on the edge of disaster in his half-ruined, haunted farmhouse in the Véxin, or evoke the melancholy desolation surrounding Guccione's studio perched on the Sicilian coast, at the very end of the world. ('*È Africa*, this is Africa,' his Neapolitan-born dealer, Sandro Manzo, mournfully intoned as we drove there over endless arid landscapes). But these are anecdotes, mere memory flash and retrieved sensation. If I had talked this much each time I hauled out notebook and set up tape-recorder, I would never have managed to get a single interview. Step aside now, garrulous critic, and let the artists speak!

---

1 In his Paris studio Bacon kept a fine, brass-bound sea chest that was always locked. As in London he had photographs and books strewn about the room, but it never became clear what was in the chest, which (unlike the rest of the furniture) disappeared back to London when he stopped living and working in Paris. I have often fantasized that his real working documents and sources were squirreled away in that locked chest.

2 The refrain was always Michelangelo, Rodin and, by implication, Moore; and it was said in a somewhat impatient, aggrieved way as if the hierarchy were self-evident.

3 They included *Réalités*, *Le Monde* and *Connaissance des Arts* in France, and the *Sunday Times*, the *Financial Times*, the *New York Times*, *Art International*, *Architectural Digest* and *Art News* abroad.

4 Although the interview is not included here because it had been frequently published, I also interviewed Francis Bacon about the 'School of London'. He began by rejecting the notion out of hand, then bit by bit came round to it, even venturing opinions that suggested he believed in it: for instance, he likened Helen Lessore's activity as the 'School of London' artists' first dealer to the role Ambrose Vollard had played for the Impressionists.

NOTE TO THE READER:

Some of the interviews that follow required new introductions to update and put them into context. All such additions appear in italic typeface. The remaining interviews have been reprinted exactly as they were, with their original introductions in roman like the rest of the text.

SCHOOL OF LONDON ARTISTS

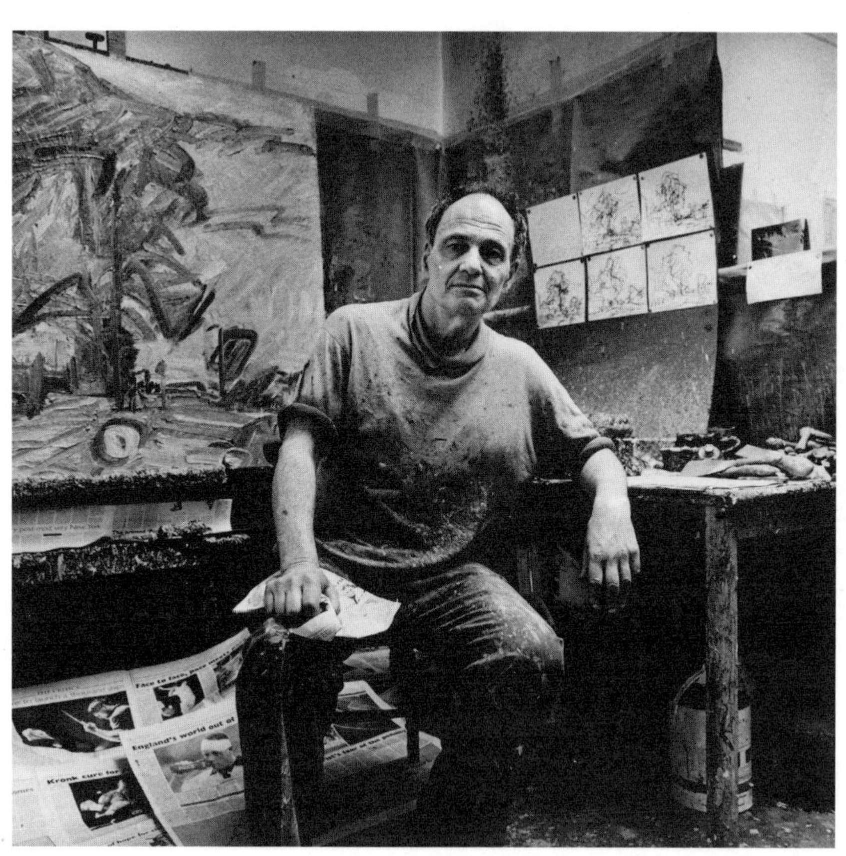
England's world out of
Kronk cure for

FRANK AUERBACH

CAMDEN TOWN LONDON 1998

The first interview I did with Frank Auerbach dates back to 1963; I did another in 1987 and a third in 1998. Slow though the momentum had been, I realized how much I enjoyed talking to the artist and thought we might continue until we had enough material for a small book. Auerbach agreed to be interviewed further, commenting – a litte ruefully, I suspect, given his demanding routine – that it had become 'something of a tradition between us'. We recorded several more sessions, all in Auerbach's small, paint-encrusted studio, then edited them vigorously via an almost daily exchange of letters until two new interviews, each more complete than anything we had done before, were ready.

Auerbach nevertheless felt 'uneasy' about the idea of publishing all our talks in a single volume, suggesting that we put the latest interviews 'on ice' until a suitable occasion, such as a big exhibition catalogue, came along. Carefully preserved now for well over a decade, these two unpublished documents gave signficant impetus to the idea of publishing the present selection of my interviews with artists.

MP What do you think of the suggestion that there is a School of London – and that you belong to it?

FA All I can say is that this concept was imposed on a number of painters. But it was not initiated by any of them. I don't think Kitaj, who thought up the name, meant it to apply to a specific group, he simply said there was a School of London as there had been a School of New York and a School of Paris. Every single title that has been applied to painters in order to classify them has been a joke title. Artists have never donned a uniform and said we're this or that, except in very provincial situations.

Unpublished interview with Frank Auerbach (1931–).
London, June 1998.

MP I'm curious to know how much fellow-feeling there was amongst the figurative painters showing at the Beaux-Arts Gallery during the 1950s. I mean, you and Leon Kossoff were close friends, and you saw Lucian Freud and Francis Bacon there quite often …

FA Yes, all that. Francis had a show there, Lucian almost did, and they used to visit the gallery. I think the situation of people who are, as it were, in the same ambience is very much like that of a political party, where the tensions between them are greater than they are with those in another party. If people have a programme in this country, they tend to keep it to themselves.

MP But you felt closer to those painters?

FA I did feel closer to them, because I saw them more often. I saw Leon a lot in those days. Mike Andrews I saw, more rarely, he was always very private, but I loved and admired both him and his work. And I saw Lucian and Francis in Soho frequently. So you could say we were in contact throughout the fifties and sixties.

MP In contact with those painters rather than with others?

FA Yes, although it wasn't exclusive. I didn't particularly think whether my friends were painters or not. It wasn't like that. Painters don't form themselves into groups and confront other bands.

MP But there was a sympathy and an admiration between you?

FA Maybe. But I think a better way of putting this would be that there was a certain rivalry between us. Not for ignoble reasons. When one's young, one's tremendously aware of everything that's going on and of anybody who is doing something exciting. One is affected by the scale of the effort, by the commitment, by the sharpness of the critical faculty …

MP So the rivalry came through admiration?

FA Exactly. But nobody thought there was a group going on, and we didn't do that thing, except possibly to some extent with Leon and me, that Picasso and Braque were supposed to have done of going to each other's studios then rushing back to try to take their own pictures further.

MP That happened between you and Leon?

FA I think it did for some years. We saw each other very frequently, and we saw each other's work as it was being produced and – I can't speak for Leon – but I was excited by what he was doing and felt that it was worth emulating the quality, if not the idiom, of the way of painting. We used to go over to each other's studios right through the fifties and into the sixties, until the Beaux-Arts Gallery closed down. Then I think we became more private, as one does as one gets older and more mature and more …

MP Oneself?

FA Yes, I think once one has discovered and defined, willy-nilly, the sort of person one is, then the battle becomes almost entirely one's own. One hopes to be stimulated by quality, but it's at least as likely to be by pictures in the National Gallery as by something remarkable being done while one lives.

MP Did you use to go to Francis's studio or to Lucian's?

FA I did use to go to Francis's studio because he lived opposite the framer's I used. If I was early, I would ring Francis around half-past seven and have a cup of tea with him and a chat. I sometimes saw things he had done. He once asked me for an opinion, which I gave him; I wouldn't have done so unasked. And he was pretty touchy. I made, in the most tentative way, a comment about what I felt about the painting, which was a triptych, and I said: 'Do you want them to look like three cones?', because for me there was something uncomfortable about the way all the figures tapered towards the top. And he was pretty miffed. But he did change the painting. And of course Lucian has been a friend for a very long time …

MP Were there any dinners after the openings at the Beaux-Arts?

FA Not at the Beaux-Arts Gallery, but in Soho Mike would meet Francis and Lucian and me, and Lucian would see Francis and Mike and me, and so on. But Leon hardly ever went to have a drink in Soho, and I think I was the only person of the four of us to see Leon regularly.

MP So that's the School of London, such as it is. But it goes on, at least as a tag.

FA People love putting painters in categories and perhaps these people are not all that categorizable. And if you want to find common traits, you will have to find them.

MP And what part did Helen Lessore play?

FA Helen's generosity and the absolute integrity with which she ran the gallery – her personal qualities – were greatly valued, but I don't think anybody always took her seriously as an arbiter of art.

MP Did she come across your work at Bomberg's classes?

FA No, she did go to Bomberg's class but she didn't like what she saw there. She actually started the gallery about two years before I had any contact with her. She was in touch with the Slade, because she had been there, but she started showing Jack Smith and Bratby and Middleditch, all of whom were Royal College students. Then she went to an exhibition of students who were leaving the college, and she liked the work of five painters – Joe Tilson, Anthony Whishaw, Michael Pope, Keith Cunningham and myself – and she wrote to each of us saying that she'd like to have a picture in her summer show. Then I got a job in a secondary technical school and, with some difficulty, finished a number of pictures in the evenings, and another gallery offered me an exhibition. I was in a pretty desperate situation, teaching three days a week and without enough money for colour and so on, so I wrote to Helen to say, perhaps I should let you know that this gallery has approached me, and she came to the studio and I showed her the work and she said, almost tearfully, 'but *I* like it'. And she bought about six pictures for £60 and said: 'No serious gallery will give you a show that quickly'. This was in October 1954, and she gave me a show the following January, and there was modest interest, modest sales, but from then on I stayed with her gallery. And I think all this is illustrative of her generosity and impulsiveness and the warmth of her response. I think she sometimes showed people because she was sympathetic to their difficulties. She never showed people because they were smart or might be fashionable.

MP Or saleable?

FA Yes, nothing like that!

MP And you introduced her to Leon?

FA I said there is this very good painter called Leon Kossoff, and she was resistant until Leon came in to her gallery with a drawing. Then she went to see him, and she was convinced by the person and the work, and very soon she began to show him. I think Jeffery Camp took in a Euan Uglow and put it in her sitting room so as to persuade her, and Mike Andrews had said Jeffery Camp was good and again she let time elapse so as not to respond right away to what anyone was saying. And Mike Andrews had been at the Slade, and he showed at the Beaux-Arts before I did.

MP And later, did Helen arrange for some of her artists to go to the Marlborough?

FA When she closed, she had absolutely no money, but she did, I think, persuade the Marlborough to show Craigie Aitchison, Leon Kossoff, Mike Andrews and myself. These were the people the Marlborough was prepared to accept. But what she really wanted was to go back to her own work, although the habit of helping artists never really left her.

MP I was wondering whether you had ever done a self-portrait.

FA I've finished two self-portrait drawings, Kitaj has one, I don't know where the other is, and I did a self-portrait painting very early on that Leon Kossoff has, but I never regarded it as a particular success. I've made attempts since then, but they haven't worked. I miss the stimulus of another person being there and, when I go round the side to see what the mass is like, if I'm doing a self-portrait, so does the subject in the mirror, so I never actually get round the side. It's a bit like working from a photograph, which I also find very difficult. You have to have a very particular sort of imagination to do that. Michelangelo said that painting is best when it's most like sculpture, and sculpture is best when it's least like painting. I like to get a very strong sense that I'm dealing with matter that is displacing space.

MP What makes you want to go on doing a particular model?

FA There are not many people who have got the commitment to sit week in week out reliably and put up with someone who often behaves ridiculously. It's hard work and disrupts their timetable, and I'm enormously grateful that I have these present five people sitting. I go on so long and the paintings take so long to finish that by the time I've finished one picture, there's already something different, geometrically different, about the sitter. As people age, they change shape. So immediately a picture has been done, I realize there's something about the sitter that I have not caught. And then something that starts as a sitting figure goes on as a head, or I turn a canvas sideways, and the colours change, the pose changes. I mean, I never do that thing of saying: 'Could you please take up this or that pose.' So it's not just that I think I could paint them in a different way: different aspects of them appear. While I'm painting the one picture, the subject for the next one is queuing up. And so I go on. The possibilities increase, and I realize how fortunate I am to have people with the courage and the stamina to put up with the whole process, which must seem endless to them.

MP Is it a temptation to try and encapsulate something of those future possibilities into the painting you're doing?

FA I don't visualize a finished picture. What I see seems to be composed of lines and accents, which means that you get the scaffolding of the form and not quite the form. And then I think 'I would like to do that head again, but without the accents'. That's a very serious technical point: many of the greatest paintings of Manet and Whistler and Velázquez are done without. I never seem to be able to do this, or to do it any more, so I am very conscious of trying – this seems to me to be the grandest way of painting – to paint by juxtaposing one area of colour against another, and hoping that that will make the form. But sometimes even Matisse had to make a scaffolding, Picasso had to make a scaffolding. It's more common than not.

MP I'm less aware of scaffolding in some of your earlier pictures.

FA That may well be the case. One does what one can. I feel very much as though I'm sleepwalking when I paint. There are things I don't want to do and things I do want to do, and I hardly articulate them – unless I'm provoked by you. And I wander on in that way. One gets impatient with what one's done. If the things have been too big, one wants to do something small. Or if the small things have become too manageable, one wants to do something unmanageably large.

MP Would it be a fair guess to say that you want to do something more ambitious, and in order to get there you use the scaffolding?

FA No. One works. And occasionally one feels one has totally forgotten how to paint – I suspect I am not the only one to have this sensation – and then a mark may happen at any time that reminds one what it's like to paint, and one tries to do the thing with the energy at one's disposal before the feeling goes. And what happens on those occasions is that in the impatience and urgency of doing this I find myself making certain marks. It's what's happened to me rather than what I mean to do, it's what's happened to me in the thrill of the chase, with the quarry in sight. I've done my best, I've forgotten myself, and this is how it has come out. I have to accept it. One thing I should perhaps stress is that the paintings are a total surprise to me. I've no idea what they're going to look like, and the thrill is not only that they seem to work but that they are totally unforeseen. I look at the paintings with the same detachment and surprise, although perhaps with a greater degree of speculative interest, as any other person. This is not the picture I intended to do. This is the picture that seems to have happened at a moment when I felt I had some sort of command over my material and some sort of inventive way of putting it down.

MP A way of trapping?

FA Yes. Trapping it. And you realize that when this happens, it's a very fraught business because if you let yourself off the hook and stop twenty seconds too soon it won't be any good and you'll have to scrape it off again. So it's a rather extreme situation.

MP It's a hair's-breadth thing.

FA Absolutely a hair's-breadth thing and a question of going on beyond any reasonable point in taking risks. And I may say this in my own defence: it's bound to seem less risk-taking for other people – that's to say, the small audience that's interested in painting – because they've become slightly used to my handwriting and idiom, which was once surprising, and whatever else I can change I can't, anymore than anyone else, change my handwriting.

MP When you have this surprise of a picture coming off, can you paint the next day?

FA Oh yes, because I've always got about eight things on the go. And that's terribly good because they feed each other. You make a discovery that you can't use in one painting, and it gives you an idea for another one, and sometimes if you're obsessed with one picture you think of it when you're painting another – in that way people think of their girlfriends when they're supposed to be with their wives.

MP You still feel you have to destroy a lot?

FA When you say destroy, it sounds melodramatic. I just scrape it down because that's the way I work. Because I can't get the living entity unless everything in the picture is in reaction to everything else. That's my idiom. And I've tried to proceed in a more measured way, and it's just bored me to tears. And there are very good painters whose work seems to me to be admirable who work in a different way. In Mike Andrews' late paintings, which I found very moving, you can see that he proceeded with enormous discrimination, and although it was unfinished, his last picture looks as though one perfect operation was superimposed on another perfect operation, that he thought ahead to such an extent, that the picture grew, as it were, with foresight as part of its development. I don't mean he didn't change his pictures all the time while he worked, but he didn't repaint his pictures from top to bottom. In my case, what you see on the canvas is the result of the last bout, almost entirely. There may be a few canvases where I have made a little adjustment, for say five minutes, a week or so later. There are good painters who don't work like that, and there are good painters who do work like that. De Kooning actually had an irrational feeling that the paint would rot unless it was one continuous coat of wet paint, and I suspect that many late Picassos are the result of one final session, although he made his transformations so quickly that it may have been one session in which twenty images paraded across the canvas before he stopped.

MP Is it a completely different experience when you paint landscapes rather than people?

FA It's become less so, particularly because I now do these daily drawings so that I come in with memories of the real thing. It is different in that I'm totally uninhibited and can carry on in any way that I like.

MP What does that entail, Frank?

FA Well, firstly that I'm working slightly more at my own pace, and I can go on as long as I like. And of course it just feels different when you're in a room by yourself. And when sitters are here, I have to be careful not to splash them with paint and that kind of thing. On the other hand, because one can do the landscapes at any time, there's not quite the urgency as when someone comes once a week.

MP The landscapes don't get up and walk away.

FA That's right. Though you'd be surprised how much landscapes change. You'd be surprised how often buildings are torn down and scaffolding goes up and so on. If you took a slow-motion film of London, it would seem like a boiling cauldron. I mean, sometimes I have put a steeple into a picture after the steeple had been pulled down, and so on. I'm making it seem that I'm totally a slave to the subject. I am in a sense. Unless I believe the picture to be true, that it feels like the subject, I can't leave it. But 'feeling like the subject' entails all sorts of inventions.

MP You seem to want to do things that are as everyday and ordinary as possible. I wonder what it would be like if you were obliged to paint nothing but a sunset.

FA A sunset I should find very difficult, because to me the magic is in the tangible. The sea would be better, because I could draw it. And if you asked me to paint Venus arising from the sea, I think now I'd have to have someone pose for Venus and some sea pose for the sea, and I think I would still feel at the end that it was rather camp. I'm so conscious of the evanescence of experience, so conscious of the fact that everything we do, everybody we know, is carried along on a tide of time and will disappear, that I do have a strong sense of wanting to pin experience down before it disappears. I find it more exciting. And it's what I admire in other people's painting as well. In the very best de Koonings and Hoffmanns and Pollocks there is such a sense of a particular moment that will never recur, of something rescued from the flood of time. I know Mary McCarthy said, referring to that phrase of Rosenberg's, 'you can't hang an action on the wall'.

Well, on the contrary, it's exactly what you can do. There's a moment of Velázquez, there's a moment of Manet, and so on.

MP Do you still go to the National Gallery as regularly?

FA Far less than I used to. One of the things that happens is that as soon as you enunciate something, you get fed up with it. I thought: they're beginning to categorize me. When I had that show there, I thought perhaps I've had enough of the National Gallery and that something more organic and less museum-like would do me good. But I still go, although I'm very conscious that I have less energy and it takes so long to get across London.

MP You must have extraordinary energy to keep up the daily battle with your pictures.

FA Well, for me it's very exciting. The reason I work in the way I do, and not the way other artists work, is that it's the very opposite of boredom. It's a little bit like being on the stage. When I was sixteen, I thought how marvellous it would be to spend all one's life in a room with paint and brushes and move the colours around, and it still seems exciting to me. There's a real stimulus. I don't say there's as much as riding a horse over the jumps, but it's exciting.

MP So that when you start, you're 'on'. You don't think of it as a rehearsal?

FA I don't want it to be a rehearsal. I want it to be the real thing. But it usually turns out to be a rehearsal. I always have this ridiculous idea that one day I might be able to pick up the brush and by some miracle paint the picture and then go and spend the afternoon in the Ritz. But it has never in all these years worked that way. So it is very much a rehearsal. There are certain things one learns, certain connections one senses, certain things that were difficult that become second nature. So in this way the performance accrues. And then, if one's lucky, it transcends itself.

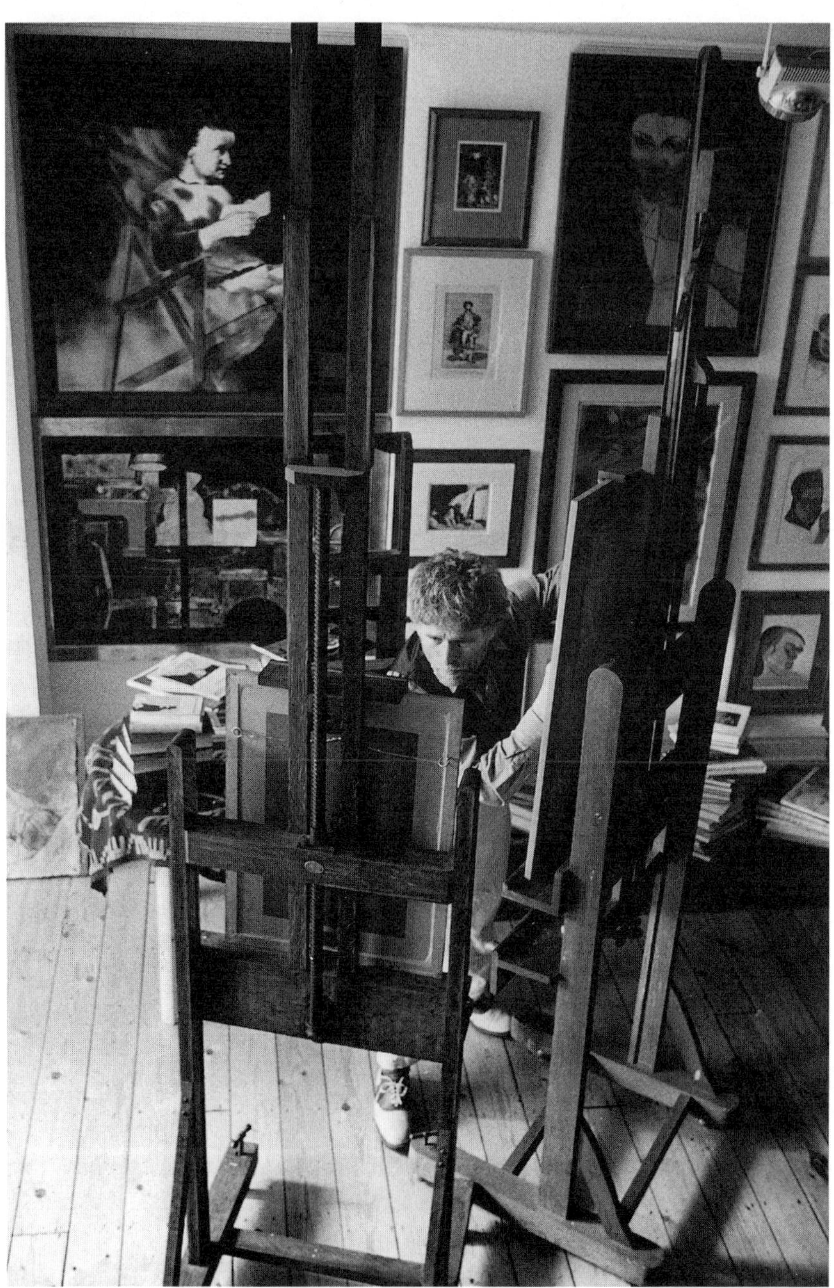

R. B. KITAJ

CHELSEA LONDON 1987

I met Ron – or R. B., as he chose to be known – Kitaj in the same year, 1963, as I met Francis Bacon, Lucian Freud and Frank Auerbach, ostensibly to persuade them to do an interview or contribute a text to Cambridge Opinion, *the student magazine I was editing. At that early stage I could not of course have known that I was bringing together the artists who constituted the core of what came to be called the 'School of London'. Kitaj not only came up with a substantial essay but also designed the cover of the issue. We met very occasionally thereafter in London and, later, in Paris, where Kitaj and his wife took an apartment for a year and assiduously visited the Louvre. What brought us together again more closely, in 1986–87, was a 'School of London' exhibition that I curated which began in Oslo before travelling to museums in Copenhagen (or just outside, at the Louisiana), Venice and Düsseldorf. This was the first exhibition on the theme since Kitaj's 'The Human Clay' show and its accompanying catalogue manifesto which proclaimed that, like Paris and New York before it, London could lay claim to a group of artists, however loosely allied, of international significance.*

Kitaj helped me define my concept, which was to narrow down the School of London to its inner core, and he gave me some valuable leads to finding the works I wanted to include. He was also on hand to discuss the exhibtion and its theme in retrospect. The interview took place in a café near the house in Chelsea where Kitaj lived and worked at the time.

MP Now that the 'School of London' exhibition has actually been put together and the pictures are there, I myself am torn between the conviction that this is a *kind* of school…

RK It certainly is a kind of school.

R. B. Kitaj (1932–2007). *Art International*, Paris, Autumn 1987.

MP But what kind is still very much open to debate.

RK I think if you looked at the School of Paris or the School of New York you wouldn't find much less spread, so there's nothing wrong with calling it a school. There's just as much spread between Picasso and Matisse and Juan Gris and Soutine and Miró as between these artists. There's just as much spread even among abstractionists – between Pollock and Rothko, Gorky and de Kooning, and yet they're known as the New York School.

MP They couldn't be more different. Exactly.

RK The concept of the school is wrapped up in the way people work on each other, don't you think?

MP I certainly think the School of London has more in common than either the School of Paris or the School of New York. The comparison I make is that these painters have as much in common as the Impressionists, in fact.

RK Certainly. They work upon each other, and that's what makes a school. That's what made Paris flower for a hundred years. It wasn't a coincidence that there were ten geniuses and twenty-five painters of real class living in Paris, working at the same time. That was because they worked upon each other.

MP And created an inventive atmosphere.

RK That doesn't mean an absolutely clear-cut influence, it means all kinds of things. It means ambition. You're up against someone else's ambition. Frank Auerbach said to me once when Lucian Freud had completed that big composition after Watteau – you know, the *Large Interior, W.11* – he said 'I think he's the master among us all – at the moment'.

MP And that atmosphere of being so keenly conscious of other artists' achievements helps to set a movement underway.

RK Take my painting called *Cecil Court*. I suddenly got a letter from Lucian Freud. Lucian had never written to praise a painting, never – you know? That's what school means. It's also very 'diasporist'. I'm sure you probably mentioned the fact that all these schools are composed of people half of whom are not born in the place where the school is formed.

MP Absolutely. Kossoff is in fact the only one to have been born in London. And the same applies to the other schools, it's true.

RK I don't think anyone's ever written properly about that. In fact, that's one of the ideas in the 'diasporist' manifesto I've been putting together: that these people don't come from the place where they finally settle or take root. There are types of diasporists, you know. There are sexual diasporists. A programmatic homosexual would be a sexual diasporist – there's enough to separate him from his peers sexually to make him like a creature from another world. My contention is that a diaspora can be a Jewish one or, in the case of Picasso, a Spanish one. I'm not talking about the period when Picasso came to Paris as an *émigré*, to be with artists and live a bohemian life, but during an exact period when it was either dangerous to go back or he refused or whatever. That was a period you could call a Spanish diaspora, when he made the painting called *Guernica*, which I call in my manifesto a 'diasporist' painting – it's as 'diasporist' as it is Cubist or Surrealist or any of the other things it's been called. So there are all these various diasporas.

MP When you look at the group that's been brought together in this 'School of London' exhibition, are there certain artists you feel are notably missing? I tried to get a hard core, as it were.

RK You did, you got the hard core.

MP Who would you add on?

RK You might find that if you asked each of the artists, each would add someone on.

MP Well, Frank Auerbach did. Who would you put on the list?

RK If you asked me I would say David Hockney. When you asked Frank, who did he say?

MP He said Euan Uglow. And if you asked Mike Andrews, he would probably say William Coldstream. Coldstream was Auerbach's second choice.

RK They would both say Coldstream.

MP David Hockney fits in very naturally, but only with the very early paintings, before he went to California. I'm glad you feel that these six painters constitute the hard core. Otherwise the choice could be extended almost indefinitely. There's also Peter Blake or Howard Hodgkin.

RK I think I would vote for Hockney and Hodgkin. They would fit very well. Hodgkin would be like the Bloomsbury, the Virginia Woolf, of the School of London. Like gorgeous little Bloomsbury.

MP Do you still see many of the London School painters these days?

RK Everyone's becoming more difficult to see now. It's only because Frank Auerbach has had this tremendous, marvellous, wonderful success in recent years that he's allowed himself to appear in public, and he does it with great verve. He leads a quite restricted life, I suppose, and he almost never leaves London. Kossoff is becoming reclusive, and Mike Andrews certainly is. But I suppose you could say that Frank is no more of a recluse than Bacon or Freud.

MP I thought Freud was fairly reclusive. Is he painting much?

RK He puts in more hours than I do because he works all night. A friend of his tells me that he hardly needs any sleep.

MP I once heard he'd cut down to a couple of hours a night.

RK I don't know how you do that, but that's what he does. And he works at night, in that studio, I imagine, where I saw him recently. I went to look at some big, beautiful new etchings he'd done. I think they are the most extraordinary etchings anyone has made in recent years. They show a power of concentration that is breathtaking. Because it's hard to continue in this way without making all kinds of mistakes that you can't correct. So all you can do when you think you haven't got it right is do another line – thicken the line the way he has in some places. I think Freud really came into this big flowering about fifteen years ago or so, and everyone began to notice what was going on, that here we had a master painter in our midst, and I suppose the finest straightforward depictive artist alive. There's no one to touch him. My idea is that this development wouldn't have been possible without that magic realist period, without that early magic realism, like that 1952 portrait of Bacon where he starts in one corner and just tries to get it right. And then continues on until he gets down to the other corner. Then you have the basis, you have the vibration, you have the power that underlies his later style, I think. What I'm saying is that this didn't come out of nowhere, it's not a middle-aged blossoming. It comes out of that highly logistical method. With that you can do anything.

MP It's as though he tried at one point in his development to make a definite break with that earlier, very controlled style.

RK Yes, but it always remained underneath.

MP It's true, looking through the works in the 'School of London' exhibition, that everyone's style is quite different. But then, what would artists who looked alike be? I think the overall impression would have been more cohesive if I had managed to find another large figure of Auerbach's.

RK There are very few of them around. For one reason, it's so exhausting for him to do something large because he has to get it all done in one session, so he has to scrape whatever doesn't work off and get it done in one go.

MP So whatever he does is all done in one session, even if he goes over it a hundred times.

RK Yes. He never goes back to it. He scrapes it all off and starts all over again. Not exactly like Kossoff, because his pictures are huge. But the two of them are close in certain ways … Most of my paintings tend to have a story. There's one you have in the exhibition called *Smyrna Greek*, for instance, that's set in a whorehouse in Athens.

MP In the port there?

RK It was halfway to the port of Piraeus. I was inspired by some poetry of Cavafy. Cavafy used to live in Alexandria, and he used to walk past brothels like these every day, they were in his street.

MP And the other people?

RK There's a girl in the doorway and this is a client coming down the stairs.

MP Those are from memory or imagination?

RK Memory and imagination. I look some details up from the vast archives I keep – to find out how this little crinoline works, or something like that.

MP Photographs that you keep?

RK I have a lot of favourite source books. And a number of them are made up of film enlargements, as opposed to stills. Movie stills are just photographs that are taken on the set by commercial photographers to advertise the movie. But I have some very rare books of film enlargements, which is the actual art of the film. And they tend to be my favourite sources for detail. If there's something I don't know, maybe a twist of a hand … The way that little border on the crinoline goes below the girl's skirt in the *Smyrna Greek* picture, for instance, probably came from one of the books.

MP The red light in the picture simply signals a whorehouse. But it looks so good there.

RK Oh yes. I put it in because I had never seen that before – in all my years of prowling round red-light districts I had never seen a district before this one where all the houses actually had red lights and red lanterns.

MP What about the picture we have in the exhibition called *The Jew, etc.*?

RK It went through about three stages of work, and then I left it and called it unfinished.

MP But it is a painting, isn't it?

RK It's got paint on it. It's drawn in charcoal, and then it's overlaid twice with greys and blacks, and then I left it. I shall probably never touch it again. I'll just keep it and call it unfinished.

MP It's based on a particular person or story?

RK *The Jew, etc.* is also a patchwork – it's basically imaginary. I might have looked up certain details.

MP Like the boots?

RK Whether I looked up the boots or just did them out of my head I don't remember. They're easy to do. I might not have looked those up.

MP And the hearing-aid?

RK The hearing-aid is the one I wear myself. I used it in a few pictures. I put the hearing-aid in the ear of some of the figures as a kind of small self-portrait. The features are not meant to be mine ... I've been writing small essays, like précis, about my paintings. Certain pictures bore me now, and I want to interpret them differently. I even revise the intentions I had when I did them. There's a whole new theory about 'deconstruction'. These fashionable intellectual trends usually don't interest me very much. But I've been reading some of the American deconstructive texts above all for their metaphorical, poetical resonance, and the deconstructive methods they use turn out to be what I've been doing myself all along in paintings for years. So I began to read more than I normally would have. Their basic thesis is that there is no ultimate meaning or interpretation of texts.

MP That texts are just open to a number of...

RK Open to any number, and they're connected in the most marvellous way with a particular Jewish tradition called *midrash*. *Midrash* is an enormous compendium – of interpretations of scripture which were evolved over many hundreds of years. Many of these interpretations contradict each other over a line of scripture. And this has been very interesting for these modern theoreticians, first in Paris and now in America. Many things in one's life – the memory, the passions or persuasions of one's youth, for instance – are subject to change, and so are the meanings and the resonances of pictures.

MP It's a little alarming at first, when you think that everything is in constant change.

RK People are alarmed by these guys – they call them nihilists. The natural inclination in human beings is to look for harmony, to look for a pattern, to look for something that's structured and that stays. So even the arguments are fascinating.

MP I find the approach very convincing. Things do change all the time.

RK Sure. The Great Zohar which is part of the Kabbalah says, 'The book changes its meaning every year'. Everything is in flux.

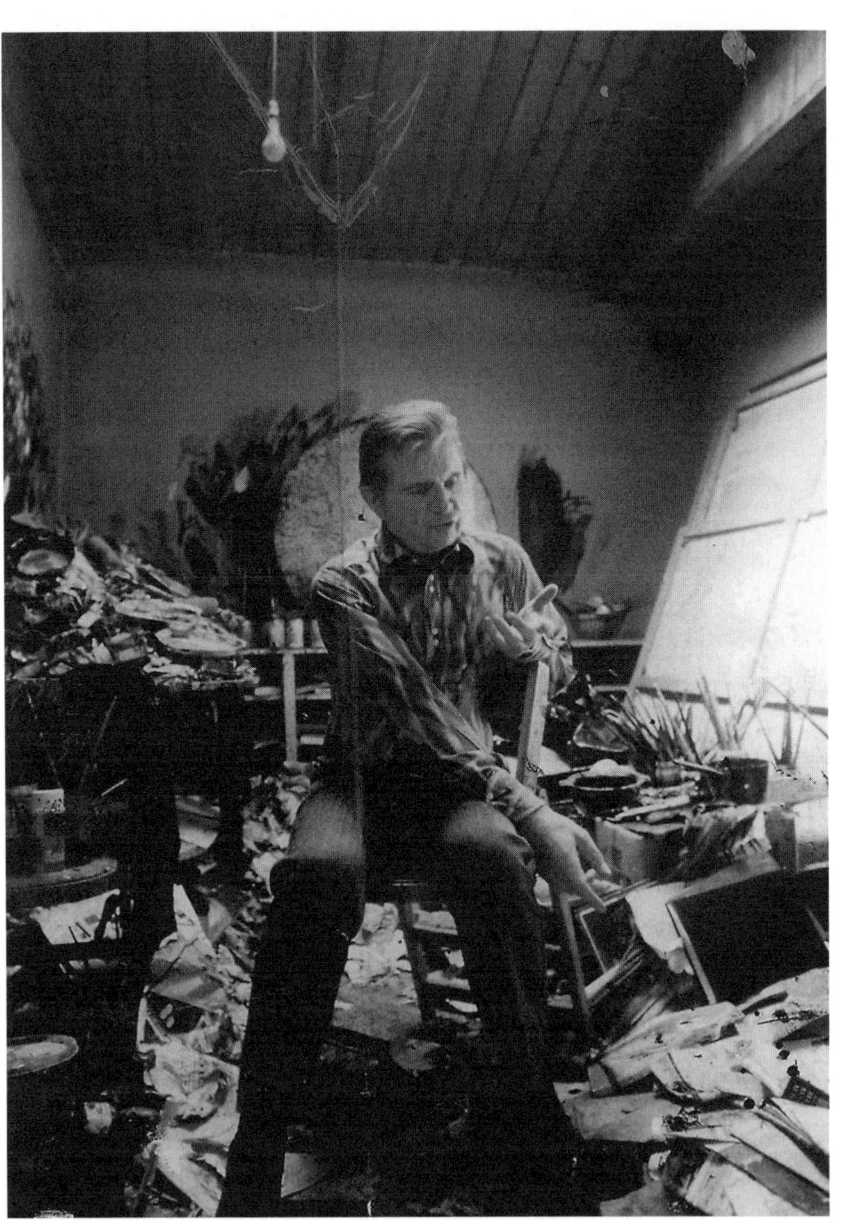

FRANCIS BACON

SOUTH KENSINGTON LONDON 1982

I did three interviews with Francis Bacon, spaced as far apart (to meet the same magazine deadlines) as those I have done with Auerbach. On the other hand, since I saw a great deal of Bacon and became very involved with him and his work, I often felt I should interview him more frequently. Generous as he was, Bacon might have gone along with the idea, but I sensed a reticence whenever the idea came up and I did not insist. I was aware that our whole friendship was in itself based on a kind of uninterrupted interview that ranged over everything under the sun for whole days and nights. And since Bacon talked to me very freely, in all kinds of moods and situations, I learnt far more than I would have done from any number of more constrained, recorded conversations.

This is the last of the three interviews, and it has been published quite widely. More recently, however, while I was working on a selection of essays and interviews for Francis Bacon: Studies for a Portrait *(Yale, 2008), I came across the original tapes and found I had omitted several exchanges – about Versailles, about Shakespeare – because they were irrelevant to the interview's main themes. In retrospect, they seem as interesting as everything else, and I have restored them and some other asides to the following version which gives a more accurate idea of the way the conversation actually unfolded.*

MP You told me recently that you'd been to the Science Museum and you'd been looking at scientific images.

FB Yes, but that's nothing of any interest. You see, one has ideas, but it's only what you make of them. Theories are no good, it's only what you actually make. I had thought of doing a group of portraits, and I went there thinking that, amongst various things, I might find something that would provide a grid on

Francis Bacon (1909–1992). *Art International*, Paris, Autumn 1989.

which these portraits could be put, but I didn't find what I wanted and I don't think it's going to come off at all.

MP Are there certain images that you go back to a great deal, for example, Egyptian images? You look at the same things a lot, don't you?

FB I look at the same things; I do think that Egyptian art is the greatest thing that has happened so far – certain periods of Egyptian art at any rate. But for myself I get a great deal from poems, I get a lot from the Greek tragedies, and those I find tremendously suggestive of all kinds of things. It's true that, not reading Greek, I don't get them in all their vitality. But there was this man who did remarkable translations from the Greek called Stanford, and he wrote a very fascinating book called *Aeschylus in his Style*.

MP Do you find the word more suggestive than the actual image?

FB Not necessarily, but very often it is.

MP Do the Greek tragedies suggest new images when you reread them, or do they just deepen the images that are already there?

FB They very often suggest new images. I don't think one can come down to anything specific, one doesn't really know. I mean, you could glance at an advertisement or something and it could suggest just as much as reading Aeschylus. Anything can suggest things to you.

MP For you, it's normally an image that is suggested though, it's not sound, it's not words sparking off words. Words spark off images.

FB To a great extent. Great poets are remarkable in themselves and don't necessarily spark off images, what they write is just very exciting in itself.

MP You must be quite singular among contemporary artists to be moved in that way by literature. Looking at for example, Degas, doesn't affect you?

FB No. Degas is complete in himself. I like his pastels enormously, particularly the nudes. They are formally remarkable, but they are very complete in themselves, so they don't suggest as much.

MP Not so much as something less complete? Are there less complete things which do? For example, I know you admire some of Michelangelo's unfinished things. And recently you were talking about some engineering drawings by Brunel and it sounded as though you were very excited by them.

FB Well, you see, this is where it's so hopeless talking about it. In a certain mood, certain things start off a whole series of images and ideas which keep changing all the time. So what happens then and what happens now are two completely different things.

MP But you are a visual person, above all. Is there a whole series of images that you find haunting? There are specific images, aren't there, that have been very important to you?

FB Yes, but I don't think those are the things that I've been able to get anything from. You see, the best images just come about.

MP So that's almost a different category of experience.

FB Yes. I think my paintings just come about. Like that *1946* picture of mine, it just came about. I couldn't say where any of the elements came from.

MP Did you ever experiment with automatism?

FB No. I don't really believe in that. What I do believe is that chance and accident are the most fertile things at any artist's disposal at the present time. I'm trying to do some portraits now and I'm just hoping that they'll come about by chance. I just long to capture an appearance without it being an illustrated appearance.

MP So it's something that you couldn't have planned consciously?

FB No. I wouldn't know it's what I wanted but it's what for me at the time makes a reality. Reality, that is, that comes about in the actual way the painting has been put down, which is a reality, but I'm also trying to make that reality into the appearance of the person I'm painting.

MP It's a locking together of two things?

FB It's a locking together of a great number of things, and it will only come about by chance. It's prompted chance because you have in the back of your mind the image of the person whose portrait you are trying to paint. I mean, there's no point in trying to make a portrait that doesn't look like the person. You see, this is the point at which you absolutely cannot talk about painting. It's in the making.

MP You're trying to bring two unlike elements together.

FB It has nothing to do with the Surrealist idea, because that is bringing two things together which are already made. This thing isn't made. It's got to be made.

MP But I mean that there is the person's appearance, and then there are all sorts of sensations about that particular person.

FB I don't know how much it's a question of sensation about the other person. It's the sensations within yourself. It's to do with the shock of two completely unillustrational things which come together and make an appearance. But again it's all words, it's all an approximation. I feel talking about painting is always superficial. We have lost our real directness. I mean if you read even in some of these translations from the *Oresteia* there are things that are so direct and so violent and so shocking in a way to us. We talk in such a dreary, bourgeois kind of way. Nothing is ever directly said.

MP But that was of course drama even then. I don't suppose ordinary Greeks went around talking like that. Perhaps they were more direct than us. Perhaps the realities of life are more hidden, more under wraps, for us.

FB Almost anything in the *Oresteia* is more interesting. And when Cassandra says 'The reek of human blood smiles out at me'. Now how are you going to make that into a painting? I don't know what it's called this kind of extraordinary figure of speech.

MP But are there things that really jolt you? I know you love Greek tragedy, Shakespeare, Yeats, Eliot and so on, but do odd things, like newspaper photographs, jolt you every now and then?

FB I don't think photographs do it so much, just very occasionally.

MP You used to look at photographs a lot. Do you still look at books of photographs?

FB No. Dalí and Buñuel did something interesting with *Un Chien andalou*, but that is where film is interesting and it doesn't work with single photographs in the same way. The slicing of the eyeball is interesting because it's in movement, though of course that kind of shock thing has been used so often since it's not really shocking any more.

MP But is your sensibility still 'joltable'? Does one become hardened to visual shock?

FB I don't think so, but not much that is produced now jolts one. Everything that is made now is made for public consumption, for money, and it's all become so anodyne. They might make it just slightly shocking, just enough for people to want to see it, so that it makes a little more money. That's all it's about now. It's rather like this ghastly government we have in this country. The whole thing's a kind of anodyne way of making money.

MP But do you still come across images that really strike you, like the nurse being shot in the Eisenstein film?

FB That was really to a large extent because Eisenstein was an artist and he made something of the whole film. That was just one influence. There were lots of other things that were very remarkable.

MP I suppose one doesn't have to be jolted as such to be interested, to be moved. One can be persuaded or convinced by something without it actually shocking one's sensibility. And I am sure that people have come to accept images that begin by seeming extremely violent, war pictures for instance.

FB They are violent, and yet it's not enough. Something much more horrendous is the last line in Yeats's 'The Second Coming', which is a prophetic poem – after all, it was written in 1920: 'And what rough beast, its hour come round at last, / Slouches towards Bethlehem to be born?' That's stronger than any war painting. It's more extraordinary than even one of the horrors of war pictures, because that's just a literal horror, whereas the Yeats is a horror which has a whole vibration, in its prophetic quality.

MP It's shocking too because it's been made into a memorable form.

FB Well, of course, that's the reason. Things are not shocking if they haven't been put into a memorable form. Otherwise, it's just blood spattered against a wall. In the end, if you see that two or three times, it's no longer shocking. It must be a form that has more than the literal implication of blood splashed against a wall. It's when it has much wider implications. It's something which reverberates within your psyche, it disturbs the whole life cycle within a person. It affects the atmosphere in which you live and move. It's a rather grandiose way of putting it, but it gets into the interstices of the body, of feeling, if it really works. After all, most of what is called art, your eye just flows over. It may be charming or nice, but it doesn't change you.

MP Are they always disruptive, the things that change you? I don't know why, for some reason I was thinking about Versailles. That's a very different order of experience, I suppose.

FB Well, when you think of Versailles you certainly think of the grandeur in which everyday life was carried on, in which people woke up and washed and shat and everything else – and the whole banality of their lives must have been offset by the grandeur and size of the architecture.

MP Do you think about painting all the time, or do you just think about things?

FB I think about things really, about images, anything.

MP I remember your saying – that's probably why I was thinking about Versailles – that when you were in France recently you spent the day in Versailles and had all these images for painting simply dropping in. Do images keep dropping into your mind?

FB Images do drop in, constantly, but to crystallize all these phantoms that drop into your mind is another thing, you see. A phantom and an image are two totally different things.

MP You never get what you imagine, of course.

FB No – very, very occasionally you get something slightly better.

MP That's real luck.

FB That's real luck.

MP Do you dream, or remember your dreams? Do they affect you at all?

FB No. I'm sure I do dream but I've never remembered my dreams. About two or three years ago I had a very vivid dream and I tried to write it down because I thought I could use it. But it was a load of nonsense. When I looked at what I'd written down the next day, it had no shape to it, it was just nothing. I've never used dreams in my work. Anything that comes about does so by accident in the actual working of the painting. Suddenly something appears that I can grasp.

MP Do you often start blind?

FB No, I don't start blind. I have an idea of what I would like to do, but, as I start working, that completely evaporates. If it goes at all well, something will start to crystallize.

MP Do you make a sketch of some sort on the canvas, a basic structure?

FB Sometimes, a little bit. It never, never stays that way. It's just to get me into the act of doing it. Often, you just put on paint almost without knowing what you're doing. You've got to get some material on the canvas to begin with. Then it may or may not begin to work. It doesn't often happen within the first day or two. You can never tell. I just go on putting paint on or wiping it out. And sometimes the shadows left from this lead to another image and the possibility of something else coming up ... But then, you see, this is a problem. Although I quite like them, I don't think those free marks that Henri Michaux used to make really work. I mean, they're better than most awful things, but they're too arbitrary.

MP Are they not conscious enough, not willed enough?

FB Something is only willed when as it were the unconscious thing has begun to arise on which your will can be imposed.

MP You've got to have the feedback from the paint. It's a dialogue in a strange sense.

FB It is a dialogue, yes.

MP The paint is doing as much as you are. It's suggesting things to you. It's a constant exchange.

FB It is. And one's always hoping that the paint will do more for you. It's rather like painting a wall. The very first brushstroke gives a sudden shock of reality, which is cancelled out when you paint the whole wall.

MP And you find that when you start painting. That must be very depressing.

FB Very.

MP Do you still destroy a lot?

FB Yes. Practice doesn't really help. It should make you slightly more wily about realizing that something could come out of what you've done. But if that happens...

MP You become like an artisan?

FB Well, you always are an artisan. This is the thing. Once you become what is called an artist, there is nothing more awful, like those awful people who produce those awful images and you know more or less what they're going to be like. What you really want is a kind of complicated simplicity – you want simplicity, but with all the implications of everything else within it. A reduction, a compression. That thing that somebody said years ago, 'what modern man wants is the sensation without the boredom of its conveyance', is absolutely true. One wants something that's so much more concentrated than anything that's gone before. But of course that almost never happens.

MP Why is it that we don't have any kind of tolerance of a slow build-up?

FB It's our consciousness of time. After all, people before weren't so radically aware that we're born, we die, and that's it.

MP Not even in Greek times or in Shakespeare?

FB Shakespeare was such a phenomenon. He seems suddenly to have had the past and the future all rolled up together at one time. He was so extraordinary, whoever or whatever he was. It's as though he knew the past and the future, because what he says and his attitude to life seems so contemporary now. Very little has become eroded by time. Of course it's so absolutely without any religion or belief. He may have put in God every so often just to widen the area, but it's so without belief of any kind.

MP Do you still get as engaged when you're painting?

FB Yes. I think age makes you more alert, in a strange way. After all, why shouldn't it? There it is. Life is absolutely nothing except what you make of it – it's what you've done and the way you've worked on yourself.

MP But it doesn't become any easier to paint?

FB No. Certainly not. I would say it becomes more difficult. You're more conscious of the fact that nine-tenths of everything is inessential. What is called 'reality' becomes so much more acute. The few things that matter become so much more concentrated and can be summed up with so much less.

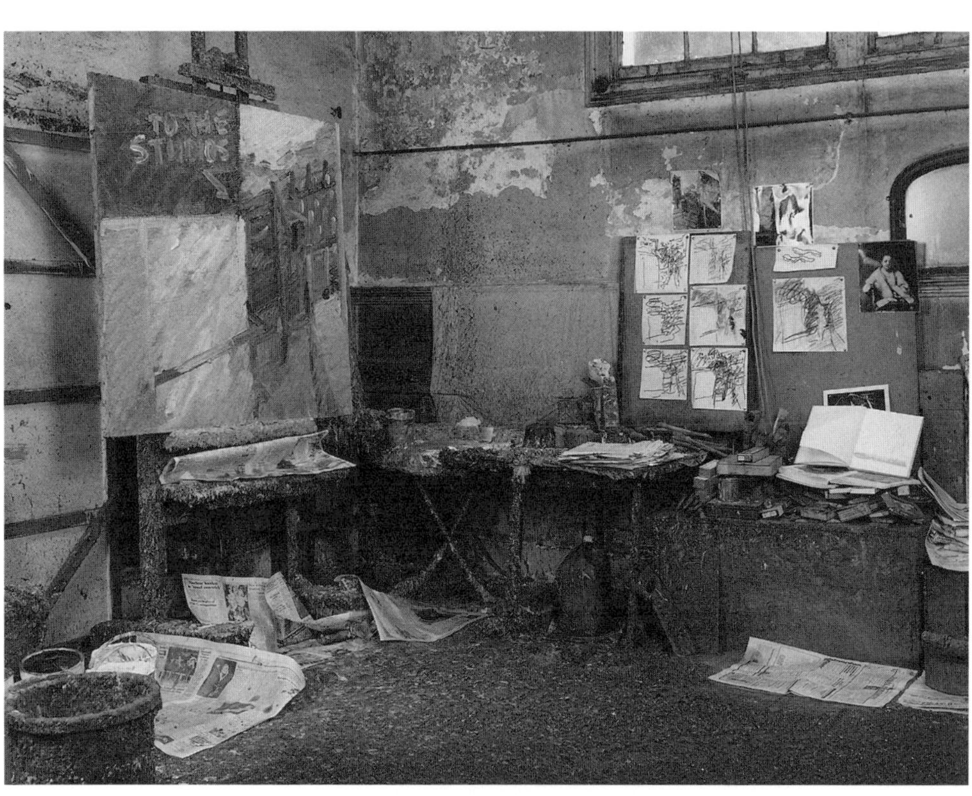

FRANK AUERBACH

CAMDEN TOWN LONDON 1999

MP If a painting came out perfectly the first time you worked on it, what would your reaction be?

FA I would be delighted! For ages, I was under the illusion that with alertness and energy and having an exciting theme, I would be able to finish at once. Then I found I couldn't. Whenever I start working from a person, I think, if they were in the right mood, if I were in the right mood, I should be able to get through all these stages, but…

MP It remains theoretical?

FA It remains theoretical, even with a drawing, which people think is quicker.

MP Not even a drawing has come out right first time?

FA I've done studies. Not a drawing done for its own sake. And even there, the ones that I've retained have been at the end of a series.

MP But in that case, if you've got the one perfect sketch, would that actually sort of stop the series? Would it mean you wouldn't want to go on?

FA No, because the study is for something. It may be that if I've got a good sketch – that has happened – it would help me finish the large painting, and I might keep the drawing. I sometimes overrun the sketch, then go back, three or four drawings in the sequence, to something that might contain the hint as to how to finish.

MP So, if you get the drawing right, it stimulates you to go straight into painting?

Unpublished interview with Frank Auerbach (1931–).
London, July 1999.

FA Yes, the drawing suggests some sort of invention which seems true. In my case, the procedure is laborious, and I'm rather passive about it until I become impatient. I do drawings, then I bring them back, and I start wondering: is the building on the right lower or higher? what does that feel like? how does this work? So I go and do another drawing. Gradually the information accrues, and as it accrues, it begins to suggest things. And gradually it comes together. Then I find I use much more paint and, even if tired, I start rushing about more energetically because the painting itself seems to animate me, and I behave with uncharacteristic decisiveness. One aims for a complete and convincing transformation.

MP So in fact it's almost a manifest of pent-up frustration.

FA Exactly. Because it seems so hopeless. I find that this is the way I've been behaving all my life. Now that I'm sixty-seven, I find the mess I'm surrounded by in my studio, for instance, is exactly the same sort of mess that I had in my cubicle when I was at school.

MP How many years did you spend at school in England?

FA Nine years. I arrived just before my eighth birthday and left when I was sixteen, after I'd done my Higher School Certificate. And at first I spent most of my holidays there as well as term times.

MP And you made some close friends there?

FA Yes. Some of them I still see. It was an interesting school. Considering how primitive it was, and how varied the qualifications of the staff – some of them were too highly qualified, really. It was kind of a tiny republic.

MP I suppose you didn't speak a word of English when you arrived?

FA No, but I don't know if any of this is relevant. I mean, I arrived at this place called Bunce Court in Kent. I felt curiously at home as soon as I arrived. There were these large grounds with unkempt kids running about, and that seemed like a sort of freedom to me. I was locked into a shed by two other boys on my first afternoon there, and even that somehow didn't depress me. And after about three weeks I was sent to the junior house, a place called Dane Court, at Chilham. It was a half-timbered fifteenth- or sixteenth-century house, full of rats, and it was run by a young woman called Gwynne Badsworth. And she spoke English to us seven- or eight-year-olds as soon as we arrived. She didn't have any of this nonsense about not speaking English, so within three or four weeks we all were able to communicate in English. And we were all enrolled as wolf cubs and brownies and did country dancing in the hall. And so, without any conscious past, we were…

MP Anglicized?

FA Yes, absolutely. And it was only because there was measles in the village that we weren't at the tenants' party during the first Christmas I was there. But we were sent great sackfuls of toys from Chilham Castle. And instead of playing cowboys and Indians, we played Greeks and Trojans, with drain rods and dustbin lids. And a small number of the more wimpish children, including me, were Greeks, but all the rougher, tougher and more able ones decided they were Trojans.

MP Do you still speak German?

FA I speak a very primitive German, with a very primitive vocabulary. I feel crippled in it. I don't have wit or allusion.

MP I believe at one point you thought about acting.

FA Yes I did, when I was fifteen or sixteen. We had a professional director with a lot of theatre and film experience at school. He had to do a 'work of national importance' and became a gardener and stoker at Bunce Court. After the War he worked as a drama director in Hull and later he launched Joan Plowright and John Hurt. He worked in a very thorough way. We did *Twelfth*

Night. But it wasn't a school play in the usual sense. We worked over each theme and used to spend hours over each speech. I was Fabian in that and by the time we had finished rehearsing we hadn't got to the point where Fabian enters – so that was that. But the next play was *Everyman*, which isn't a long play, and we managed to do the whole thing, and I was Everyman. I remember a rather heady moment. We worked in this man's painstaking way to get everything right and to understand, then we came to a point where Everyman finally realizes how wrong his life has been and says: 'I will make my testament, here before you all present'. This speech hadn't been rehearsed. And I did it, it was only about eight lines, and he said: 'Sometimes one does get it right without the rehearsal.' I think, because of all the training, I had perhaps managed to make some sense of it. Then when I came to London, I first joined something called the Tavistock Theatre in Islington, where BBC Radio actors used to act, and I got a couple of tiny parts. One of them was in an American play called *Beggar on Horseback*, and I think that was because when I filled in the form, I said I could do an American accent – which was stretching it a bit.

MP Were you a mimic at school?

FA Yes. I think I was better at it forty years ago than now. Then my friend Frank Marcus set up a semi-professional company, and I joined that. We did Peter Ustinov's first play, *House of Regrets*, and a production of Goldoni's *Servant of Two Masters*, and all the while I was going to art school during the day. I sometimes slept in the Torch Theatre in Knightsbridge when rehearsals went on too late. There was a very brief period in Ireland where I went after answering an advertisement in *The Stage*. That was more or less the extent of it. Then the acting began to fall away.

MP So you had already started going to art school?

FA Yes, I started to go to art school as soon as I came to London. I only did theatre in the evenings. The first art school I went to was the Hampstead Garden Suburb Institute – I was only there for a term, and by that time I realized it wasn't much good. So I took my portfolio, still sixteen, and went round the London art schools with it. At St Martin's they said: 'We'll take you, but we only start in September'. But at the Borough Polytechnic, there was a very kind man, a Mr Patrick, who said: 'Yes, you can come, I'll make up a timetable for you.' I went in January 1948, and David Bomberg was teaching there one day and two evenings a week. So I found myself in his class. I think it was very lucky that I was so young, because if I'd been older, I might have found it more difficult to accept him and get used to his ways.

MP Because he was overbearing?

FA No, he wasn't so much overbearing. He was totally unbiddable. And his language was his own. Bruce Bernard attended two or three classes and he heard Bomberg say to a student: 'This drawing's just like a Holbein.' And Bruce, who was older and more mature, was so offended with this that he didn't come back to the class. But gradually, one realized that part of the message was: 'You're not a student, you don't need to walk before you can run – in fact, children do run before they walk. If what you're doing is to have any validity at all, it's going to be on the level of these Masters that we admire.' It might have been a gnomic way of conveying that message, but it was part of his message. I must say, for me, apart from the idiom, which I believed in, and which was helpful, there were certain other lessons which have stayed with me. There were lots of good, intelligent painters teaching in art schools in those days, when hardly anybody could make a living out of painting, but most of them suggested that you should not be too excessively vehement and ambitious, and things would come to you.

MP Whereas Bomberg himself was excessively vehement and ambitious?

FA Yes, he was. And so was the work.

MP And that struck a chord in you.

FA Absolutely. I didn't make a conscious decision but I kept going to Bomberg's evening classes every week throughout my time at St Martin's and during my first year at the Royal College as well. So I suppose it must have struck a chord, and I must have felt that what was going on there was on the proper level, and that elsewhere there was a feeling of dilettantism, of a certain proper modesty. Although there were all sorts of useful things to be picked up at the other schools, I thought that what was going on in Bomberg's class was much more likely to produce something valid.

MP What initially drew you to art? Was it looking at pictures? Presumably it began at school.

FA Well, if you were in a school where you never went anywhere else and spent all the holidays there as well, you could do all these things, and I did paint all the time.

MP There were materials around?

FA Yes, there seemed to be. Poster colours, and so on. And I wrote poems. I know I wanted to do something that interested me, and I had an absolute horror of going into an office – really, it seemed to me like being sent to prison. I would much rather have been a tramp. That's the sort of thing you say when you're an adolescent, but I'm sixty-seven now and still feel the same. When one starts one doesn't know the difficulties, and there is a certain amount of showing off and attitudinizing. But as you go on, it's the work itself that becomes interesting, and everything else becomes fairly irrelevant, even a bit irritating. And you just want to work and be left alone.

MP I sometimes wonder if one could look at your paintings as a kind of diary.

FA They may record what I feel like. All the painting I think of as authentic does that. My work is certainly less comprehensive a diary than that of Matisse or of Picasso. If you want to know what it felt like to be sitting in a café in Paris in 1909, to be surrounded by people talking brilliantly, to be living on a level where you don't need much – you have a drink, and a cigarette, and the newspapers – and everybody is quite extraordinarily brilliant, you've only got to look at Picasso's Cubist paintings. In a sense, the geometry is incidental.

MP All you yourself need is this area immediately outside the studio.

FA I know everything about this place. And it helps to know what's going on behind things, I'm certain I'm not alone in this. There are superficial landscape painters who paint effects. And some of them make great art out of their effects. But there are other landscape painters – Constable may be the prime example – who became very familiar with their material and actually tried to convey within the forms how things interlock, even where you can't see them. If you've painted a nude of somebody whom you're in love with, you would know what they feel like. And that could certainly inform your painting. And if you've been walking about a landscape or a street, and know everything about it, that does inform the painting, and, of course, the actual subjects can be wildly different even though they are within a small geographical compass.

MP Even by moving a few yards left or right?

FA It can be entirely different. And understanding means understanding the way the forms within your painting cohere. If you move a bit, you try to make a unity out of a different set of data.

MP Until at one point you get the maximum amount of information?

FA It is not a routine. Each painting has its own character. In the end I am not certain that it's good, but I hope it feels finished. And then the next one becomes a new enterprise. The reason why my paintings are totally unpresentable, before they're finished – although some people might say afterwards too – is because I start at the beginning. I actually worry about how many windows there are, and how the road comes round exactly. I know all these things are going to get moved around. I do a drawing every day because every day I get a little bit more data – partly about a unity, and partly simply gathering information. You might draw a street with all the chimneys, but you might not draw the television aerials. You see what you're looking for. And so you go out again, and again, and again, and you actually notice different things. In the case of trees, an exciting thing happens – in the painting I've just finished, I started the branches in December and kept on drawing. And then, suddenly, it only took three days for the branches to turn into a complete feather-duster of a tree.

MP You've seen the skeleton before the flesh.

FA Yes, and this makes the thing interesting to do. I try to recognize and perpetuate something that means something to me. If somebody is doing the most magnificent image, and it doesn't, for me, have some sort of pang of genuine experience, it leaves me cold. On the other hand, if somebody copies, however devotedly, some humble fragment of autobiography – their wife or their kitchen – and the thing doesn't take off and blossom into an image, that too leaves me cold. And what one tries to do is to make that move – one could actually do it in ten minutes – from a recording to an independent explosion or expression or celebration in the one painting. Some paintings fail by being arbitrary and not sufficiently exact. And others fail by being insufficiently independent and grand. I still hope to be a formal inventor. I never thought I would be a recorder of my environment. But I was affected the first time I started painting somebody I was close to. Everything about it, the experience itself, and the result, and the degree of judgement I was able to have of it was so entirely different from what I'd done before that it really conditioned my work for the rest of my life.

MP At what point was that?

FA That was 1952. I'd been painting nudes for five years but painting an intimate, familiar person was an entirely different experience. One of the legs in the picture was tiny, and the other was big. But it was true. It only seems an authentic invention when I know that, however nutty it might look to someone else, that it is actually true, for me.

MP I know that you've done paintings of the outside of the studio. Have you ever done a painting of the inside?

FA There are many things that I haven't done because of practical difficulties. Before the studio was rebuilt, I used to work on two big pictures at one time. I would turn one to the wall and work on the other one, and change them about, so that I would come to each one fresh. Since the place is even smaller now than it was then, I work on one big one, and I may do a small one related to it. There's no way in which I could record the inside of the studio, partly because I have people sitting every evening and the place is rearranged, partly because the logistics of doing that in this space are so difficult. So I paint what is close to me, people I know.

MP Surely, the studio's interior is the closest thing to you.

FA Yes, but there's no room to paint it because it's so close. Even when I'm drawing a person in here I have to swivel round. Because if you're drawing anything, even a person, your head goes up and down and swivels. What you're seeing is in fact lots and lots of different linear perspectives that interpenetrate. So you've got to invent.

MP Didn't you once liken the moment when a painting seems to be going well to a domestic row where suddenly you blurt out the things you've been holding back?

FA Yes, it feels very much like that. You find ways of cutting through all the fudging.

MP Do you leave a finished picture for some time to make sure it's finished?

FA I leave it for some time, but not for long. I often put it in a box, and when the model – if there is a model – comes again, I take it out and it becomes clear whether it's finished or not. Then when it goes to the gallery, I wait for a black and white photograph – and quite often I brood over that. It's a little bit like when a writer sees his handwritten work typed out.

MP Are you conscious that your own images will appear strange?

FA Well, as you paint, you're certainly waiting for something strange that will suggest an image to you, and you work backwards and forwards. This has been going on in oil painting, at least, for centuries – Leonardo talks about it. You attempt to record, then you get impatient with the recording and start making irrational marks, and the irrational marks actually seem a better record than the literal ones. They suggest things, and suddenly in a corner of the picture you get a little bit of truth, which might actually expand into a whole truth. You don't know where it's going to come from, you see. What happens is that the painting begins to speak back to one. One has more energy when there's a bit of hope within the forms. The painting gets one out of one's chair, the painting makes one take the brushes in one's hand, the painting makes one go on working. In the end one has stored so many sensations in it that it begins to come alive.

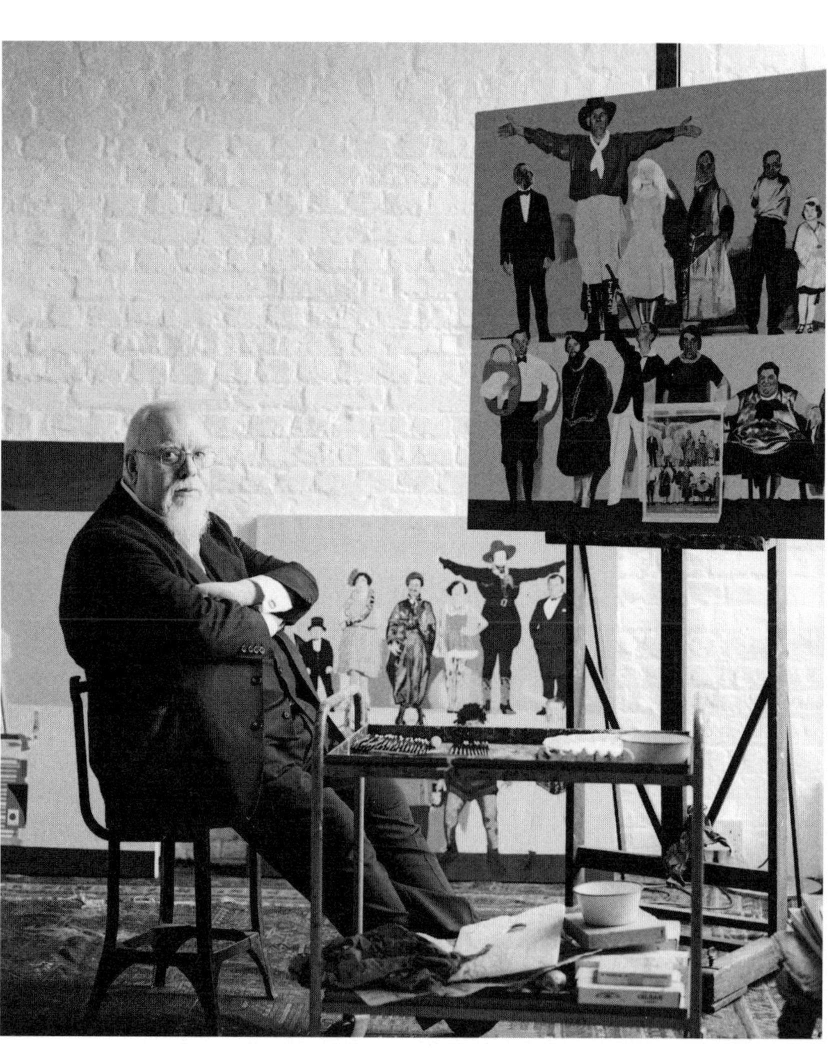

PETER BLAKE

HAMMERSMITH LONDON 2009

When the Galerie Claude Bernard asked me to write a preface for their new Peter Blake exhibition, I accepted immediately because I had long admired the wistful fantasy and subtle, poetic irony of Blake's pictures. Although I had met the artist a few times and seen several of his exhibitions, I didn't feel I knew his work and the world out of which it had sprung well enough to write something that was sufficiently new and worthwhile. Looking through the numerous, accomplished books about him merely reinforced the impression that I would do much better (as I had done often in the past) to invite the artist himself talk about his work, particularly if I could combine this with a short description of his studio, which I'd heard was a kind of Aladdin's Cave filled with all kinds of discarded treasure and kitschy memorabilia.

Blake did indeed talk far more revealingly and wittily about his work, both past and present, than I could have done – which was proof once again, especially for a foreign audience, that drawing an artist out on the background to his work and the themes that preoccupy him served as the most direct and useful introduction. Blake's studio also exceeded all expectation, speaking volumes about the way this highly imaginative yet infinitely painstaking and methodical artist has mined vein after vein of richly suggestive imagery, to create a richly patterned, scrapbook-like evocation of whole areas of our lives over the past half century.

One knows that Peter Blake has created an entire world of his own, peopled with tribes of jaded pop stars and pin-ups, pensive chimps and Mad Hatters, Shakespearean heroines and battered boxers. Yet this is revealed as barely the half of it, the tip of an iceberg of delectable oddities, when one is lucky enough to visit the artist and

Peter Blake (1932–). Published in *Peter Blake*, exhibition catalogue, Galerie Claude Bernard, Paris, October 2009.

be taken round his vast, cluttered studios. There, in a modest street in Hammersmith, the whole archive of an imagination run riot is open to view. Elephants of every size and in every material plod dutifully past stacks of minutely engraved heads culled from old encyclopaedias and kitschy white sculpture lovingly retrieved from flea markets, while a large hyperrealist prize fighter (Sonny Liston), formerly in Madame Tussaud's waxworks, guards the treasure with impressive fists about to flail.

Upstairs in this cavern of curiosities lies a warren of small rooms put together by an obsessive collector as neat as he is eccentric. Shrines to Elvis give way to orderly arrays of bizarre signs and furniture, Baroque driftwood, assemblies of shells, once important hats, Punch and Judy puppets and enough period toys and whatnots to satisfy whole lifetimes in search of the strangeness surrounding us all the time – if only we have the eye to find it. Like the artist and his work, the studio is a celebration of the unexpected, the unlikely and the freaky – sourced with all their weirdness intact from everyday life. Against this background of hilarious diversity, Peter Blake, as befits a master of ceremonies and a master magician, is a picture of courteous calm and benevolent ease. What gives the everyday life so poignantly encapsulated in his work an extra charge is the artist's acceptance of all the oddity around him. In viewing it with the wonderment of a child, Blake has extended the childhood he never had into a childhood we never had – and are delighted to share with him.

MP Something that always strikes me when I look at your work, Peter, is that it's this marvellous mixture of naïve and sophisticated. It's between ironic and child-like and full of wonderment – and yet it could be *very* ironic at the same time. For me, that's its particular fascination: one can't work it out because it's a bit of both.

PB Well, I think there's never any cruel irony. If there is irony it's gentle irony. So I don't think there would be any trick irony in there, or any attempt to fool people or to make them look silly.

MP There's something unusually touching about the work, and it comes across very immediately. I think probably everybody can respond to your work, at some level or another, which in itself is a very rare thing.

PB I think you're right that there is this child-like feeling, and it's probably to do with my childhood and with being evacuated during the War and things like that. I suppose I've retained a feeling for childhood right through my life – for the childhood that I didn't really have.

MP Because you were moved out of your home when you were small?

PB Yes. I was seven when the Second World War started. So in those very important years, from seven to fourteen basically, I was either evacuated or at least the War got in the way of any normal life.

MP So you were away from your parents and your family?

PB I was away from my parents, yes. So I think there is an element of going back. For instance, you couldn't buy toys then, and you didn't see a banana or other fruit or any number of things right through the War. They seem unimportant now, but when you're living through a period like that and you look back at it, it was nevertheless a strange time. And then I went straight from that to going to art school when I was fourteen. So in a way art school was a direct extension of a childhood that hadn't in fact taken place.

MP Was it tough? Did you feel cut off?

PB It was difficult, yes – at the age of seven to be suddenly taken away from your parents. I was with my sister, she was evacuated, too, and she was only five, so it was much more difficult for her. But there was no cruelty. I was never…

MP Maltreated?

PB Maltreated or abused.

MP But you were lonely, and I suppose you had to reinvent your life.

PB Exactly, yes. So I think that childish element in the work is probably there because of that. Perhaps the mixed media work I did in 1962 called the *The Toyshop* is about the toys that I didn't have. Maybe. And then on the other hand, there is, I suppose, a natural sophistication or intelligence that's nothing to do with education – it's either there or not. So, hopefully, my work is a combination of the two things.

MP And did you go into that kind of subject matter right from the beginning – reinventing, as it were, a lost childhood?

PB Probably not. What happened was that my art education began at fourteen when I went to a junior art department and then did something called the intermediate examination. For a year I was taught by Enid Marx, who was a great scholar of popular art, so my love of popular art was instilled then. But this searching for childhood probably didn't emerge until after the first year at the Royal College of Art in London. The first year was life drawing, and you had to be in the life room. After that you were left alone. And at that point in 1954 came the first pictures I did of children reading comics, and badges, drawing on my background and on popular culture.

MP Was that because at the Royal College you felt able to do what you wanted to do? Was the atmosphere 'do what comes most naturally and what you're interested in'?

PB It was the first point where it occurred for me because my life up until then had been junior art school, art school and then national service for two years. I originally applied to the Royal College as a graphic designer, having gone half-way through the graphic design course, but I actually got in as a painter. So when I arrived at the Royal College in 1953, I had no training in painting. It was only after I'd spent a year in the life room and the training had started that I felt at all free to think about what I might really like to do.

MP You actually became a painter by a series of flukes – you would normally have gone into a trade?

PB Completely. My family background would have suggested going into the building trade.

MP One might say you've actually had a longer childhood than most people. You've had your revenge on your lost childhood because you've been able to deal with child-like things for years and years.

PB I think so, yes. Perhaps in the way that Picasso did during a certain part of his life – he became very child-like, didn't he? He wanted the work to look like the work of a child, and he made those wonderful sculptures where he put toys together and made sculptures from that. So hopefully it's the same kind of playfulness.

MP Yes. I think Nietzsche said something about the artist as being someone who has the seriousness of a child at play.

PB Exactly.

MP Do you reflect a great deal before beginning a new series, or do new ideas pop up spontaneously the whole time?

PB They do now. The older I get and the less time there is left to work, the more there is to do. I don't have to think of anything new to do any more. And the most exciting possibility I suppose is this concept that I announced a while ago that I was now in my late period and this would give me, at the age of seventy-five – two years ago – carte blanche if I wanted to go a bit barmy and to do anything I wanted to do. But I could anyway you know.

MP *(Laughs)* It's an old childhood, a senior childhood.

PB Yes, an old childhood. But if I wanted to do a Jackson Pollock, for instance, this would be the time to do it, in my dotage. So that element has been introduced as well.

MP So you feel very free?

PB I just thought seventy-five was a reasonable time to start a late period, and I thought I might as well impose it on myself rather than have it imposed by art history at a later point. I mean poor old Aubrey Beardsley's late period was in his mid-twenties, wasn't it? I've got this far, so with any luck I'll go on a bit farther, but from seventy-five is my late period. Hopefully, I might go on until ninety even.

MP I hope so too. Do you get a lot of feedback from your studio which is almost like a museum of your fascinations and your interests and obsessions?

PB Yes, one thing leads to another. I suppose a good example would be the series of panels with objects stuck to them, which started off being called 'Museums of the Colour Black and White'. And in buying the white material I realized how many things were also black and also black and white, so that's been extended into becoming 'Museums of the Colour White'. So that was a natural progression. There were more black and white things around and the white things were running out. That's an example of how one idea leads to another.

MP Your studio has all those rooms full of different objects: found things and bought things and collections, whole collections, whole curiosity cabinets. It's almost like a reference library for certain types of visual inspiration.

PB Yes. Some of it has settled down into being almost a museum and those things won't be used in my work. In other areas there are stacks of wood or driftwood or folders of paper or marbles or whatever it might be, that will be fed into the work.

MP And do you continue to add to it?

PB All the time.

MP You look around. Do you go to flea markets?

PB I go to the Portobello Road still quite often, and there are certain stalls there. There's a stall where I buy lead figures for some of the work I'm doing, and there's a stall that has children's kind of ephemera. I've become rather like Joseph Cornell towards the end of his life, who would come in from Hoboken, or wherever he lived, and go into Manhattan, and he knew a shop where he would buy music and he knew a shop where he would buy bits of this and bits of that.

MP You know the places now.

PB Yes, I know the places. And my journey is rather like his. I enjoy going out to look for things as he did.

MP And you're consciously looking for things to put into your work?

PB Certainly. I also discovered boot fairs about a year ago. I only go to the one local one, but I'm looking mostly for Elvis Presley stuff. I'm also looking at the moment for the black and white pieces and I'm looking for – I hate the word 'kitsch' but it's the only word to describe them – I'm looking for a series of small white sculptures that have a kitsch quality, little white sculptures of pretty children, for instance. And I'm making a series of sculptures of those.

MP And you also still buy things simply because they fascinate you and you'd like to own them?

PB Sometimes. I collect elephants, toy elephants, so if I see a particularly nice one I buy it. I started to collect elephants as a safety valve for my other collecting. If I went to the Portobello Road and I came back with a little elephant, that was a good day because it would have stopped me from maybe buying a complete kitchen or an old bicycle or something that was probably ludicrous. So that's how it started. But then I bought every elephant I saw, and there's a lot of elephant material around. I've cut down on the elephant buying now, but if I see a good one I will still buy it.

MP When you cut back, do you then get rid of the sort of surplus elephants?

PB No, I never get rid of anything. But I stop adding to what's already there.

MP And you've got it all here in the studio?

PB Yes, it's all over. On all the shelves as well, even here in the kitchen. There are a few little elephants just there beside your head.

MP Oh yes, of course, I hadn't really taken them in.

PB I'm also planning to make some jewelry, so I'm collecting little elephants for that. There'll be a necklace of small white elephants which might be ivory or they might be plastic, some will be broken but it will be just a whole lot of little white elephants. And I might want to do a necklace of Ethiopian silver crosses which I've put together. I've also got a series of cufflinks in mind.

MP So you're still producing right across the board – everything from graphic art to sculpture, including jewelry making and silversmithing. Early on, you were taught in all those disciplines.

PB Yes, they're all there at the back of my mind still. The intermediate examination I mentioned earlier consisted of the following: life drawing, costume life drawing, architecture, anatomy, perspective, wood carving, joinery, stone carving, modelling from clay and lettering. It was an incredibly diverse course. There was also wood engraving and silversmithing. And most of those things I've gone back to, years later.

MP So you've used all those disciplines?

PB Pretty much. It's mainly silversmithing now. I don't have the facility to actually make the pieces, but I'm putting them together and the silversmith will put loops onto them and put them onto a chain. So I'm not actually beating the silver. But I did, and I still could. And if we're talking about diversity, I've designed a fabric for Stella McCartney, and I've designed the carpets for the new law courts in Parliament Square that the law lords are moving into. I did the latter quite consciously in the spirit of Pugin. And I'm almost certainly going back to making some more wood engravings. So it's still very diverse.

MP And you enjoy that variety.

PB I do. After all, none of it is compulsory. I only take on commercial art things that I'm interested in doing.

MP Yes, of course. So you've actually got no reason to do a Jackson Pollock, you've got all the variety there already.

PB Exactly, except I used to share a flat with Richard Smith when we were both very young students. And while I would be in my room with a sable brush fiddling about on a panel of wood, Dick would be up a ladder kind of throwing paint at the canvas. And I harbour just a bit of desire still to do literally just that – throw some paint at something. So there's no reason why I shouldn't.

MP No absolutely, there's no law against it, is there?

PB No *(laughs)*. And who knows what might happen!

MP So you're ready to experiment – but you always have been, haven't you?

PB Well, now that I'm old and I've publicly declared my late period, everything has opened up completely because I've got such a marvellous excuse. It used to be called 'retirement'.

MP *(Laughs)* Right.

PB We haven't talked about it yet, but when I was at the National Gallery for two years as artist in residence – and that's a very long, complicated story and there's no reason to go into it now – but along the way I did a painting which needed a chimpanzee in it and I became acquainted with Cheetah, the Tarzan chimpanzee, and so the show ended up with me incorporating some of Cheetah's paintings into my exhibition at the National Gallery.

MP It was Cheetah who actually made the paintings?

PB That's right. He was the original chimpanzee in the first Tarzan movies. And he retired to Palm Springs, and on his retirement he took up painting.

MP How long did Cheetah live then?

PB This is a big discussion that goes on because there is more than one Cheetah. And he's died three times in the last ten years but he's still talked about as being alive.

MP *(Laughs)* I see.

PB And there's this wonderful image of him, in retirement after a day's painting being taken by his trainer on the back of a scooter with a cowboy hat on, a glass of whisky in one hand and a cigar in the other hand, driving around Palm Springs.

MP How extraordinary.

PB Anyway, that story has nothing to do with anything. But then a year after that and more or less as I moved here into this studio I was sixty-five, which as you know is the British age of retirement. So I announced my kind of conceptual retirement which at the time meant I'd retired from the unpleasant side of the art world. So I retired from ambition and from avarice and from jealousy of other artists.

MP So you took yourself out of the running as it were, so that you could do exactly what you wanted.

PB Yes, and I still kept working. I mean it didn't change the work, it was pretty much a kind of emotional and psychological thing and it was only to do with me. I didn't need to tell anyone else except that it became a bit of a story in the British press so I was asked about it.

MP And has your way of working changed? Do you simply come in the morning to the studio and work through until the evening? And you work alone, you don't have an assistant except for an occasional handyman?

PB No, I work alone. I have someone who comes about every two months for a week. He hangs pictures for me and organizes things. There was an enormous pile of papers here on the table when he came and he's gone through that and filed it.

MP But you work alone.

PB Yes, I work alone. And I also have a framer who makes my frames and if I need a box made or a piece of woodwork that's more practical for someone else to do then he does that.

MP Right.

PB But I've never had an assistant here in the studio.

MP But do you work regularly?

PB Yes, I certainly try and work regularly. I've eased back from working at weekends. I decided that I'd try and take Saturdays and Sundays off. So I don't work every weekend now as I used to. But I try and get here by about half ten and I work until about half six, so that's my working day. I'm concentrating on my Paris show at the moment so I'm primarily working on collages.

MP And collage is an important part of the Paris exhibition?

PB It's *the* important part. It started off as being an exhibition of collages only and then we added some sculptures. But in my mind, it's above all a collage exhibition.

MP And collage is a form, a genre, that you've been doing for a long time.

PB Yes, again it's a very specific story. Very early on I shared a flat with the artist Richard Smith, as I mentioned, and he had a girlfriend whose uncle and aunt had come from Germany and had been friends with Kurt Schwitters. So the girlfriend would have talked to Dick Smith about Schwitters and collage and Dick Smith passed the information on to me. I'd probably stuck things together before, but I actually learnt about collage in about 1955, so it really started from then.

MP And you've been doing collage on and off ever since?

PB Yes, in various groups of works. Originally there was a group about the circus in 1955 and then a group of abstract collages and then over the years ... As for the ones for the show, there's a group about Paris and another one about Venice. And these are based in the main on a collection of postcards. The Paris ones, for example, came out of one of those concertina-type, Edwardian packets of postcards.

MP That you found in Paris?

PB I probably did. So the postcards are stuck at the top of the sheet of paper and then in the space below the collage things are added, and that's the way the stories are told.

MP This is a series that you've done specifically for the Paris show?

PB Yes. I did the Venice ones first and then I did the Paris ones and then I started another group of Paris ones and a group called 'World Tour' of different cities. There's also another group of larger ones which are kind of like the 'World Tour', but there are only four of those.

MP Are the collages themselves quite arbitrary or are they very planned? Do you just make them up as you go?

PB They make themselves up often, and then a theme starts to emerge. The Venice ones for instance are quite dark, you know, they're quite sinister, some of them: aeroplanes flying in low and slightly sinister things happening. And then for some reason, the Paris ones are much more cheerful and much jollier. And there's dancing and children play games, and ideas emerge so that I might for instance decide to buy a book about physical exercise, and then suddenly I've got a whole book of children dancing or exercising. So from this big library of collage material all kinds of themes emerge.

MP The big library is stuff you've cut out over the years from various ... did you say you bought a whole Larousse?

PB Yes, quite recently. When I lived in Bath I went to an auction for the very first time and it was a book auction. And as you know in auctions, sometimes lots just don't go. And I couldn't resist these incredibly low prices and buying things I didn't really want. So I bought a whole run of *The Cornhill Magazine*, which is a kind of Victorian magazine, and I bought a whole twelve-volume set of the French Larousse dictionary which I was rather proud of owning. But about a year ago I looked at them and thought 'well, you don't speak French, you don't refer to them as a dictionary and they're full of wonderful imagery, so why not cut them up?' – which is what I've been doing.

MP So you cut them up and then spread them out and sort of choose characters that begin to suggest a theme?

PB Well, the process with them is that I take each letter at a time, and then I go through every page and if there's something on that page that I could use I tear the page out. So I then have a stack of pages and I go through each page and divide it into categories: so there's a category for portraits – and there are thousands of beautifully drawn or engraved portraits – and there's a category for fish and another for birds and so on.

MP Yes, they're beautifully drawn and very detailed.

PB They're wonderful! They're beautiful engravings. And so I put them into stacks and then into envelopes and I sit at home, for instance, cutting out four hundred little heads. And then that will probably suggest a crowd. So then I'll make a crowd of the heads. So that's the process at the moment and I do refer to other books like *Wonders of the World* or ethnographical books, and I'll find images in those. I just found a particular one of *Peoples of the World* that has very lurid colour reproductions, early colour reproductions, so I've been working with those.

MP You sound as though you have such a good time!

PB I do! *(Laughs)* I have a wonderful time, yes.

MP I'm full of envy, I mean there's no anguish here, is there? You're at play in a sense.

PB Well, there's the anguish of actually making a painting. That's never easy. People assume that it's easy, but we all go through our own anguish, Frank Auerbach in his way and me in my way, but it is similar. I don't scrape the paint off at the end of the day, but there's lots of re-painting and over-glazing, and it's hard and it doesn't get any easier to paint.

MP Do the collages get easier?

PB They are easier than painting.

MP Painting is *always* as demanding.

PB I think so really.

MP And do you always feel that you haven't quite got what you want?

PB Well, this is the frustration eventually too, that I never ever have achieved what I try and achieve.

MP That's why you go on, isn't it?

PB Yes of course, but within each painting you think 'maybe this time I will' and what I have always attempted to achieve is a kind of ultimate realism, which is impossible in painting. And you can't pin it down. Velázquez in a way makes a realism which couldn't really be any more realistic but it doesn't do what Van Eyck does in turn. So the ultimate would presumably look photographic – it would be as much like the person as it could be. And that by implication would probably look rather photographic. It would have the exact proportions, the exact skin tones, it would depict every hair, it would catch their character, it would catch that twinkle in the eye, it would catch the mood of the day. And it's impossible!

MP Of course it is, otherwise you'd be re-creating life, wouldn't you?

PB Yes exactly, and you can't. I used to have this thesis that the closest anyone got to it was Madame Tussaud: a very good head by Madame Tussaud was the closest you would get to sculptural realism, but of course at the time I was laughed at for saying that. But I'll never achieve that. In painting I can never do it. But in collage there's a beginning and an end. As you stick the last piece on you have actually completed it.

MP Like a jigsaw.

PB Like a jigsaw puzzle, exactly. So that is much more ... relaxing is the wrong word, but it does have an ending each time. Whereas a painting ... is never finished.

MP I was just about to say you've taken back paintings and gone on working on them for years?

PB I have, yes. And I still am, I delivered this portrait of Christopher Frayling to the Royal College of Art last week because he's leaving as Rector there but I've asked to have it back during the summer holiday because I know it's not right even to the point where I could take it.

MP Does that ever get dangerous? Do you go too far and have to abandon a picture?

PB Well, I never abandon anything anyway. Things are always put to one side as a work in progress. So the abandonment will only be when I can't work on it anymore. I've never thrown anything out.

MP You've never got to a point where you feel you've taken it too far and you've lost it?

PB Sometimes there are pictures that I suddenly see I don't like. They've become too harsh or the colours are too bright – so there is a point where you go too far. And not far enough. That's the real problem, I think. There's always a certain beauty to a work in progress from that very first mark, and then there's a point where it becomes more established and there is a time to stop, because I know I can't achieve what I'm trying to achieve – and sometimes I go beyond that. And you do spoil it, it goes too brittle perhaps.

MP So it's lost some of the spontaneity it had and goes a bit dead. And the sculpture? What kind of role has that played in your work – has that been a parallel activity?

PB Yes, it's pretty much three-dimensional collage. I've attempted to model in clay but I don't do it very well and in a way there's no point, so again I use found objects. They're really kind of sculptural collages.

MP And you've been doing this for a long time?

PB Yes, I've done that since the late fifties. Some of them exist still as collages, pieces like *The Family on a Bridge* was from the late fifties. Some of the work I've had cast into bronze over the last few years. But the pieces I'm showing in Paris ... well, I suppose one of them is a carving, it's of an endless column, the Brancusi column. I carved a basic section of it from wood, I whittled it, and then the casters made four or five of these and welded them together. So although the scale is about an inch across it's about three feet high. And this is another whole thing that I think about, gigantism and – is there such a word? – about Lilliputism.

MP Scale.

PB Well yes, scale. That by making the endless column smaller you can make it more endless than Brancusi could. So I have twice as many units in mine as he could get in his, but each of his is bigger than a man, so you're using gigantism. For instance, I could make a bigger Richard Serra by making it small than he can make a big Richard Serra.

MP Yes, because it becomes big in the imagination?

PB Well, the scale becomes bigger. If you make it tiny you can make it bigger in scale. Do you see what I mean? It's a silly idea really but it's questioning gigantism, I think. That's really all it's about.

MP Yes, and you're as happy doing sculpture as anything else?

PB Yes, I enjoy it very much. I enjoy the little bit of physical work, I enjoy cutting the wood and I enjoy the little bits of carving it entails.

MP Do they take a long time?

PB They can do, carving the little endless columns, which I'll show you later. It was quite laborious although the whole thing is only like a foot long.

MP To go back to the collages, the difference between Venice and Paris was that because of a mood you were in, do you think? Or did it just happen that way?

PB Well, looking back, it was probably simply because I hadn't been to Venice for fifty years. I went there in 1957 when I was on the scholarship and we went back to accompany Tracy Emin to the Biennale two years ago. And then we went back very soon afterwards, later in that year, and it was a disastrous trip. We lost our luggage so we were at Venice airport for like three hours, someone was meeting us but we couldn't get to them to tell them and didn't have their phone number. So we went to catch a waterbus and my foot slipped and I fell into the water bus. Luckily I didn't fall into the water, but I fell about four feet onto my knee which has troubled me ever since. So looking back, it wasn't a happy trip. I was nervous afterwards about going on any other boats and my knee hurt the whole time.

MP That doesn't sound much fun. And you bought the postcards there or did you find them?

PB I had them already with me. I probably bought them, maybe on the first trip or maybe I just had them. But there is a darkness about those which maybe comes out of that bad experience. It didn't occur to me until I'd done them. In fact, it didn't occur to me until I'd done the Paris ones which I realized were so much lighter, you know – the skies were bluer and there weren't those sinister aeroplanes flying down low.

MP Is Paris a city you go to relatively often?

PB Pretty often. I lived there on a scholarship for a period of about six weeks to two months. And then I came home for Christmas, and then went back. So I got to know it pretty well then.

MP In the fifties?

PB Up to Christmas '56 and back in January '57. It was still a kind of war-time city at that point, the American writers were still there and whoever they were I met them but I didn't know who they were at the time. So I probably met Hemingway and Ginsberg and Kerouac.

MP They were all holed up in little hotels on the Left Bank.

PB That's right. And Ellsworth Kelly was in Paris at the time. Ellsworth Kelly is a friend now anyway, but I met all the other American painters who were there as well. But I always enjoy going back to Paris, and all the more so now that we have this show coming up.

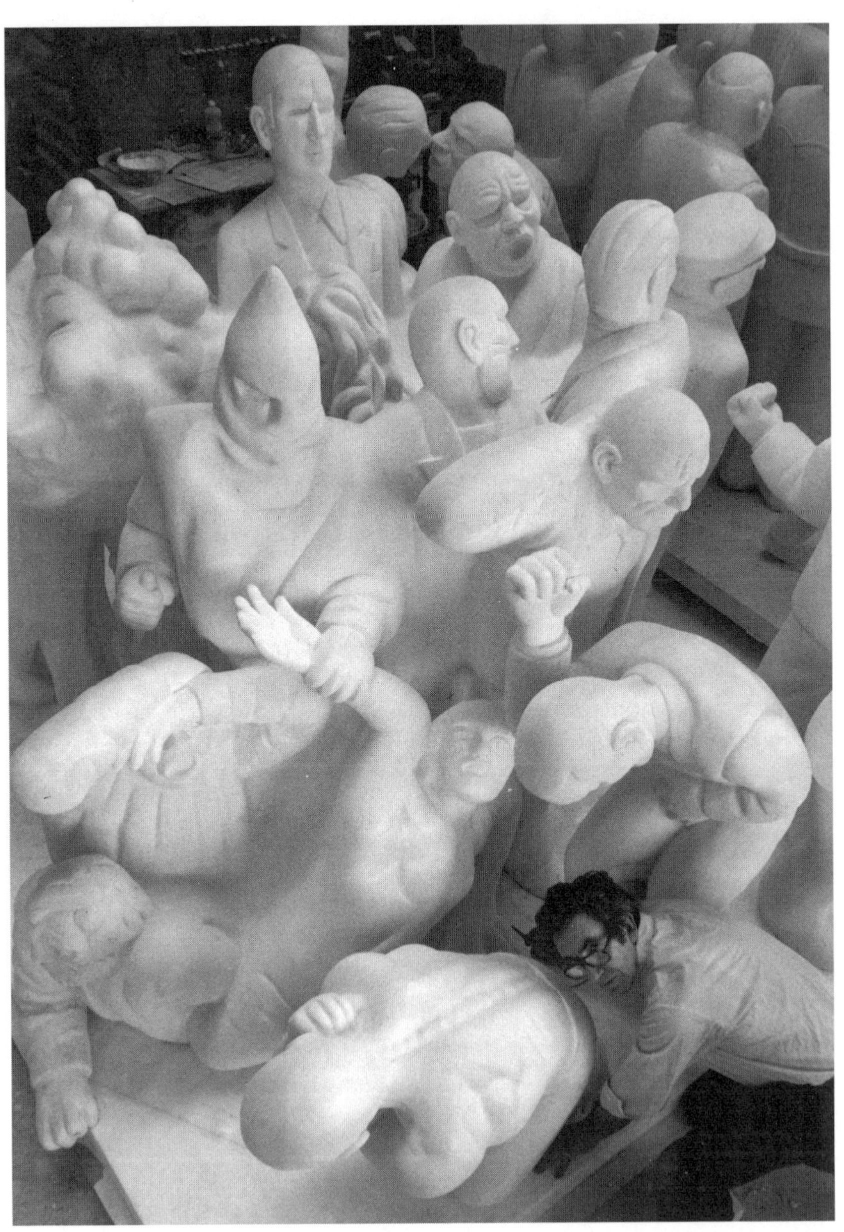

RAYMOND MASON

LUXEMBOURG GARDENS PARIS 1982

Although Raymond Mason thought of himself as very French, he remained for all his decades in Paris quintessentially English – and an artist of that vintage that considered most things French superior to their English equivalents. Another of his contradictions was that although he led a hermit-like existence in his studio near the Luxembourg Gardens, he also seemed to know everybody of any cultural interest in the city and to be abreast of all the latest art world news and gossip. He was, in fact, despite his rough manner and harsh tongue, not only extremely sociable but extremely witty, able to tell the funniest stories about himself and his uncanny ability to put his foot in it with just the wrong reaction or remark.

When it came to his sculptures or any aspect of his work, Mason was like a lioness with her cubs. He was suspicious even of those who actively supported his work and, needing them though he did, often managed to alienate them. Having poured himself so whole-heartedly into his monumental coloured sculptures, and having suffered so much in the process, Mason jealously guarded them against anyone else's interpretation or way of exhibiting them. I did an interview with him, which might well have been included here had he not taken it and rewritten not only his answers but the questions I had originally asked him. The result read like a manifesto, as did most of the texts that accompanied Mason's exhibitions since he himself tended to write them, just as he tended to insist on both the choice of the works and their presentation in the shows he had. The following article, which appeared while the show I had 'curated' under Mason's total direction for the Serpentine Gallery in London in 1982, nevertheless was not subjected to his manic strictures since it was written, with a degree of independence, for the Sunday Times.

Raymond Mason (1922–2010). Published in the *Sunday Times Magazine*, London, 12 December 1982.

'Lunch?' the voice barks.

'Well, a drink then, Raymond.'

'Look here Peppiatt, you don't ask a man who's half-way up the south face of the Annapurna to come down for a drink.' The voice crackles over the telephone with the bitter glee of hardships willingly endured. 'You've caught me right at the most crucial stage.'

It is early spring in Paris. The dank passages and narrow streets of the Latin Quarter where the sculptor Raymond Mason has lived since 1946 have at last begun to lighten, but when you get inside the ground-floor studio, there is only one season. The old stove smoulders on in a large, shed-like space that years of plaster dust keep a perpetual, snowy white. Of the sculptor himself, you see only a tousled head of hair and spectacle frames as you come in. Dominating the space is the dead, bright white of the latest big sculpture, *Grape Pickers*, with four life-size figures at work amid thick, rich – but still white – vines. The hair and spectacles come into focus on a plaster-splattered face.

'You see what I mean? The work involved?' Mason demands, bearing down on you and hooking a finger round the nearest bunch of grapes. 'Every single damn leaf, every grape and clod of earth has to be carved out and given its own unique life.' You gaze at thousands of small shapes awaiting completion. They blur and recede into the white mass of the whole. 'Then every single damn leaf and grape and clod of earth has to be painted and given its exact individual tone.' The spring morning falls flatly, blankly, through the studio skylight. It is indeed a most daunting exploit.

Grape Pickers is the final exhibit in the retrospective of thirty years of sculpture, painting and drawing by Raymond Mason at the Serpentine Gallery in London's Hyde Park. To many visitors the exhibition will come as a surprise, not to say a shock. One obvious reason for this is that the work radiates a powerful vision unlike anything else in contemporary art. The other is that, although he has exhibited regularly in Paris and New York, the sixty-year-old, Birmingham-born Mason has not been shown in Britain for over a quarter of a century.

This is quite as much Mason's doing as anybody else's. He virtually exiled himself from England until a few months ago, not really by deliberate choice but because he had found everything he needed for his art in France and saw no particular reason to return to England.

By temperament, he is in any case a classic example of the outsider. Otherwise he would never have escaped his definitely unartistic, working-class background so quickly and effectively. By the time he was 15, the young Raymond had made it clear that he was not going to learn a 'useful trade'. He then enrolled at the Birmingham College of Arts and Crafts – and never looked back.

After a short spell at the Royal College of Art in London, Mason got himself accepted in 1943 at the Slade, where the far-sighted principal, Professor Schwabe, persuaded him to try his hand at sculpture. The Slade had been evacuated to Oxford and, to help make his way, Mason found employment as a fire-watcher at the Ashmolean Museum. Long summer evenings alone there among the marble sculptures of classical antiquity gave him an opportunity to ponder the glories and the snares of this most tradition-bound art. But although he got a useful technical grounding in Oxford, it was not until he had left England and settled in Paris, in 1946, that Mason encountered the master influence that was to spark off his own individual development as a sculptor.

That influence was the work and personal example of Alberto Giacometti, who was already established in certain perceptive circles as the artist destined to renew the vocabulary of figurative art. On his first evening in Paris, Mason got a glimpse of the legendary Alberto at the Café de Flore. A lively friendship grew up between them which lasted until Giacometti's death. Mason's stylistic debt to the Swiss-born artist is obvious in the cityscape sculptures in low- and high-relief which he modelled throughout his first decade in Paris.

The key work of this whole early period was *Barcelona Tramway* (1953), a bronze relief which shows some figures seated in an open-windowed tram while others stand in a loose queue in front of it. The surface is so incisively etched and the compositional space moulded with such cunning conviction that the 4ft-long work acquires a haunting grandeur – a grandeur all the greater for emanating from the most commonplace of scenes: people in the street.

'I am a worshipper of the visible world,' Mason says of himself. And although it is difficult enough nowadays to prise him out of his studio, he spent his first decade in Paris roaming the streets with a sketchbook. 'Paris had a bracing vigour in those days. It was marvellously spontaneous,' Mason reminisces with obvious pleasure. 'There was real freedom, too. I mean, you could live or you could die and the French couldn't care less.'

However strong his liking for the city, Mason admits that day-to-day existence was 'pretty grim'. He was frequently penniless, but his talent and very energetic sense of survival nevertheless ensured that his work began to gain an audience. The first one-man show of Mason's sculpture and drawing, nevertheless, was organized in London in 1954 by the exceptionally discerning Helen Lessore at the Beaux-Arts Gallery. Two years later, a second Mason show took place at the Beaux-Arts, but from that time until the present exhibition at the Serpentine Mason disappeared from the British art scene.

Definitive recognition in France came with the large show put on at the Galerie Claude Bernard in 1965. The works chosen began with the *Tramway*, but the focal point was *The Crowd*. This new monumental piece was Mason's most ambitious work to date, since it dispensed with background and set out to turn a mass of figures into a tensely organized, dynamic sculpture. The challenge pushed Mason's gift for rapid synthesis to new heights: in *The Crowd*, the eye is kept constantly moving by the interlocking of volumes and an insistent repetition in the forms. Strenuously articulated composition had always been one of the sculptor's major concerns, but from then on it became his ruling passion.

A man as gifted and as torn by contradictions as Raymond Mason – whose power to convince is matched by ferocious doubts – was unlikely to stick to one style or technique. Once the bronze reliefs had been well received in Paris and then in New York (at the Pierre Matisse Gallery), Mason might have been tempted to work the same vein until he had exhausted its possibilities. But he was always conscious of a fundamental dichotomy. He had begun as painter, and his love of colour remained. What he sought, unconsciously enough, was a means of uniting his passion for sculpted form with his painter's delight in colour – a synthesis rarely achieved, and as rarely approved of, in the West today.

The answer came with the discovery of a new technique. Mason found a casting-shop where sculpture could be moulded in synthetic resins. Having had a piece cast in epoxy resin, he added touches of acrylic in an attempt to recapture the intensity of his plaster original. The result gave him the combination of painterly colour and sculptural volume that most excited his visual imagination.

A subject worthy of this radically new technique soon came along. In the centre of Paris the marvellous food-markets at Les Halles were about to be obliterated. Baltard's soaring iron-and-glass pavilions were going to be ripped up and the whole night-world of porters, prostitutes and insomniacs banished forever. Mason saw this as a unique opportunity to commemorate his love for Paris's hub of human appetite. Over the following two years, from 1969 to 1971, he sketched the vanishing scene furiously, then slowly translated it into plaster models before beginning to build up the final sculpture. A vast fresco eventually emerged, measuring over 10ft by 10ft. Contained within that vibrant slice of Paris between the market pavilions and the Church of Saint-Eustache was a crowd of Halles characters carrying off the last crates of fruit and vegetables.

The finished plaster was greatly admired by the chosen few invited to the sculptor's studio to see it. But when Mason began to colour the immaculate epoxy mould, reaction became considerably more mixed.

'I wanted to make my sculpture as vivid, as human and warm as possible,' Mason says. 'Well, it's obvious that a sculpture in colour is more human than one in marble or bronze. I know some people are horrified by the vividness of the colour. But where a painter might tend to harmonize his colours, a sculptor uses colours which fight, red against green for instance, because then there's a sort of bang and they separate and the space is filled.'

The *Halles* sculpture was filled to bursting point. Between the towering and minutely detailed pieces of architecture, there brimmed scores of faces and an endless profusion of fruit and veg. This great spawn of images could only be kept together by the tautest compositional organization. Each window, each head, each apple and leek had its part to play in holding the overall balance. Mason had painstakingly plotted a complex graph of cross-references, but as the sculpture neared completion all kinds of unforeseen ones cropped up. A potato found an unexpected echo in a fleshy nose; a clearly-veined cabbage leaf rehearsed the delicate tracery of the church behind.

The stage-by-stage planning of each large sculpture has enabled Mason to aim not only at a maximum coherence of form and colour, but also at a maximum of factual information. The *Halles* constitutes a real document about what the famous night-market looked and felt like. Content, in Mason's view, is indispensable to a durable art; his insistence on cramming as much hard fact as possible into his work has kept him at loggerheads with the many contemporary movements that reduce actual content to a minimum. 'For me, art should be a means of intercepting thought,' he says. 'It should give it the weight and body to hold out against the centuries. Real art should have enough substance to satisfy everybody, old or young, cultured or not, who looks at it. I want an art that stems directly from life, not from other art.' This credo was amply borne out in Mason's next large sculpture, *A Tragedy in the North: Winter, Rain and Tears*, based on a mining disaster of 1974.

The *Tragedy*, which made a tremendous impact at this year's Venice Biennale, shows people overcome with grief streaming out of the mine. Behind them rise a red-brick building and the ominous tip of a slag-heap. Each of the sharply characterized figures tells of an aspect of the disaster. The sculpture's perspective involves the spectator right away, leading his eye through the figures to the mine, then back to the foreground along the cobblestones.

Mason's sculptures are plainly narrative, and the story they tell is aimed at the widest possible audience. That is why the artist has always chosen the most easy-to-understand, not to say humble, of subjects. The *Grape Pickers* is as close to his own experience as one could imagine, since the vineyard stands opposite the small summer house he owns in Provence and the grape-pickers are his neighbours. It is also a universal theme par excellence, one with which virtually anyone in the world can identify. The subject has been treated with absolute simplicity, but each detail of form, every fleck of colour, makes a specific contribution to the overall effect.

The Serpentine exhibition will be a moment of truth for Raymond Mason, since it is the first time that all his most important works have been brought together and the first time they have been shown in a public museum. He has long maintained that a large section of the public has a hunger for art which cannot be satisfied by the purely aesthetic concerns of most contemporary work. Whatever the public's reaction to the Serpentine show, it is likely to be loud, for the sculpture is too powerful, too bristling with life and conviction, and too provocative to be passed over in silence.

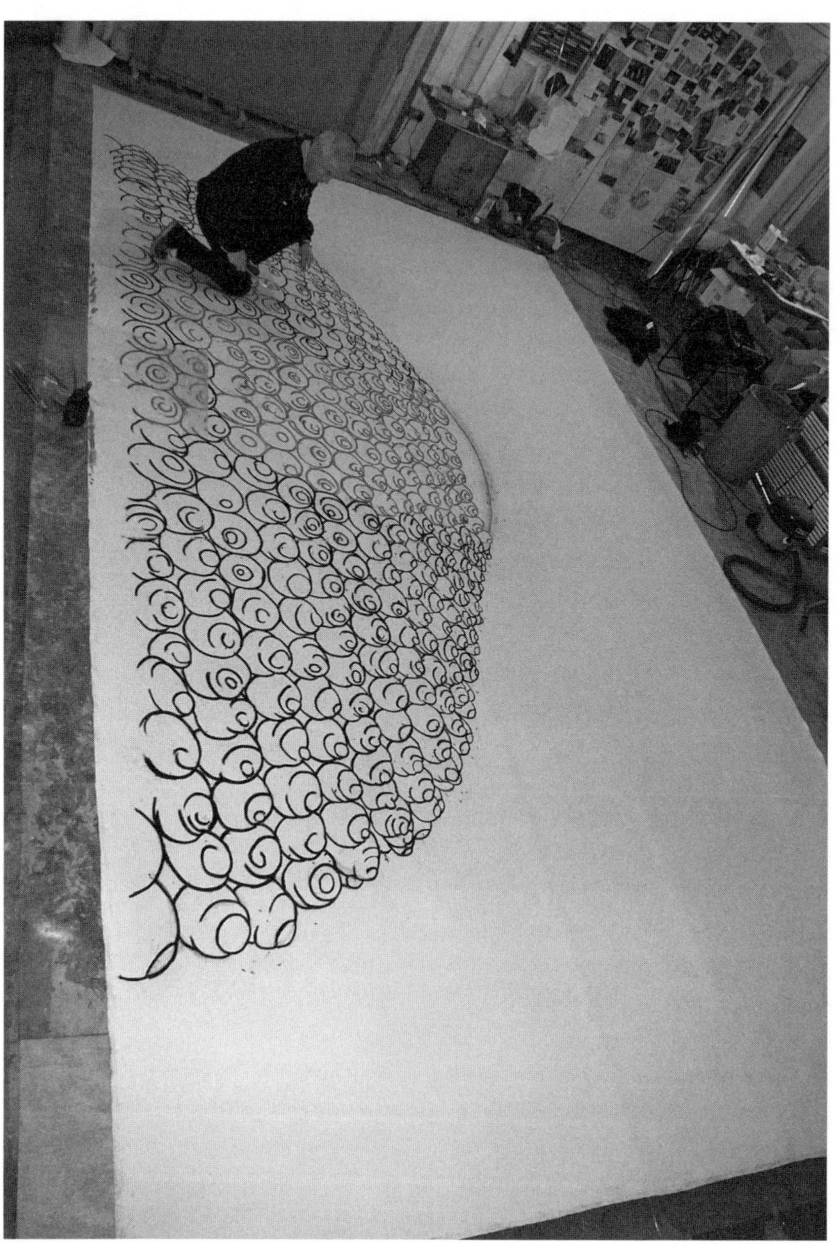

TONY BEVAN

DEPTFORD LONDON 2008

It is early August 2008 and Tony Bevan's studio in South London is unusually light and silent. Two chairs have been found and dusted down and placed opposite each other for our talk. Otherwise there is nothing in the high-ceilinged, functional space that does not relate directly to Bevan's activity here. A half-completed canvas and a couple of charcoal drawings lie face up on the concrete floor, while several finished paintings hang high overhead and others stand face inwards against the whitewashed walls. Among the bottles and brushes, the pyramids of bright pigment and pyre-like stacks of charcoal sticks, there are more homely objects: paint-spattered shoes, odd rags, knee-pads for working on the floor. Pinned to the back of the studio door are a few photos and postcard reproductions, alongside odd notes and letters. Anonymous though it seems at first, the studio becomes more and more like a Bevan painting as the conversation gets under way: a space opening on to other spaces where assumptions of normality are questioned and everyday identity goes slowly out of focus, its habitual contours seeping into the calm, absorbent light.

MP Your paintings talk very powerfully for themselves, but I wanted to listen to you talk about them because I think it might reveal things that critics and observers are bound to miss. For a start, I'd be particularly interested to know how you began as an artist.

TB I think it had a lot to do with growing up in a house in Bradford with my parents and grandparents where there were all kinds of African artefacts around. My grandfather spent most of his life in Africa as a trader and explorer, and each time he came back he brought lots of these carved figures with him. They were all over our house, and I think they had a huge

Tony Bevan (1951–). *Tony Bevan: New Paintings*, exhibition catalogue, Ben Brown Fine Arts, London, September 2008.

influence on me because I realized they were very alive and had nothing to do with decoration. And they kept changing because my grandmother didn't like them and she'd put them into the saleroom once he'd gone back to Africa, and then eventually he'd bring back another shipment. It was very odd because my grandmother painted, and what she really liked was copying her favourite Victorian paintings, and of course they were genteel and indirect and about as far from these African carvings as it's possible to get. I was also fascinated by all the paraphernalia she used. She had these extraordinary wooden boxes that folded out into easels, and there were folding stools and folding boxes with all the paints she used laid out in orderly coloured rows. It was real experience for me to see all the tools and materials that went into painting, and I was very impressed by them.

MP You were a very visual person right from childhood – perhaps unusually visual?

TB Maybe. I do remember doing lots of drawings from the age of three or four. And that continued, I got lost in it, and I think just by drawing a lot you actually become quite good at it. But I was also a painfully shy child, I don't really know why, and I actually kept my drawing ability under wraps because the first time somebody found out I could draw quite well I was asked to stand in front of the class to draw a rearing horse. I can remember the heat of all this embarrassment and it was a terrible trauma.

MP But you felt totally at home in the world of drawing – that's what you took refuge in?

TB I suppose so. My great-uncle, my mother's uncle, was a stained-glass artist. You know, you paint the oxides on the glass, then it's re-fired so you can do the shading on the details. And the unusual thing about him was that he disappeared one day. He just didn't come home from the workshop. Every now and then people thought they'd sighted him, and there were all sorts of speculation that he'd started another family and so on. But he never reappeared, and later on, when I wanted to go to art school, my parents, particularly my mother, were very encouraging because they thought it was almost this person and his interest in art resurfacing.

MP What sort of things did you draw? I mean, apart from the horse, did you draw your family at all or imaginary things?

TB It was mainly imaginary things. But there was a broad range, drawing was such a big part of my life ... So then I was able to go to Bradford Art School to do a Foundation course, and I stayed there for three years. I was interested in everything, the whole gamut of art, from cave painting to contemporary art. We saw endless slides in the art history course, but they almost put you off because there wasn't enough in them – you couldn't see the quality or the scale. I remember seeing all these slides of Giotto, but it was only when I had been to Padua and seen the frescoes in the flesh that I developed a real love for them.

MP So you got a grounding in Bradford but quite early on you had your eyes set on London and you came up and looked round the art schools.

TB Yes, Goldsmiths struck me most and that's where I ended up going to in 1970. Coming from Bradford to a city like London and leaving home for the first time felt like a huge liberation. And while I was in the painting department at Goldsmiths, there was an opening up of all the different disciplines within the school and we were encouraged to work in different departments. So I was making films, installations and photography, casting sculpture and even working in the psychology lab. But after a while I actually found this 'freedom' quite restrictive, because while I was painting I didn't have to reason things through all the time, but when I worked with other media, I was always caught up in a reasoning process.

MP So in fact this exploration of other media sent you back to drawing and painting. Drawing is the basis of what you do, isn't it? I mean everything is charted out and explored with drawing.

TB Yes, it's a kind of grounding for everything I do. And when I left art school I went back to drawing and painting full time, and around 1979 my partner Glenys Johnson and I started spending half of the year in New York. So for a number of years we divided our time between the two places. As you can imagine, the New York art world was, compared to London, compact and lively and we got to meet and become friends with many painters, film makers, performance artists and musicians. Painting was back in fashion there. Remembering it now, it was very difficult surviving in London during this time and being in New York gave you a charge of energy.

MP What sort of things were you painting at the time? Were they particular themes?

TB I did figure paintings, mainly large single figures. We're talking about 1982, 1983, and I brought back a lot of those paintings and showed them at Matt's Gallery. Matt's had always been very supportive towards me and I was able to show those paintings as well as others that I did directly there on the floor of the gallery – which wasn't always easy because Matt was actually the name of the gallery's dog and it was very difficult to keep him from walking all over the paintings . . .

MP But during this time whose work did you admire most? Were you influenced by any particular artists or by a wide range of people?

TB I think it had more to do with a lot of people.

MP But surely certain things had a lasting, formative influence on you? You mentioned Giotto, for instance.

TB Yes, but there are so many artists, when you start naming them you're bound to forget some. I'm reluctant to make a list. But I suppose if I had the luxury of having just one painting I could see every day, it would be Mantegna's *Dead Christ*. I've seen it on three or four occasions in Milan, and I think it would be a fantastic thing to be able to view that on a daily basis. I find it an incredibly emotional painting: there's all the intensity of that relationship between the mother and the son, as if all that had been unsaid between them was held there. It's the power of the unsaid. It's a small painting covering such a huge area it's endless. Death has never been painted with such intensity as this.

MP And even though you don't really like seeing works in reproduction, do you look at a lot of books, or do you just try to go to certain exhibitions and museums to see things?

TB I do look at things in books and you do get an approximation – you can actually fill in the gaps sometimes. I try to see as many paintings and exhibitions as possible. The act of looking at a painting is a contemplative thing, I think. It's a slow process and you tend to try to build a relationship with the painting, over a period of time.

MP So you are constantly feeding your imagination by looking at the work of others?

TB Yes, and I think that is what all artists do and need to do. We're not just restricted to painting, of course. There's also sculpture and just everything else around, whether it's films and photography or whatever. I couldn't live as a sort of hermit where I was denied access to all this other information, because all sorts of things that you see stimulate your work and get incorporated into it. Things feed into painting in an unconscious way.

MP You told me the other day that something had come completely out of left field and interested you visually, even though you hadn't been aware of it when it happened.

TB It happens quite often. You make a particular decision when you're painting and you're not sure of the reason why. I mean, I was doing a self-portrait once and the whole figure was in violet and I was very sure I wanted a silver background. I mean I'm not even sure if silver is a colour, I'd never actually worked with silver and it was just a very curious background for me to work with. Anyway, I painted it in silver, and the violet and the silver worked very well. Then a week or so later, I realized that when I'd been walking past the window down the corridor to my studio there were these people in the distance who were painting a roof and they'd been painting it silver for the last few weeks. And I'd never actually consciously taken that in, I'd just been glancing at the silver out of the side of my eye. These things happen and surprising elements come up. I actually like that feeling, I like the sensation of being slightly out of control. And to come back to an earlier point, that was one of the interesting things I've always found in painting – that you don't have this constant need to pin down why something is actually happening. You simply create a kind of a space where these things can surface and become part of the painting.

MP And that's really one of your prime motives for painting, this freedom to wander and let things surface?

TB Yes, and sometimes things surface and you wish they hadn't and you have to confront them. And I certainly want that kind of spontaneity, but at the same time I tend to do lots of preparatory drawings before I start on a painting. They help me to take the first steps, to get to a stage where I feel I can go straight into the painting. This thing of spontaneity is very strange. When I went to Oslo to visit the Munch Museum, I'd always thought *The Scream* was something he'd painted very urgently, in a very short space of time. And then I saw that he'd done these masses of drawings and colour studies before he did it, and yet it still seems a very spontaneous image.

MP Are you aware of specific origins for your own images?

TB Well, you're never really sure where paintings come from. Things hit you and get stored, and they're often combinations of all sorts of things. When I was travelling in China recently, I went to see a very large Buddha, and I had to climb a hill to get there, and when I got to the top I saw this other hill which eventually turned out to be the back of this enormous Buddha's head. And that interested me and amused me – to think of heads in terms of hills and vice versa, and thinking of heads in terms of pure mass ... And these kinds of surprises happen when you're painting. All sorts of things go on within this pictorial space, and that has always amazed me. Your imagination enters into this space and starts on this particular journey. I think when you look at my paintings, you're not looking at some stage set but at a kind of space we all inhabit. You're drawn into them and they demand a response. I inhabit this space while I'm painting, it's an extension of me both mentally and physically. Since I'm very involved in it, I think that intensity comes through.

MP But does your hand sort of almost get in front of you and start doing things that you're not absolutely consciously aware of?

TB I think that happens quite often. And you get a situation where your thoughts are down one particular branch line and your physical actions are down another, you know? There are many occasions when your painting or drawing is way ahead of what you're thinking, or it's done something that you hadn't foreseen at all. It's often a whole state of flux. I like there to be a certain degree of disorder, and I suppose I need disorder for things to happen. If a kind of surgical precision creeps in, nothing can actually take place.

MP And if things are going a bit too much to order, do you feel you have to break out of it? Do you paint over or scrape off?

TB If something is becoming too tight, too restrictive, I have to start the whole thing over again, on a fresh canvas. Sometimes I can paint over, but often the marks I've made are actually embedded way into the surface. One of the things that I've been doing for many years, for some thirty years, is painting on the floor. At a certain point I found I needed that physical contact to be able to put pressure on the painting and I needed the assistance of gravity and I found that working on the floor helped. I've always felt a need to be in close physical contact when I'm working. And very often on the work you will actually see where my knees have been, or where my hands have been. They've become part of the process. And you can see the debris from the charcoal still there on the surface, so that the actual process of the making still lingers. You can work out what materials have been used, you can trace what's been going on. And I have always had – probably every painter does – a particular interest in the materials I use and the way they behave.

MP We're talking about drawing and painting?

TB Yes. And I suppose the materials I tend to use are very basic and raw. When you draw with charcoal, for instance, you realize each piece is quite unique. You have all these different pieces of burnt wood, and no two pieces are alike. You can actually tell by looking at them, you can gauge their behaviour or quality. A particular stick of charcoal might be incredibly soft or hard or it might scratch. And you've got these different woods. There's charcoal made out of willow or vine or poplar, and they're all different colours and they have different behaviours. This whole business of how one works with different materials fascinates me. Pigments also have different behavioural qualities. You're very much aware of the weight of colours, whether they are metal-based, when they have that heavy metal colour, or plant-based, when they tend to be a lot lighter and float in a different way. My paintings tend to revolve around a small number of colours, but within each colour there are endless tones and contrasts. So things are actually suggested in the process of painting just by the behaviour of these colours alone.

MP Are the process and the materials as important to you as the subject – or part of the same thing?

TB Well, the subject I'm dealing with is not just about the material, it's the other way around. What I'm really concerned with is the whole process of working, the process of painting. I mean, there's an obvious difference when I'm painting a 'Head' or a 'Studio Furniture' subject, but there's a similarity between them in the sense that you're entering a space where the 'Head' becomes some kind of internal landscape or the 'Furniture' a kind of mental threshold or construct. I see all these things as constructs for an extension of myself and an exploration of the world around me.

MP Do you move freely between these subjects or focus on a single theme?

TB I usually have several themes on the go at any one time. One painting tends to metamorphose into another, or one theme sends me back to another. They go in cycles, but the cycles frequently overlap. The 'Studio Furniture' and the 'Towers' simply came out of looking at all the props and objects and debris that I have around me here in the studio. Again, it's what's closest to me on a daily basis. They started out as drawings, and I was very interested in the way you can draw an object and watch it lose its initial identity, so that it goes into a kind of flux, a kind of free fall, and it becomes multi-faceted, with multiple existences, transforming from one thing into another and back again, so you can't actually put a label on it any more. I mean, I see some of the table tops I've done transforming into hill tops, then back into just junk on a table – or two lines within them suddenly meeting to suggest a crucifix.

MP It's a process of giving and withdrawing identity?

TB Well, it's a process of finding what gives that object its identity, or how much identity is needed and how much can be taken away or reduced. You tend to lose the initial identity as you work. It moves into something else as you're making decisions about what is essential and how it can transform. And it's surprising what happens sometimes, because you're not sure why certain things appear. I like these constant shiftings and transformations. But you can only take them so far, and even though sometimes all these other suggestions come up as to how to go forward you realize they're for the next painting or for another one down the line.

MP So one painting suggests another in the series.

TB I tend to think of them as cycles, because for me a series means a beginning, a middle and an end, and these are more chaotic. They go off into orbit or they come back to something previous. But of course certain things do suggest others. I think the 'Studio Towers' developed out of the 'Studio Furniture' paintings. And you're not sure what they are, I think, these imaginary towers, because they inhabit a very particular space and it's not clear what scale they're on or what they support or how they themselves are supported. They're gouged into the canvas, into the surface, so they're very physical and there's a sort of awkwardness in the way they lock and form. I see them as chaotic and contradictory, with whole other worlds stacking up within them, right at their core.

MP Have the materials you use been pretty much the same all the way through, or have they been whittled down and refined?

TB I suppose they've been refined, but refined in a kind of reversal of refined. I mean I make my own paints now, and initially I worked with ready-made paints. You understand the behaviour of paint better when you work with pigments you've made. Years ago, when I was at art school, there was a tradition of always making your own paints. You had these three or four black pigments and then you had the linseed oil, and it is only when you started measuring the French black against the vine black or the Mars black that you realized the incredible difference between blacks. Sometimes the particles would be incredibly light or they would be very heavy. So you could alter the colours of black with these particular pigments. And later when I started working with bought tubes of paint, I found they had this ready-made quality, and around the late 1970s, early 1980s, I had to go back to the basics and make my own colours. These things just come about as you're working. When I painted on an easel, for instance, the canvas had a tendency to move around or fall because I pressed so hard. With some of the recent paintings, like the 'Towers' and the 'Studio Furniture', the lines have been almost gouged into the canvas, with brushes where the bristles have been almost completely cut off, it's like a gouged line, you know, through the pressure from the brush onto the surface of the canvas. It would be quite impossible to do that if the canvas was actually on a stretcher or on an easel.

MP What sensations do you have when you are gouging like that?

TB Well, on those particular paintings, it was the physical nature of the line – the line had a very strong physical presence. It wasn't to do with the line being a description, it existed in itself. It became an object in itself and the lines constructed the pictures.

MP And you wanted it to have its own existence because that gives you a space to inhabit, to explore. So the technique also opens up formal possibilities.

TB Well, it's a twin-track thing. We were talking about the process of painting and being out of control in terms of thoughts, and of allowing things to happen and the unexpected to come through. These are kinds of unconscious things, coming through while I am working and also in the way the materials are reacting, especially when they're getting out of control. So things are suggested through the painting process and how the colour is behaving. The two elements come into play. And I think the speed your mind goes at and things that are suggested become quite extreme on occasions.

MP Which means that some paintings are done very quickly and others take a great deal more input.

TB Yes, with some paintings I'll have to put them to one side and come back to them three or four months later, just because I may have lost them, lost the kind of vision I had, and I know I can't work with them any longer. Some paintings can take a couple of days and others much longer. On average, I tend to do about sixteen to eighteen paintings a year. And quite often, you can't really see a painting until years later, and you realize it's a lot stronger or a lot weaker than it seemed when you did it.

MP Do you think you're your own best critic? You obviously know more than anyone else about your own work.

TB I'm not sure about that. When I come to see a lot of my paintings together, in a retrospective exhibition, or if I have to give a talk and there are a lot of slides, I do see elements and subjects that recur. And when I'm working I'm never that conscious of this thing re-occurring. It's really curious when you see things resurfacing ten, fifteen, twenty years later. And you realize there's a degree of chaos and contradiction in the works. But also there are elements that are almost like props that you carry around with you. And I think you're always drawing on things that you are used to as well as things you probably didn't know about. I mean, I use myself a lot as a source, possibly because it's what's closest.

MP Your own appearance?

TB Well, probably not so much my particular appearance, but the kind of way my own body is. I use elements of my body. I'm reluctant to say 'appearance' because it's not to do with the outward look of any particular person. And I wouldn't actually call them self-portraits, because it's not to do with reflecting a particular state at a particular time.

MP Would you say it's more an exploration of yourself and a sort of transmission of feelings about yourself?

TB I think so, yes, but not feelings about myself, feelings about other things. If it was a part of me, such as the head, the whole body would be contained within that head, for instance.

MP So this is really a kind of interior drama, as it were. You're inhabiting your own inner space and acting out things.

TB I suppose there's a certain degree of that. But it's not a direct expression of something particular going on. I don't profess to know myself fully what the actual content is of any particular painting. For me the endless fascination is with pictorial space, even though that is a concept that is often dismissed. Painting is unique and endlessly fascinating. After all these centuries it still has the ability both to elevate and to plumb the depths. For me, painting remains the most exciting, accurate way of exploring sensation and awareness.

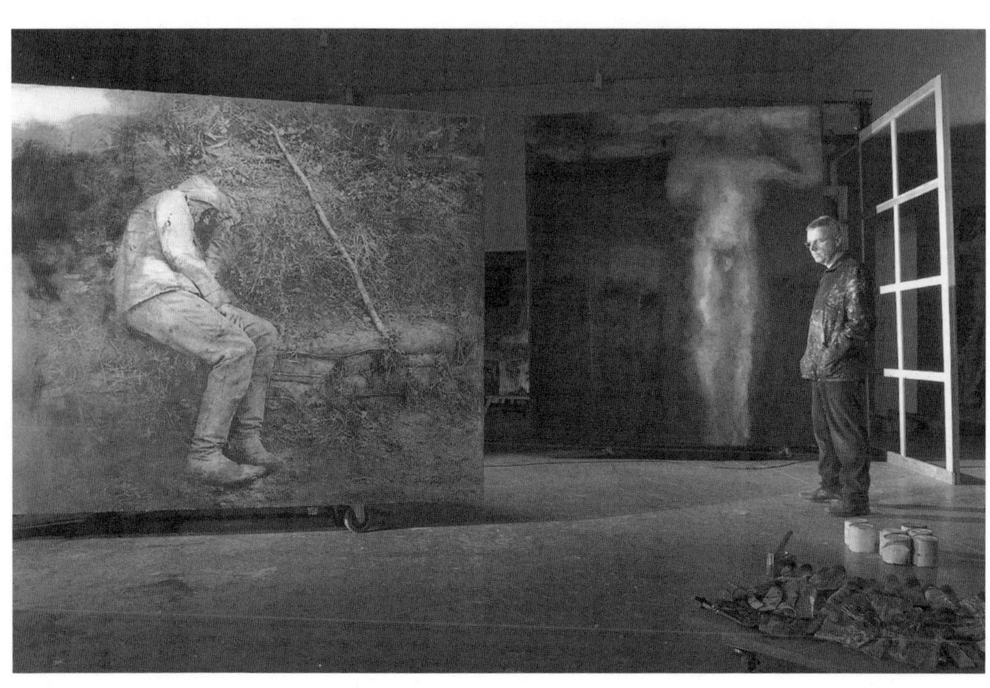

HUGHIE O'DONOGHUE

GREENWICH LONDON 2009

The following conversation took place during an almost tropically hot, heavy afternoon in late June 2009 in Hughie O'Donoghue's vast studio, a former chapel set at the end of a cul-de-sac in Greenwich. O'Donoghue and his wife, Clare, had just settled back in after one of their regular migrations between London and their other home in the Irish countryside. Several recent large-scale paintings, including a 'Yellow Man', hung in regular intervals around the walls, while upstairs, on a mezzanine level, dozens of small works in progress, incorporating a mass of old photographs, lay around with various paints and tools on the floor. From the windows in the vaulted ceiling, light flooded down in almost tangible waves into the lofty, silent, white space. Speaking softly and concentrating intently on each phrase, O'Donoghue talked with practised ease, but also warily, in a directly questioning spirit, as if he were exploring his own work and its implications anew.

MP Hughie, the word 'memory' comes immediately to mind when I think about your painting. It's a key word when you or anybody else talks about your work. What do you think memory is? What is memory for you? And why do you think you're so drawn to it, so interested in it?

HO'D That's a difficult question because it's something that emerged in my work rather than something that I made a conscious decision to investigate. And quite early on someone observed that my work was probably more about *re*-membering or trying to *re*-construct an idea, as a kind of recovering process through memory. I think memory is like an intangible archive that we carry with us, and it's primarily about how we feel about things. So in my work, I'm trying to make some kind of equivalent for

Hughie O'Donoghue (1953–). *Hughie O'Donoghue: The Journey*, exhibition catalogue, Leeds Art Gallery, Leeds, September 2009.

feeling and also to make sense of the world: to put things back together, to try and reconstruct things and see whether they add up. That may sound a bit vague, but the process was something that was gradual. I suppose it emerged from having made paintings that had come to an end: a body of work that was on the subject of the Passion had come to an end, and I was making new paintings. It was shortly after my father died and I was going through a lot of archive material that I'd inherited – not with the intention of it being source material for work, but it fascinated me, and it became subject-matter.

MP It's a very curious thing when you try to differentiate between memory and feeling. You might almost say that feelings are a form of memory, because feelings are rooted in memories and they are often sparked off by a specific recall.

HO'D Yes, by smells or by sounds or things that are familiar, recording something that's visceral, that affects us. And that's what I think the language of painting is as well. That's not to say that painting is without intellectual content, but if the ideas in a painting can be understood in a text before the painting is looked at, the painting itself is redundant. So the painting has to actually act in some way as a trigger for memory. It has to trigger an emotional response and I think the way that meaning is arrived at in painting, in many ways, is connected to this process. When I begin a painting I don't have an absolutely specific, nailed-down, hard-and-fast idea of what the painting's meaning will be. In fact, I would argue that I don't actually control that – what the painting is and its meaning. I think meaning is a product of the encounter with the painting, ultimately by the person who receives that painting. I'm sure everybody has had the experience of going back somewhere that they remembered or seeing something that they feel they knew intimately, and being shocked by seeing how little it resembles or corresponds to their feeling. In a way I think that's how the painting relates to its subject, it's an equivalent but it doesn't illustrate its subject.

MP Are you saying that, in other people, a painting might spark off memories different from those you had in mind when you were making it?

HO'D Yes, I think that the meaning of a painting is not fixed. In my view meaning is a product, it's the result of a process. I would certainly acknowledge that, although I say I don't entirely control that meaning, there are certain subconscious elements that will emerge in the process of painting. I'm aware of that – in fact I see that as inevitable.

MP Well, obviously an adolescent is going to have other reactions to your painting than, say, a Second World War veteran.

HO'D Yes.

MP But your themes are actually quite varied. I noticed that you talk about individual and collective memory. Is there some sort of bisection of the two that you occasionally find in a particular subject that catches your interest and that you want to explore by painting?

HO'D One of the subjects that emerges in my painting is history. In the nineteenth century, history painting was the epitome of what artists aspired to, and it died because essentially it was fake and phoney.

MP A kind of costume drama?

HO'D Yes. It became basically something that was highly manipulated. History painting was there to tell a particular story the way people wanted it to be told, and that's never the currency of art. The currency of art is some idea of truth, whatever that is, but the artist in a sense has to be true to himself. So my take on it is that history is very personal, and one way of understanding the Second World War, or the legacy of the Second World War, is to understand it through a very personal story, through the everyman story rather than the stories of the campaigns or the big events. That particularly interested me when I began to make work that took my father's chequered history in the Second World War as its source, so I decided to follow that path wherever it led. Even the banality of the time, the boredom and the frustration – having to fill out your tax returns just after you'd come through the Battle of Monte Cassino, for example! Or at the end of the War just being welcomed back to the railway, as my father was, and being told to get back on with his job. To me, that kind of ordinariness seemed to be a possible route towards a universal human experience.

MP So how were they welcomed back?

HO'D At the end of the War they were just sent a letter saying: 'Thank you for your contribution, look forward to seeing you back in the office next Monday'. All of that became very interesting to me because it was human. I was very aware of the dangers of the kind of assumptions that people would immediately make – things like 'you must have admired your father greatly' – which was absolutely not the case. That's not to say that I didn't have any respect for my father, but I wasn't in any way trying to elevate him. It was the fact that I had this subject . . . it's like Cézanne painting the Mont Sainte-Victoire, you don't actually learn much about the mountain – he's not telling you about how big the mountain is or anything like that, he's telling you more about himself than he's telling you about the mountain.

MP Do you yourself consciously search for subjects?

HO'D Yes absolutely, yes.

MP So they have to meet a certain number of requirements in a sense? I would imagine you're always looking to see if they cut into enough areas to give you enough material, because the denser the subject is, the more it interests you?

HO'D Yes it does. And in a way I'm interested in the human, in anything that really tells a human story. I suppose I'm of a generation where the idea of any kind of narrative or story-telling had been so purged out of art, it was so unfashionable and so old hat that it actually became interesting again. In my formative years the first serious paintings were really very minimal, they were purged of references to the outside world. But now, actually, I'm very interested in returning to themes that are about human experience.

MP I suppose purging of content and of narrative was exactly what you were saying about nineteenth-century painting, when it became so contrived that any kind of narrative was seen as potentially false and to be avoided. And that's been done and now there is a void again to be filled.

HO'D Yes, there was an exhibition at the Royal Academy a number of years ago on American painting, and at the end of the exhibition it came back to various kinds of minimalism. Whether it was Ryman or Reinhardt, or what have you, everything had been purged from the paintings, the only thing that changed was the text next to the painting.

MP *(Laughs)* Yes, right.

HO'D Even now when I look at contemporary painting, I realize as a young artist you're trying to make work that's relevant to the time you're in. So my turning-point, I suppose, was 1981 at Goldsmiths. Almost overnight, I lost that belief in formalism and what was formal painting and decided to go back to subject-matter.

MP And how did that Pauline conversion come about? Had it been building up?

HO'D It had been. Goldsmiths was very much a talking shop and a conceptual school. I arrived there as a formalist painter, and all the assumptions that underpin formalist painting were put under close scrutiny, and the conclusion I came to was that I'd painted myself into a corner in a way. I think I probably thought about people like Rothko, late Rothko, the way the paintings aspire to so much but they become emptier and emptier of possibility. Then over the summer of 1981 I was in Brittany for a holiday and I came back with some drawings of menhirs – they were the first where subjects emerged in the painting again. I suppose that archaeology has been a kind of constant motif really, the references …

MP The unearthing of the past?

HO'D The unearthing of the past, whether it's stone sculptures or maps of how places were. The work is about trying to understand …

MP And yet, your painting isn't like a diary, is it? I suppose to some extent it must be. How would you define it? Picasso said his work was a diary, Bacon said his work was a diary. I suppose all work is a diary to the extent that you record the daily, but is your painting a kind of experiment, a kind of unearthing, in itself an archaeology?

HO'D I often see it as the analogy of archaeology. An archaeologist digs somewhere where he doesn't know what's there, but something leads him to believe that in this place there may be something of interest. In a way my painting is like that. It's always been quite time based, and it's often a process of beginning with a subject and allowing the process of making the painting to define the painting itself. Ultimately it has a life of its own and that's when it's finished. But the process of doing it is all about refining one's idea. When I begin a painting I make my first stab at it, and it's that desire to correct it, to refine it in some way and it is very, very difficult to articulate that when I'm actually doing a painting. I'm quite articulate in talking about my work when it's some time after the event: I can usually point to things that were conscious or even subconscious. But when I'm making it, it's the actual struggle with the material, and I'm looking for a time that is almost like a kind of flow where you're not particularly aware of time. You're certainly not trying to put meaning or to put obvious triggers or signs or symbols into a work.

MP You're caught up in a process, a dialogue …

HO'D Yes, with the work itself. I feel that's very much why a reaction to the culture of conceptual art set in. I feel that the idea has to be in some kind of tension with the form.

MP But how specific is your idea when you start a painting? Do you work in a series, with one work sparking off another?

HO'D Yes, invariably I have more than one work going on at the same time. Sometimes I begin a work with a very specific idea and abandon it for a long period of time, and then possibly return to it or change it. One of the paintings that's in the exhibition at Leeds has undergone many, many changes. It's a painting called *Course of the Diver* that was originally entitled 'Tomb of the Diver'. A number of sources fed into the idea; one was the actual remaking of a painting from antiquity. The 'Tomb of the Diver' was a work at Paestum discovered in the 1960s – it's a very unusual early fourth-century BC painting of a diver. It's meant to represent the tomb's occupant passing into the afterlife.

MP This was dug up?

HO'D It was dug up and it's a tomb slab. On the inside there are other images of the tomb's occupant. It's a very free painting, and the archaeologists think that what looks like a diving board actually represents the Pillars of Hercules at the edge of the Mediterranean. So the idea is that he's diving into the Atlantic, the unknown sea. It's about the passage into the after-life. When I saw that, it was the first trip I made after September 11. I had been very affected by those images of people leaping from the World Trade Center towers, I saw it as a very positive thing. I know it was a terrible event, but it was the action – not awaiting fate but acting as a diver, a leaper, a jumper – not just passively awaiting fate, I was interested in that. In that painting there are a number of ideas: the idea that the tomb can contain a portrait of the individual, and they often did allude to myths in the iconography of the tomb, but they also included objects that were there to represent the individual, so the painting initially began with objects. So in this case I took the individual as my father in the first version, in the second version the image is of my son, so it's people I know. I suppose I'm far enough from the image now to say what it's actually about: it's about the spiritual journey people have to make in life. So it's meant to be a metaphor for growth, and for enlightenment and for the growth of the person. That's often in literature, the features of a journey, the idea of the journey into the self. So that's my subject, but the form it takes in that particular painting underwent many, many changes: the painting was enlarged, cut down, parts of it removed and the imagery changed three or four times.

MP And it ended as something quite …

HO'D Something quite unrecognizable from what it began as, but that's not always the case. The only reason to go back to a painting is if you want to improve it or if something in it just irritates you or distracts you, or if part of the subject that is there is nevertheless distracting, drawing you into a section of the painting that's destroying the whole thing. And that is difficult when you're trying to deal with specific subject-matter rather than with more formal painting, because I'm trying to resolve …

MP Because there's form and meaning.

HO'D Content. Yes absolutely, specific content.

MP Do you ever find you have to stop a picture and start it all over again?

HO'D Yes, or even abandon it, although I rarely abandon a work. What often happens is that I've invested so much into it but it isn't working, and what I normally do is I hide it away somewhere and forget about it, and then at some point I'm able to pull it out and have the distance required to destroy something that was perhaps too precious to me at the time to get rid of, because I wasn't able to distance myself enough.

MP Do you discuss this with anybody else or is it just with yourself?

HO'D I discuss it with my wife, Clare. It took a long time to arrive at that. I was very defensive about showing my work in progress, but for the last ten years or so she regularly comes into the studio.

MP That can be very useful, can't it? It's another gaze.

HO'D It's absolutely fantastic.

MP And so then the work isn't just yours, it's begun to take on a life of its own, because somebody else has looked it at.

HO'D Yes, and she's very good at immediately noticing something that isn't working, that I may not see because I'm too close to it. And because she points that out to me I'm very good at resolving things when I can see what the problem is, but often I can't see the problem, I can only see the content. I think similar strategies have been used by artists for hundred of years: I mean, there are stories of Titian turning his pictures to the wall. In the past I've used the shock of seeing a photograph of the painting, because you've got that distance of a photograph, and I still use that as a distancing method.

MP Taking a photo and then taking the painting away and looking at the photo?

HO'D Yes, because it's like something else then. In many cases I think because of the very, very large size of my pictures and the very worked surfaces, there is a tendency to be sucked into the surface.

MP And no longer being able to see the whole. Is there a process of drawing or anything like that, or do you go straight into the canvas?

HO'D I go straight into the canvas. I don't draw as much now as I used to. I used to make large-scale charcoal drawings but they were usually after the paintings. It was almost like something had emerged in the painting and then it was in the drawings. There'd be one painting and either five or six drawings –

different possibilities of the painting, rather than drawings as a preparatory stage. There was a phase, after I'd been living in Italy, where I picked up this tendency to draw on the canvas with a sort of sepia, like a thinned-down burnt sienna, almost like a sinopia drawing. I was making very ambitious figure compositions at that time, and it was a disaster, technically, because it just was a complete impediment to what happened in the painting. I just went in too early.

MP Before you knew where you were going and what you wanted to do? Or before you knew what the scope could be? All of this is not that different from writing. It's a process, isn't it? You're constantly testing yourself and then suddenly, sometimes you can find a freedom that you never realized you had. And those kinds of preparations ... well you just want to throw them out because it's not the way to go. Do you look at things while you're doing your paintings? Do you continue to leaf through books and read?

HO'D Yes. It's my process of drawing really. I would include reading around the subject extensively, researching what I'm doing, getting familiar with it, going to the place ...

MP Taking photos?

HO'D Taking photographs, yes, I've always taken photographs. Even the taking of them, rather than necessarily referencing them, just that immersion in the subject is key for me. It's traditionally how artists familiarized themselves with the subject, by focusing on it, concentrating on it. In my case, I'm not sitting in front of a model and drawing the model, but I'm immersing myself in the subject-matter.

MP It's a real intellectual occupation, an endeavour. The voiding was no doubt a necessary stage, but it sometimes does seem slightly absurd in retrospect.

HO'D I feel it was a massive reaction to the invention of photography. It was about separating and finding what painting could do. It was felt that photography took away from painting something that…

MP It became a competition.

HO'D Yes. I'm very interested now in the way there is a kind of dialogue in my painting, and that's probably mapped out in one of the substantial paintings in the Leeds exhibition called *Wrestlers* about the relationship between photography and painting. Everybody reads photography, so without thinking we read a photograph, whereas the language of painting is a slightly more rarefied language. And in that particular painting I wanted the painted component, which is an image of the Roman sculpture *Wrestlers* – it's a bas-relief made in lead white and graphite – to completely overshadow the photographic image, which is obscured. It's of a soldier at Cassino who is up to his knees in mud digging an artillery piece out of the quagmire. The references are quite overt; it may be because the painting was made while I was living in Oxford in a very academic environment. The references were to the idea of archaeology, but also to digging and unearthing. The sculpture is a symbol of memory, of something coming out of the ground and being recovered.

MP Almost out of the unconscious…

HO'D Yes, and I'm not sure whether that sculpture was known, but certainly the *Laocoön* was known about when it came out, it was talked about in Pliny and various commentaries. They knew about this famous thing and then it emerged and it set up a dialogue with the artists at that time. So this was being paired with the soldier at Cassino, and in a sense with the idea of this recent memory coming out of the death of my father. I suppose there are these various subtexts about the results of not learning from history.

MP As all these things have been unearthed, do you take a great deal of pleasure in the actual medium of paint? Is it a voluptuous thing?

HO'D Absolutely.

MP Has that set up a certain tension too? I mean the actual pleasure of manipulating the paint and the pain of the memory … ?

HO'D It has to. That's why I became a painter, because I discovered I had a very intense response to the physicality of paint. At first I largely knew paintings through reproduction, but even so I was drawn to people like Rembrandt, to Caravaggio, to Cézanne, to really painterly painters. One of the first oil paintings I made, when I was sixteen, was a copy of the National Gallery's *Saskia*, which was done from a reproduction. I saw my painting again a few years ago, and what was shocking about it was the density of the paint on my canvas compared to the one on Rembrandt's, it was so much denser.

MP *(Laughs)* Right, he achieved the effect without having had to pile it on.

HO'D Yes, exactly. But what I'd taken from that was not so much the image, but the physicality of the painting – that interests me. And at various times I had moments of connection. I think a lot of artists connected with Titian's *Marsyas* painting when it was shown at the Royal Academy exhibition in the early 1980s. That painting emerged then, and the absolute physicality of late Titian is something that has also been a great source of inspiration for me. So I'm trying to make painting that, although it lives in the modern world and it references the here and now, also draws upon the extraordinary potential that oil paint has. That's what a lot of the works in the exhibition at Leeds are, there's this dialogue with the photographic image, the painted image and how this more vernacular way of seeing can be brought into painting.

MP And you literally absorb photos?

HO'D Yes.

MP It's curious. It's almost the revenge of painting – it comes back and actually swallows the photographic image, and manipulates and mediates it.

HO'D Well, I like to think about it like that. I'm very clear about what I'm doing: I'm bringing photography, I'm bringing the mechanical image into painting. I thought long and hard about this. At first it crept up at the edges and appeared in the background, but photographic space is quite different. We read depth in photographs in a kind of coded way, and in painting you read it in a different way: the way that the tone or the form is emphasized or de-emphasized, and that's what I'm trying to do. I'm bringing the photograph in the form of ... almost like a membrane, it's like one layer contains this information but it's not giving you drawing necessarily, or colour, it's not giving you tone or depth, it's not giving you design or balance – there's all that other armoury of things which painting can do.

MP Interesting, it's like a subplot...

HO'D Yes. There are different ways in which it functions; in some pieces it clearly functions like a documentary dimension, so that the narrative is being told. In the painting called *The Last Summer* you clearly know that what you're looking at is something that has been adapted from an earlier photographic form, and although we know that the photograph can lie, I think what you understand when you're looking at that picture is that there are no lies being told, no intentional lies.

MP You have de-constructed them all in a sense, when they're absorbed into the matrix of the painting.

HO'D Yes, certain things are clearly left there. For instance, where the glass of one of the glass negatives is broken, that's left on the print – it's not tidied up on Photoshop, it's tidied up with a paintbrush. There's a difference to that, I think it gives you certain valuable information. It's used in more of a documentary way there. In other paintings where the photographic source has been something that I've set up, a photographic scenario where I've taken a photograph and used it to make the composition of the painting, and then emphasized certain things, then it's more like a *tableau vivant*, you know that what you're looking at is a construction, and it's different.

MP Do you think that photos will always be in your work or do you think they might fade out at a certain point?

HO'D At the moment they're fading out, or there's a dichotomy developing in the large work that I'm making about the Second World War. It seems to me that the photograph is appropriate for that material because it's about documenting. But in the most recent paintings there is a return to pure painting, particularly in the *Yellow Men* paintings – there are three of them in the Leeds show. Two of them have a small photographic component: I was looking for a model of the head of Van Gogh and arrived at that very blurred image of a shell-shocked Canadian soldier at Dieppe, which I used. In the fourth picture that's in the Leeds show, I've not worked from a model other than from the memory of that – there's no photographic dimension in it. So over the last few years, there's been this dialogue which is sometimes very much to the fore and sometimes I'm trying to find out what the photograph gives that's important, if anything, and what painting gives, and at the moment this division is taking place.

MP And you're still looking a lot at the traditional art about? I mean are you a big museum guy, gallery guy?

HO'D Yes, I am. The idea of tradition has often made people run a mile, the idea of something being a tradition, but I see it as an accumulation of experience. One of the great things about painting is that as well as it being contemporary, you are obviously in a dialogue with all the other painters who've ever made paintings.

MP From the moment you pick up your brush really.

HO'D Yes, and you either do it in ignorance or you do it from the point of view of being aware ... I suppose a critical moment for me was when I did a residency at the National Gallery in 1985, that really accelerated that process.

MP What did that consist of, actually being in the Gallery?

HO'D Yes, there was a studio there. It's much like the associate artist scheme they have now. You have a studio and the brief was that you were there to interface with the general public and you open the studio once a week or so – it was actually at the time when Francis Bacon was doing the 'Artist's Eye' exhibition there – but also that you made a body of work, which I showed at the end of that time.

MP I see, so people could wander in?

HO'D They couldn't wander in, no. They could come on a Friday afternoon for three hours to talk – that was very intense. You had three hours to talk about your work. It was actually very good because what I learnt from that was that it's good sometimes to just look and talk, not to work.

MP Did you walk round the Gallery then or were you just in your own studio?

HO'D I was in my own studio and I had access to the Gallery whenever I wanted, so I did.

MP It was like living in a house of painting?

HO'D Yes absolutely, but also being right at the centre of tradition. Particular pictures came, they loaned at that time the *View of the City of Toledo* from the Metropolitan in New York, and I made a very large charcoal drawing from that which is still in the National Gallery. They had the Rembrandt Deposition and I did some small drawings from that. I tended to make drawings from paintings and my own paintings were …

MP Actually in front of it? Or sitting in front of it?

HO'D No I didn't. I've never been …

MP It's a bit embarrassing, isn't it?

HO'D It's just the self-consciousness of it. If I'm self-conscious, I'm never going to do anything worthwhile. There's a kind of showmanship I think also of standing in a gallery and . . . I didn't really feel it was necessary anyway because I was trying to make an equivalent of the painting, rather than a copy of it. Those were probably the first serious figure paintings that I made there.

MP What about literature, Hughie? I suspect you're a literary man – you write well, you write naturally. I can hear your voice when I read what you write, which to me is always a sign of somebody who's at home in language. Do you read very widely, I mean outside the sources that you consult?

HO'D I don't really get enough time to read widely, although I'm reading all the time. It's a great surprise to me that I write reasonably well; I suspect it's because I was never burdened with any talents in that area so that I could only give my own voice really.

MP That's a talent already (*laughs*). But you have read quite widely, I was impressed that you'd read things like Xenophon's *Anabasis* which is not on everybody's bedside table – unless you're trying to learn ancient Greek.

HO'D No, that was probably the only classical book I read when I was younger. I did read that, and the Pelican version of it had a picture of a Greek soldier on the front that I was quite taken with, and that drew me in. It was a book that my father was interested in. The story of the *Anabasis* interested me, again, because it's a journey and a return, as it emerged. I have read relatively widely and I do have quite a big library, my own reference library is quite extensive, but it's rare that I would read a novel. Once I get into a subject I read around it, that's part of my drawing really, I look at the subject and immerse myself in it. I also love books; as a child I grew up in a council house in South Manchester in which every wall in the house was literally covered in books.

MP Because of your father?

HO'D He loved books and he collected books. I think probably my elder brothers hated them because they were forced to read them, but by the time I'd reached that age my dad had kind of eased off a little bit, so I actually developed a love for them. It was that idea that knowledge or tradition could be learnt from a book, something that's slightly magical.

MP All these doors around you that could lead you into other worlds.

HO'D It's like that idea of the space a child grows up in perfecting the shape of his mind. And although this was a small house it seemed to be cavernous in a way.

MP Leonardo said that small rooms concentrate the mind.

HO'D Right, I didn't know that.

MP And the moment I saw your work I thought of the writer, whom I like very much, called W. G. Sebald.

HO'D I have read Sebald and I greatly admire what he writes. I haven't read all of it, but I've dipped into it and felt great empathy with that.

MP There is a link with your work there, the way it's delving into the past – into collective memory and personal memory.

HO'D Yes, I think my dealer at the time, Rebecca Hicks, gave me a copy of Sebald's *The Rings of Saturn* after I had made a number of works that used texts and photographs. I was very interested in the fact that he was using photographs to augment the text. I felt that I was working primarily with images and using words to augment. I put the text in with these works to give more information, to almost give a parallel correspondence to the work. The little bits of writing that I have made have sometimes been misunderstood by people who expect to read some commentary on the work. My writing isn't a commentary on the work, which would be totally inappropriate. Hopefully what it is, is a window on the subject from a different point of view, so by reading the text one becomes aware, in a different way, of the themes that are emerging in the painting – that's how I saw it.

MP Is there much accident in the process of working? Do you suddenly stumble on things or do things reveal other things that you hadn't in any way foreseen?

HO'D I think there's accident.

MP Surprise, whatever you want to call it, or discovery.

HO'D Well, I prize the accident and discovery in a work, the chance discovery of something. In a way though this idea of chance can be misleading, in that I would find something anyway. It's a chance but I'll find it.

MP That's what it's all about, isn't it? Sometimes it takes longer and is more laborious and perhaps less exciting, but it's about discovery.

HO'D Yes. The works that were made from the first set of glass negatives, which are a group of pictures around the idea of the Prodigal Son, they're about…

MP These are in the works on show…

HO'D There's none of them in the Leeds show, but *The Last Summer* would be a very similar piece. I found these glass plates in a car-boot sale, and I didn't even look at them really, I glanced at one or two and decided to acquire them.

MP Do you do a lot of this wandering around, seeing what you can see? In flea-markets?

HO'D Yes. Habitually in the bookshops on the Charing Cross Road and markets – Bermondsey Market occasionally, or anywhere. I'm always curious to see what might be there. It doesn't always come to something, but if I'm looking that's where the source material comes from in a way.

MP You're got a whole archive, haven't you?

HO'D Yes, and I suppose for me one of the things that's interesting about it is that it's been discarded, and that gives it added significance because it references back to what we choose to remember or what we don't choose to remember. It illuminates things differently.

MP To come back to this whole concept of memory that we talked about at the beginning, the more I think about it the bigger the word grows. Because we are memory aren't we? In a sense that's all we are. As we sit here, we are just an accumulation of memory – whether the memories have been transformed or whether we've improved on them in our own minds – but we are just volumes of memory.

HO'D Yes, I think Lucian Freud used the expression the 'tyranny of memory'. I think memory is who we think we are. Our reactions to everything are governed by our sense of ourselves: who or what we identify with, the view we take of history. I became increasingly interested in that after moving to Ireland and the different take on history there, that is filtered through a sort of collected national consensus of the world. A lot of the time in my work I'm trying to slightly subvert those cosy assumptions about things, that's possibly the only thing I own up to in a conscious way, to point out real inconsistencies in things.

MP You mean in accepted versions of history?

HO'D Yes, the accepted views of things. I'm looking to tell a story, but to tell a story that …

MP That queries the accepted versions?

HO'D Yes. You know things get really simplified, myth takes over very, very quickly, and so we don't have to think about it, we don't have to remember any longer. So, in a way, I suppose the idea of choosing history as a subject in painting now is to arouse curiosity. The painting might have an emotional impact, which subsequently arouses intellectual curiosity about events, rather than feeding you a version of events. It's to try and tell the story in a different way – a way in which you start to look at and question everything again.

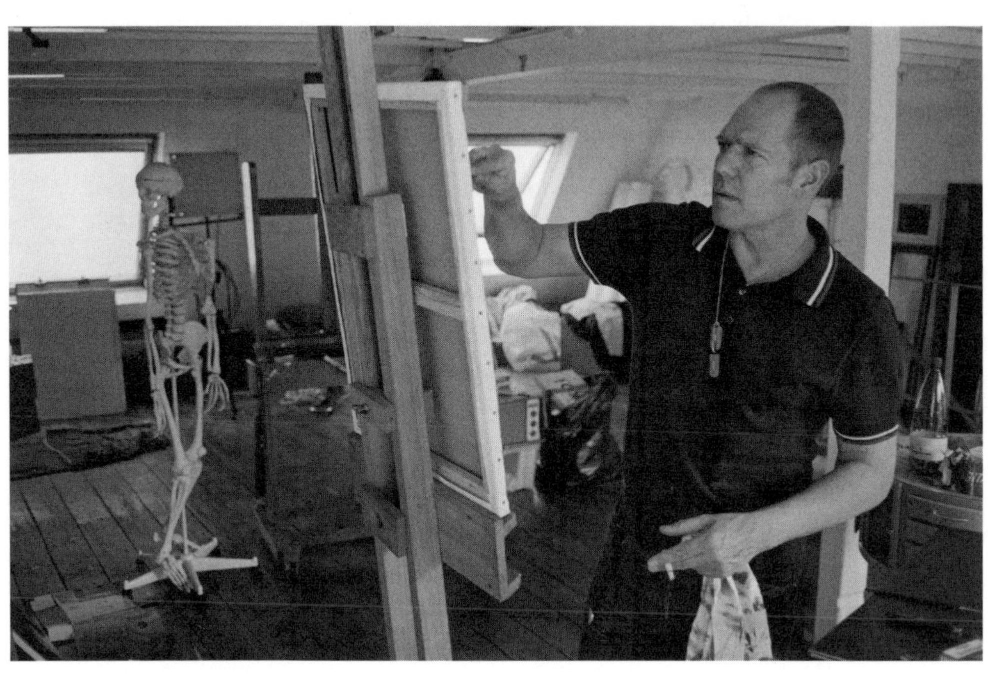

PAUL SIMONON

PADDINGTON LONDON 2008

This conversation with Paul Simonon served to introduce an exhibition of his recent paintings in London in 2008. Although I knew, vaguely enough, of his career as bass guitarist for The Clash (I lived abroad throughout their heyday), I had no notion that he had ever painted. Since the text was needed urgently, there was no way but to plunge straight into the deep end, with no preparation, and visit Paul directly in his studio. Where I had half-expected an unreconstructed raving punk spewing substance-induced gibberish, I found a charming man wholly engaged with the art of painting and able to talk about it lucidly and unassumingly from an unusual angle. What I particularly liked was the freshness of Paul's whole approach, as if he had come to painting anew (as indeed he had) without any of the baggage that a career in the art world saddles most artists with. At the opening of the show, attended by ranks of hoary rockers and more recent luminaries such as Lily Allen (whose presence won me momentary esteem from my teenage children), I was impressed, but not altogether surprised, to find Lucian Freud edging round the crowd to peer intently at Paul's new pictures.

MP Paul, I feel as if I'm just about to walk into one of your 'Bullfight' paintings. There's a lot at stake, a lot of ground to cover ... You spent most of your earlier career as a musician, then you went back to your first passion for drawing and painting. Was that a difficult transition? How did it happen?

PS I was living in Los Angeles, I came back to London in 1986 for a weekend or a week and it was raining and I looked up at the sky and the gasworks and thought, God, that's so beautiful, and I went straight outside with my sketch-pad.

Paul Simonon (1955–). *Paul Simonon: Recent Paintings*, exhibition catalogue, Thomas Williams Fine Art, London, April 2008.

MP And you hadn't actually drawn for years apart from designing the odd album?

PS No, next to nothing. I just went out on the canal and did a drawing of the gasworks and that was it, I was lost – lost and back.

MP And then you decided to stay and go on drawing? You didn't have much in the way of training.

PS Well, I'd gone to art college for about a year and a half. I got a scholarship to the Byam Shaw, when it used to be in Notting Hill Gate. But the thing was that life drawing wasn't really encouraged at that period because the teachers were very influenced by the American abstract movement. All I wanted to do was to have a plaster cast put in front of me and be told to draw it for a year. I would have been happy doing that.

MP A totally traditional way of learning.

PS Yeah. I remember reading as a child that Matisse had his own school of art, and everyone turns up saying this is fantastic, Matisse has set up a school, and Matisse just says, 'Here's the paint, here's the canvas, I'll be back in a week'. And everyone's getting really carried away, pushing paint all over the place, and Matisse comes back a week later to review all the work and he looks at it and says, 'It's all rubbish', and he gets one of the students to wheel in a plaster cast and he says, 'Right, you need to draw this because you need a foundation to bounce your ideas off'. And that's really stuck with me. That's why I realized that drawing's very important, for me especially.

MP That's been basically the accepted way, the only way, for centuries. And the recent thing, the idea that you could just throw drawing and the whole preparation out of the window was, in the end, wrong. There's a language you have to learn, and to do the other things, the more inventive things, you've got to learn the language.

PS And I'm sure Rothko and Pollock and the people from the American abstract movement actually learnt that language in the first place.

MP But, in your painting, you seem obsessed with the real.

PS Well, I've got to a point where I'm trying to capture the thing I'm looking at but with a lyrical element to it rather than just a straightforward representation – you know, not just something that looks like that bottle of vinegar. I want to go beyond that. I'm influenced by so many painters. And there's that whole period of English painting, around Christopher Wood, that's like poetry done through paint, more lyrical, with another ingredient. To a point, painting's like making a cake, it depends very much what you put in. Sometimes when I'm working I can look at something, like a Constable, and get annoyed because what I'm doing begins to looks like Constable and I don't want to be Constable, I want to be me.

MP You're a very committed artist. It's a bit like, as a musician, when you learnt the bass guitar by practising to reggae tunes on the jukebox right through the night. You know you have to study and you've spent a lot of time in the British Museum, for instance – copying what sort of thing?

PS Horses, mainly Greek and Roman, giant feet, anything.

MP And all this since that cloudy day. But you'd picked up enough from art school to know you had to go back to the source?

PS Well, it was from reading that thing about Matisse and from spending a year in Italy with my mum and my stepfather when I was a young boy of ten, going to lots of cities and museums and films. It was like a paradise for a kid who'd only known Brixton. There was pasta and wine, grapes and melons – I'd never seen melons before – and while we were in Siena all the preparations, all the drumming and the costumes, for the Palio, the big horse race round the centre. I refused to go to school because the kids wore this blue smock with a big black bow in front of it. 'But we're from Brixton, Mum,' I said, so I got to wander round the streets, and my mum taught me and my brother in the evening. And my dad, who I lived with later, was a Sunday painter and the room I used to sleep in was his painting studio, so I was surrounded by props and whatever pages he'd stolen out of books that were all pinned up on the wall around me, so I was aware of Vlaminck, Rouault, Van Dongen. Also as I was growing up I realized that there were quite a few artists, and they were either called Pablo or Paul, so I sort of figured, Picasso, Cézanne …

MP Rubens, Veronese … So this was predestined (*laughter*). And when did you start doing life classes?

PS When I was a teenager, I went to life classes in the day and in the evening. For me life drawing is like discovering a new country, insofar as there's the form in front of you, you're aware that the patella is poking through the skin there, it's held up by the thigh bone, but when it's slightly to one side then it takes on another form and it's immensely fascinating to draw and that's why I really admire sculptors because they've got this complete grasp of three dimensions. I hope my own painting absorbs a bit of that three-dimensionality, because I wouldn't want any of it to be so thin it might float away. I did spend a lot of time drawing Rubens paintings, fascinated by the sweep of his lines. Drawing from a Rubens painting your arm sort of ice-skates over the page. There's so much movement, heads turning and arms reaching up …

MP Of course the colour's so fabulous you tend to forget how sinuous the line is. The drawings are fabulous too, and even the oil sketches are wonderful things, so spontaneous.

PS Yes, they're fantastic. I've been influenced by so many things, but I've also been lucky because along the way I've had a lot of encouragement. And when I went back to painting in earnest there were two people in particular, a friend of mine called Sophie de Stempel – she was a really big help – and she introduced me to someone called Anne Dalcombe who's a teacher at the new

Byam Shaw. And so I've spent a lot of time with her and Sophie, drawing together, over about five years, in her studio, drawing and painting. And what I like is the environment and realizing that one doesn't need to be precious with your HB pencils, you just have your bit of charcoal, and you do your drawing and then rub it out and you've got the ghost of it there. And it's not like trying to make a nice drawing, it's like trying to understand what's going on. I mean, how can I make that hand look like it's really holding that chair? That's the great thing about charcoal. I've done drawings, probably like a hundred drawings on one bit of paper, rubbing them out, exploring.

MP And then you get the ghosts of these things coming through a bit.

PS Sometimes, but then the ghost changes and then you just work on that.

MP So it's in perpetual movement.

PS Yes, but the way I paint is quite different from the way I draw.

MP But do you use these drawings in preparation for the paintings or are they separate entities?

PS At the moment they're separate really. They're for learning and understanding. Painting's more like composing in some ways, elements, some real, some taking advantage of knowing how to look at things maybe.

MP So in your nudes, for example, do you use photographs?

PS The subjects tend to be ninety-nine per cent in front of me.

MP Are these professional models?

PS No, they're friends, or shared models. I did have one situation where Sophie and I whizzed down to Brighton to see this stunning girl called Amanda who lay on the beach for us and we just painted her and it was fantastic.

MP Did that attract a crowd?

PS No, which is surprising since she was topless, but the painting came out really well because the light was amazing.

MP Did you ask her to take a particular pose?

PS Just to relax really. That's the problem with professional models, they have these fixed airs. But I don't find that when I go to life school because the models are actually actresses and they're playing into the role.

MP They're more active in a sense, not just passive, and they haven't grown that protective 'second skin' Lucian Freud says professional models get. What about actual painting techniques?

PS I sort of learnt many years ago the basics while I was living with my dad.

MP So technique is not a problem.

PS No, not at all, I understand paint. The best thing to paint on for me is hardboard because the paint slides around. You know that thing Francis Bacon said about the paint becoming the subject, and the subject becoming the paint – the interlocking. Anyway, that's sort of an idea I have in my head. That's not entirely the way I'm heading but I do enjoy all the possibilities of paint and its deliciousness. I can see it and I can feel it – it's a sensual experience. Moving it you realize the paint's coming off more on this side, and you can turn it like skiing or riding a motorbike. You can control the movement yourself.

MP I know you've done this series on London.

PS Well, coming back to England and painting the gasworks and the sky I got really into Constable's sketches at the Victoria and Albert. Auerbach said something about painting what's on your doorstep and that resonated for me and I started doing more and more Thames paintings, large canvases. But it's impossible to copy what you see because it's changing all the time.

MP And so are you and your perceptions. It's a courageous thing to do, just to go out with a canvas and start trying to paint London …

PS But what you've got to understand is that from seventeen or eighteen years old, when I began in music, it was a real us against them situation. People used to chuck things at us. I remember coming off stage one night and the techie pointed out to me that there were three darts in the backdrop … We hadn't been aware of them. That's just one little incident. But, anyway, from working with lots of people to being very much on my own, painting, was a bit scary. What kept me going was being outside with the rain, the wind, the elements.

MP What about the bullfight paintings?

PS Well, there are so many aspects to this spectacle of man and beast that are fascinating. It's like being at the Coliseum, you know, with the Christians and the lions. Then you've got the bullring, which is like a huge frying-pan – and the shadow that creeps across as the sun goes down, with all these characters trying to dance with the bull, and from time to time they get chucked around like a rag doll, and we know that in the end the bull's going to die. A couple of years ago I went to see a bullfight and a man got chucked around by the bull and the whole atmosphere in the ring changed in an instant. Suddenly someone could be dead, and he was actually carried off in his own cape. It reminded me of Christ being taken down and laid out in the shroud. I did lots of drawings, and then I went back a week later to the bullring in Madrid, and I got to know lots of the people involved – the matadors, the people who handle the bulls, the people who make the capes.

MP So you made lots of drawings and started painting when you got back?

PS Yes, I started to paint when I got back, from some of the drawings I'd done. Then I went straight back again and did more pen-and-ink drawings of all the smaller situations going on in and around the bull-ring... It's funny because the bullfights came by chance. After doing the exhibition of my Thames paintings, I just wanted to paint nudes – and then I did this trip to Spain and I thought, forget the nudes for a minute, I've got to paint this. I just got right into it and tried to understand exactly what was going on. For me, if it's going to work, the painting's got to be convincing to a Spanish person. So you have to be aware of a lot of details. For instance, when the bullfighter takes his hat off and throws it into the arena, if it lands this way it's really bad luck, and if it falls this way it's good luck. Little things like that, you know, if he's being chucked through the air and his hat's on the ground, open side up...

MP The symbol's got to be right otherwise it looks as if you don't know what you're doing.

PS That's it, you've got twenty matadors over there, moving around, and you've got no idea where to put them unless you know what they're there for. It's a whole thing that you've got to understand. Like doing the Thames paintings and trying to understand as much as you can about the movement of sky. That's why Constable is such an interest to me.

MP How about the nudes? They're as eternal a subject as landscapes.

PS I actually see nudes like a landscape. It's the most exciting thing to paint, especially when it has that bit of magic, which is what I really strive for in painting. Sometimes it happens, sometimes it doesn't. When it doesn't, it's really annoying because you've just got to scrape everything you've done off – even the good bits – and start again. But I've just done these two nudes, and the magic has been there each time, which is unusual. Then you get this exhilaration. It's like a warm wind blowing over you.

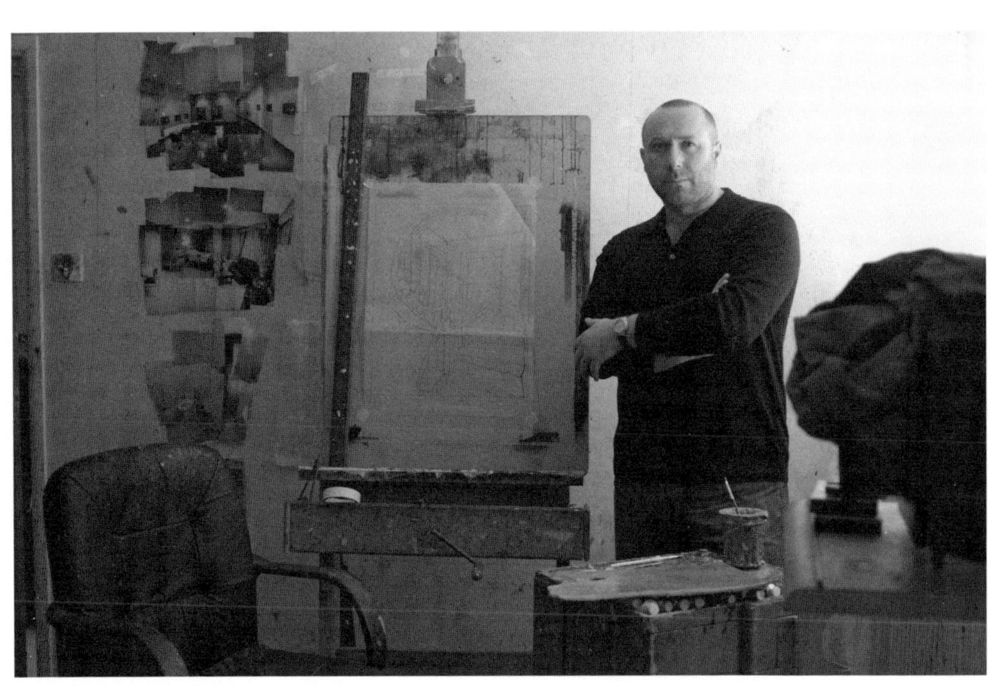

ROBERT PRISEMAN

HOLLAND PARK LONDON 2008

I came across Robert Priseman's eery recreations of interiors inhabited by Francis Bacon by chance on a website. I found them unsettling at first, then curiously moving. These interiors – the Wivenhoe studio, the Paris hotel room where Bacon's lover died, the Madrid clinic where Bacon himself died appear to have been emptied of every trace of life or emotion. But this emptiness fills up with our own feelings and associations that are slowly, inevitably, sucked in to the void. The paintings appear almost malevolent because they contain a stark truth about the nature of existence which we attempt to shut out of our everyday lives.

Priseman and I met and enjoyed talking together so much that, one afternoon in London, we decided quite spontaneously to record a conversation that was later published in a catalogue about his work.

MP What I wanted to ask you first of all, Robert, was how your interest in Bacon – you might almost call it an obsession – came about. Did it develop over a long period of time?

RP All my painting projects take years to develop. There's an interest you mull over for a number of years which eventually crystallizes into an idea, which then just sits there for probably two or three years until you act on it. It's probably just the same with writing.

MP But before it crystallized, was it simply that you'd seen a lot of Bacon and you'd realized he was an artist who interested you?

RP I had seen a lot of Bacon. For me he's one of the greatest painters and I'd learnt a fair bit before then about his work, and I liked the School of London in a broader sense as well. I suppose when you're looking at a lot of art you become aware of the

Robert Priseman (1965–). *The Francis Bacon Interiors*, Seabrook Press, Wivenhoe, 2009.

conversation that's going on in art and that fascinates you, and then you reach a point where you want to have a go at participating in it. That's really the crux of it. That's why I gave up the portrait painting I'd been doing before. I felt I understood it enough and had enough courage to have a go at it.

MP So there was a kind of dialogue set up and after a time you felt you'd like to speak, to join in.

RP It felt like an open forum. And obviously there was also the thing that Bacon had lived in Wivenhoe where I live, and had a studio there. I used to walk past it every day and it always intrigued me. I knew that I liked to work in sets of pictures, so I was thinking, well I'd love to do a painting of that studio but I don't know how I'd do it as a series ... I'm generally interested in what you'd call more anonymous spaces, but I thought I could do it because I'm not a gestural painter in the sense that Bacon's a gestural painter. If I worked in a gestural sense or any vaguely abstract way then I couldn't do any more than produce a pastiche of Bacon, so I wouldn't have done it at all; it's because I work in a completely different way. But I see lots of overlap, of similarity, between the core of his *oeuvre* and what fascinates me. I'm interested in rooms that are enclosed, sealed, artificially lit, in places where human trauma takes place. Those are environments that fascinate me.

MP They're sort of empty but inhabited spaces. They're empty but there are traces ...

RP Yes, traces of the human presence, I suppose. But it's more specific than that for me. I'm interested in places where trauma has taken place or extremes of emotion have happened. I'm interested in the idea that that emotion leaves a resonance behind. And so initially, when I abandoned portrait painting, I began working on these hospital interiors.

MP And were they empty of people?

RP Yes, always empty of people.

MP But full of them in a different sense.

RP Yes, exactly. I'm interested in the idea that these places are clean, clinical, cold and expressionless. They're empty of emotion but they're where extremes of emotion have taken place. Previously, when I was doing portraits, I did a painting of one of the Sheriffs of London and he took me into the condemned cell in the Old Bailey, and it had a really powerful effect on me because I walked into it and I kind of braced myself and I was thinking – it's going to be like walking into a dungeon and you're going to feel the screams coming out of the wall and ... it was just nothing, it was just completely cold. It's the only cell in the Old Bailey that has two doors, one to go in and another one to go out. And you're thinking, well the walls, they're just white tiles – and it's just like walking into a bathroom or a kitchen or something. No feeling, no emotion, nothing.

MP How strange.

RP Now that really fascinated me. So I was looking at the way Bacon handled those things.

MP Let's go back. You were living in Wivenhoe. When you went to live in Wivenhoe you didn't even know Bacon had had a house there, or did you?

RP I didn't know about Bacon's Wivenhoe house when I first moved there for a spell in 1988–9 – but I did know about it when we subsequently moved there as a family in 2002 – that, and the fact Constable who is another painter I have an enormous respect for, had lived and worked up the road in Dedham – made me feel very comfortable. Because it's like you're living in the same place as friends or familiars. And what particularly interested me about Bacon's house is it's just a little two-up, two-down cottage. And as you walk past it, you'd never know it had been used as a studio. The only clue is that the sash windows have been removed: Bacon took them out so that he wouldn't get a shadow on the canvas while he was painting. So it became really intriguing to me that one of our great artists had worked there – that this great artist had produced great works in this humble little house in the middle of nowhere. I found that quite compelling because it makes you think, you know, yes I could have a go at doing something that maybe would hit the mark, maybe would achieve something. As an artist, what's the point of doing it if you're not going to have a go at doing something…

MP You really want to hit as high up as you can.

RP Exactly. There's no point doing it otherwise, I don't think. I was interested as well in Bacon's asthma and how that might have influenced his work. I mean, reading your book was really interesting, because of the idea of how personal biography affects the public work. Bacon's work is a public aspect of his personal life. And I myself have epilepsy and that affects the way I think about the pictures. Partly that I have this sense that when you have a fit – not that I have many because I'm on medication – but when you have a fit you do have this sense that you have a soul that's being yanked out of your body. It's very disturbing, and when you come round from a fit you feel completely disorientated, so you don't know where you are, you don't know what time of day it is, you don't know what day of the week it is, you don't know why you're there. I had a fit once when I was on a ship going over to France, and I came to and I thought where am I, why am I here, what am I doing, you're completely lost and you have to mentally re-construct the world you're in to make sense of it all again. I suppose that is like a real sense of the uncanny. You know this idea of the uncanny – that really intrigues me because I suppose the uncanny is an artistic exploration of something which through epilepsy I can feel in a very real sense. So looking at Bacon's work thinking about the screaming and then there's that idea that maybe it's a gasp for life rather than a scream, I mean it's open to interpretation but just the fact that there are those thoughts there interests me. So I've got all those sorts of overlaps of thought that made me think, yes, maybe I would like to tackle Bacon's interiors. The other thing I thought is that, since I don't know enough about painting, if I dived in completely on my own and tackled Bacon's material and spent some time in his world maybe I would learn something. That was another sort of undercurrent of thought I was having at the time.

MP Like a sub-text.

RP It's like spending times under the wings of the master, if you like, seeing if you could pick up something from this.

MP So you used to walk past in front of the house and you managed to get a bit of a dekko.

RP Oh yes, you can peer through the window. But I didn't want to start work on it because I thought, well, it'll just be a one-off and it wouldn't make sense.

MP You liked the idea of a series.

RP Yes. I was working on the hospital paintings and I was doing this painting of a critical care bed and then I saw the Arena documentary and it showed the Clínica Ruber in Madrid, where Bacon died. And then I thought: Ah! There are two pictures. And I realized there must be a series I could do: his studio, the room he died in, and I bought some books and worked out a whole list of rooms and came up with about twenty. I thought there must be at least half a dozen of these I could get access to, so I decided, well, I'll just get cracking on it.

MP So to date you've done the studio in Wivenhoe, the staircase in the Hôtel des Saints-Pères in Paris where he and George Dyer were staying in 1971 for the opening of his retrospective at the Grand Palais, the bathroom where poor George was found dead on the lavatory, and then the room at the Clínica Ruber in Madrid where Bacon died, and then finally the transposed studio that's gone to the museum in Dublin with that strange kind of apparatus for listening and the studio sealed off very much like another room that's sort of died.

RP That's right. You see, I find that really fascinating because it's like looking at a ghost in a box. That's how I feel about it. It's as though his ghost has been trapped and then put on public display. I find it a very strange installation really.

MP I quite agree, it's sort of sealed it off, like something that's been bottled up.

RP Yes, that's right … a genie in a bottle. And everything's so clean and clinical on the outside and sort of chaotic and …

MP … messy and turbulent and emotional inside.

RP Yes, that's exactly it.

MP If one has an interest in a person who has burned a kind of myth into our consciousness, or subconsciousness, as Bacon has, these interiors reverberate with a presence which is no longer there. But it's his presence alone that makes them significant.

RP Yes.

MP And you like the idea of re-creating the traces of somebody in a kind of vacuum? Is it a vacuum?

RP Yes. For me, it's a kind of vacuum that you are sucked into as the viewer. So you are stepping into something like an abandoned stage set. The drama has already taken place.

MP How do you go about recapturing these interiors?

RP Well, I use perspective in a particular way. I go and visit the rooms, I take photographs of them, and they come out in this slightly fish-eye, fragmented way. I then translate that into a perspective drawing, like a perspective plan, which takes quite a lot of effort. I'm thinking of the early Renaissance perspective windows, that's what I was originally thinking of when I started to do these paintings – the one-point perspective of Alberti's treatise on painting. I like the idea that the perspective creates this sense of drawing you into the image and so opening out the image. There's no block in the foreground, there's nothing preventing you as the viewer from feeling your way in …

MP Almost toppling in.

RP Exactly, you're toppling into the picture, you're sort of drawn in, almost compulsively you're being sucked into the space. And so for me the perspective has that quality, there's no barrier there for you. But, unlike Alberti, who sees perspective as a window onto the world, I view it more as a window onto the subconscious. Perspective has a way of objectifying the external world whilst placing the viewer at the centre of it. For me this mirrors an idea of both inner and outer concepts of reality and so I suppose perspective is acting as a kind of bridge between these two worlds. And then I'm trying to use the paint as a way to act as a sort of metaphor for the emotional traces – so I'm trying to use the paint in that sense.

MP What I find very strange and very difficult to define is the way your painting is very clinically exact, there's an almost repellent sense of exactitude – you know you can't touch it, because it's done so perfectly – it draws you in but it also forces you back again because it's so complete in itself.

RP Well, that's exactly what I'm after. Although I don't know why.

MP The pull and the push. It's like you go towards it because, as you say, spatially you're drawn in, but there's also a finished aspect to it which actually repels you, so there's a double movement and it's very interesting, it's difficult to put one's finger on why that's fascinating. It's fascinating beyond the fact that you know this is where Bacon worked, this is where Bacon died, this is where his lover committed suicide, this is where his studio is incarcerated. There's something else, and of course you've done many other things, like the places of execution, which I think have the same thing. They draw you in and it's not even the fact that people are killed there that's repellent, it's the fact that it seems so complete in itself and therefore you can't get a grasp on it.

RP Yes. Well, I also try to strip out a lot of the detail, so perhaps it's the simplification that enables you to get a mentally easier access. I also try to harmonize the colours – and make them more attractive than they are in reality, more soothing and beautiful. So I'm trying to create the whole environment to be somehow ... enticing yet disconnected. I'm thinking also of what Joshua Reynolds said in his 'Discourses on Art', that an artist should paint pictures as they appear in the mind's eye, as he put it – to exclude particulars. He believed that removing details enables the viewer to approach a painting on their own terms, and therefore engage with it more fully.

MP Do you want something that's both attractive and sinister?

RP Well I suppose I want a sort of punchy feel. I want the viewer to get a sense of feeling something. If they're not feeling something then I'm not doing my job.

MP One of the things that I find slightly sinister is that it's not a kind of neo-reality, it's not a reproduction of something, it's its own thing. It's very, very close to an absolutely visually accurate record, but it's something else. The French have got this word *décalage*, which they use about things that have slipped out of their normal contours. There's a kind of slippage into another kind of universe that is very disquieting.

RP Well, I'm pleased you say that, because I feel I'm hitting the mark. I go out of my way to try and achieve that. I mean I'm not making a huge effort, because it's something to do with the feeling that I carry inside myself, if that makes sense.

MP Yes, and you think that's linked to some extent with your experience of epilepsy?

RP I think it is, yes, I think it's also linked . . . it's difficult to say, I know the epilepsy is part of that, but I had this experience when I was eight as well, which I think distanced me from the community I grew up in, so I've grown up with a sense of disconnection if you like, certainly as a child and young adult, from the adult world. I don't know how related the epilepsy is to that.

MP Well, I was going to add that if I'm fascinated by these pictures it's because I have that sense of not being related to things, to people and situations. I used to get it much more strongly when I was younger, and it used to worry me enormously, I thought I was losing my mind. I'd be somewhere, for instance, in a crowded restaurant in Paris, and suddenly I'd get this terror of thinking that I wasn't part of where I was, I was sitting in a sort of glass cage, and everything else was happening outside of me and it was unrelated to me. And I was dissociated from it, I was witnessing it but I myself was dissociated from it and therefore I was different and to say it made me feel very spacey is putting it mildly. It made me feel, I wouldn't say paranoid, but it made me feel very afraid.

RP Yes, that's very much it. I think I've had that feeling most of my life.

MP Freud wrote a whole essay on this sensation, I think. It's called *das Unheimliche* in German.

RP It's dissociation, but it becomes threatening.

MP It's the slide. I'm sure for a lot of people it's a phenomenon of everyday life. It's an experience …

RP What brought that on for you do you think?

MP Well, one thing that happened to me was that I took some drugs once that made me feel very, very strange. I was doing an interview with a sort of commune of American actors called the Living Theater and they kept giving me these things and I felt to be cool I just had to keep taking them, and then I just sort of flipped and I thought I'd lost my mind completely. I think that brought to the surface perhaps something that was already there. It took me a long time to recover from that experience – because I was in a state of complete paranoia, I thought that that police were after me and that my head and my whole life had gone wrong. And I don't even know what it was, it was meant to be some sort of marijuana, whether they'd laced it with something or it was particularly strong or whether I had so much, or whether I was simply very tense anyhow because I was meant to be doing this important interview with them. I was a young man in my mid-twenties and the magazine I was working for in Paris had sent me there, it was one of the first things they'd let me loose on and I thought I'd better make a good story out of it, and I'd half lost my mind with them. And I went back to the flat I shared with my girlfriend and I remember just sort of crouching under the shower for hours and hours, hoping it would all sort of wash away; but of course it didn't. And I didn't dare talk to anyone about it, and it took me years to absorb the anxiety. So that's the strongest feeling I've had like that. I don't get it as much any more, if I get it I treat it with much more distance, and I say you're just having a bit of a funny phase, don't worry. If it comes back, it's usually because I'm under pressure or there's a worrying sense of déjà vu. It's the slippage we were talking about. Things look slightly distorted, slightly unfamiliar. You know, suddenly the walls look rather whiter than they should do, or someone's face keeps reminding you of someone completely different. You start getting more and more anxious. That's what it is in me, I think, a form of extreme anxiety.

RP Right. That would make sense actually, wouldn't it? That would make sense from my point of view as well.

MP Would it?

RP Yes, it would. I'd not thought about it in that way before.

MP I think being self-conscious and then suddenly it's as though things are continuing to go like a film that's being played but you step to one side, and it continues. You're no longer in the frame; you're no longer part of it even though it's part of you.

RP That sense of the uncanny is central to me. I realize that a lot of the art I enjoy looking at, or am fascinated by, has it or evokes it.

MP Who else is in that category?

RP Some of Hopper's paintings, like *Automat* or *Gas*, or Magritte where he has figures looking in the mirror. It's also people like Caspar David Friedrich – *The Chasseur in the Woods* or *The Monk by the Sea*. All those pictures are doing that same sort of job. Actually, in a slightly different way but in a beautiful way, there is a painting by Pisanello, *The Vision of St Eustace*, in the National Gallery, that's both very beautiful but slightly unsettling. So it's those pictures which have that slightly unsettling quality that I'm drawn to. And I suppose when you're looking at art or when you're thinking about art you come to realize that it's when people push whatever is at the core of what they're doing to an extreme that it becomes more interesting. And then when you look at Bacon it's like he's doing that over and over and over again, over decades, and for me that's what marks him out head and shoulders above all the others.

MP I see. Do you think part of the experience we're talking about is at all what people call an 'out of body' experience?

RP I would have thought so, yes.

MP To the side of the body in my case, it's not sort of hovering up over things and looking down.

RP To me it's like I'm not actually in reality but it's just there in front of me.

MP I see, you're the observer. When it happened to me, I'm glad it doesn't happen so much any more, it's really, very, very unsettling… I used to think I was just losing my mind, losing my grip on things. How do you think it comes about?

RP Have you seen a film called *The Firm* with Tom Cruise – the Sydney Pollack film? I find that quite interesting because there is an uncanny moment in that. Tom Cruise lands a job in a law firm, he's working hard, doing his exams, and he can't believe his luck: he's landed on his feet, then he goes into the office one day and suddenly there's this moment when he finds out the only client they have is the Mafia. Then he has to walk out of the office, it's the same faces, it's the same building, it's the same furniture, but suddenly everything's disturbed.

MP How interesting – you mean the set's slightly different, off-key as it were?

RP No, it's the way it's acted and directed. It's not like the film is distorted in any way; it's all exactly the same, yet the perception is completely different. Everything's changed, and it's become unsettled. And that for me is the uncanny sense.

MP He has this revelation, it's seen through his eyes, therefore everything's sort of shifted.

RP Yes, everything has changed and become unsettled. There's the guy who's been mentoring him – suddenly he's seen as being connected to the Mafia and our view of him switches from that of being a benign presence to a threatening one.

MP Oh yes. Except this is in a different degree, isn't it? Because it's the whole notion of reality, it's not a situation, not the firm or an interior, it's actually the universe or your perception of the universe that has shifted ... It occurs to me that we go along in our little corridors of space and time and occasionally I try (and this doesn't make me feel unsettled but I just try) and have sort of antennae out because I know there are all sorts of things going on out there, and I have disquieting ideas that something's gone badly wrong. I try to have these antennae out, beyond normal perception, as it were, to try and pick up what's really going on – behind appearance, behind the drone of the day-to-day. In my own little corridor everything seems neat and orderly and happy, but I get the sensation that outside it's quite different – and of course things really do go wrong all the time, terribly.

RP Yes, but we try not to think about it!

MP Perhaps that's it. Perhaps that's what Bacon meant when he said that he thought he cleared away a few screens. You know, he said: 'I don't think my paintings are violent, I just think they're about the way things are, the reality of experience, and if people think they're violent it may be that most people tend to live their lives behind screens, a kind of screened life, and possibly my paintings have removed some of those screens'.

RP Yes, I think before I started looking closely at Bacon's world I would have said I thought Bacon's work was violent or that there was a violence underlying the superficial appearance of things. But I don't think they are violent any more.

MP No, they're intense.

RP Yes, very intense.

MP And it's strange, we see Bacon's imagery so differently from the way people saw it in the fifties and sixties. You know, they said it was 'Grand Guignol' horror, a sort of Punch and Judy show with nothing but blood all over the place and guts and things. There is that, of course, but the real intensity is the intensity of being alive.

RP I was thinking about that quite a bit. I think what is at the core of Bacon's work is the idea that you explore so thoroughly in your own work on him – that he brings together the two concepts of the sacred and the profane. He seems to be fascinated by Christian iconography and classical myth and what you see in his painting is like a road crash of these two great strands of western thought. He creates out of it a world which seems to acknowledge the existence of a soul – and I'm thinking here of his *Three Studies for Figures at the Base of a Crucifixion* where he lifts the head on the left-hand panel directly from the Schrenck-Notzing book *Phenomena of Materialisation*. In doing this, in taking a photograph which claims to show ectoplasm, he acknowledges a soul but then gives it nowhere to go by removing the central icon of Christian hope for a life after death, the crucifix itself. What we see instead are figures locked in a universe without forgiveness or redemption. It is like looking at a post-Christian vision. I know people found his work difficult when it first came to public attention and it didn't take off initially. And I can imagine that if you'd been through the War you wouldn't want to look at anything else that was horrible or challenging... And I can imagine that's why abstract work would have been so prevalent postwar, because there's not much on the whole to challenge you intellectually or emotionally, I wouldn't have thought.

MP Well, also perhaps the actual disappearance of the figure was significant. What happened to the human figure? Had it been so badly treated throughout the War that it was generally off-limits – a disturbing subject in itself since it had been so mutilated and tortured and destroyed?

RP It's something beyond people's ability to deal with, the subject of the past.

MP What's interesting in your case is that, having painted so many official portraits, commissioned portraits, suddenly you've gone as far away from that as you can, and you've abolished, you're emptied the interiors of any actual human forms.

RP There is this idea of the 'absent portrait' which I find interesting, and I'm thinking here of paintings like Van Gogh's boots or the paintings of his bedroom in Arles. But I wish to take this idea a step further and make the viewer the figure.

MP Ah... yes, I see.

RP I'm trying to get you to be an active participant.

MP So I'm inhabiting these spaces as I look at them?

RP If I'm getting it right, I hope you are, yes.

MP And you've put them so that I or any other viewer will walk into them, will be drawn towards this door or this bed in the clinic...

RP Yes.

MP The series doesn't stop there because you've got one under way of Bacon's former studio in Paris, which of course I'll be very interested to see. And that's presumably less a thing of extremes of emotion. When you talk about extremes of emotion, of course, both the bed and the toilet are places where a death has occurred.

RP Yes, I suppose the Paris studio is more of a contemplative piece for me. Because I know from what you've told me that he painted there in the seventies.

MP From 1974 until the early eighties, yes.

RP That makes me feel it's a more reflective space. Whereas with these other ones, with the staircase, for example, I was wanting to engage directly with his famous triptych *In Memory of George Dyer*. For me that's a direct engagement with one of the greatest paintings in the world. It's my attempt to try and engage and understand more fully what I really admire.

MP And of course you actually stayed in this hotel, didn't you? You stayed in that particular room.

RP Yes, I went there with my wife and she thought it was a very odd thing to do.

MP Did you take the photos while you were there?

RP I did, yes.

MP And did they know in the hotel?

RP They suspected, yes, they kept asking me why I wanted this room particularly. And I just told them that Bacon had stayed there, I just kept it at that. I didn't want them getting too upset about what I might be doing.

MP Do you think other people have stayed there because of that?

RP I believe so, yes.

MP How interesting. Isn't it strange, I was just talking about this yesterday to Peter Conrad, who's doing a long article on Bacon for the *Observer* and he said it's extraordinary that there are all these people who've been in contact with him and for whom he became the most important person in their lives.

RP Well I wouldn't have done these pictures if I'd ever met him.

MP Oh, I see – because...

RP His personality would've been in the way. It's really about my tracing something... my reaction to something.

MP Yes, of course. So it's a very strange powerful thing that's affected many people who never came across him at all, who know him only through the paintings.

RP Going back to the uncanny, I'm reading this book of Margaret Iversen's at the moment called *Beyond Pleasure*, where she relates pictures, cinema, things like that to being like mirror recognition that babies have. I thought that was quite interesting – because it gives you a sense of control. Mirror recognition is the moment when babies start to recognize their sense of omnipotence. After that you start to gain a sense of there being an outside world and an inner reality, and that these are two separate things. Your inner reality is contrasted to the outside world, and you also start to build up this sense of a past, present and future. And that gap between outer reality and inner reality is where the imagination takes place – the space that play, the creative arts and religion occupy as you become an adult.

MP Are you aiming at a feeling of control?

RP Yes, I'd say for me painting is about control – taking something that's in some way frightening and having a sense of control over it. I think it's related to the imagination of an outside reality and the threat it poses. And there's this thing that Lacan explores about language – words – being labels attached to our memories of things from our past, and that we use language to project an image of ourselves into the future to alleviate the thought of the inevitability of our own deaths. The void in art for me represents that inevitability, and painting as we are talking about it here is an attempt to control our underlying and suppressed sense of dread at that.

MP You think that's what Bacon was doing too?

RP I think he's controlling something that is quite terrifying and I think when he talks about removing screens for people, I think what he means is that he is removing some of the illusions we create for ourselves that we are in some way immortal, that death won't visit us and our lives will continue as they always have done.

MP And you are too?

RP Yes, I am. And what I most admire about Bacon is that he was able to do that consistently for decades, not just for a few years, not just over a few pictures. And in your book you talk about this, how he grew from a weakling into someone who had the physical constitution of an ox, and I think he must have had the emotional constitution of an ox as well, to have visited that visual world over and over again in that unrelenting way. I have a huge amount of respect and admiration for that. For me, tracing all those spaces has enabled me to think about taking the next step in my own development. So going on to do, say, the execution pictures, I feel I've drawn from Bacon's strength, from looking at him, admiring him.

MP His ability to confront, to probe and to control.

RP Yes.

MP In a sense encapsulating deep fear and anxiety and horror, extreme emotion – putting it outside himself.

RP He's putting it outside himself, yes. I don't know quite if I understand it, but it's something about what you'd loosely describe as the eternal void, when you're looking at pictures, say like Rothko's *Seagram* paintings. For me they are the ultimate in abstract painting. I don't normally like abstract paintings, but I'm overwhelmed by those paintings and I think that is like an abstract version of looking at the void. And I think if you're looking at, say, the *Automat* painting by Hopper, there's a figure in front of the void. So, quite often I think in art where you've got this sense of a void, you've got the figure in front of a void, often contemplating it. And I think what's interesting in Bacon is you've got that void over and over and over again but the figure is being sucked into it – it's like they've stepped over the threshold. So I think that's why they're not violent pictures but they are terrifying pictures. And the figure is cracked open, like an egg with the yolk seeping out, you've got the stuff of the soul seeping out but it's stretched over the threshold of the void, it's not in front of the void, it's not completely vanished into the void either, but it's being sucked into it. And I think that gives you as the viewer a bit more space to step into the picture, you don't have the proxy of the figure in the picture to take your place. And I think that's what makes them as paintings much more challenging and much more engaging.

When I'm thinking of Bacon's paintings I often think of the chaos he was able to live with, with the physical, emotional and sexual extremes he embraced in his life – with his ability to live with huge amounts of uncertainty. It demonstrates his ability to live outside the norms and rules of society. And I think being able to dispense with rules is one of the things that makes Bacon so engaging an artist. He treated painting as a game defined by rules which he wished to either disregard or adapt in whichever way best suited his purpose.

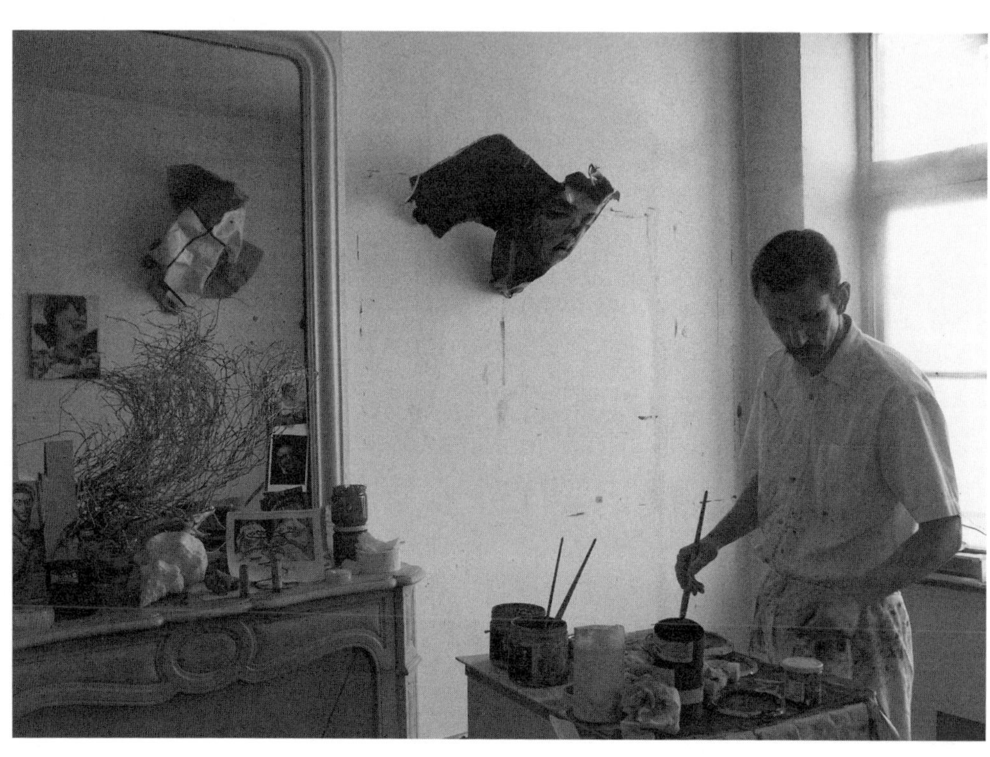

RUPERT SHRIVE

CANAL SAINT-MARTIN PARIS 2010

The following conversation took place in Rupert Shrive's studio beside the Canal Saint-Martin, an area of placid waterways and footbridges where Paris momentarily turns into a mini-Amsterdam. Every morning by first light Shrive shuts himself away in his functional, glass-roofed room to juggle fragmented memories into images, testing the possibilities of painting anew.

Shrive has lived and worked in many of the places I know best, from Soho to Spain, Venice to Paris. Our talk began as if we had all the time in the world, continuing over lunch in a funky, canalside restaurant and touching amiably on everything from mornings-after at the 'Coach and Horses' to fireworks in Valencia, until all of a sudden – like a photographer who knows he will only get his picture if he releases the shutter now – I snapped the tape recorder on.

MP Rupert, I feel a strong sense of mortality in the works you're showing in London. They come across as frozen and full of fragility.

RS Well, I try to capture fleeting moments, fleeting presences, like the faces you see flickering up in a fire. So the impermanence of things is certainly there, but for me they're like people you glimpse for a moment, people who suddenly rise up out of the dark – as they do in a nightclub, for instance – then fade away. So it's also about the mysterious way appearance blurs. That fascinates me, and it's very difficult to capture in a painting.

MP So they're more to do with taking portraits into a different dimension. You said that seeing a Rauschenberg show at the last Venice Biennale kick-started a new series.

Rupert Shrive (1965–). *After St Theresa*, exhibition catalogue, Morton Metropolis, London, March 2010.

RS Absolutely. I call that series 'configurations'. They're collages made from pieces of paintings that I failed to turn into one of the crushed paintings. I've got lots of these things lying around the studio, and I was going to throw them out. But then I started playing around and reassembling them, and that came out of Rauschenberg's 'Glut' series. Rauschenberg picked things up from the junkyard and composed them into structures which he then stuck on the wall, and I found them very moving.

MP So are yours a junkyard of faces, would you say? (*Laughter*) I see them as very tender, sensitive things, as if you're peeling back the skin of appearance to show the strangeness of a human face and the head beneath.

RS Well, I myself sometimes wonder if they don't look as if they'd been to too many plastic surgeons ... But what I'm always after is some kind of connection between the various elements, whether it's the eyes being aligned in a certain way or other features being connected by a colour. Something has to tally, so you push these things around until you get a harmony between the parts, where they lock together.

MP The collages form one part of the exhibition, and then you have the 'crushed' paintings.

RS Yes. I've always been interested in trying to extend the normal life of a two-dimensional painting. One of my great interests is portraiture and I did very classic portraits at one point. But since then I've wanted to take portraiture to another place, another level – to find an extra lease for it. I tried doing this first years ago when I was working in Soho. I ripped up some drawings in a rage and when they were on the floor I realized that if you shuffled five or six pieces around you could turn them into what I then termed 'visual anagrams'. The variety was extraordinary.

MP I suppose you have an extra freedom in the sense that you've already done the hard work of actually trying to capture a likeness or whatever it is when you're painting a portrait classically, and then you have these discarded images which you can shuffle into a new pack of cards.

RS Exactly. That's what it felt like, that's where things began and I realized that having explored the visual anagrams I was lucky enough to come across another method – of screwing things up, crushing them, and that seemed a more violent and dynamic way of re-creating things.

MP Is it a pleasurable process? You don't feel any pain in the way that you're maltreating your own work. Is it sadistic – or masochistic?

RS No, no, it's not pleasurable. Generally if I'm working on a series I prevaricate on the day when I'm going to start crushing. Because I know I've got, say, six paintings ready, flat paintings, and I know I've painted them as well as I possibly can …

MP And you're fond of them …

RS Yes, you've put a lot of feeling and thought into them. So I prevaricate, I lie to myself about when I'm going to deal with them.

MP But you know you're going to do it?

RS Well, I want to do it. Because I've discovered this way of working, and I know for example if I've got a crushed painting on the wall next to a flat one, when I look at the flat one there's something missing. The extra dimension the crushed one has got is asking me to pop it out into that multi-faceted thing. So I know I want to do it, and yes, as you say, it is painful and I'm always very scared when I start crushing them and it's very risky because you only have so many movements you can make before you've lost the big dynamic crush that you're going for. I want it to look as if it's been crushed in one strong movement, one bold movement, not fussily …

MP Do you think you've become an expert crusher now?

RS *(Laughs)* Well, you know things go wrong sometimes, and then they're irretrievable, they're completely doomed . . . but there again they end up in the pile which might be recycled into the configurations.

MP So you have to gauge very carefully the moment when you stop crushing.

RS Yes, it's very tricky, very hazardous, because at the beginning it sort of feels all right, and then as you're doing it you become increasingly aware that the more you move it around the less dynamic it's going to look, the more fussy it's going to look, so the tension mounts and it's not an agreeable feeling. You feel very anxious.

MP You worry you could take it over the top yet at the same time you've got to be bold.

RS Exactly, and that's the real pleasure. If it works it's a very sharp surprise. It suddenly jumps out at you. It's a very precise, tangible thing. It is quite fragile but it's also a physical thing, you're wrestling with it on the floor, with a corner of it under one foot . . . I do a preliminary sort of large crush and then I attach it at the back and put it on the wall and shuffle it around a bit further if I can.

MP How long does this process take?

RS Well the first main crush might take ten, fifteen minutes. But I might then leave it on the wall for a little bit, then tinker with it every now and again.

MP And by definition you've no idea of what you're going to get or what you want. You just want some kind of image coming out that you feel is right . . .

RS Yes, the image just seems to assert itself. I mean there are things you look out for. I always try to preserve the features, I want to be able to see the eyes, and obviously crushing can blot out the eyes. What I'm looking for is an image that the spectator has to walk round. I think El Greco, who's a painter I particularly admire, wanted that too. El Greco didn't believe in the static spectator. You know how with Piero della Francesca, with the *Baptism* in the National Gallery, say, there really is a particular point where you have to stand and then this glorious geometric harmony falls into place. Well, you don't get that with El Greco, his compositions catch your eye as you walk past, they're flickering flames of composition that take your eye up, largely heavenwards, and I like that very much, and it's something I particularly want to explore.

MP I suppose that was a change in the history of art, I mean you've got the Baroque age where movement comes into play. It's a change of faith, a change of man's position in the world even – that God rather than being in one fixed place in a fixed harmony is everywhere. It's a kind of dissolution of fixed values ... But in the show there are some collages, the crushed paintings ...

RS And some photographs. They're compositions I make on the studio floor with objects, but it's all largely related, if anything they're more like fetishes or 'primitive' art. You're looking out for images by shifting around bits of fur and plastic bags, twine and leaves, bits of food and string, anything that you happen to find.

MP Do you feel a bit like a child at play? Nietzsche said that as adult writers or artists or philosophers we have to find the seriousness that we had as children at play. A kind of total engagement. But to come to something a bit different, am I right in thinking that you do almost exclusively women?

RS There are a few self-portraits in the show.

MP Just you and the women ...

RS That's how we like it (*laughter*). I have painted men but less successfully, I just haven't been very pleased with them. The reason I've used quite a lot of geishas is that they already have a mask – a very perfect mask of red, black and white. And of course white is very good for crushing because it creates very strong cast shadows. And also just the immaculateness of it, the purity, creates a dynamic tension when one actually despoils or abuses it as it were.

MP So your primary sources are geishas as well as St Theresa.

RS Yes, the St Theresa of Bernini's sculpture in Rome – *The Ecstasy of Santa Teresa*.

MP Are all the women ecstatic in some way?

RS There is an element of that.

MP Do you think they're erotic?

RS I hope so, I want the girls to look strong and ... what do I want ... (*laughter*) ... I was going to say I want them to look challenging but no, I want them to catch your eye, I want them to look at you.

MP Do women react sometimes in a negative fashion to your crushed portraits?

RS Not as much as I feared.

MP They don't think you're attacking them?

RS I certainly don't like to think I've got anything particular to say like that.

MP You don't feel aggressive towards them?

RS No, Lord no, quite the opposite. There is an element of idealism in them, but as I say I want them to look fleeting, almost like spirits ...

MP Are they heroines? Or saints?

RS They're distributed about the wall in a way that seems like a constellation ...

MP So they are goddesses to an extent, you're putting them in the heavens as it were.

RS I quite like them fairly high on the wall, yes.

MP And are they destroying themselves in their ecstasy? I mean I wonder if this is their last moment. You've disfigured them as far as you can ...

RS Well no, I think they're enhanced.

MP You're their admirer.

RS To an extent. I'm trying to listen to them, they talk to me in their own way. It's difficult to talk about it because I don't have many benchmarks, I can't look at many other artists for clues, so sometimes I really don't know which way they're going and that's why I say they do talk to me themselves. I feel that there are moments when something happens and it seems to have come from nowhere really. Again it's all about listening to chance and accident and responding accordingly. You know all about that.

MP But you create your own chance and accident.

RS You set the scene ... I don't know if it happens to you as a writer, but it happens to me all the time. I discover something in the studio, some way of working, some shape, some combination of something, and I promise you within half an hour of leaving the studio I see the same thing there on the street that I'd never noticed before.

MP That is a state of grace and it's very exciting.

RS Exactly, you're trying to set a scene where these things can happen.

MP And then they do happen.

RS If you're lucky. They don't happen every day.

MP Do you mean that you see something that you can incorporate in your work? Life gives you the clue ... Have you ever done any commissioned crushed portraits?

RS No, I haven't. People have asked me but I'm very reluctant to do that. You get caught up in the situation where people want to look good, and although I like to think that they do look good, if I was expected to do this it would be strangulating. You'd be worried about preserving particular features, you wouldn't want to make their nose too big or too small or whatever.

MP And you want to create the excitement of a portrait that changes as you move around it, you see different angles and different shadows being formed. And you use a paint that catches the light as much as possible …

RS I sometimes use metallic paints, but I certainly use lots of varnishes, thick acrylic gels which catch the light wonderfully and combine with the works' three-dimensionality. And if in the end they don't quite work I know I can then recycle them into configurations.

MP Well, Rupert, I think that brings us full circle.

THREE ARCHITECTS

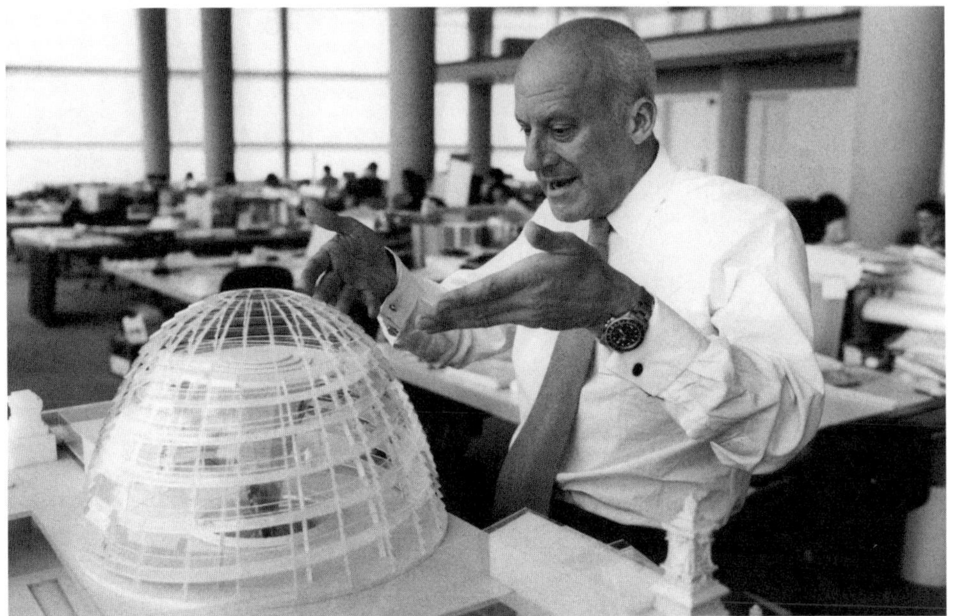

RUDI MEISEL, BERLIN

NORMAN FOSTER

BATTERSEA LONDON 2000

Norman Foster believes that everyone should be part of the architecture around them. And the minute you enter his huge, light-filled offices overlooking the Thames at Battersea, you are taken to a mezzanine café buzzing with architects where you immediately feel involved. An impressive array of scale models of Foster and Partners projects lines the walls, while on the vast, open floor below a sea of heads are bent over designs or locked in animated talk.

One of these heads is instantly recognizable as belonging to Lord Foster himself, who has exactly the same desk space as the scores of other architects. Foster sticks out so clearly not only because media coverage has made his face familiar, but because one has come to associate that domed head and intense gaze with some of the most radical, ambitious buildings of our time. Most of the projects Foster undertakes are on a monumental scale, ranging from corporate headquarters to airports, from bridges to subways and museums. Thus his most acclaimed buildings in recent years have all been public spaces, and they have been unusually attentive both to environmental issues and to the needs of the large numbers of people who use them. Much of the innovative thinking behind the Third London Airport at Stansted, for instance, the Metro in Bilbao or the Canary Wharf Station in London has focused on making mass travel as stress-free as possible. Similarly, the glass cupola which crowns the new German Parliament in Berlin allows visitors not only to gaze across the city's changing horizon but to keep an eye on the politicians below.

Casually dressed and relaxed amidst the controlled chaos of his office, Foster talks about his work with ease but also with a genuine desire to share his enthusiasm. He has recently completed a radical redevelopment of the British Museum, which will be officially inaugurated by Queen Elizabeth this month, and at a lithe sixty-five, with worldwide projects as well as a Pritzker Prize to his credit, he is

Norman Foster (1935–). *Town & Country*, New York, December 2000.

clearly at the height of his powers. But he seems sustained by a kind of long-term anxiety, as if he were still at the outset of his career, and he gives no signs of letting up.

'Architecture is a highly risky and competitive profession,' he says in his softly decisive voice. 'You never know whether there's going to be enough or too much to do. And each project takes up the most enormous amount of time because you have to come at it from so many angles, whether you're starting from scratch or transforming an existing building. Take the British Museum. When it was completed in 1852, it had a huge central courtyard the size of Hanover Square. A little later the Reading Room was built in this Great Court, and the remaining space was filled with book stacks. What we wanted to do was to rediscover this lost space.

We had to go back through many layers of time to find out exactly how the museum had become the way it was. Then we had to decide what was precious, what had to be kept at all costs – like the Reading Room itself – and what could be done away with. We also had to think how we could incorporate new materials and technologies in this project – how we could stretch the limits, by making greater spans and bigger domes. Because that is what architecture has always been about: stretching the limits.'

'What was most important', Foster concludes, 'was to find a solution that would satisfy all these demands yet look so simple, so obvious, that it seemed inevitable.' It is too early to say how 'inevitable' the redesigned Great Court and Reading Room look, but there is no doubt that, thanks to Foster's radical, £100 million transformation, the British Museum – still the finest example of nineteenth-century Greek Revival architecture in Britain – can look forward to a new lease of life. What Foster has done essentially is to clear a considerable space all round the old Reading Room, thus creating a hub from which visitors have direct access to the museum's different collections – such as the Egyptian Galleries or the King's Library – then cover the whole with a vast transparent roof. This newly liberated area has been planned as a 'cultural plaza' with its own exhibitions and sculpture displays, as well as shops and restaurants. The Reading Room, whose famous dome has been reinstated with its original pale-blue and gold paint scheme of 1857, will now serve as an information centre and reference library for the museum and its collections.

Foster is of course no stranger to the special demands of building or transforming museums. The Sainsbury Centre for Visual Arts, which he built in 1976–7 to house the remarkable art collection given by Sir Robert and Lady Sainsbury to the University of East Anglia in Norwich, brought Foster international recognition. In the mid-1980s he designed the Sackler Galleries, an extension to the Royal Academy of Arts on Piccadilly, and the Carré d'Art, a contemporary art space in Nîmes. But the British Museum, which draws some six million visitors a year, is no doubt the most prestigious project Foster will ever undertake in this field. He himself sees it as more than merely the transformation of a museum. Since the new court, already billed as 'London's first covered square', will be open as a public thoroughfare from early morning to the evening, Foster hopes that it will be used as by pedestrians making their way from Bloomsbury to Covent Garden, Trafalgar Square and the Thames. 'What I think we have found', Foster has declared, 'is not just a new heart for the British Museum, but a great new plaza for London.'

Not all Londoners have been won over by Foster's achievements. When his elegant Millennium Bridge, built to link St Paul's Cathedral to the new Tate Modern and the Globe Theatre, had to be closed temporarily because the number of pedestrians crossing it caused it to sway, the press had a field day, eventually demanding that the 'wobbly' bridge be kept open as an attraction on a par with the Leaning Tower of Pisa. More recently, when it was discovered that the south portico in the British Museum's Great Court had been mistakenly built in a light French stone rather than the original, more weathered Portland limestone, another furore ensued.

Although he prides himself on his attention to every detail of his buildings, Foster is unlikely to be fazed for long by such unforeseen mishaps. He has numerous other commissions under way in London, most notably the 40-storey offices of the insurance company, Swiss Re, in the City (its unusual shape has caused it to be called everything from a 'giant gherkin' to a 'post-modern Strawberry Hill'), the riverside headquarters for the Greater London Authority and the elegantly spare, new Wembley Stadium. In these, as in all his previous projects, Foster has concentrated on making spaces whose beauty derives from their adaptability to people's needs and a concern for the environment as a whole. One of Foster's current, cherished plans is to pedestrianize London's traffic-clogged Trafalgar Square. If he succeeds, it will allow Londoners to stroll about in one of their finest architectural ensembles. It will also enable Foster to change further the face of the city, a radical and welcome transformation for which he will be remembered long after 'wobbly bridge' jokes have faded away.

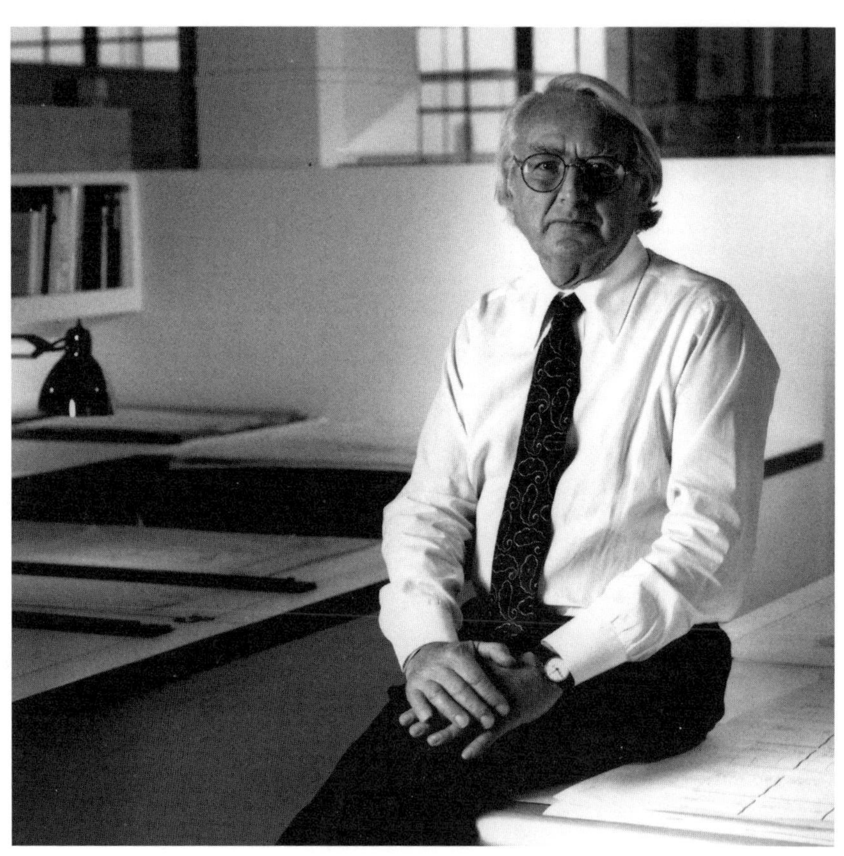

RICHARD MEIER

CHELSEA NEW YORK 2000

The first glimpse I had of Richard Meier's office on 10th Avenue in New York struck me as saying a great deal about the architect and his basic aesthetic. Filling the entire top floor of a landmark building that overlooks the Hudson River, Richard Meier & Partners hums with intense activity. Dozens of architects and assistants pour over drawing-boards or computers, working on urgent projects in most parts of the globe. Yet where one might imagine feverish haste and chaotic clutter, an extraordinary tranquillity and order prevails.

Despite the manifest activity, everything appears to be under control. The central mass of architects' desks, each of them unnaturally tidy, is ringed round by an impressive array of scale models representing the many, ambitious projects currently in hand. They range from a court house in Arizona to a church in Rome, a department store in Düsseldorf to a private residence in Kuala Lumpur. The almost supernatural neatness of these tiny, meticulously executed models is accentuated by the sparkling Manhattan light that bounces off the Hudson River and plays over the office's huge white walls.

White is the dominant colour, as one might expect in the offices of a man who, because everything he builds is predominantly white, has been dubbed the 'white architect'. Oddly, when we meet, what first catches my eye is the whiteness emanating from Meier himself. The only things whiter than the all-white conference room where we settle down to talk are Meier's expanse of snowy white shirt (he is an impressively big man), his mane of silver white hair and his very American, very white smile.

'It's true I love the colour white,' Meier explains. 'That's because I'm interested in light, in the way it changes throughout the day, and from season to season. I think of light as the best and most versatile building material. Space changes as light changes, and nothing shows the modulations of light, the play of light and shadow, as clearly

Richard Meier (1934–). *AD*, Paris, July 2000.

as white. Above all, I think white expresses in the fullest way the architectural ideas inherent in a building.' White also has a wholeness and a purity that is clearly inspirational to Meier, who is fond in this context of quoting Goethe's phrase that 'colour is the pain of light'.

For a man who is responsible for important, often controversial and expensive buildings going up all over the world, Meier comes across as unusually relaxed as he fields one question after another with disarming simplicity. Nowadays he seems doomed to be forever on an aeroplane, visiting sites or shuttling between his New York and his Los Angeles offices; and the range, size and cost of his architectural undertakings would keep most people awake at night. The Getty Center, which Meier completed in 1997, is a case in point. The architect's largest project to date, this huge arts complex built into the hills above Los Angeles is designed as a series of interlinking buildings punctuated by a series of open and closed spaces. Looking and functioning very much like a small, albeit futuristic, town, the Getty Center took fourteen years and a billion dollars to complete.

Born in Newark, New Jersey, in 1934, Meier reckons that his life as an architect began the moment when, at the age of fifteen, he helped to build a family house. As a result, he began training in an architect's office and knew from then on that he had found his vocation. While studying architecture at Cornell University, he was especially drawn to the work of Le Corbusier, Frank Lloyd Wright, Louis Kahn, Alvar Aalto and Mies van der Rohe, who have continued to be major sources of inspiration. But, as Meier himself freely admits, he has been as deeply influenced by the architects of the Renaissance and the Baroque, from Bramante to Bernini, as by twentieth-century architecture. 'You can see elements of structure in those periods that expand your mind because they are so brilliant,' he says. 'Their purity may be clouded over with decoration, but there is a relationship of light to structure which is unforgettable.'

After three years working for Marcel Breuer, Meier set up his own practice, and by 1967, when he had completed the now-famous Smith House – a characteristically transparent, white structure – in Darien, Connecticut, his reputation was well established. Over the three decades since, Meier has been unusually prolific, designing a wide variety of buildings both in the United States and abroad. Among his best-known projects, apart from the Getty Center, are the High Museum in Atlanta, the Museum for Decorative Arts in Frankfurt, Canal Plus Television Headquarters in Paris and the Museum of Contemporary Art in Barcelona.

As this list suggests, Meier is particularly sought after in Europe, to the extent that in America he is often described as a 'European' architect. 'I think one reason why people here think of me as 'European',' Meier reflects, 'is because I'm particularly sensitive to what already exists in the environment where I am building. Another reason, perhaps, is the scale of my buildings, which – by American standards – are relatively small. You know, I don't do forty-storey skyscrapers. Although of course,' he adds, with a laugh, 'I'm always happy to consider doing something I haven't already done …

'I think that's what excites me most. Because a new kind of project – like the bridge I'm doing for Alessandria in Italy, or even more, the Church of the Year 2000 that we're building on the outskirts of Rome – forces you to rethink everything. You know, I'd never built a church before. And suddenly you have to consider all the implications: what does a church mean today, and how can that be expressed spatially? It seemed to me above all that it should not be confining. And the basic concept I arrived at for the church was an atrium enclosed by curvilinear elements that leads through a passage to the adjoining community centre, which by contrast has a rectilinear organization. The idea was to create a relationship between something which is free-flowing and something which is more defined. And, of course, the whole building is built to be seen from every angle, to be looked up to and looked down at, because it is surrounded by high-rise apartment blocks where everybody gets a bird's-eye view.'

We look at a few other on-going projects, including a very handsome private residence in Malibu, California, and I begin to wonder what Richard Meier's own house might be like. Does it have all this space and light and whiteness? Did he design it himself?

'No,' says Meier, with a rueful laugh. 'I live in an apartment in New York, and on the weekends I go out to an old farmhouse on Long Island. I've never built for myself. I don't know why. The idea certainly interests me, and my children have asked me often enough to build a family house. Perhaps it's because I'd be too difficult to please – my own nightmare client!'

*

With ambitious building projects under way right across the globe, Richard Meier has little time to devote to anything outside his highly successful architectural practice. But at the beginning of his career, when he was still working with Marcel Breuer, Meier cultivated another passion, which has never left him.

'I started painting at night, when I got home from work,' Meier explains. 'For a time, I was really torn between wanting to paint and wanting to do architecture. And a friend of mine, Frank Stella, said I could work in his studio. That was wonderful, and I began making these large abstract canvases until Frank said to me, 'You're taking up too much room, Richard. You'd better get your own space.' So I did some other large things in my little, two-room apartment. But it got awfully cramped, and there was simply nowhere to store the works once they were finished. So I decided to do small-scale things that would fit on my drafting table. And that's how I started trying my hand at collages. I found they gave me terrific pleasure, and that's why I'm still doing them today.'

Unlike the collages of Kurt Schwitters, which juxtapose sharply contrasting images, Meier's compositions tend to be carefully focussed and harmonious. 'White architect' though he may be, Meier gives free rein to a dramatic sense of colour in his collages. Whole series have been done in subtle variations on red, black and white; and at one time or another he has used virtually every colour in the palette. Most of the material that goes into the works has been collected during his numerous travels, along with bits and pieces from newspapers, magazines and his own daily post. Not surprisingly, the collages are predominantly abstract, with fragments of posters, tickets and invitation cards, which are frequently over-painted. But they refer, however cursorily or obliquely, to Meier's movements around New York and across the world, and occasionally an odd photograph or recognizable image creeps in.

'I try and get rid of any specific reference so that the collages have a more general relevance,' Meier says, 'and I'm always conscious that, although I organize them to some extent, they basically come about by chance. That's what I love about them. I hoard all this material, which I collect the whole time, in a special box. I take it with me when I fly, and it fits perfectly between the armrests of an airplane seat. So when I'm tired of reading, I take out various fragments and play around with them until I think I've got the beginnings of a stimulating composition. I find it very absorbing and terrific fun. Of course, everybody around me thinks I'm totally crazy. But I love to do these things and then keep them in books – I must have forty or fifty books filled with them now, mostly dating from the last twenty years. And in a sense, although they are above all formal compositions, they've also become a kind of diary of my life.'

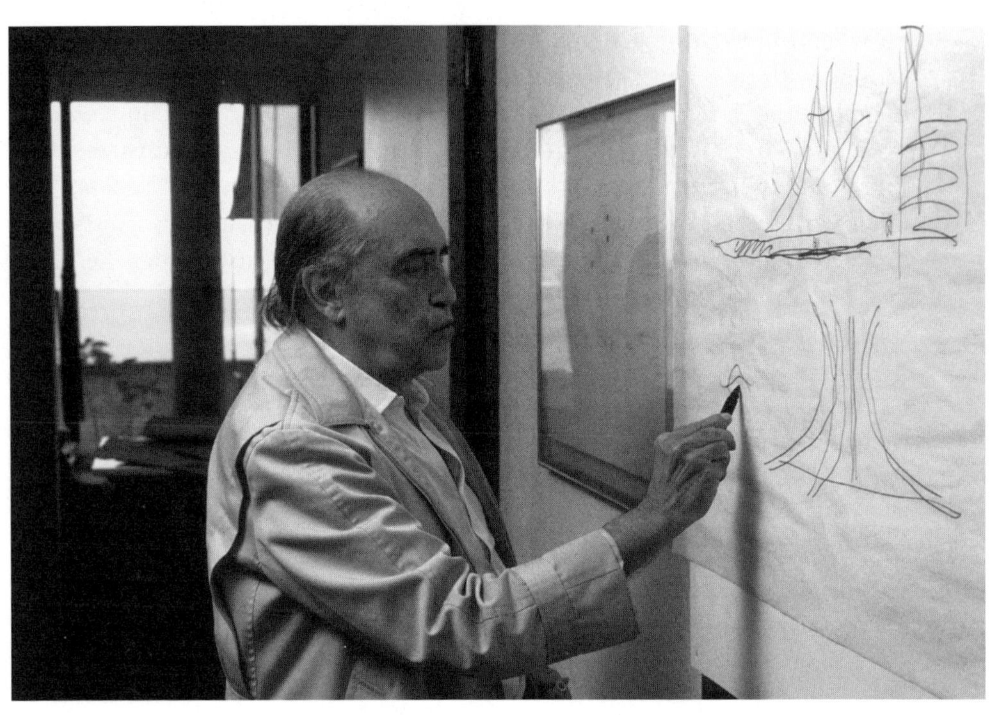

OSCAR NIEMEYER

COPACABANA RIO DE JANEIRO 2000

Oscar Niemeyer is sitting in the bow window of his office in Rio de Janeiro looking out over his favourite view: the sea and the sky over Copacabana beach. 'Whenever I can, I come here and daydream,' he says peacefully. 'I love to watch the clouds change shape. They take on the most marvellous forms for a moment – huge cathedrals, Roman chariots or a woman smiling down at you. I've always been attracted to free form – to free-flowing, sensuous curves. When he talked about my architecture, Le Corbusier often used to say to me: 'Oscar, tu as les montagnes du Brésil dans les yeux.' But I prefer to say that I have everything I love in my eyes – not only the mountains, but the rivers, the waves of the ocean or the body of a woman. And it is out of all those things that my work has evolved.'

For a man who was born at the beginning of the last century, in 1907, Niemeyer – whose full name is Oscar Ribeiro de Almeida de Niemeyer Soares – remains extraordinarily energetic and alert. While we talk, he occasionally complains of old age ('De Gaulle was right,' he says, 'L'âge, c'est le naufrage'),[1] but shows few signs of his advanced years. Small, slender, and dressed entirely in white, he moves briskly around his large office, frequently going from the bay window to the drawing-board to illustrate a point he has just made with a sketch. The drawings are extraordinarily fluent, with Niemeyer's pen racing with apparently careless ease across the large sheets of paper, conjuring buildings already designed and others under way. Occasionally, with impish humour, he will draw a naked woman and have her lying invitingly beside a museum he has just outlined.

'I've always drawn,' he continues in slow, clear French. 'In that sense, I've always thought with my hands. But I didn't really get serious about architecture until I got married. Up until then, I'd really only been interested in amusing myself: hanging out with my friends, playing sport, looking at the girls – the kind of things all young men do.

Oscar Niemeyer (1907–). *AD*, Paris,
January 2001.

Once I had a family, though, I realized I had to support them, and I set about qualifying as an architect. I was very lucky because the director of the School of Fine Arts where I studied here was Lúcio Costa, a wonderful, generous man and a fine architect, and I went to work at his office in 1935. Then very soon afterwards I met Le Corbusier, and that was of course a major turning-point in my career. Little by little, I began to have commissions, mainly for public buildings, both in Brazil and abroad. But I have always followed *my* route and done *my* architecture, which I think is like nobody else's.'

Niemeyer's career seems in retrospect to have been charmed from the start, since he was able to absorb Le Corbusier's influence and develop his own distinct style, combining the curving, organic forms of his native country with the demands of international modernism. Having designed the Brazilian Pavilion at the New York World Fair, several public buildings and a remarkable house for himself in Rio, the architect achieved world fame in the late 1950s when, with Lúcio Costa, he began work on Brasilia, the country's brand new capital. His designs included everything from government ministries to a cathedral, a theatre and a hotel, all of them marked by a drive towards a sheer, soaring simplicity. Even though Niemeyer is less than enchanted with the way Brasilia has evolved over recent years, his conversation often touches on it. 'I think architecture should always be different. It has to work, to function perfectly – but it should always surprise,' he says. 'Nowadays everybody has got used to Brasilia. But when it was built, it did come as a surprise. Nobody had seen forms like that before. I have never liked straight lines, so I used free-flowing curves. For me, the universe is made up of curves.'

Early on Niemeyer had joined the Brazilian Communist Party and, as he became increasingly respected both at home and abroad, he never made a secret of his passionately held political views, drawing attention above all to the plight of the poor. Once the military gained power in 1964, Niemeyer found himself isolated and his career severely hampered. A couple of years later, the architect left for Paris, where his work was already well known and where he was to live throughout the 1970s. During this period, Niemeyer set up office on the Champs-Élysées and designed, among other things, the Mondadori publishing headquarters in Milan, the Maison de la Culture in Le Havre and the building for 'L'Humanité' in Saint-Denis. He also began to make his own highly simplified and elegant furniture.

At the end of the 1970s, with a Légion d'honneur and a retrospective exhibition at the Centre Pompidou to his credit, Niemeyer returned to his beloved Rio and resumed his place as Brazil's leading architect. With the country's military dictatorship at an end, he soon became as busy as he had ever been, even if none of the projects had quite the awesome responsibility of Brasilia. In fact, he was able to indulge the lighter, more fanciful side of his nature in 1982 by creating a 'Sambódromo' – a stylish stadium for the samba parades that are an essential part of Rio's Carnival ritual. While designing an impressive variety of public buildings throughout Brazil, including the ambitious and intensely sculptural Memorial da América Latina complex in São Paulo, Niemeyer has found time to write several books, make sculpture, receive numerous international honours (including the Pritzker Prize for Architecture) and help the many museums which have put on exhibitions celebrating his long lifetime's work.

Niemeyer shows no signs of slowing down. Every day sees him arrive at his office and begin work on one of his latest projects. In 1999, for instance, the buildings he designed ranged from a theatre in Ibirapuera Park in São Paulo to the administrative centre in Betim, Minas Gerais; and over the past year he has concentrated on a series of daycare centres. 'The essential thing is to remain free,' he says. 'You can only create if you feel completely free to do whatever you want to do. I have always wanted to make forms that were beautiful. I took a lot from nature. I saw columns as trees, for instance, and I'm fascinated by the way you can change a building by changing the space between the pillars that support it. But I also often think that architecture itself is not so important. In fact, very little is important. We ourselves are very small and insignificant. You only have to look up at the sky to understand that. Life is an instant. There are tears and smiles. Then it's over.'

Yet Niemeyer makes sure, even in his mid-nineties, that he enjoys that passing instant to the full. Every day towards noon his office begins to fill up with venerable looking gentlemen of a similar age to his own. One by one they settle down beside him on the bow-window banquette. As in the best clubs, a familiar conversation, part banter, part gossip, starts up. The large central table is cleared of drawing materials and set for lunch. Drinks are served. It is clearly part of Niemeyer's philosophy not to let work get in the way of the pleasures of life. And indeed as these old companions begin their meal, they can see a large inscription in Niemeyer's hand looking across at them from the wall. 'Le plus important, ce n'est pas l'architecture,' it reads. 'C'est la vie, les amis et ce monde injuste que nous devons modifier.'[2]

1 'Old age is like a shipwreck.'

2 'What is most important is not architecture, but life, friends and the injustice of the world that we must change.'

STUDIO VISITS

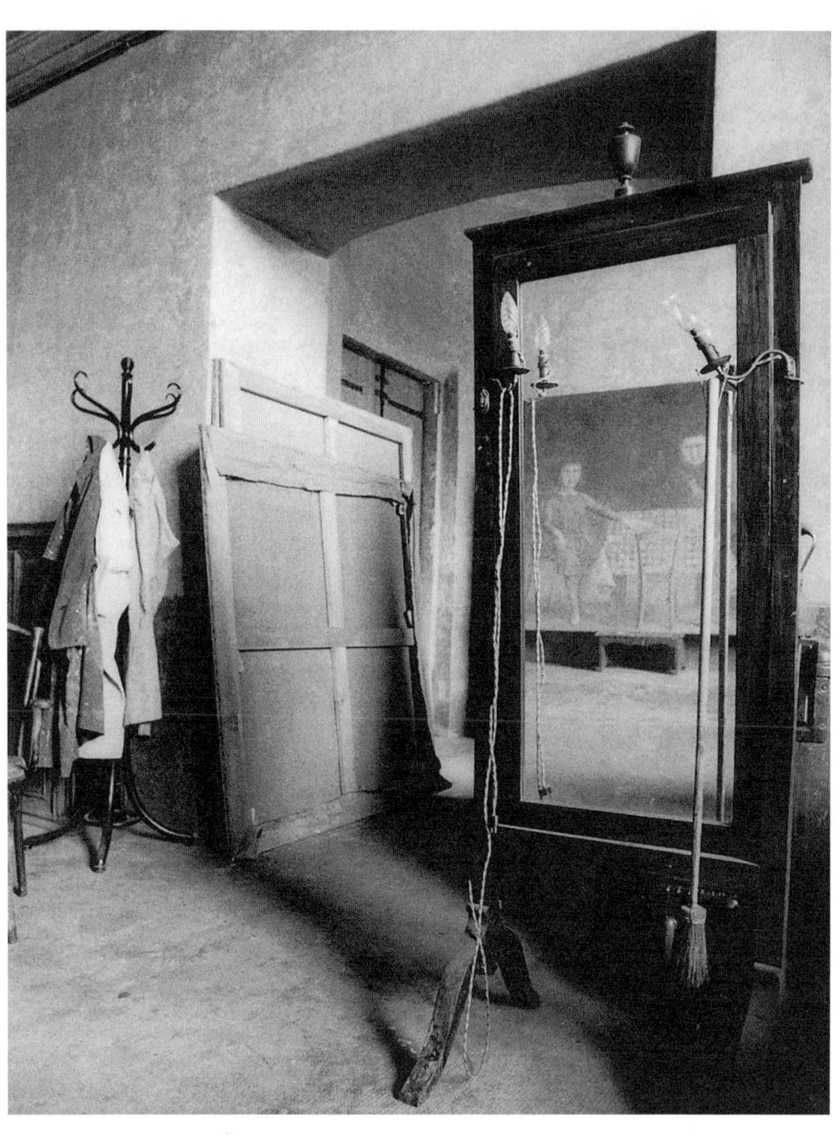

BALTHUS

VILLA MEDICI ROME 1966

Being sent to interview Balthus at the Villa Medici in Rome in 1966 was the highlight of my early career, occurring shortly after I arrived in Paris to take up my first job at Réalités *magazine. I was too young and inexperienced to know how to get behind the artist's carefully stage managed, aristocratic hauteur; and of course seeing him preside over the magnificent villa with its historic gardens, virtually unchanged since Velázquez painted them c.1634, did nothing to make my account of the visit and this grand personage more critical or probing.*

Balthus – or I should say the Comte Klossowski de Rola, to call him by the bogus title he insisted on – appears here pretty much as he wanted to appear (even though, when the piece came out, Balthus grumbled to the art critic John Russell that I had talked too much about the artist and not enough about the art). Yet I was not so naïve as to fall for some of Balthus's wilder fantasies, such as when, having shown me round the villa's impressive, vaulted and frescoed rooms, he let drop casually that he was descended from Lord Byron. Rather than express polite scepticism, I joined in the make-believe and enthusiastically speculated about the tartan Balthus would be entitled to wear (with his love of dressing up, Balthus warmed visibly to the idea of kilt and sporran); but I did not of course include this particular flight of fancy when I came to write up my visit. Later, when Balthus was stripped of his aristocratic pretensions by his biographers, I felt a little sorry for him. The titles, the gaunt châteaux *he had inhabited, the coats of arms he had embroidered on his kimonos (after his marriage to Setsuko) had all been part of the fantasy world, along with the day-dreaming pubescent girls, from which he derived his art. And without that fantasy world those gorgeous images of indolent adolescence caught in a golden light would never have been dreamed into existence.*

Balthus (1908–2001). *Réalités*, Paris, October 1967.

For over 250 years the French Academy for Fine Arts in Rome has been housed in the Villa Medici, and for the last six of them, Balthus – the painting name of Count Balthazar Klossowski de Rola – has been its director. Under his guidance, this lovely late Renaissance villa has made a step back towards its former glory: a series of seventeenth-century frescoes, drawn from Old Testament themes, has been discovered beneath its whitewashed walls.

'I've become a sort of works' foreman,' Balthus said wryly, as we sat in the villa's vast and barely furnished drawing room, high up above the deep snarl of the city's traffic. 'Because of that, I have been unable to give proper attention to my painting. I haven't even started on anything, in fact, since spring last year.' Balthus's most recent paintings, both finished last year, are *The Three Sisters* and *The Turkish Room*. The latter, a large picture of a pale Oriental girl lying in a brilliantly patterned bedroom, took three years to paint.

'Each picture I do,' Balthus continued, 'requires a lot of forethought and planning, so that when I eventually begin I know exactly what I am going to do.' A glance at Balthus's work tells one enough to sense, above all, the deliberateness with which it has been conceived. Beneath its softly fused surface, there is a composition as hard and inevitable as bones beneath flesh. It is as though one were watching a dream pinned onto reality. But not even these dreams seem left to chance.

We walked from one massive, high-vaulted room – where only proportions and a lean-looking bust by Giacometti were noticeable – into another, where the table was set for lunch. The conversation only rarely touched on art. 'I don't see what one can say about my paintings,' Balthus remarked at one point. 'After all, if they are any good, they should say whatever it is for themselves. It's very exceptional that writers on art actually help one to see. And poets – Baudelaire apart – are particularly dangerous: they tend to use others' work to talk about their own.'

In discussing the reviews published on his work, he mentioned the case of an article in which he had been ridiculously misquoted. 'The trouble is,' he continued, 'that people have become so much more interested in the artist's 'personality' than in his work. What can it matter how Picasso eats?'

Balthus is extremely wary of the publicity boom in modern art. He believes it can do nothing but harm to the artist and the meaning of art. And especially dangerous, he feels, is the belief that art is for everyone. 'It is part of the modern sickness that craves a report on everything that is happening, irrespective of its importance. Why, for instance, do tens of thousands of people crowd into art exhibitions? One would think they were trying to fill some kind of terrible inner emptiness.'

The same lack of belief in modern methods affects Balthus's view of painting. Rather than explore present chaos, he looks to the time when painting was intimately dependent on its own heritage. No living painter, he says, has influenced his style; but his admiration for great artists of other centuries – Piero della Francesca, whose works he once copied, Ingres, Courbet and Bonnard, whom he knew – is a prime motive in his creativity. Throughout his career, Balthus has preferred traditional values to the modern one of the artist's lonely flight into the unknown.

One approach to the rare quality of Balthus's pictures lies, in fact, in appreciating his use of a traditional pictorial vocabulary. His constant reference to masters of the past taught him how their technical excellence can be kept alive in new contexts. Having this background, he is naturally ill at ease with the contemporary conviction that art is a private adventure, a way of walking one's personality. He believes that the artist should appear anonymous – to the point where, to quote his beloved Courbet, he creates 'a suggestive magic, containing both object and subject, both the world outside the artist and the artist himself.'

But there is another, more immediate way into Balthus's world. One needs no art history to become absorbed in the quietly haunting atmosphere of his pictures. That atmosphere – as familiar yet unexpected as a remembered fragment of a dream – has become a constant and quickly endearing aspect of his vision. The subjects he chooses are commonplace – a street scene or a girl asleep – and represented in a very literal way, but they have the mystery of things that lead a secret existence. As soon as one turns away from them they might, one feels, begin to breathe.

Elusive as they are, these paintings repeatedly follow certain themes. The most frequent, and perhaps the best loved, is adolescence: Balthus delights in the uncertain, equivocal moments of life that divide childhood from early maturity. Caught unawares in the full bloom of a daydream or an unguarded, self-absorbed gesture, his adolescents cling jealously to their childish state, as though they already resented the pace of time. 'Childhood,' Balthus remarked with a distant stare, 'is the heroic age of man.' His own childhood, spent in Switzerland, was free of parental interference and perfectly happy. 'I have never felt any transition from childhood. Everything seems to have followed on in the same way. But then,' he added with a smile, 'perhaps I never really was a child.'

Balthus finds his attachment to childhood and adolescence closely echoed in Emily Brontë's *Wuthering Heights*. In 1933, when he was twenty-one, he made a series of drawings on scenes from the novel; one of them turned into a large painting of himself as the jealous Heathcliff watching Cathy dress. The first part of this story, tender and violent in swift succession and haunted by a feeling for the precariousness of happiness, comes wonderfully near to the atmosphere in which Balthus evokes his theme of adolescence.

Towards evening Balthus took me through the gardens of the Villa Medici. The sunlight had deepened, and the gardens' palm and pine trees threw shadows along the paths. 'You should not forget,' Balthus remarked, 'that I am also a landscape and still-life painter. I find them just as interesting as figure painting. They are similar, in a way. Painting one tree in relation to another and painting two figures have a great deal in common.' Balthus's attention to everything he paints is uniform. Objects find as careful, full-bodied a place in his work as people.

We climbed a sharp flight of steps to the small, classical temple that serves as the villa's belvedere. The city's skyline, heroic and familiar in the reddening sun, rose towards us. 'And yet,' Balthus mentioned, 'one is always conscious of how much more beautiful Rome must once have been.' As we turned to go back to the villa, he said: 'I don't know why I paint – I really don't want to know. But sometimes, when one sees what happens to one's paintings, the question becomes: why go on painting? I am, in any case, very pessimistic. Perhaps there is no more art – only illusions about it.' This reflection was cut short by the thunderous arrival of Balthus's two dogs, still possessed by some adventure in the gardens' undergrowth. And I was left wondering whether the secret and richly invested beauty of Balthus's painting did not contradict that pessimistic outlook.

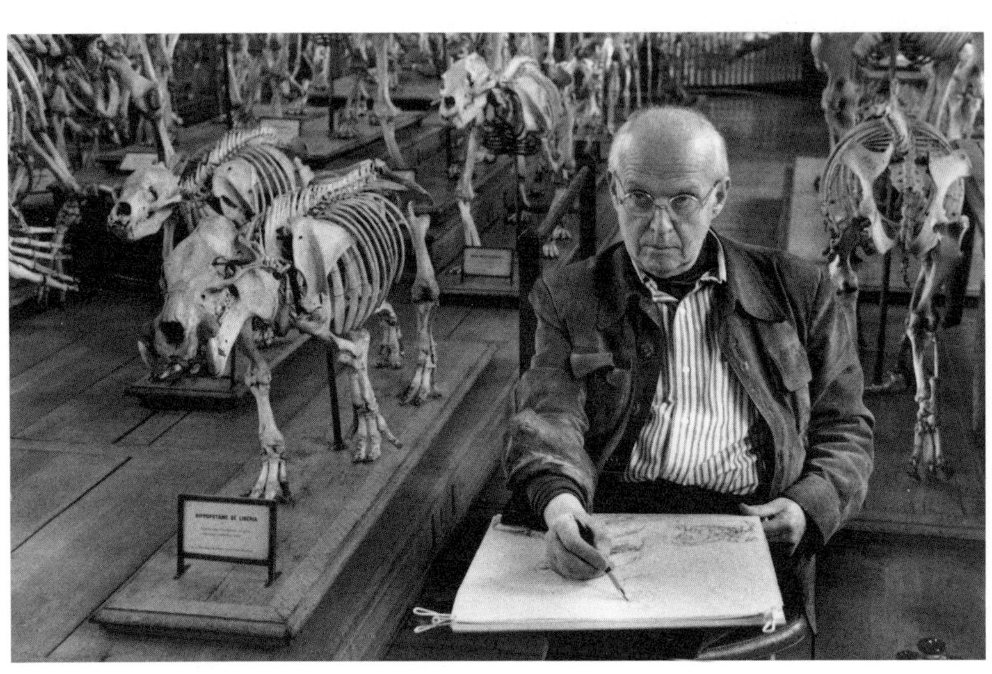

HENRI CARTIER-BRESSON

RUE DE RIVOLI PARIS 1987

Henri Cartier-Bresson's conversation was as quick and to the point as his photographs – and as universal, since it ranged over an astonishing range of subjects. Although he had long been considered as one of the world's greatest photographers, Cartier-Bresson was regularly dismissive of his enviable reputation. At first this came across as a rather extreme affectation, not least because the great photographer tended also to dismiss photography itself as a medium, above all when compared to drawing, insisting (as he does in the following interview) that: 'Photography is instant drawing, really, like instant coffee'.

But it was a real dilemma for him, and throughout the latter part of his life Cartier-Bresson made a heroic attempt to succeed as a draughtsman. To some extent he was constantly thwarted in this by his own reputation as the creator of some of the most memorable photographic images of the century. But like all true artists Cartier-Bresson thrived on conflict and contradiction. In the following interview, he gives vent to his frustrations, but always elegantly, taking us rapidly and decisively to the heart of his creative dilemma.

The pale blue eyes stare – a bird's sudden, inquiring gaze – blink, then stare elsewhere. The hands flutter in swift, nervously expressive gestures. The words multiply, sketching quick portraits of people and times past, or gleefully dismantling set notions about life. But it is to the eyes that attention returns. Their questioning restlessness invests the most ordinary scene with significance. After a few minutes in Henri Cartier-Bresson's company, everything becomes intensely visual.

It is natural to wonder whether each quick glance has composed – then accepted or rejected – a photograph. A fat man presiding over a large beer on a tiny café table, a succession of deserted courtyards,

Henri Cartier-Bresson (1908–2004). *Architectural Digest*, Los Angeles, January 1987.

or a child open-mouthed in sleep all come to look, when he is there, like potential Cartier-Bressons. The name is inseparable from a flow of images – taken in every country, in every form of society – in which the poetic irony and chance beauty of everyday life stands revealed. The name is, quite simply, that of the best-known photographer alive. But for well over a decade this prodigiously resourceful man has channelled his best energy not into photography but into drawing. 'I've gone back to what I wanted to do at the beginning of my life,' he says. 'My first passion was for drawing and painting; photography came much later. One day I thought to myself, I've said whatever I had to say in photography, so why shouldn't I try my hand at drawing again?'

While photography allowed Cartier-Bresson to travel the world and capture the unexpected, drawing keeps him at home and forces him to concentrate on the familiar. Paris is his richest source of inspiration, above all the magnificent views of the Louvre, the Tuileries and the Seine from the window of the comfortably bookish apartment where he lives with his wife, photographer Martine Franck. He returns to these obsessively, as to his own Mont Sainte-Victoire, attempting in a flurry of soft lines to fix the impermanence of appearance.

'One great advantage about a drawing,' Cartier-Bresson points out, 'is that you can go over it time and again. Photography is the opposite. Once it's done, it's done. I think of photography as an extroverted activity, whereas drawing is much more introverted. It's a form of meditation, really, because it makes you close up on yourself and concentrate.'

Cartier-Bresson's photographs possess the calm eloquence of fact stated without hesitation. The drawings, on the other hand, come across as masses of contradiction and doubt. In certain sketches, each line seems unsure of itself, as if it were questioning both its own existence and the object it attempts to represent. But as in Alberto Giacometti's drawings, which Cartier-Bresson deeply admires, so much doubt in the end takes on an air of heroic affirmation. The frail tree and the faintly outlined face appear to have resisted overwhelming odds to have stayed at all on the hostile blankness of the paper.

'Up until World War II I'd always imagined that my whole life would be devoted to drawing and painting. My uncle had been a painter and I started taking lessons with a friend of his when I was only fifteen, in 1923. I went on to study at André Lhote's studio, but a year later I destroyed all the canvases I'd done. In the thirties I began going around with the Surrealists and trying my hand at photography. But it was painting that fascinated me. Even at the end of the War, after I'd managed to escape from a P.O.W. camp in Germany, I thought I was going to be a painter. But I wanted to travel everywhere and have an adventurous life. And I saw that photography – especially reportage, which is what has always interested me most in photography – could give me that kind of life.'

Cartier-Bresson's passion for drawing is so intense that he tends to make light of his achievements as a photographer. A biography, in the catalogue of an exhibition of his drawings held in 1981 at the Musée d'Art Moderne de la Ville de Paris, states, baldly enough, that 'from 1946 to 1973, photography played an important role in his life.' He himself is similarly given to such laconic statements as: 'Photography is a kind of instinctive drawing. It's instant drawing, really, like instant coffee.' And he repeatedly underlines the fact that his visual sense was formed by looking at painting.

'Nowadays,' he says, warming to a favourite theme, 'people come to photography from all kinds of different disciplines, such as anthropology or sociology. In my case it was from painting and drawing. They gave me my real basis. Other photographers get annoyed and say I've turned my back on photography. They didn't mind when I made films – when I worked for Jean Renoir, or more recently when I made a couple of documentaries. But the idea that I'm drawing seems to infuriate them.'

Contradiction and controversy are natural elements for Cartier-Bresson. He is most at home, however, talking and laughing with his friends, who are as varied as they are abundant. But although his sense of the uniqueness of other people has stood him in good stead both as a draughtsman and a photographer, it has not proved infallible, as he himself recounts wryly: 'I once had to take the portrait of a famous and rather formidable lady here in Paris, and I was worried because I'd photographed her many years before and realized she might make the inevitable comparisons. Portraits are difficult enough to do at the best of times. You only have to say one thing out of tune with the other person's mood to lose a good portrait. She seemed rather tense when I arrived, so when she asked how long the whole thing would take, I tried to make a joke by saying, "Oh, rather longer than the dentist, but not as long as a psychiatrist." That didn't amuse her. And we lost the portrait.'

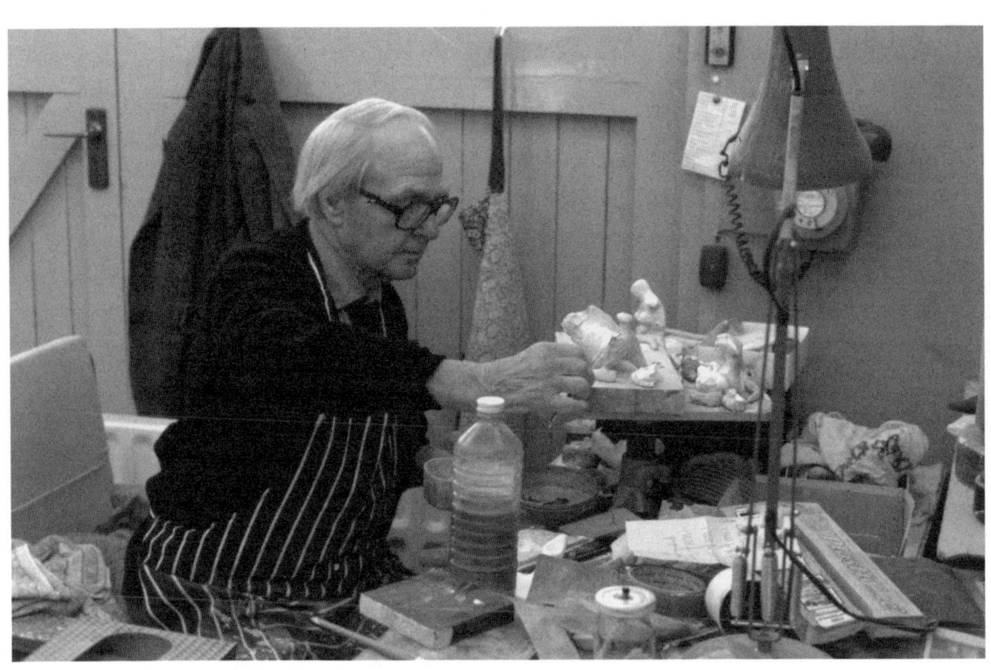

HENRY MOORE

MUCH HADHAM HERTFORDSHIRE 1983

The following preamble below served to introduce this interview with Henry Moore (which begins on page 189) when it was brought out as a small book in French in 2010 by L'Echoppe, a specialist publisher in Paris.

The interview was originally written in English, then translated into French for Connaissance des Arts *magazine. Some thirty years later, search as I might, I could only find the French version, so I have been obliged to translate this back into English, often guessing as to how I might have phrased certain comments thirty years ago.*

By the time I met him in 1983, there was no more established figure in the international art world than Henry Moore. Radically innovative and controversial as he had been in the 1930s (his sculptures provoked such outrage they were vandalized), from mid-century onwards Moore became the accepted and increasingly official face of modernism in England. After the War, retrospectives of his work, organized by the British Council and transported by the RAF, encircled the globe,[1] while his monumental bronzes proliferated to such an extent that no important new building appeared complete without a 'Mother and Child' or 'Lying Figure' set prominently athwart its façade.

Similarly, the man himself became laden with distinctions and honours. Although he wisely turned down a knighthood, Moore accepted (exactly like Lucian Freud) the more prestigious Order of Merit and Companion of Honour. Bolstered by such powerful art world friends as Kenneth Clark and Herbert Read,[2] he officiated as a trustee of both the National Gallery and the Tate (where he proposed – unsuccessfully – that a wing be devoted to his own works). As his fame grew, so did his wealth, much of which he channelled into a Henry

Henry Moore (1898–1986). *Connaissance des Arts*, Paris, September 1983.

Moore Foundation, set up principally to 'advance understanding of his work'.

For me as for many young people of my generation, Henry Moore lay like a monolith, both metaphorically and literally, across the landscape we grew up in. A backlash against such wholesale public recognition was inevitable. In becoming so dominantly Britain's Official Artist, Moore was now bound to stir up controversy of a very different kind. As an art critic who had been exposed to countless works by Moore, I experienced not only a numbed response to roomfuls of unwieldy, gaping organic forms – often patently derivative of Picasso's bone sculpture[3] – but a resentment at the implicit expectation that I would join unthinkingly in the widespread chorus of praise.

In my case, scepticism about Moore had been accentuated by a long, formative friendship with the other heavyweight of British art, Francis Bacon. The two men could hardly have been more different in everything from their art to their lifestyle. Irritated as much by Moore's stolidity as by his success, Bacon rarely missed the opportunity to aim a jibe at the Yorkshire-bred sculptor. Once, when they were both attending a reception, Bacon suggested they join another group of guests. Moore resisted, saying 'I think I'll stay where I am'. 'Where you are is usually where you stay, isn't it, Henry?' Bacon retorted as he strode off. I also remember an interview transcript in which Bacon talked about artists rarely being satisfied with their work, adding waspishly, 'although I believe Henry Moore is' (an aside he withdrew before publication).

So as I wended my way to Much Hadham in Hertfordshire (plane from Paris to London, train to Bishop's Stortford, followed by a hair-raising car ride down narrow, leafy lanes with my mother, who lived nearby, nervously clutching the wheel), I realized that, although I was sceptical about Moore's long-term claim to pre-eminence, my less-than-adulatory attitude towards him and his work would be unlikely to dent the carapace of self-confidence (cast in bronze, surely) that the artist and his cohorts of supporters had constructed around him for over half a century.

When I arrived at Hoglands, the farm he and his wife transformed into a sculpture studio and home after their London house had been hit by shrapnel during the War, I was disarmed by the rustic simplicity of the surroundings: sheep grazing among the sculptures in the fields, the cluttered, workmanlike studios and the Moores' modest living space. Somewhat stooped and fragile, Moore himself also came across as unpretentiously direct, even if he could not quite disguise his impatience at being interviewed for the nth time. Yet although he was then about to turn eighty-five, Moore threw himself into the game with surprising vigour. This flattering interest stemmed partly, I thought at the time, from the fact that the interview was destined for a publication in Paris, where as a young artist Moore had made a vital discovery in the Trocadéro Museum: the plaster cast of a pre-Columbian Chac-Mool figure whose pose, in recline with its head turned towards the viewer, made a lasting impact on his own sculpture. But as we went from studio to studio looking at drawings, clay models, piles of bones, stones and other evocative 'found' forms, Moore soon shifted the interview onto lines that he must have established decades earlier; rather than answer the questions I came up with, he produced pre-prepared statements. Only once, when I referred a little sarcastically to the fact that he had long left the actual production of his sculpture to assistants, did Moore break with his monologue and give a more spontaneous reply. But this, too, proved eventually to be self-serving. By comparing himself indirectly to Michelangelo and to Rodin ('We all know Michelangelo had assistants, we all know Rodin had assistants'), Moore managed to turn an implicit criticism into an accolade. My interview was over. The carapace had indeed not been dented, but for what it was worth neither had my scepticism been in any way diminished.

Since 'An Afternoon with Henry Moore' appeared in *Connaissance des Arts* in 1983, I've rarely thought about him or his work, apart from the odd visit to the Henry Moore Foundation, which also runs a gallery in Leeds (where Moore first attended art school) with an independent exhibitions programme. It is also true to say that, since his death in 1986, Moore's reputation has declined steeply from its erstwhile peak, with his work being regarded as notably less significant and influential in the wake of two new generations of British sculptors (Caro, Chadwick, Paolozzi et al. and Cragg, Woodrow, Kapoor et al.)

having made their mark. And that might have been the end of my limited involvement with Moore but for two roughly simultaneous events: L'Echoppe's decision to republish the interview that follows nearly thirty years later, and a new exhibition at Tate Britain[4] purporting to show the darker, edgier, erotic aspect of Moore that we had either forgotten or completely overlooked.

Mindful that I had agreed to write a preface to introduce this interview for L'Echoppe, I went along to the exhibition and found the most convincing presentation of Moore I had ever seen – although that reaction was clearly induced in part by my not having seen any Moores in a long time (and no doubt by my having to write this preface). The curator had wisely limited the choice of work to Moore's early and middle period, roughly from the early 1920s to the late 1950s, thus avoiding the repetitive nature of the sculptor's late output – those vast outdoor commissions that seem to follow one another over the globe like a line of elephants.

This struck me immediately as a mercy ('Moore is less' as some wag once put it), because in the past the elephantine nature of Moore's big bronzes tended to blot out the often anguished complexity of his earlier work, as well as the finesse of the hand-carved sculpture – the way Moore revealed the underlying nature of the materials he worked with, such as the beautifully grained elmwood he favoured ('truth to materials' was the rallying cry of his early years). The largish pieces that were on show took on an added aggression, even malevolence, in the dramatically lit rooms. Since quite a few small pieces were also included, a sense of scale – vital to any good Moore exhibition – kept the eye and the mind moving.

Most satisfying was the way this focussed and relatively confined selection illustrated Moore's development concisely, from the influences of Eric Gill and Jacob Epstein through Michelangelo and Aztec sculpture to Rodin, Picasso and Dalí. It became clear how receptive Moore had been to a variety of cultures before settling down in later life to a 'signature' style that came to overlay and obliterate all the more complex inventiveness that had come before. In this sense, we have all been victims of Moore's success.

This younger, edgier, unsettled Moore is the Moore I should have liked to interview, rather than the Grand Old Man of Sculpture that I actually had to deal with, dishing out dogma to the presumably converted. But, of course, in that earlier, angrier part of his career, Moore was neither giving nor being asked to give interviews. Rereading it thirty years later, I think the following conversation captures Moore perfectly at the summit of his fame. It was a memorable afternoon, and it has now allowed me quite unexpectedly to discover the inner Moore, the rawer, more tortured and troubling Moore I would otherwise never have known.

*

If there is one place in England where sculpture reigns supreme, it would have to be Henry Moore's farmhouse with its sprawling complex of studios just outside Much Hadham in Hertfordshire. Although only an hour's drive from central London, Moore's demesne is surrounded by lush, unspoilt countryside. A few kilometres before one arrives at 'Hoglands', the road suddenly narrows, the dense, overhead foliage darkens and the last thatched cottage slumbering in gentle sunlight disappears from view. It would be easy to lose one's way amidst so much luxuriant vegetation were it not for the fact that every last farm labourer in the area can indicate the direct route to their local celebrity.

On these winding, leafy roads that have been travelled by so many previous visitors to Moore's studio, one becomes uncomfortably aware of how difficult it will be to obtain new information or even spontaneous remarks from an a sculptor who has given more interviews and been more widely written about than any other in the world. Once the bucolic 'Hoglands' heaves into view, that very fact seems as good an opening gambit as any.

'Quite possibly,' Moore replies a little testily, 'but it's less than a tenth of what has been written about Picasso!'

After this brief exchange in Moore's simply furnished sitting-room, we move to the 'drawing studio', a small building set in the middle of the expansive, park-like gardens behind the family house. Several other studios are dotted around the property. In one of them Moore makes the models which are then taken to another to be enlarged, while a third, larger studio houses monumental sculptures which are eventually manoeuvred into a fourth studio to be polished and photographed.

Given Moore's prodigious output, the studios look almost deliberately modest: rather cramped, workman-like spaces without the slightest hint of comfort or indeed of the worldwide fame and fortune the sculptor has enjoyed for several decades. It seems barely credible that this little cluster of makeshift buildings, run by an elderly sculptor and his two assistants, has sufficed for the creation of the large numbers of Moores that now adorn so many landscapes, city centres and international organizations across the world.

An immediate key to this extraordinary activity lies in Moore's own undiminished energy and sense of purpose. At eighty-five, he continues to put in nine hours of work every day. Whenever the wide range of visitors or the manifold administrative problems connected with his work so overwhelm him that there is no time left to model or to draw, he admits that he is 'really upset at the end of the day'. Moore rapidly settles down to be interviewed in the drawing studio, but as he talks his fingers pluck at the armrests of his battered old chair with barely contained impatience, or fiddle restlessly with the bones and stones and little plaster models scattered all over the work-table in front of him. Very clearly, the interview will be brief, and the questions will have to get right to the point. Of all the usual ways to get the ball rolling, the innocuous one of 'influences' comes most readily to mind.

'Everything I've ever liked has influenced me,' Moore replies, immediately hitting his stride. 'But if I had to make a list I'd have to include all the great Italians from Giotto to Titian – by way of Michelangelo and without forgetting Bernini. Then Rembrandt and Velázquez. I'd have to include whole periods like Romanesque and Gothic architecture as well. And after that classical and primitive art, since both of them have influenced me enormously. Literature would have to have a big place as well. Writers like Tolstoy, Hardy and D. H. Lawrence have had a huge impact on me. Their novels have deeply affected my life – my life rather than my work, perhaps. Then of course there are all the modern artists from Ingres to Picasso that have been important to me.'

The reply comes unhesitatingly, almost mechanically – not surprisingly perhaps from a man who has been questioned regularly about his work for well over half a century. Looking round the drawing studio more closely, one is struck by how small Moore's models are, especially when compared to the monumental sculptures most of them are destined to become. Once the sculptor is satisfied with one of the small models, he entrusts it to one of his assistants, who then enlarges it to the required scale. Thus most of the towering works by Moore that one knows either from museums or public places have been made – in the purely material sense – by assistants and anonymous workmen. The fact that Moore's direct participation in a work is limited to the original model has provoked a certain amount of criticism. Is the sculptor not the person who actually executes the sculpture? This notion clearly touches Moore to the quick, and he begins to talk in a somewhat piqued, less rehearsed fashion:

'Listen, you don't expect an architect to mix his own mortar and lay his own bricks, do you? Of course I've got assistants to do the enlargement. All artists have had assistants, right through history. Everybody knows that. Michelangelo had assistants, that's quite obvious. If he hadn't had any while he was painting the ceiling of the Sistine Chapel, he'd have to have wasted half an hour going down the scaffolding every time he dropped a brush! Rodin had lots of assistants as well, including some very gifted sculptors like Maillol and Bourdelle.

'Everything I've ever done has been done with a large scale in mind. Even when I'm working on the models, I see them on a large scale. If you can't automatically picture things on another scale, you're not a sculptor. Scale is everything in sculpture. What would the pyramids or the Sphinx mean if they were tiny?

'The very small models I've got here are nothing more than the idea. What I really like about them is that you can hold them in the palm of your hand and turn them round and see them from every angle. I put them to one side for a time, then I come back to see what I really think of them. I sometimes get them made on an intermediate scale and have them cast in bronze. After that I like to live with the result for a while before deciding whether or not I want to make them bigger still. Sometimes, when I'm looking for a particular project – a sculpture someone has commissioned, for instance – I take a model I made a good while ago. And it's only then that I decide on its scale. That's the most important thing. Not the enlargement process itself, which is merely a technical problem. I'm sure you remember the story about the assistant who pretended that he was the real creator of a work that he had produced for Michelangelo? Well, Michelangelo got rid of him.

'Personally I adore carving, and that's why I preferred stone and wood to bronze when I was a young man. But carving takes up a huge amount of time. I've had assistants myself since the end of the 1930s. You have to, you know. You have to have help, even if it's only to get a sculpture moved from place to place. At one point I had five assistants. I've only got two now. They are excellent, but there are certain nuances in the models that they might not pick up on. I oversee the enlargement of my models every day. Sometimes, for instance, I have to show my assistants exactly how the various angles relate on a piece. I can spot problems like that right away, because I haven't been working on that particular piece like them all day and I bring a fresh eye to it. And of course since I actually make the model I know all its finer points. That's obvious.'

Moore becomes visibly more relaxed as he develops this theme. Yet his hands are constantly in motion, rolling the smooth pebbles on his table, picking up various models and weighing them in his palm, or sketching the outline of this or that sculpture rapidly in the air. And one feels that, for all his well-practised ease in talking about his work, he would be happier drawing rather than searching for the right word to explain what comes to him instinctively.

Because of a recent injury to his back, drawing is in fact the only work Moore is currently able to do. But this does not dismay him too much since he finds drawing a fully satisfying activity in itself. And he talks about drawing with an Ingres-like enthusiasm.

'I draw for the pleasure of drawing rather than with a view to producing new sculptures', he says, lining up several very recent sketches on his table. 'I love drawing. It's the basis of all art. Drawing should be obligatory all the way through art school, in my view, because it's by drawing that you learn to see. People think they know what a tree is, for instance, but once you ask them to draw it they realise they have never really looked at it – never seen it – before.'

Yorkshire people (Moore was born in Castleford in 1898) are well known for their plain speaking, and everything Moore says is delivered in a tone of no-frills, no-nonsense common-sense. This notion is clearly dear to him, and as he expounds on various aspects of his work he regularly uses such phrases as 'nine-tenths of art is simply a question of common-sense' or 'Michelangelo was above all practical. Artists are not dreamers. They are the most practical people on this planet.' Being eminently practical himself, Henry Moore glances significantly at the large alarm-clock that has been loudly ticking off the minutes of our brief interview. The telephone rings and his secretary reminds him that a shipping firm is awaiting his last-minute instructions, that a group of architects have assembled for a studio visit and that a collector has arrived to take a look at the new work. With courteous firmness Mr Moore takes his leave, manoeuvres himself with some difficulty into his bright yellow Rover, then shoots back up the garden path to his house.

The most famous, and clearly the busiest, sculptor in the world has gone. But he has allowed you to linger on in his world and explore the rest of his professional universe. Not far from the main house and immediately apparent is the Henry Moore Foundation, a clean-cut, modern building with a library dedicated mainly to books about the sculptor, as well as photographic archives in box-files with titles such as 'HM with Visitors', 'HM in Studio' and 'HM with VIPs'. Here and in the adjoining secretarial offices the considerable administrative business of being Henry Moore is carried out. It is here, for example, that each huge new retrospective of Moore's work – he has already had over one hundred of them at all points of the globe – is organized with the attention to detail of a military campaign. Here, too, that each new doctorate, national award or foreign distinction is filed away and each new commission carefully vetted and recorded. But the real work of actually producing this eminently exportable British product is restricted to the far more modest buildings further down the garden.

In one of the enlargement studios, Michel Müller, Moore's French-born assistant, is at work transforming a little model into a large version in polystyrene – a material that is both lighter and easier to work than plaster. Once an enlargement has been made and received Moore's approval, it is sent to the foundry to be cast in bronze. A complete tour of Moore's studios allows one to follow the whole evolution of a work, from its genesis among the shells, stones and bones that the artist has collected throughout his career to the ultima mano, when the final patina is applied and the sculpture is ready to leave for the outside world.

Moore much prefers his sculpture to be seen against a natural rather than an urban background, and the property's extensive, well-maintained gardens display an excellent selection of his monumental pieces. The serenity of the setting would seem to offer an ideal opportunity for re-evaluating Moore's work. Yet the sculptures appear so familiar that they have become quite literally part of the landscape, and it is almost impossible to look at them afresh. No doubt because of this over-familiarity, the admiration one has for the powerfully straightforward humanism radiating from these massive forms is tempered by the feeling that Moore's work has been both overproduced and conceived on too monotonously monumental a scale.

Indeed many of Moore's later works are striking if not solely, then essentially, because of their imposing scale. That may be considered as already an achievement given that most contemporary sculpture leaves the viewer indifferent, however large or small it is (César's much-vaunted *Thumb* comes immediately to mind). But however significant Moore's contribution to this century's sculpture has been, it is surely time to dismiss the chorus of unquestioning praise his work now automatically elicits and attempt to place it in a durable historical perspective. This more critical approach might lead to the view that Moore has become the victim of his own success and that, in creating too many sculptures for too many sites, he has progressively dulled the intensity and vigour of his original vision. In the not too distant future we shall be able to distinguish quite clearly between the imposing but ultimately hollow works engendered by overproduction and those – made mainly during Moore's early career – which this master of instinctive synthesis created with the freshness of his convictions and talent intact.

1 I remember being struck at the time that the RAF had been called in as official carriers for this valuable cargo, but I must add that I have not been able to corroborate the fact since.

2 Respectively the Director of the National Gallery in London and the most influential English art critic of the day.

3 John Richardson dubbed Moore the 'petit maître of Picasso's bone-surreal'.

4 The exhibition, which ran from February to August 2010 at Tate Modern, traveled to the Art Gallery of Ontario, Toronto, then returned to the UK for its final venue at Leeds Art Gallery.

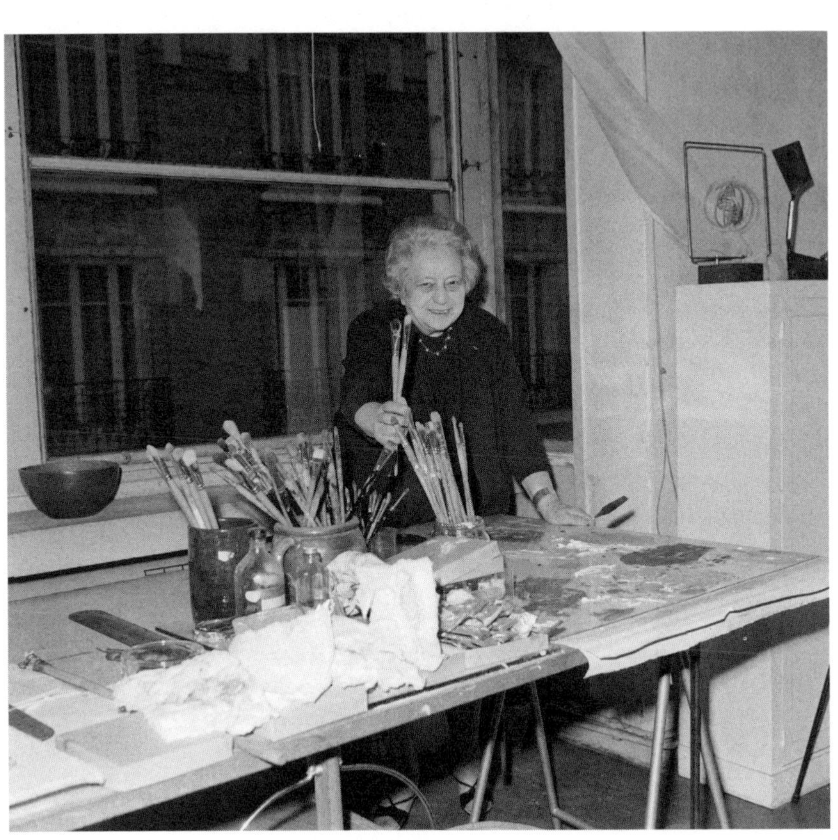

SONIA DELAUNAY

RUE SAINT-DOMINIQUE PARIS 1975

Sonia Delaunay seemed very old and very grand. She was nearly ninety by the time of this interview and, although she had lived a very turbulent life in several countries and through two world wars, she looked as if she were about to attend a duchesses' tea party or a défilé at one of the top couture houses. Despite her elaborate dress and jewellery, Madame Delaunay did not beat about the bush. She had not only been at the centre of much that was new and revolutionary in the century, she had also held her own amongst many of the men who had shaped the course of events. She was formidable and, I remember, rather cruel towards her studio assistant. But her wealth of experience and her very tangible instinct for survival immediately commanded respect. When she talked you listened.

At 89, Sonia Delaunay retains her passion for painting. 'I want to get back to painting *large* pictures,' she said recently in the high-ceilinged apartment that adjoins her studio, just off the elegant rue Saint-Dominique on the Left Bank. Her conversation ranges from her late nineteenth-century childhood in St Petersburg to the gouache she has been working on that morning. The only constant factor in that long, troubled, intensely vital span of time seems to have been her devotion to painting. Now, as always, the best part of every day is given over to new work.

Sonia Delaunay was born in 1885 and spent most of her childhood in the house of her uncle, a prosperous lawyer in St Petersburg. The family spent several months of each year abroad, and when Sonia was fourteen and on a visit to Berlin, a painter friend of her uncle gave her her first paintbox. The gift was to have a determining effect on her life; in 1903 she was back in Germany studying contemporary painting and taking drawing lessons. Two years later, she arrived in Paris, when the Salon d'Automne was holding the first Fauve exhibition.

Sonia Delaunay (1885–1979). *Art News*, New York, March 1975.

Sonia's earliest paintings were influenced by Van Gogh and Gauguin. During a short-lived marriage to the dealer Wilhelm Uhde, she met Picasso, Braque, Derain, Vlaminck and, of course, Robert Delaunay, whom she married in 1910.

Sonia's first abstract work, a patchwork quilt, coincided with the birth of her son, Charles, for whom it had been made. In the years before the First World War, she illustrated a long poem by Blaise Cendrars and created clothes that were regarded as wildly daring by those Parisians who, like the Delaunays, went to dance the tango at the fashionable Bal Bullier in Montparnasse. Apollinaire, a close friend of the Delaunays (who cared for him during the difficult period after he was publicly accused of stealing the Mona Lisa), describes Robert as appearing there in a 'red cloak with a blue collar, red socks, black and yellow shoes, black trousers, a green jacket, sky-blue waistcoat and a tiny red tie.'

Colour and painting were the Delaunays' entire life ('They wake up talking about painting,' said Apollinaire). Robert referred to Sonia's sense of colour as 'couleur slave,' of the kind shared by Kandinsky, Jawlensky, Malevich and Chagall; and Sonia herself has a vivid childhood memory of staying in the country at a friend's house where 'all the colours seemed so unusually bright'.

By force of circumstance, their sense of colour was about to be even further intensified. War broke out while the Delaunays were taking a holiday in Spain, and they stayed for a while in Madrid, then settled in Portugal. The luminous quality of the southern light helped them to develop their theories about chromatic contrasts and, in Sonia's case, inspired a magnificent series of paintings based on Portuguese market scenes. While they were there, another upheaval transformed their existence: the Russian Revolution meant that Sonia, formerly well provided for, was abruptly made penniless. 'It was a good thing,' she says now. 'Before, we lived like children. We were just playing at being alive. After the Revolution, we were forced to make our own way.'

After their return to Paris in 1920, the Delaunays got to know the members of the new Surrealist group and slowly began to see their own reputation as innovators confirmed. For most of the following decade, Sonia devoted herself principally to designing decors, costumes, fabrics and clothes; it was during this period that such arbiters of fashion as Gloria Swanson and Nancy Cunard wore clothes that Sonia had created for them. Her joy and skill in colour had gained wide admiration; her designs were seen on film, exhibited at the Grand Palais and discussed in a lecture at the Sorbonne.

During the 1930s, Sonia devoted herself once more almost exclusively to painting. The major elements of her style had become fully apparent, and now – as ever since – it was a question of expanding and refining the vast lyrical possibilities of contrasted warm and cold colours. Much of her time was spent on an enormous joint project with Robert: the execution of huge mural paintings for the Paris Exposition Internationale of 1937.

After Robert's death in 1941, Jean Arp invited Sonia to live with him and Sophie Taeuber in Grasse, in the South of France, and it was there that she spent the remaining War years.

From her return to Paris until the present day, Sonia Delaunay's considerable energy has been directed towards developing various aspects of her work and obtaining full recognition for the work of her husband, whose approach to art she long ago made to a large extent her own. Thus, as well as painting and designing new works (including tapestries), she has been occupied in helping to put on shows of her husband's influential artistic legacy. Nowadays, the organizational work that such exhibitions involve is taken care of by her Paris dealer, Jacques Damase. One of her major preoccupations is a foundation devoted to the work of both Delaunays. She hopes for a site on the Left Bank overlooking the Seine; but the project is still under discussion with the Ministry for Cultural Affairs.

Once she has talked about the future – which includes a travelling retrospective of her works in the United States this year – she is quite happy to plunge back again into her long, eventful past. She knew virtually all the important painters who lived in France during the first half of the twentieth century. But her views about them tend to be highly exclusive, and many heads roll on the way. Matisse is the only artist (apart, naturally, from Delaunay himself) to be accorded full honours. He remains, she says, a 'great man', whereas Mondrian, whose work she finds 'quite interesting', is summed up as 'a bit limited', and Picasso is dismissed as 'above all, a bluffer'.

Among younger, living artists, she finds no one in particular to single out for praise, although she does concede that 'a few of them have begun to understand the importance of colour'.

'Mine is an optimistic painting,' she says. 'Oh yes, I carry all those colours around inside me, and each of them has its own life.'

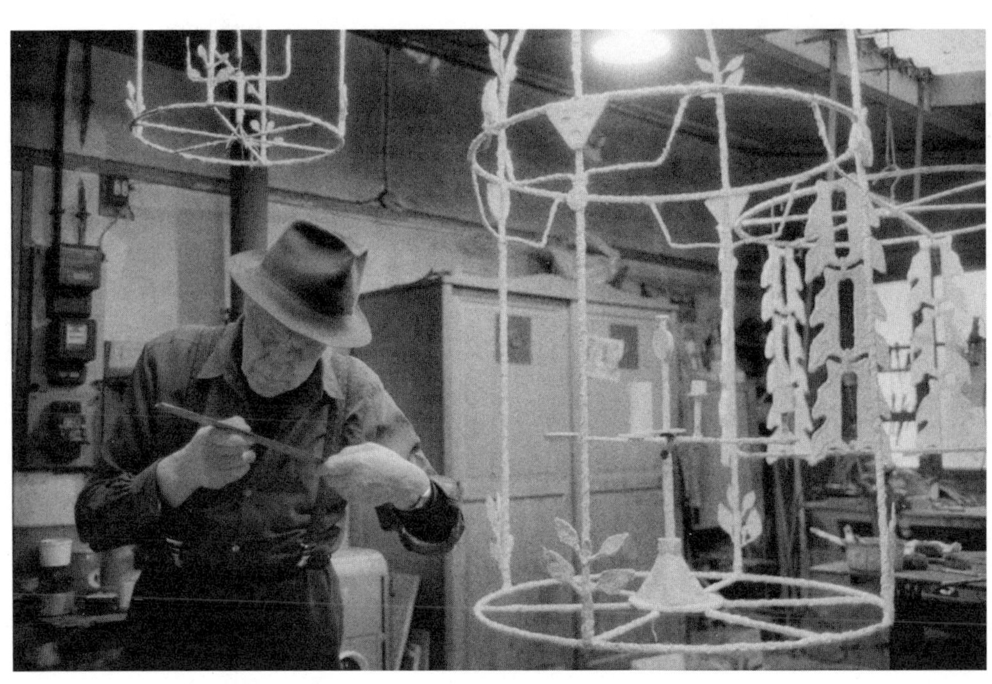

DIEGO GIACOMETTI

ALESIA PARIS 1985

Having narrowly missed meeting Alberto Giacometti in his sculpture-crammed studio when I arrived in Paris in 1966, I was all the more pleased to get to know his brother and right-hand man, Diego. Very different in some ways, the two men were very similar in others. Where Alberto talked endlessly, loving nothing more than to begin an intense discussion on any subject, Diego was notably taciturn; indeed if Alberto had been an ideal interviewee (as existing interviews with him appear to attest), then Diego was the interviewer's nightmare, rarely venturing an opinion and mostly shrugging his shoulders when pressed to reply to a question. On the other hand, the two had the tough individuality of men bred in a harsh mountain climate, and both shared a simple nobility of outlook and a natural courtesy that even a lifetime rubbing shouders with the international art world had not erased.

In the course of this interview I saw Diego several times and felt I had got to know him reasonably well. If he had not died shortly afterwards, I think I might have been able simply to drop by his studio unannounced from time to time, in the way visitors did when he and Alberto shared premises just nearby. That is what I should have done, and I regret it now. Little by little, particularly if we had shared a few drinks, Diego would have opened up and talked more freely, and no one could have described as accurately and poignantly the fast-disappearing world that he and Alberto had shared.

'What's that?' Diego demands, dredging something formless from the sauce on his plate. His craggily noble face has grown stern. 'I think it's veal,' I say.

'Veal!' Diego snorts. 'Veal is *blanquette de veau*. That's a real dish. Not this nouvelle cuisine nonsense. What have you got?' I peer into my

Diego Giacometti (1902–1985). *Connoisseur*, New York, March 1987.

plate. 'I think it's beef,' I say. 'Beef!' Diego snorts. 'You want a *boeuf bourguignon*. That's real food. All you get nowadays is decoration.'

Only the claret seems to find favour. Another bottle is brought. 'This used to be a good restaurant before it got so fancy,' Diego continues, on a note of gruff triumph, carefully sweeping breadcrumbs onto the floor. 'Alberto and I used to come here often. You could get *boeuf bourguignon* then, you know,' he says, glancing at me suddenly with amusement.

All the talk so far has centred on food and drink.

'Diego,' I venture, 'I like real food, too. But what I really want to talk to you about is your furniture – your sculpture.'

'But there's nothing to say about it,' Diego says, for the third time this evening. His hands rise in a gesture of helplessness.

'But Diego,' I insist, 'I can't just tell the readers we both like *boeuf bourguignon* and leave it at that. No one will ever ask me to write an article again.'

He smiles at this. At eighty-two he still has an expression of child-like candour. And now, quite visibly, the game is called cat and mouse.

'Oh, you'll manage, you'll think of something,' he says easily. 'It must be marvellous to write, to have words just coming to you like that.'

A hundred yards down the street in this agreeably crumbling, village-like *quartier* behind Montparnasse, Diego's little shed of a workshop lies locked up for the night. Early tomorrow morning he'll be there, in workman's clothes and a battered felt hat, pottering around, drawing a little, modelling a little – doing all the things he thinks it unimportant to talk about. It's clear he takes the fame that has come to him so late in life with a big pinch of salt. When I arrived in his modest living quarters, just behind the workshop, he was thumbing, not for the first time, through a glossy magazine full of glamorous colour photos of his cramped, dusty living room. 'That's meant to be this place,' he said, jabbing a calloused finger at the brightly lit, wide-angle shots, then laughing in disbelieving glee.

Why, indeed, should he take seriously the fuss now being made of him? For sixty years of his long life, Diego was simply the 'other' Giacometti, the one in the background, who helped his famous brother with the more manual tasks – building armatures for the sculpture, preparing the moulds for casting, then applying the various coats of patina until the bronze took on the right finish. He became almost literally a second pair of hands for Alberto, with whom he worked, day after day, for forty years. The rapport between the two brothers was so strong that they rarely needed to communicate by words. Nothing testifies better to their deeply instinctive understanding than Alberto's busts and portraits of Diego. Alberto began making them, under the watchful eye of their artist father, when they were boys together in the Swiss village of Stampa, and continued from his arrival in Paris in1922 until he died in 1966.

It has been said that Diego's own creativity could not develop while his brother was alive. Alberto's obsessive vision and relentless drive certainly dominated the relationship; and only a man of Diego's unusual unassertiveness could have borne so secondary a role for so long. Nevertheless Diego had, as he says with characteristic diffidence, 'always thought of making objects'. And from 1950 onwards, whenever the growing volume of work for his brother permitted, he designed a great variety of furniture, from tables and chairs to lamps and chandeliers, from staircases to door handles, usually made to order for well-known interior decorators, art collectors or museum-like institutions, such as the Fondation Maeght in the South of France. After Alberto's death, Diego found himself not only with time on his hands but also at liberty to indulge his own sculptural fantasy – which the presence of a forceful, famous brother had inhibited. While he continued to incorporate the sparse tautness of his brother's vision, the furniture took on new accents of pure playfulness that were Diego's alone.

Though this master craftsman has lived at the hub of Europe's intellectual and artistic life for sixty years, his imagination remains rooted in the mountain-encircled valley in Switzerland where he grew up. Surrealism and existentialism, the conversation of Sartre and Picasso, seem nothing to him compared to a youth spent wandering the rugged countryside and getting to know the ways of animals – of watching the dogs and horses, the owls, frogs and foxes that now move freely among the knotty branches of his furniture. They people Diego's mind and spring up so naturally in his sculpture because, a lifetime later, it is still with animals that he feels most at ease. 'I used to keep a fox in the studio,' he says shyly, as if revealing an intimate secret. 'It was an extraordinary animal, always playing, particularly at being dead. I used to come in, and the fox would be lying inert on the studio floor. I'd pick it up and it would pretend to be dead, with its head falling to one side and its tongue hanging out. So I'd put it back on the floor and turn around and pretend to start working. Then suddenly the fox would leap onto my back. I'd liked having it around, even though it smelled very bad. But one day it wandered off, I don't know where. Where would a fox go in Paris?'

Two cats – one of whom has the run of his living quarters, the other, of the studio – now keep Diego company; and among his happiest inventions is a birdbath held by a Jeeves-like feline in sleek bronze. A shy and extremely modest man, Diego seems at his happiest in this whimsical menagerie, producing an ostrich whose basket-like back serves to hold its own egg, or a tiny filigree stag so realistic it seems to be sniffing the air – as well as any number of wise owls, squat toads and solid mice. A more public project of special note has been the commission to design furniture for the new Musée Picasso, in its splendid, seventeenth-century Paris mansion. One of the roles of Diego's tables, chairs and chandeliers is to serve as a stylistic hyphen between the classical grandeur of the town house and the audacious modernism of the Picassos it contains.

Diego was an inspired choice for the Musée Picasso, since his furniture derives from ancient sources, notably Etruscan and Egyptian, while seeming wholly contemporary. Such well-known pieces as the bronze table with a cat's head at each corner, for instance, immediately recall the deities of Egypt (a country that Diego visited during his footloose youth); yet the table looks at home in the most starkly modern interior. Other examples, whether chairs or lamps, have an archaic simplicity of form that puts them outside time and place; it is interesting to see how well they accord not only with modern but with every kind of 'primitive' art. Their ability to blend with different periods and cultures stems from the most finely gauged proportions, from a universal sense of harmony.

This remarkable combination of grace and craftsmanship has brought Diego an international reputation and far more demands for his furniture than he can hope to satisfy. While he concentrated on completing the work for the Musée Picasso, the waiting list of those who dream of having their environment enhanced by one of his delicate consoles or sculptural chairs grew ever longer. True to his calling, the master craftsman is concerned above all that each piece to leave the studio corresponds to his exacting criteria of workmanship; whenever pressures to produce become too great, he growls about not wanting to be turned into a 'factory'. Rather than court fame and wealth, Diego has turned his back on them. With characteristic modesty (and a hint of weariness), Diego says he can see no point in publications and shows, but he has lived to see a curator at the Musée des Arts Décoratifs begin to organize an exhibition celebrating the unsuspected range of Diego's achievement – the event duly documented with a splendid book about the artist.

Although a degree of affluence has come to Diego willy-nilly in recent years, he maintains the Spartan style in which he and his brother always lived. Proverbially tough (his cure for a toothache a few years ago was to extract the tooth with studio pliers), this mountain-bred man spurns most domestic niceties beyond a good bottle and the pleasure of getting into dandy clothes after a day's work. While Diego's daily routine has altered little, the area he has lived in for half a century has changed beyond recognition. Not only can one not find the *boeuf bourguignon* of yore but, more sacrilegious, the cafés that were the brothers' daily haunts have become banks; high-rise buildings have started to tower over the once eminently human maze of little back streets. Diego appears to be the one feature of the quartier not to have changed.

He puts his elegant felt hat on at a rakish angle, and slowly we move out of the restaurant, into the familiar street. 'This used to be a paradise, you know,' he says, stopping to let a car go past. 'It was full of gardens when Alberto and I arrived. There were goats. You could even get local goat cheese. Imagine that! And the place was full of craftsmen. You could get anything you liked, any tool you needed, made for you right away. Imagine, for sculptors – a real paradise! But, of course,' he adds, looking almost embarrassed, 'all that was so long ago.'

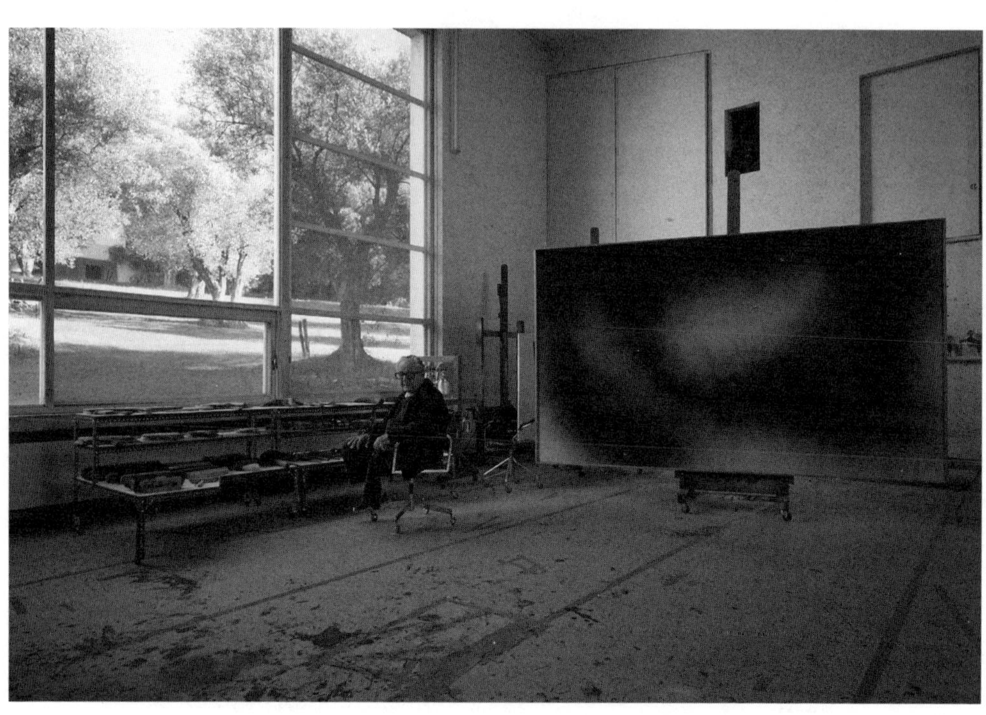

HANS HARTUNG

ANTIBES 1986

Although he was confined to a wheelchair (having lost a leg fighting against the Nazis), Hans Hartung had lost none of his boisterousness when I went to visit him just outside Antibes in 1986. We hit it off immediately because he seemed so delighted to have a new young companion for the day with whom he could share stories, jokes and several bottles of red wine. We visited his beautiful Bauhausian house, looked at pictures and had lunch. Hartung's enthusiasm was so extreme it bordered on the excessive. At one point he delivered such a powerful slap on my back (with an arm grown unusually strong from manoeuvring a wheelchair) that I almost fell headlong. I was caught completely off-guard and would no doubt have got angry had I not been immediately disarmed by Hartung's triumphant explanation: 'I like you so much I wanted to hit you!' From then on, our conversation became literally no holds barred. I think back on this interview, in one of the most idyllic settings imaginable, as one of the most liberating and enjoyable I have ever done.

'Whenever lightning was about to strike,' Hans Hartung says, 'my grandmother used to shoo me into a dark corridor until it was over. I grew as frightened of lightning as she was, especially as I'd never seen it. Then one afternoon – I must have been six years old – I forced myself to go out and confront it. I was terrified, but I had pencil and paper with me and I knew that if I could draw the streaks of lightning before the thunder broke, I'd be safe. So I covered page after page with lightning flashes, and instead of being afraid I felt tremendous exaltation.'

What was true for the boy of six in Leipzig before the First World War still holds good for the eighty-two-year old artist in his retreat at Antibes in the South of France. Hans Hartung has lived much of his

Hans Hartung (1904–1989). *Architectural Digest*, Los Angeles, October 1986.

life on the edge of catastrophe, and if he has kept the thunder at bay it is by his unshakable belief in the transforming power of art. His mature paintings have continued in the vein of his lightning sketches to capture the beauty and often terrifying mystery of the universe. In the limitless scale created by his pictures, the sudden ripple of wind on water is as impressive and enigmatic as a distant explosion of stars, since the questioning involved is equally profound.

'Whatever I've done, I've always done with absolute conviction,' Hartung says. His bespectacled, professorial air belies a sense of humour so lively as to be impish. 'When I was an adolescent, I had a religious crisis and was convinced that I had been chosen to spread the word of Christ. So I came down one morning and said to my poor father, "I must leave you now. I have decided to become a missionary". My father had the clever idea of putting a book on astronomy by my bedside that evening. I got so engrossed in it that I built my own telescope and spent hours studying the night sky – and soon forgot my religious calling.'

As an artist, however, his course has been unwavering. Not only did he draw incessantly – 'I always sat behind the boy with the largest back in the class,' he recalls, 'so I could doodle all day' – but his fascination from the very beginning was with abstract forms. 'I used to play endlessly with blots of ink and find all sorts of things in them. Of course our art teacher couldn't stand them, and even my school friends used to say, 'Oh, any baby can do that'. I couldn't stop experimenting with them, but I also began to doubt whether they had any real value. Then I saw that extraordinary Rembrandt – his *Family Group* – in Braunschweig, and I was so moved I literally almost fainted. I'd noticed that the folds of the clothing were made up of completely abstract shapes. From that moment I knew I was a painter.'

For many years thereafter Hartung was to experience all the solitude and hardships that an artist breaking new ground is traditionally believed to undergo. In Paris he countered lack of money and loneliness by copying at the Louvre and visiting the galleries. Increasingly, reduced funds drove him from France to the then rarely visited Spanish island of Minorca. With Anna-Eva Bergman, the Norwegian painter whom he had just wed, Hartung set up house alongside the Minorcan fishermen and devoted himself to painting. The idyll was short-lived, for as the Second World War loomed nearer, foreign residents became suspect. 'The local authorities began to think we were spies and that our paintings were in fact diagrams of the island,' Hartung says. 'They were also convinced we had connected our cellar to the sea so as to harbour German submarines.'

Far from aiding his fellow Germans, Hartung had such strong anti-Nazi convictions that he fought against them. He joined the French Foreign Legion and survived most of the War without serious accident. Then, in 1944, while attempting to rescue a comrade who lay wounded behind enemy lines, he was shot in the leg. The injury worsened as a result of insufficient medical care, and eventually grew so bad that the leg had to be amputated.

Largely ignored before the War, abstract artists increasingly occupied centre stage in Paris in the 1950s. Hartung began to exhibit and to build a reputation. Once his role as a forerunner was recognized, prosperity and fame followed. Having long been attracted to the South of France, he decided to build a house there in which he could work undisturbed. As his basic plan, he took the simple white cube of the Minorcan fisherman's house where he had been so happy before, then multiplied it around a swimming pool set in an olive grove outside the ancient Mediterranean city of Antibes.

Hartung's insistence on perfection in every detail has produced a house in which maximum simplicity coincides with maximum comfort and the elegance that comes from being in complete harmony with the landscape. There is little furniture in the big, silent rooms and no paintings on the walls. 'I don't need paintings,' the artist says. 'If I want to look at something, I look out of the window at the trees. Do you know something that made me feel very proud? When the architect Marcel Breuer came to visit us, he said to me, "I envy you, Hartung. You have exactly the house I myself would like to live in".'

To live, but above all to work, was the artist's reason for choosing seclusion. In the vast studios, a semi-industrial quantity of brushes and paints stands neatly aligned, in constant invitation to the painter to produce. The latest works have the freshness of a new departure: the joy of suggesting order within chaotic explosions of colour. After a long, often harsh life, Hans Hartung still has the eye of a child – the child who looked out at the storm-crossed world in fear and exaltation.

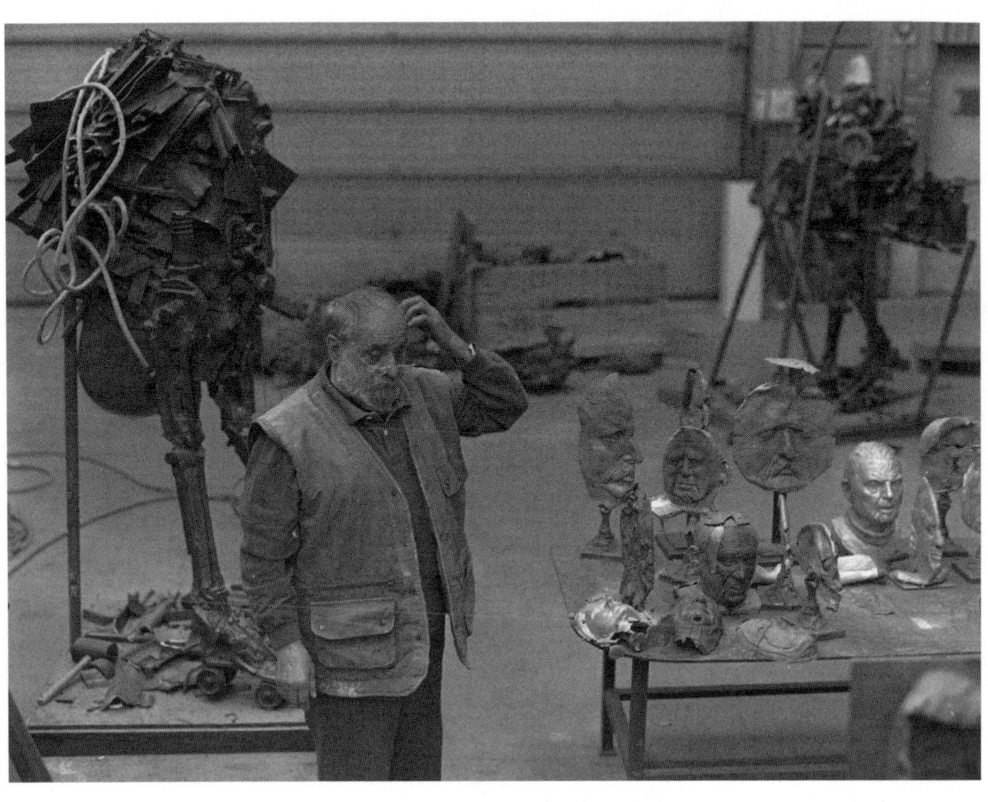

CÉSAR

MONTPARNASSE PARIS / SAINT-PAUL-DE-VENCE 1988

César was an elusive character. By the time we did this interview, he had become a media personality quite as well known for his quick-witted buffoonery as for his sculpture. In the end, the former came to overshadow the very real inventiveness of the latter. As well as the visual shock of the first 'compressions' César made of cars, I remember how mesmerized I was when I visited an exhibition of his 'Heads', all of them recognizable portraits made of freshy baked bread. Once you got to know him a little, César's clowning diminished, gradually revealing a shy, vulnerable, anxious person who was convinced that his success both as an artist and a performer might vanish overnight. Although he was constantly agitated, he was amusing company, although I never became at all close to him as I did to quite a few of the people I interviewed. Something of this inability to get beneath César's skin, as it were, comes through in the following short studio visit.

'If I had to live my life over again,' says César, France's best-known sculptor, 'the only thing I'd really want to change is my height.' But even if the diminutive artist had been taller, he could hardly have radiated more energy or appetite for experience. The artist's studio behind Montparnasse in Paris and his home in the South of France both mirror this unbounded curiosity for the outside world, as well as the skittish sense of humour that characterizes so much of César's sculpture.

In the large, sky-lit working space in Paris, Houdon's anatomical study of a flayed man dominates an amiable chaos of welding tools, finished works, dolls, toy cars, skeletons and such arresting oddities as a crate filled with eye-glasses. 'I never throw anything away,' the sculptor admits, needlessly enough, as he picks his way through the

César (1921–1998). *Architectural Digest*, Los Angeles, February 1989.

studio's intriguing jumble. His collages of watch-straps and Métro tickets attest to the fact that there is plenty of method to his mania, and that even the most disinherited seeming objects have a potential future life as works of art.

The room's workaday atmosphere is regularly interrupted by telephone calls inviting César, one of the most sought-after personalities in the Parisian art world, to various events and celebrations. 'I love being surrounded by people,' he says, as his assistant notes down another engagement, 'but I also need time to be completely cut off from the world.

'Obviously, that's something you can't do in Paris. The only place for me to get away is the South of France, where I was born. I've always gone back and kept up with old friends. Picasso used to say, every time I saw him at Mougins, 'What's the matter with you? Why don't you get yourself a house down here?' So in the end – it must be twenty years ago now – I came across a place near Saint-Paul-de-Vence that was more of an outbuilding than a house. But I liked it and I love the area, since it's far enough back from the coast not to be completely overrun with tourists. Yet there are plenty of interesting people from all over the world living nearby or passing through. And for the following couple of years, I threw myself into making it my kind of place.'

Set in a large, rambling garden of pines, olive trees and wildflowers, César's house now fully bears his mark. Most of the furniture and decorative elements came from flea markets and demolition sites, but they have been chosen with such uncanny flair that the result is both picturesque and stylish. 'I got the marble floor for the terrace from a casino they were pulling down in Nice,' he says. 'I liked the idea of putting something that had been inside there outside my house. I was born in a poor family, you know, so I didn't know what 'good' furniture was. Now I can appreciate a fine Louis XV commode, but I can't say I'd want to live with one. I prefer the kind of stray objects you pick up in the most unlikely places.

'I combed the entire area for things. Some of the tables and chairs were thrown out of an old café at a Nice railway station. I rummaged around local junk stores for days at a time – until I'd not only furnished the house but filled a couple of barns. It was like an illness – I couldn't stop picking things up and carting them back. But that's quietened down a bit now, I'm glad to say.'

Although the artist's hand is plainly apparent in such details as the seashells that encrust the living-room beams, there are no signs of sculptural works in progress. 'Everything I need to work is at hand,' César admits. 'I've got those barns filled with things that are crying out to be turned into sculpture. But I've decided that the house has to remain a place to rest in and see friends. I like to do the kinds of things you can't do properly in Paris. I cook when I get down here, because you have all that marvellous produce and it reminds me of the food my mother used to make – simple food, cooked with olive oil and herbs. I like to improvise in cooking as in everything else, but basically I make the dishes she did. There's nothing better than sharing the food you liked as a child with old friends.'

Meanwhile, as in Paris, the telephone rings constantly. Directions must be given to complete the *Monument to Gustave Eiffel*, a vast structure made up of scrap metal from the Eiffel Tower that greets visitors to the Cartier Foundation just outside Paris. A huge new cast of César's famous *Thumb* sculpture has to be prepared for shipping. A Scandinavian museum director is interested in a retrospective, while a French government official discreetly negotiates a state acquisition. The artist handles each call with good-humoured verve, but he is clearly eager to get back to his herb-scented terrace, where a group of local friends is waiting for him to finish an anecdote and start lunch.

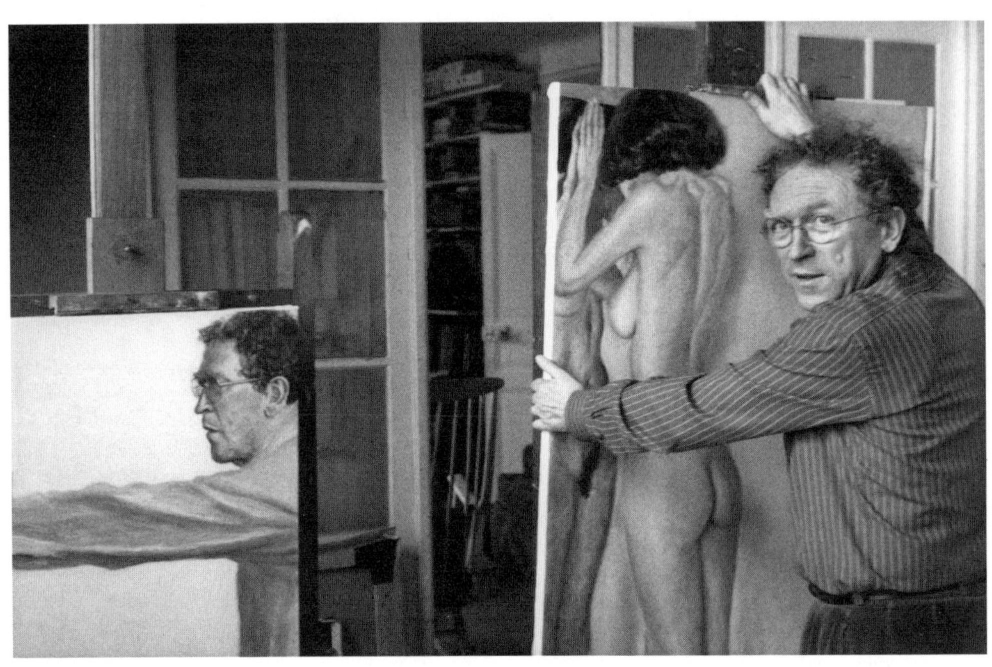

AVIGDOR ARIKHA

MONTPARNASSE PARIS 1982

Avigdor Arikha presented a formidable face to the world. Known not to suffer fools gladly, he was erudite, opinionated and quick to fly into a rage. When I began visiting him in his Paris studio, I tiptoed round the irascible artist hoping not to provoke him. At one point, however, he said something so outrageous that I replied, without thinking, in kind. He paused, looking at me for a moment in amazement, then burst into laughter. From that moment the atmosphere became more normal and we got on well, with Arikha rapidly sketching me as we talked (he very generously gave me the portrait afterwards). Nevertheless, I remained wary until the final version of my 'portrait' of him had passed muster since I knew that a single small error of fact could unleash his wrath.

To be simple in life is difficult enough. To be simple in art, without in any sense being naïve, requires unusual courage allied to a fine awareness of the ever-present, never resolved complexities of expression. Only children or undeveloped adults are naturally simple. Mature artists may achieve simplicity by an unconditional attempt to give their experience its most direct, essential form. But the attempt involves an important risk: by cutting through preamble or sophisticated disguise, it quickly indicates how much or how little the artist has in him to convey.

This is the revealing and uncomfortable position, it seems to me, that Avigdor Arikha has always sought – as if only a tight corner could make him sing. Endowed with an enviable natural facility, he has spent much of his artistic career abandoning what he could achieve easily. The fifty-three-year old Israeli artist-cum-philosopher-cum-curator might have used his encyclopaedic learning and gift for synthesis to elaborate the content of his art. Instead, he has progressively narrowed

Avigdor Arikha (1929–2010). *Connaissance des Arts*, Paris, May 1982.
Republished in English in *Art International*, Lugano, September 1982.

it and so created some of the sparest figurative canvases in existence. Given the ability to undertake the most ambitious themes, how does one come to make pictures containing a solitary broom, a section of anatomy or a piece of bread? The question concerns Arikha directly, but it also touches on the vital dilemma of art today.

Part of the answer may lie in the artist's background, which has been marked by extremity and conflict. Born in 1929 in German-speaking Bukovina, Arikha was imprisoned from the age of twelve onwards in a series of Nazi deportation camps. The precociously accomplished sketches he had done of the desolate life around him were discovered and – by a miraculous twist of fate – they secured his release via the Red Cross in 1944. Arrangements were made to send him immediately to Israel, where he lived in a kibbutz. In late adolescence, he fought and was severely wounded in the 1948 Israeli War of Independence. By that time Arikha had already spent two years at art school in Jerusalem, where the official style was so heavily dominated by Cézanne that, the artist ruefully admits, 'it took me twenty-five years to get it out of my system'. From 1949 to 1951 he followed the traditional course at the École des Beaux-Arts in Paris; and although he returns regularly to Israel – of which, he says, 'every stone in that country speaks to me' – Paris has remained his home since 1953.

Arikha's stylistic background is equally chequered. He continued for a while as a figurative painter, moving towards a freer, more personal handling of form than art school had prescribed. As a parallel outlet for his teeming mental energy, he studied philosophy under Jean Wahl at the Sorbonne. The Paris of the mid-1950s vibrated with new styles and attitudes, of which abstraction was among the most alluring; beside it, figurative art looked compromised and constricting. 'I thought that painting could equal music in the sense that its real content was its own structure', Arikha recalls. 'I believed in a sort of transcendental art.'[1] By 1957 Arikha had embarked on wholly abstract compositions: anguished shoots of colour half-swallowed by a black ground, like great fires climbing into the night.

That Arikha became abstract is far less surprising than the fact that, having developed his style and his reputation considerably over the eight years that followed, he found it imperative to change once again. Characteristically for this impassioned student of art, already as learned as many a professional art historian, the new volte-face was triggered by an encounter with Caravaggio's dramatically realistic compositions in a large show at the Louvre in 1965. 'I suddenly realized that we were in the same kind of situation as when Caravaggio started out. Our art was Mannerist – painting done from painting, not from life. It became clear to me that we had to start again from the beginning...'

The return to 'life' proved more exacting than the lyrical conversion to abstract art. If he was to start from scratch, Arikha felt, he would have to accept certain self-imposed limitations. He decided he was 'not yet ready for colour' and restricted himself to black and white (while not unmindful that Tintoretto found them the most beautiful colours of all). The desire for predetermined limits was also manifest in Arikha's choice of subject and format. Both were strikingly modest, announcing that the artist's renewed raid on the real was to be made in small, hesitant steps – letter by letter, as it were, until the first words of a freshly proven vocabulary could form.

Clearly announced, too, was the absence of any hierarchy among the subjects Arikha treated. A pair of collapsing trousers received the same scrupulous notation as, say, a self-portrait. Essentially, in fact, there was only one subject. Each drawing recorded its own difficult emergence – as though squeezed through the artist's belief that only by deliberate restriction could valid, new, figurative images be made. The images emerged criss-crossed with doubt, as if in perpetual questioning of their real existence in the bright, blank air of the paper. The fundamental difference between one Arikha drawing and the next lay in the intensity achieved, in the relative success of that strange venture that Samuel Beckett has described as 'Eye and hand fevering after the unself'.[2] And there an empty armchair or socks lying strangled on the floor proved as poignant as a portrait.

However humble in pretension and scale, each drawing constituted a work in itself: not a sketch or a study, but a complete statement – in fine yet sumptuously gradated black ink – about a passing moment of precise visual content. 'I used to be very general in my abstract work', the artist remarks. 'But now, on the contrary, I try to be extremely specific and get in every molecule.' The desire for factual precision – prompted by the 'hunger in the eye' Arikha felt at the end of his abstract period – meant that thenceforth the artist would never draw or paint without continuous reference to a model, whether inanimate, a member of his family, a friend or a professional. 'Everything I do is from life', he emphasizes. 'That's the whole basis of my work. I wouldn't allow myself to do a dot that wasn't from life. In fact, I consider drawing from memory or imagination a lie – an impossibility. To believe you can record a living instant with the memory of this instant is to me an aberration.'

The attitudes and practices that Arikha had developed throughout his chosen 'exile' into black and white naturally carried over into oil painting, which he resumed in 1973. A similar range of subjects also prevailed. Still lifes (of what was nearest to hand), the immediate landscape (the studio, or what could be seen from the window), and portraits (of friends, the artist himself, his wife, Anne, or their children) formed the main reach of his themes. Nothing was imagined, nothing recalled: only what the artist could maintain under his rapid, pale-blue eye throughout execution qualified.

Arikha tends to work in short, furious bursts, alternating his activity as a painter with another as art historian and guest curator.[3] Although the impression they give of balance and completeness seems to belie it, the paintings are usually executed in a single session, without any preliminary study, and then never reworked. Arikha believes that the only chance he has of capturing the ever-elusive spark of life is by trying to seize it in one go (which may last from one to five or more hours). This strictly observed convention and Arikha's insistence on having his subject always before him puts one in mind of the unities of time and space in classical drama. It is as if the artist had looked round at the unstructured proliferation of contemporary art and decided that, to have a game worth playing, he would have to invent (or re-establish) some rules.

Arikha's theory and technique of painting are deeply anchored in tradition. His parallel career as art historian not only allows him to compare attitude and method with all the major periods of western art; it also makes him aware to the point of anguish of everything that has been achieved – for once and for all – in painting. 'There's an element of entropy in culture that gradually reduces what's credible in art', he says. 'And when what's credible shrinks, what's expressible shrinks too. But since the *need* to express stays constant, we continue to try … It's impossible, of course, to capture the totality of an image. But if you feel intensely about what you have in front of you and attempt to follow what you see truly, you may produce a suspended trace of life – a series of seismic marks of your feeling.'

As he expounds his theory (as complex as his art is apparently simple), Arikha is never still. In the studio near Montparnasse, which he has drawn and painted with such fidelity, the artist steps back to deliver a well-prepared definition, darts forward to peer and squint at a recent oil on the easel, hurries off to the adjoining study to check a reference from the rows of highly specialized tomes, or pads with unflagging enthusiasm up to the split-level platform, which he uses for storage, in search of another portfolio of drawings. In all the provocative intelligence and undoubtedly contagious excitement that emanate from this wirily energetic man, one senses a compulsion to persuade, convince, even convert.

'The pictorial code has been broken', Arikha continues, shifting from French to an emphatic and perfectly mastered English. 'Painting had to be learned. Now it's been unlearned … though I get the impression that the new generation is interested in learning again. Art is not simply a question of feeling, obviously. Take colour. Colour is also a question of intelligence. You have to *think* how you are going to achieve the right pitch, the precise tone. A picture, after all, has to be both a painting and the truth, without falling into the trap of illusionism … I myself want to reunite with tradition but not, naturally, without taking modernism into account. I could not paint the way I do – with these planes', he says, pointing to a still life in which a knife, some cheese and bread appear pressed almost vertically to the picture surface, 'if Mondrian hadn't come before. Just as Mondrian could not have painted the way he did without Vermeer. By the way, have you noticed how Mondrian helps one to see Vermeer … ?'

Arikha's personal experience of changing radically from one style to another has combined with his historical connoisseurship to give him a special awareness of the dilemma of contemporary art. Now that the return to figuration has become so marked, the fundamental problem (largely shelved during the abstract period) will become increasingly obvious: what can painting still say? what areas are left to it to explore? Arikha's answer, not unlike his friend Beckett's in literature, has been to reduce: to limit himself to the barest elements of the knowable, record them with humbled passion, and from there – perhaps – move out with a renewed eye towards a wider vision of the universe.

---

1 From the informative interview with Arikha by Barbara Rose published in the catalogue of the artist's exhibition at Marlborough Fine Art, London, in May to June, 1978.

Also of special interest is Robert Hughes's preface to Arikha's exhibition of *Inks, Drawings and Etchings* at Marlborough Fine Art, London, February to March 1974.

2 The brief text that Beckett wrote in December 1966 for Arikha deserves to be quoted in full: 'Siege laid again to the impregnable without. Eye and hand fevering after the unself. By the hand it unceasingly changes the eye unceasingly changed. Back and forth the gaze beating against unseeable and unmakable. Truce for a space and the marks of what it is to be and be in face of. Those deep marks to show.'

3 Arikha has organized several exhibitions, notably of the work of Poussin and Ingres.

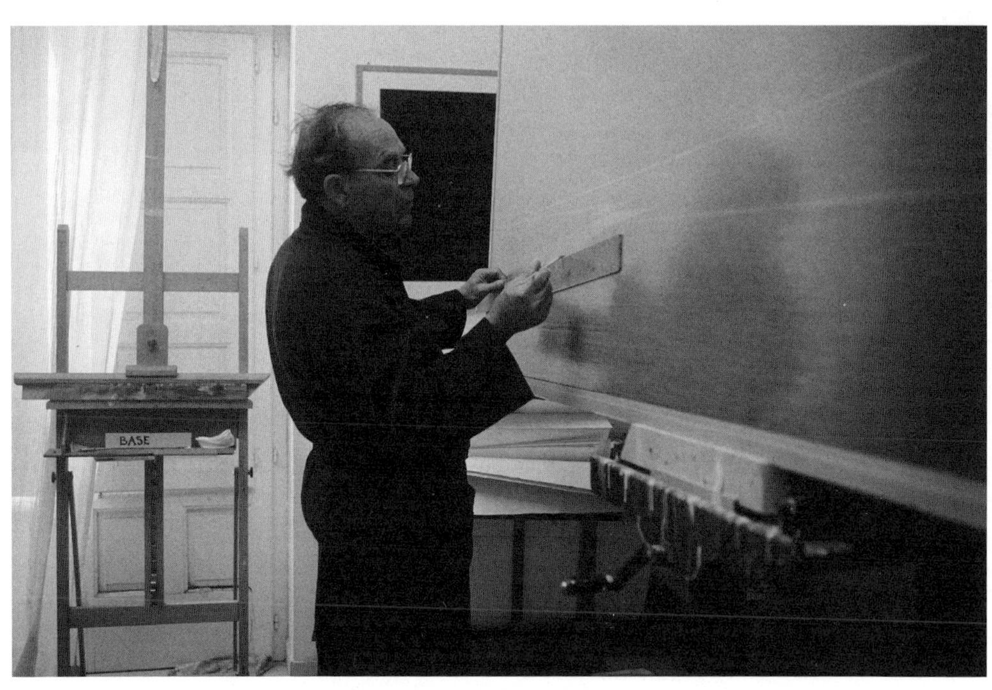
BASE

PIERO GUCCIONE

SCICLI SICILY 1988

Since writing about this visit to Piero Guccione in 1988, I had had no particular reason to think about him again until last summer when a young Italian film-maker who was making a film on him asked me to talk about my visit to Guccione on camera in Rome. The whole experience came back very vividly. With his dealer who had come especially from New York, we had driven over a parched Sicily (cracked earth scattered with black carob pods) to its southernmost point where Guccione had withdrawn to devote himself to endlessly attempting to capture on canvas the endlessly changing mirrors of sea and sky. The whole impossibility of his endeavour – of fixing an instant that by its very nature could never be more than fleeting – immediately won my admiration. Having gazed at the sea with Guccione, then having gazed at his shimmering azure canvases, I attempted thirty years later to recapture and fix the ever-changing impressions of life on the equally fluid medium of film. In the awareness of this incessant movement, I am hugely comforted to know that Guccione is still there, at the other end of Europe, patiently recording the transience of light on wave that will outlast us all.

The world is circumscribed by places where a world ends. Scicli, on the southernmost coast of Sicily, is a town where a civilization reaching back to the Greeks comes abruptly to an end. On that scorched outpost overlooking the Mediterranean towards the Libyan shore, Piero Guccione lives his isolated artist's existence like the last exemplar of a great abandoned culture.

An exile in time, Guccione continues to pursue the ideal of beauty that transfixed his classical forebears: how to give durable form to the floating, formless grandeur of the world? What shape should those

Piero Guccione (1935–). *Architectural Digest*, Los Angeles, March 1989.

greatest gods, Zeus and Poseidon, the sea and the sky, assume? The poignancy of Guccione's task is that he pursues what can never be caught: the shifting dazzle of light on the water, the sky's imperceptibly changing play of depth and shade.

In his own country, Piero Guccione has become a legend, publicly praised by its leading writers but almost never seen. Cut off from the world in his Sicilian studio, he spends months, sometimes years, on a single image, obsessively reworking the precise subtleties of its tones until, he feels, it has captured the essence of the arid mountains and glittering Mediterranean that make up the boundaries of his world. Only then will he allow it to join the works patiently assembled for one of his rare exhibitions in Rome, Paris or New York.

Although born in Sicily (in 1935), Guccione has spent most of his adult life in Rome, where he first studied, and later taught, at the Academy of Fine Arts. His work, as he himself describes it, has traced a complete 'arc', leading from the highly gestural painting of his twenties to the painstaking realism of his maturity. This development proved so all-consuming that life in the city became a hindrance. Some ten years ago, with the eagerness and relief he had felt on leaving it as a young man, Guccione went back to Sicily in search of the space and the light, as well as the time, that would best serve his exacting vision. He eventually settled for an austere country house surrounded by a walled garden, beyond which sparse fields end abruptly at a horizon of sea and sky. Those two vast, endlessly changing and by their very nature indefinable elements are exactly what Guccione longs to define in paint.

'That's probably why I take so long over a painting,' the artist admits. 'The sea is never the same from one instant to the next. I look at it all the time. When I'm painting, all sorts of different viewpoints and movements of light come back to me. I think it's the final sum of these that, after months of changing the whole image, makes me think I might have caught something of the subject's inner reality. For me, a painting is finished only when I'm convinced there's nothing more I can add or take away.'

Each infinitesimal change of colour that Guccione brings to one of his marines or landscapes or night skies enforces a delicate, painstaking revision of the picture's overall tonal harmony. In changing one note, he is obliged to change the whole. This maddening quest is undertaken with grace and good humour by Guccione, whose gentle manner belies the iron will that enforces such unswerving application. 'I need to stay on a subject for years to find its underlying meaning,' he says. 'To my mind, it's when the real and the ideal come together that you get a compelling image.'

When Guccione stares out of his window at the endlessly changing sea and sky, he is indeed gazing straight at North Africa. After a long drought, with the lean cattle huddled for shade under the carob trees, this dusty coastline seems more than ever the last reminder of Europe. To see it first in the flesh and then recreated on Guccione's canvas is to be made acutely aware of the transformation brought about by the artist's incessant raids on reality. A great intensity, a stronger, more timeless presence comes through: this is the sea, the shore and the night sky that both Norman invader and Greek sailor knew.

But Guccione's painting is also created out of and nourished by art. However close his vision appears to come to topographical fact, it draws constantly on a highly informed visual culture. 'There is no end to the number of artists one admires,' Guccione says, 'but Cézanne is the most essential point of reference. There's Munch, too, who in a certain way represents the other 'face' of Cézanne.' The influence of Caspar David Friedrich has also been directly acknowledged in a series of pastels devoted to themes borrowed from the great German Romantic; and in his recent series of drawings of Matisse and his model, homage to the French master's calm – that precious lull before the full storm of twentieth-century modernism – is equally evident.

'The sea occupies a space, the wind creates a space,' says Guccione. 'What interests me is to try to give durable form to those spaces, to recreate them with their own inner structure.' The intricate compositions that result from this ambition are built out of a mass of sketches and notes that the artist makes while out walking on the beach or surveying a chosen theme from his window. Gradually all extraneous detail, all anecdote, is excluded, leaving a single main theme, conveyed with a magical feel for the grandeur of the natural world. 'Guccione does not paint what he sees,' the Italian novelist Alberto Moravia has suggested, 'but what he wants to see.'

Something, certainly, which Guccione is obliged to see with great sadness and anger is the massive deterioration of the Sicilian countryside. Its severe beauty is scarred by cheap new buildings and dumps of semi-industrial waste. A sense of abandon lies heavily on the island, and it accounts for some of the melancholy that Guccione's landscapes communicate. 'I often have the feeling that we have ruined things beyond repair,' the artist says. In recent paintings of local scenes, Guccione has incorporated bits of black plastic into his paint. 'It's a kind of realism,' he remarks wryly. 'There's masses of this black plastic all over the countryside. It has, quite literally, become part of the landscape.'

Periodically, to escape the long-term labour that each new oil painting imposes, Guccione concentrates on pastel. The change of medium frees him and, since he masters it so naturally, allows him to catch a more instantaneous side of the reality – the infinitely changing face of Nature – which obsesses him. Sooner or later, however seductive the soft, grainy touch of pastel proves to be, he will return to oil. It is in this richly, unexpectedly changing substance that he best achieves the illusion of having stopped the universe for an enduring second before our eyes.

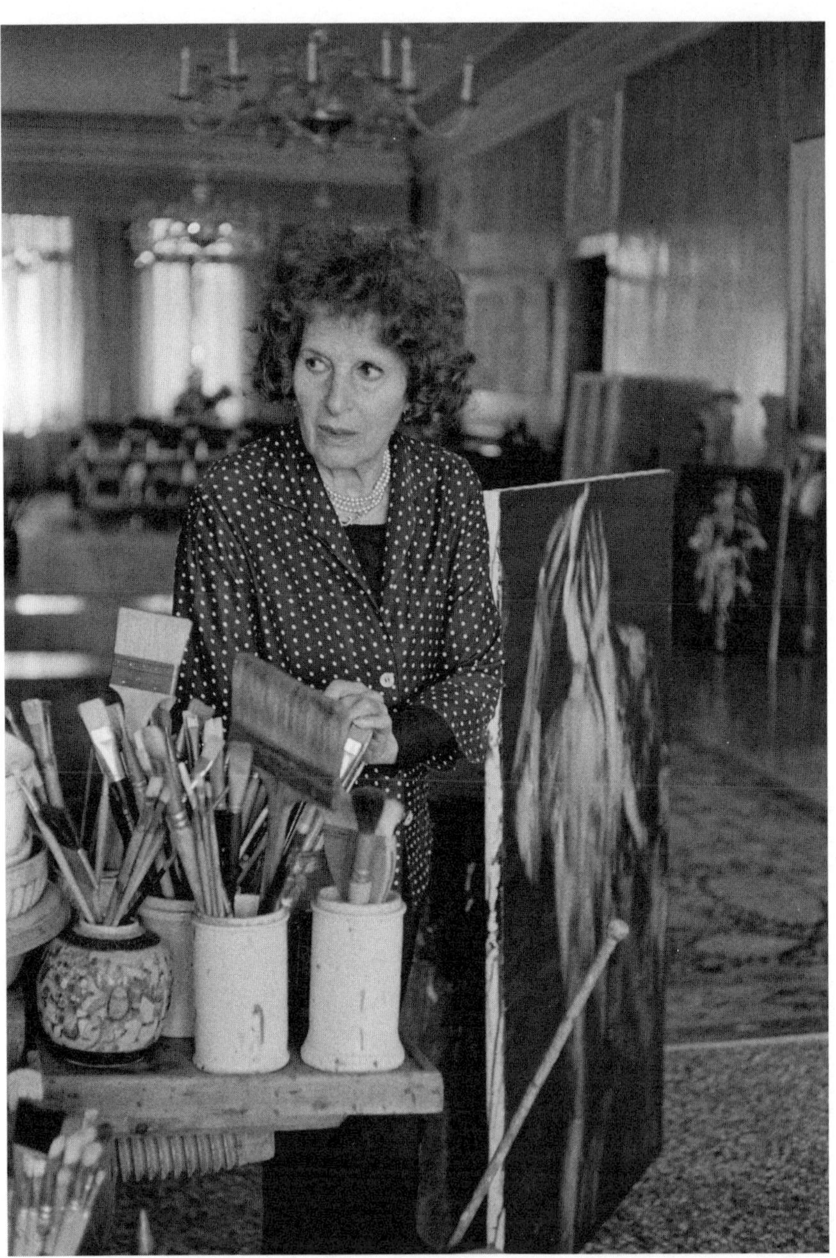

IDA BARBARIGO

DORSODURO VENICE 2000

Throughout their long marriage Ida Barbarigo and Zoran Music lived between Paris and Ida's native Venice. If Paris was the capital where they kept in touch with the international art world and developed their careers, Venice became a haven where they could work more tranquilly and entertain their many friends on a princely scale. No one who was lucky enough to be there will forget the sumptuous New Year's Eve parties in Ida's palazzo overlooking the Grand Canal or the grand dinners that she organized in her vast marble-lined studio.

In Venice, where she lives and works entirely today, Ida has become an extraordinary link with the city's artistic past. Although her own work is resolutely modern and forward-looking, Ida draws instinctively on centuries of painterly awareness and technique. A visit to her studio is a voyage not only to the heart of Venice but to the very heart of art history.

The more time one spends with the painter Ida Barbarigo in Venice, the more she seems to embody the strange, elusive magic of her native city. Vivacious and articulate, she talks about Venice's great heritage of art and architecture with admirable intimacy, as if she had been personally present as this sublime church was designed or that great image grew from preliminary sketches into a painting. There are in fact good reasons for this. Ida Barbarigo comes from a long line of distinguished painters, sculptors and architects who have been at work in Venice since the Renaissance, and she herself was brought up in a family of cultivated artists where a sense for the techniques and achievements of the great masters had become second nature.

'Our family house had studios all over the place,' she says. 'There was always an uncle or two painting or sculpting, and my mother or an aunt playing the piano. The house was called the Ca' Briati, and

Ida Barbarigo (1925–). *AD*, Paris, September 2000.

the parties that were given there in the eighteenth century became so famous that Casanova wrote about them. Something of that atmosphere remained, and I must say it was a wonderful place to be brought up in, full of fun and very easy-going. What's more, my father, Guido Cadorin, was a well-known painter as well as director of the Accademia, and lots of interesting people came to the house to see him. Even as a little girl I used to spend hours in his studio, grinding his colours for him or doing my own drawings. So from childhood on, painting seemed to me like the most natural activity in the world, and it never really occurred to me to become anything but a painter myself. But the other thing my family had given me was a taste for freedom. I knew that, however much I loved Venice, I couldn't develop unless I got away from it. I also knew that I would always have to come back to this extraordinary city regularly.'

Having finished her studies in Venice, Barbarigo began to travel in Europe, visiting the great museums and developing her already markedly personal approach to painting. By the early 1950s, after several stays in Paris, she and her husband, the painter Zoran Music, had found a studio in the rue Mazarine, and from this moment on both artists began to divide their time between the French capital and Venice. Freed from the influence of the Accademia and her own beloved family, Barbarigo began to work more directly from her own experience, and by the end of the 1950s she was well launched on a series of paintings of 'Chairs', which were to remain an important theme in her work. Several exhibitions and monographs on her work through the 1960s began to establish her reputation in France and abroad.

In 1974, Ida's father died, and the family decided to move from the Ca'Briati to another grand house, the Palazzo Balbi Valier, on the Grand Canal, where the artist established the studio where she works today. Built on foundations dating back to 1100, this splendid Renaissance building underwent a total 'modernization' during the 1870s. The *piano nobile* where Barbarigo lives and works during her stays in Venice is above all remarkable for its vast central room, which stretches from one set of windows over the Grand Canal to another set that looks out over a private courtyard filled with pieces of ancient sculpture. This space is large enough to accommodate Barbarigo's studio at one end, a sitting area in the middle and a dining room on the courtyard side in perfect comfort. With its huge dimensions, marble walls and elegant chandeliers from Murano, the main room would be overwhelming were it not for the relaxed and natural way in which Ida Barbarigo has chosen to live in it.

'For me the studio is the very heart of the house,' she explains. 'So I set up my main studio in this room, directly overlooking the Grand Canal. I feel totally at home here, with perfect light and space, and I've been concentrating on a series of pictures on the themes of Dionysus and Saturn. Once I've found a theme, it usually takes me about two years to work my way through it. The 'Chairs' went on longer, but since then there have been 'The Persecutors', 'The Beaches', 'The Self-Portraits' and 'The Sphinxes'. But I think of them in a way as a single theme with variations. The 'Chairs' became a little bit more human and turned into the 'Persecutors', and so on …

'Each series starts with a jolt – a sudden, unexpected emotion. I remember very clearly how 'The Sphinxes' were triggered off, for instance. It was in Vienna and I'd been very struck by an Egyptian head I'd just seen in the museum. But it was raining and I was in a bad mood, so I decided I'd go back to my hotel. Then when I got to my room the memory of that head was so insistent that I couldn't stop myself doing drawings of it. And that's how the whole series began. I don't know why, because I've seen thousands of Egyptian heads in my life, but that one made such an intense impression on me that I had to draw and then paint it.

'Those moments are very rare,' Ida continues. 'But when they come, they mark you for good. I think other artists have experiences of that kind. Do you remember that story about Giacometti in the cinema? Giacomettii had just settled down to watch the film when he noticed a large black man sitting next to him whose head seemed so enormous in the dark that from then on he couldn't take his eyes off it … At all events, I can get back to work the moment I come in here, because everything feels so familiar. Curiously, many of the objects you see around – the easels and the wooden sculpture stands – come from the studios that were in my parents' house and they have been used by several generations of my family before me. The same is true of the furniture and the paintings that you see on the walls – most of it not only belonged to but was actually made by one or other of my relatives.'

With so many creations – landscapes and allegories, busts and terracottas, faïence and carved furniture – by parents and grandparents, aunts and great-uncles, this sumptuous space might have turned into a worthy, somewhat lugubrious family museum. But the very quality of the works and the naturalness with which Ida Barbarigo displays them give the house an extraordinary resonance. Within these ancient walls, another history of Venice stands revealed: the styles and aspirations of several successive generations of a family which during the Renaissance had its own flourishing workshop in the Santa Croce quarter of the city. And in this way the house, like Ida Barbarigo herself, comes to resemble Venice. For everything here, from the seventeenth-century mirrors to the Fortuny fabrics, evokes other epochs and other associations – not unlike Barbarigo's own works, which hark back incessantly to the great tradition of European painting.

'Clearly Venice and Venetian art have influenced me deeply, since I myself am Venetian through and through,' Barbarigo says. 'But I have been influenced by so many things that if I mention Giotto, I would also have to mention Cimabue and Cavallini. The list is far too long, because I would have start with the first glimmerings of civilization, with cave paintings and things like that. But what seems self-evident to me is that all art grows out of something, and that to be a painter, today as in the past, you have to be able to refer to a specific culture. Nothing, after all, comes from nothing.'

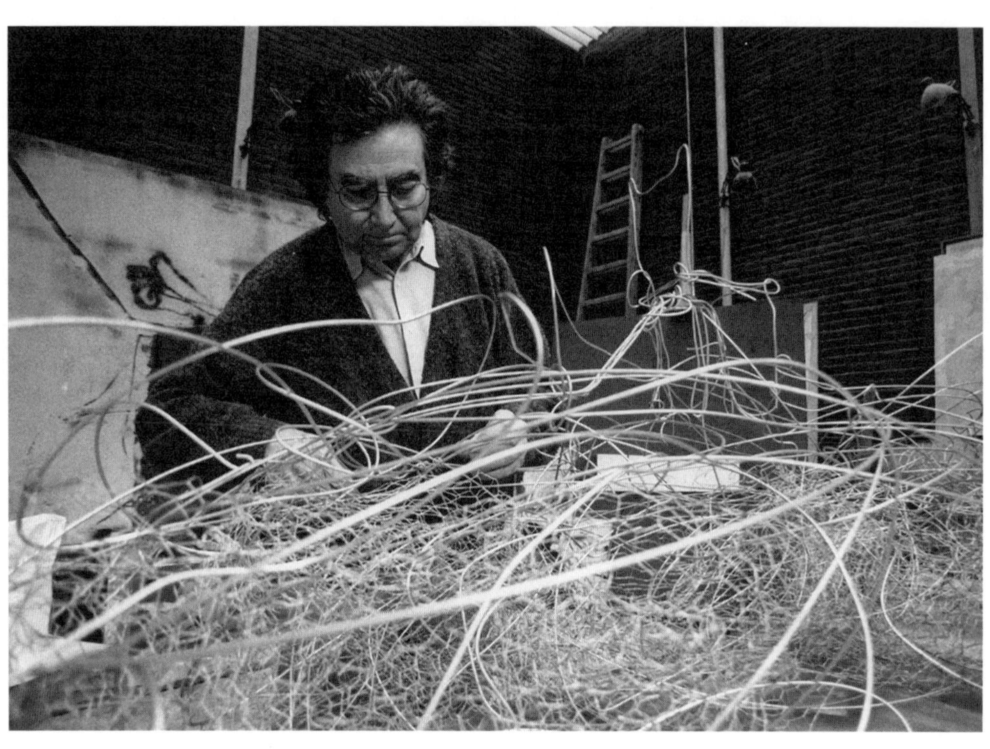

ANTONI TÀPIES

EL PUTXET BARCELONA 1987

You could not have even dipped into the Paris art world during the 1970s or 1980s without being aware of the latest developments in Antoni Tàpies's work. Regular exhibitions, notably at the Galerie Maeght, barely sufficed to keep up with the inventive proliferation of his large canvases and sculpture, which incorporated a variety of materials, most of them 'poor' and normally considered junk: bits of twine and rusty wire, the odd sock and battered chair leg. I became fascinated by Tàpies's ability to create with so much rawness and fluency and watched how he constantly pushed back the barriers of his art, focusing on such disparate themes as bath tubs and feet while always succeeding in making his admirers uneasily or humorously aware of the contradictions of contemporary mankind.

I had met Tàpies on and off at gallery openings but it was not until I went to Barcelona to interview him in his studio that I began in any real sense to get to know him. During this first visit, I was struck by the artist's rather sombre, bonze-like bearing – an impression reinforced by the collections of rare books and oriental paintings that filled the adjoining house. By the time I went back to do another interview (see page 413), our relationship had become less formal and I saw another, much more exuberant side.

The journey to Antoni Tàpies is a long, labyrinthine one. As if on a separate plane to the bustling Ramblas downtown, his Barcelona house stands in a residential area so quiet birds can be heard singing in discreetly walled gardens. A visit through the artist's house reveals rooms that are like a series of self-enclosed worlds, filled with oriental art and well-chosen examples of the painters Tàpies esteems most – from Klee and Kandinsky to Picasso and Miró. But the large, functional studio contains nothing but working materials and the artist's

Antoni Tàpies (1923–2012). *Architectural Digest*, Los Angeles, August 1987.

own canvases. Stacked around the walls, these images seem to defy all verbal description, so that the baffled eye returns again and again to find a way to the heart of their enigma. It is here that the real journey to Tàpies begins.

At first all signs point east, to lands that Tàpies knows only from books and pictures. 'For a long time now I've felt very close to oriental art and thought,' the sixty-three-year old artist says. 'I've been collecting paintings from the Far East since the 1950s, and eastern philosophy has always fascinated me. Occasionally my works come out like Chinese calligraphy, in a single stroke I don't need to retouch. But more often I paint over what I have done time and again.'

To one side of the main studio there is a smaller drawing studio. 'Many of my works, particularly the larger ones, begin here as drawings,' Tàpies says. 'But they're like notes – simply points of departure. When I work on the paintings themselves, I never stay with the image I've drawn. I improvise, because I want to come up with things that surprise me, images I'd never dreamed of. Often I make things difficult for myself, simply to get out of certain intellectualized attitudes. Sometimes I mix marble dust into the paint, which means it dries very quickly – so I have to work fast, without thinking about the consequences. The basic problem is one of renewal. You have to renew constantly in order to communicate. There's a Taoist saying that sums it up perfectly: "When everyone agrees that something is beautiful, it becomes ugly".'

The problem is all the more acute for an artist who has been in the public eye since he was a young man. After an initial 'heroic' period of solitary invention, he began to exhibit widely, showing for the first of many times at the Martha Jackson Gallery in New York in 1953. His career since then has been studded with retrospectives, monographs and honours such as France's Prix Nationale de Peinture, which he received quite recently.

The drawings provide the best introduction to his paintings, which prove increasingly accessible as the eye grows accustomed to their hermetic language. Gradually they disclose quite unsuspected traces of the artist's own life. 'There are – it's probably inevitable – certain biographical details in my paintings,' Tàpies concedes. 'For instance, the stitches in that composition were probably prompted by an operation I underwent recently. In any case, I have always been obsessed by the 'visualness' of stitches. But these images can have their starting-point anywhere. This one, for example,' he says, pulling out a large composition of bold, black masses joined by an airy calligraphy, 'comes out of a story about Bodhidharma, the founder of Zen Buddhism. Bodhidharma is said to have contemplated a wall for ten years, and one of his disciples was so intent on attracting his attention that he cut off his arm. That story and all its implications continue to impress me and to suggest images. In this one, you can see the two figures quite clearly, as well as the wall.'

Walls have loomed large in Tàpies's *oeuvre* since 1945, when he became fascinated by the graffiti Catalan patriots were making all over Barcelona, at considerable personal risk, to publicize their separatist cause. Much of his work may in fact be approached as apparently random 'writings on the wall' that look as if they have been simply lifted out of their usual context in the street. Moreover, as he likes to point out, the word *tàpies* means 'walls' in Catalan.

Although his career has been built up mainly in Paris and New York, the two real poles of Tàpies's life are Barcelona and a farmhouse one hour's drive away, in an area he describes as 'intensely Catalan – grey-green holm oaks, grey-blue mists and ochre-coloured fields'. There, in a large wood-beamed studio, he is able to work uninterrupted by the business of being a famous artist. 'It's wonderful,' he says. 'I wake up, cross the courtyard in my pyjamas and go straight to work in the studio. In the afternoon I take a siesta, work a little more, then listen to music.'

Born into a cultivated family, Tàpies has been steeped in music since childhood. Another passion he inherited from his parents is one for books. He is a reader of impressive range and is also a discerning collector. The top floor of his Barcelona house is given over to a library that would make the most expert book-lover's heart quicken.

Tàpies seems so firmly rooted in his life, and so widely acclaimed in his art, that one wonders what he can still aspire to. Two things, at least, it appears. One is a foundation for his work, and negotiations have long been under way to have it established in a fine building of the artist's choice in Barcelona. The other is the far more difficult, far more elusive 'desire for constant renewal'. But that has been a lifelong preoccupation. 'When I was a young artist,' Tàpies reflects, 'I went to see Miró, whom I admired tremendously, to talk about painting. He said, "Listen, everything's been done in art. What can you come up with that's new?" But I didn't lose hope. And I think I've been able since then to find a new language – a language of my own.'

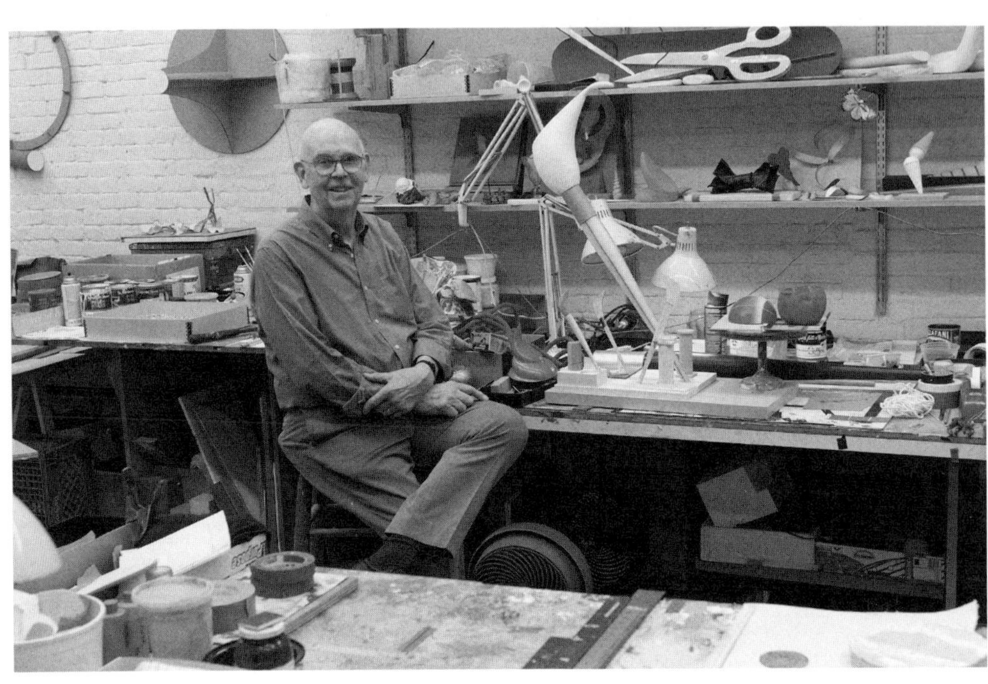

CLAES OLDENBURG

MADRID 2010 / WEST SOHO NEW YORK 2011

The first time I met Claes Oldenburg and his wife, Coosje van Bruggen, was at their summer home, a splendidly restored, white château *in the Loire valley. We shared a beautifully prepared lunch, wandered through the gardens where several of their monumental works (such as a giant 'Clothes Peg') loomed amiably into view and had a long, lively conversation. Several years later, I was lucky to catch a show of Oldenburg's works at Elena Foster's Ivorypress Art + Books gallery in Madrid. The works were there, Claes himself was there: it seemed too good an occasion not to build on our previous conversation and do a more complete, formal interview. We duly met at Claes's hotel and began talking over a borrowed tape-recorder. I had not had the time or means to prepare the kind of properly researched, searching questions that, one hopes, elicit the most revealing replies. I need not to have worried since Claes's well-ordered mind and remarkable memory took over and gave very complete answers to my lame queries.*

Claes is a strict perfectionist, however, and once he received the transcript of our Madrid conversation, he decided there were areas that required further elucidation or rephrasing. Several emails later and after a visit to his wonderful studio in New York, we agreed on the final version. The interview has taken on depth and solidity, and since it has been almost entirely created and reviewed by Claes I won't be blowing my own trumpet if I say that I think it may be read as a fresh, personal and authoritative account of the artist's early career.

MP You can look back on a long career now, Claes, but when you started off, you had a fairly classical education and you went to Yale, didn't you?

CO I did, but I didn't study art much. The first two years I was in a special programme called Directed Studies intended to

Unpublished interview, Claes Oldenburg (1929–). Madrid, February 2010.

introduce the student to all types of education from Physics to Literature – but not, as I recall, any Art. Later I focused on drama and literature. *The Waste Land* dominated poetry study. Eliot lectured but renegades were drawn to Dylan Thomas. The Yale Art School was very conservative: Prix de Rome studies of classical sculpture. I took a course for non-art undergraduates in which models wore bathing suits and we did compositions on 'Jack and Jill Climbed up the Hill.' This was long before Albers.

I took my first art course in summer school at the University of Wisconsin, after my sophomore year. I studied Perspective. I returned to Yale in the fall with a major in English and Art – because so many of the students were returning veterans, the University had relaxed major requirements which normally had been in a single subject. Unfortunately I switched into straight English for my senior year for which I was not completely prepared. I walked away from the final examination to sit on a bench near New York's City Hall reading *Moby Dick*. Instead of studying I had gone to New York as often as I could on weekends.

MP Was that to look at art or something less edifying?

CO I went to look at the world. Art was still a mystery to me. The closest I came to it was Art Students League Ball.

MP I was trying to find out – perhaps too indirectly – what got you going as an artist. Nothing we've talked about so far actually predisposed you to having a whole life in art.

CO I was born in Sweden but came to New York before I was one year old. My father was the Swedish vice-consul there. Later when I was six he was assigned to Chicago and that's where I grew up.

I had a talent for drawing, but no one treated it as an entry into art. Instead I used it to document an imaginary country I had – doing maps, advertisements, photos, comic strips and newspapers combining Swedish and American. American eventually took over. I went to as many movies as I could, especially Saturday serials. I spent a lot of time making model aeroplanes which satisfied my sculptural inclinations.

After Yale, I returned to Chicago and took a job as a newspaper reporter. I had returned to my aim of becoming a writer and felt that this was an important preparation. The job was very good for me, taking me into worlds I knew nothing about. At the same time a deal was struck with Yale that I could return to my original major of English and Art if I were to take some additional courses in art to qualify for a degree. I began to attend night classes in Figure Drawing at the Art Institute of Chicago.

MP How did the decision to become an artist come about?

CO In early 1952 I was drafted but I wasn't accepted due to my age and flat feet. My newspaper job had grown boring because in order to attend the evening classes I had to give up reporting from the street. I was put on re-write in the office, a far less adventurous duty. Also I suspected I could never become a writer. Instead I asked myself, walking along Lake Michigan, what can I do best. My drawing had begun to show promise and I decided to try and become an artist. I gathered my drawings and showed them to commercial art studios which resulted in a job over the winter drawing boll weevils for an insecticide firm. In 1953 I used my accumulated salary to enrol in day courses at the Art Institute, where I met Robert Indiana and John Chamberlain. I had my first show of drawings with Indiana at a restaurant in March 1953. My favourite course was doing watercolours from street life in different parts of Chicago. I also enjoyed figure drawing and started oils from still life – until the school removed the fruit and pots, saying 'from now on we're going to work from the imagination'.

My approach to art was analytical: what is it and where is the best environment for it? I continued my art education by taking a job washing dishes in a summer art school on the opposite shore of the Lake in Saugatuck, where, inspired by Soutine, I began to use oil paint freely. I had the theory, common to a Chicagoan, that New York should not have everything. In the fall I boarded a Greyhound bus to explore other places in America where art might be. I went to New Orleans, to Houston, to Los Angeles and to San Francisco. I was a little early in San Francisco; the City Lights book shop was just opening with only one book on the shelf, about Francis Bacon. When I ran out of money I moved to Oakland where the landlady in a boarding house provided me a basement apartment in return for a watercolour a week. I drew constantly, determined to be self-taught and work out of my own experience. My only friend was the new director of the Oakland Museum who lived in the boarding house. I realized my landlady had figured out that if I talked about art with him he would be more likely to remain a boarder.

MP Europe didn't sort of cross your mind?

CO No, Europe, what's that?

MP It's a sort of small island floating.

CO Well, of course, most of what I was reading and seeing came from Europe, but I wasn't to get back to Europe until 1964. I was firm on establishing myself as an American.

In the end of 1953 I returned by bus to Chicago to receive my American citizenship. In 1954 I returned to the Art Institute for the last time in a painting class taught by Paul Wieghardt who had been a professor at the Bauhaus. I worked alongside Cliff Westerman. I had first met him in an evening drawing class in 1951 when he challenged the teacher to a fight in the hall. He was an original in the most opposite direction imaginable who first made me conscious of outsider art. Summer I sold candy at the Dearborn train station. I had for the time being decided that Chicago might have possibilities.

I moved into a studio on Chicago's Bohemian North Side and eventually got to know artists of the Chicago School such as George Cohen, and the printmaker Richard Tyler. I volunteered to help organize the Momentum exhibition, to counteract the conservatism of the Art Institute Annual. I moved in with Marjorie Oplatka, who taught me to read Freud and Whitman. I worked evenings at an uncrowded record store listening to Stravinsky and Ravel. I showed my paintings in restaurants and my drawings in the annual outdoor Chicago art fair. What I showed was figure work, either metamorphic or street sketches. I longed, however, for more experience, excitement and ideas than Chicago could provide. Resigned to the inevitable, I boarded another bus on May 31, 1956, this time to New York. I did what I imagine everyone does on arriving, stayed at the YMCA for the first week – it's near the bus terminal. Then I looked for a little apartment; first it's one room and no bath and the next one is two rooms with bath and finally I found an apartment large enough to use as a studio. In those days it was cheap. For sixty dollars a month you could have a five-room apartment.

MP My God!

CO Yes, but it took a year to find! And it was on the margins, the far end of the Lower East Side. Bob Indiana, who had not yet changed his name from Bob Clark had arrived in New York before me. He advised me to apply for a job at the Cedar Bar, which I did. I could have worked there but a more promising opportunity came up, a job in the library of the Cooper Union. My first residences were all near Cooper, where I had to put in four hours a day. I was in the Department of Decorative Arts which had all kinds of wonderful art books, an elephant edition of Audubon for example. Most of my work was pasting up clippings and not many people came into the library.

MP So you were free to roam.

CO I really got an education there and I discovered the French eighteenth-century architects like Boullée. Every day I found something new. Of course, this move meant starting all over, and with a higher opinion of one's possibilities.

MP New York was already very hip?

CO Always in one way or another, but this was New York in 1956 and with much underground that would soon be released. I settled in and continued my search, but it would not be until 1958 that I had my next exhibition. My first loft space was heated by a wood stove, so I was obliged to hunt the streets for wood each evening of the first winter. Windows let in the autumn light in which I drew the pail, the broom, and other simple objects on the premises. On 14th Street I bought magazines and cut them up into compulsive patterns which I called *Strange Eggs*. And I wrote poetry about life in the city. It was the city in New York which dominated all, the city as theatre and I spent many hours walking the streets, day and night, noting sights and making lists. Occasionally I ate at the Cedar Bar, observing the notorious artists in action at the bar.

MP Did you feel Abstract Expressionism weighing very heavily on you?

CO No, I liked de Kooning, especially I got a lot from his line and sense of space. I tended to connect Abstract Expressionism with the look of the city's surroundings, street art, movement...

MP But there was a feeling something new had to happen.

CO Yes, everyone was looking for a solution. Were we going back to figure painting in a loose way or were we going back to collage and assemblage, or would junk sculpture take over? I did a lot of figure painting from models, especially in 1958, influenced by Bonnard and Degas, Manet and Corinth, but I also practised a metamorphic approach to reality, like the *Elephant Mask* of newspaper over chicken wire or the *Lady* made of a coat rack with many pieces of painted wood.

MP Was performance a big part of it already?

CO Performance was waiting in the wings. I did not see my first performance until late 1958 when a friend of mine who was also a friend of Dick Bellamy and the artists of the Hansa Gallery, took me to George Segal's farm in New Jersey to see a performance by Allan Kaprow. Kaprow had written his famous article on the development of Pollock's work into performance the same year.

MP Was this an attempt to bring back a personal or everyday reality? I mean Abstract Expressionism was quite far removed from what you might call everyday reality.

CO I wanted to integrate what I saw in my work. Every morning I would walk to Cooper Union from my place far out on Avenue C and through the neighbourhoods at night. This way I got to know a world I had never seen before and that contributed to not only what I call the context, but to the actual materials I used like plaster, chicken wire and cardboard which gave form to the expression.

MP And people living rough?

CO I saw people living in cardboard boxes who set them up like houses every evening and removed them when daylight came. The streets of New York are not as crazy as they were then. Then you could look down on the streets and you saw drawings and you saw poems people had written. Some poems I copied literally into the drawings I made. And the walls were relatively free of placards and posters. I put up some of my own and they stayed uncovered and visible for months until they peeled away by themselves.

MP So this was really the source of your early imagery. Did you feel you were very much alone or did you discuss it with other artists?

CO The artist I saw most often was Dick Tyler, the woodcutter and printmaker I had met in Chicago and who had come to New York with his painter wife and lived in the same house as I with a studio in the basement. He was also the janitor of the building. It was Dick who had tipped me off to a vacancy on the top floor. A very complicated person, again like Cliff Westerman an artist on his own terms, outside art. He sold his woodcuts and tracts from a pushcart in the courtyard of the Judson Church near Washington Square.

MP And was your work accepted quite easily? Or was there a reaction against it?

CO My work had not yet been discovered at all. In those days you could bring it to galleries, but few galleries would take the time to look at it. You could leave it in the smoking room of the Guggenheim where J. J. Sweeney came in for an occasional cigarette. That produced nothing after several months but a nicotine odour on the canvas.

My chance finally came when I showed my drawings of the figure to the head of the library in early 1959. She arranged to give me a show in the gallery of the Cooper Union art school. The show was seen by Tom Wesselman, who along with his wife-to-be Claire Selley, were students. Wesselman asked me if I would show with a group that was starting a gallery at the Judson Church. Its minister was interested in developing an art and theatre presence in addition to social services such as helping drug addicts. My first one-man show in New York City was held at the Judson Gallery in May 1959. At the last moment I made a radical decision not to show the oil paintings and drawings of the past year, but to concentrate on the metamorphic works which seemed more original. The contest between the two would continue the remainder of the year. In Lenox, Massachusetts where I spent the summer, I reverted to figure painting. Back in New York in the fall, I took up the metamorphic again. A two-man show with Jim Dine in December combined works in both styles. A month later with the performance of *The Street*, I stopped figure painting from life altogether. The natural strangeness of the streets melded with the metamorphic vision. My companion Patty and I became the figures; later many others did as well. I had found a style composed of the ingredients of my experience, the first of several. The sixties had begun. Red Grooms had done a wonderful performance at his Delancey Street Museum called the *Burning Building*, Kaprow had his *18 Happenings* at the Reuben Gallery. At the Judson we organized a series of performances, *Ray Gun Spex*, with Jim Dine, Bob Whitman, Dick Higgins, and others ... *Time* magazine featured a full-page photo of Patty and I performing in *The Street*. The fact that they did it was taken as praise even if the comments were negative.

MP That must have helped.

CO People said, 'Oh, *Time* put it down, it must be good.' It was an important moment for the Judson and the whole movement into new territory.

MP Were you experimenting a lot technically at the time, using street materials and so on?

CO *The Street*, which was redone as an exhibition at the Reuben after the Judson performance in 1960 was entirely made of found cardboard and burlap trash bags, string, materials from the street. It marked the transition from figure to object, and figure also became performance.

It was followed the next year by *The Store* in which reliefs and sculptures based on store objects and ads were made of canvas dipped in plaster and placed on forms of chicken wire, then painted with enamel – materials of the hardware store, consistent with the notion that *The Store* resulted from lifting your eyes off the street to the side of the street, where you encountered a different sort of material and forms.

MP When one talks about realism, it seems to me that these are things that are taken out of an everyday reality and given an unexpected reality, an unexpected existence.

CO Yes, the subject is something seen in the surroundings, which for reasons that are not at first clear, stand out and can absorb a number of interesting approaches, imaginatively, and in rendering, formally. *The Store* is sometimes written about today as if it were a real store, where you went to buy soap or a toothbrush. In fact, there was such a store after my store, assembled by Paul Bianchini – a Duchampian found-object concept two years later which was very different, often brought up in connection with my *Store* and confusing. My *Store* was art form, even if it was a disturbing form, strongly painted, colourful, irregular wall reliefs derived from advertisement and shapes of clothing from the neighbourhood, together with objects made with more attention to sculptural form than representation; also freely painted, never mixed, only superimpositions of a limited palette of hardware store bought enamels. Very few people of the neighbourhood dared to come in, it was too strange-looking for them.

MP They knew you were on acid at that point and completely out of it.

CO I guess. Those who dared were dealers, collectors, or artists. Henry Geldzahler and Andy Warhol each bought a shirt. Prices were very low: $50–100 and sometimes people paid half and I never got the rest.

MP What date was that?

CO *The Store* had three different installations. The one I'm describing was the second, in December 1961. Before that, a number of the pieces had been shown in *Environments, Situations, and Spaces*, a show at Martha Jackson Gallery in 1961. The 'I am for...' statement was written for that show. Then in the summer of 1962, after *Ray Gun Theater*, Dick Bellamy gave Patty and me the Green Gallery on 57th Street to use as a studio. We worked there on larger pieces and downtown as well, including large pieces like the *Floor Cone* and *Floor Burger*, inspired by the scale of piano displays on 57th Street, all new work which became the final installation in September accompanied by a performance – *Sports*, commissioned by the Italian producers of Mondo Cane, done in the context of the show. People said, 'Oh, he's sold out, *The Store* is no longer Lower East Side. Now it's 57th Street and gentrified.' But it was just a continuation of the

Lower East Side. The Green Gallery – in this and other shows, you could say – had brought downtown uptown.

Sixty-two for me was the final year in a frenetic period that began in the end of 1959 with *The Street* and *Ray Gun Spex* in the Judson. Afterwards the Reuben, first shows and performances in their 4th Avenue location, then a performance in their second location on 3rd Street, followed by the versions of *The Store* and *Ray Gun Theater*, and interplaced exhibitions at the Martha Jackson Gallery. All the artists of the new movements were fully employed. After *Sports*, a kind of pause set in as if a goal had been reached. We had been recognized and that in New York meant exploitation. Audiences formed of 'Thrill Clubs' appeared at the performances; police questioned me about the erotic significance of plastic forks thrown into water. Dalí complained that he had invented happenings. I began to feel as if I should seek new territory ... The last piece I did in '62 was the *Lingerie Counter*, for an exhibition organized by Sidney Janis called *New Realism*. Early in 1953 I decided to accept an invitation to do a performance at the University of Chicago, which put performances 'on the road.' Three performances were done that year and each one in a different place dealt with the surroundings of that particular place. The *Gayety* happening in Chicago was followed by Stars in Washington and finally *Autobodys* in Los Angeles. By the time of *Autobodys*, I had relocated to Los Angeles, living with Patty in a bungalow on the canals of Venice, California. While doing *Autobodys* I was also preparing an exhibition at the Dwan Gallery, which contained the first of the so-called soft works. Venice was then run down, relatively undeveloped and not an art destination. An abandoned bank on its main street became my studio.

The first soft sculpture was the *Giant Toothpaste Tube*. Of course being a soft thing, it was more of an example. Then I selected light switches, which – in the example that I chose off the wall in our living room – involved redoing a hard geometric form into a soft sagging one.

MP Was Surrealism at all influential?

CO Not really. The *Soft Typewriter* for example, has been called surrealist, but it's not. My intentions began as an experiment, to take a subject and do a very simple thing, substitute the surface, change it from a hard to a soft one – so that it still retains the potential of an outline. Just that move within a realistic concept enabled you to see the thing as an unrealistic form. Factual Surrealism. People could buy a 'toaster', a soft toaster and take it home and they could push it around all they wanted. Every day they could change the shape of it if they dared. The soft pieces were based on the idea that you could take a normally hard piece and transform it by the simple act of sewing it.

MP How did that original idea come? Was it just by sort of messing around in the studio?

CO It probably started in the performances, because a lot of the props were sewn. Patty could sew beautifully and it continued out of the performances into the first large soft pieces done for the Green Gallery show.

In Los Angeles sewing became the main means of transformation, along with scale, of course. The technique became even more eloquent when vinyl came in about that time. Early vinyl was very beautiful, it was thick and rich and colourful. I had a source on Lincoln Avenue in Venice that could supply any kind and design, Lincoln Fabrics, at a reasonable cost. The place bought leftovers from designers. There was nothing you couldn't get. The vinyl from then still has its colour, it hasn't cracked or anything. It was even more convincing if you did a metal object out of vinyl, very convincing.

MP So that it sort of slips into another reality?

CO Yes, right.

MP And then in a sense, hell is let loose, isn't it? Because it changes the rules.

CO That's the important thing. It changes the rules.

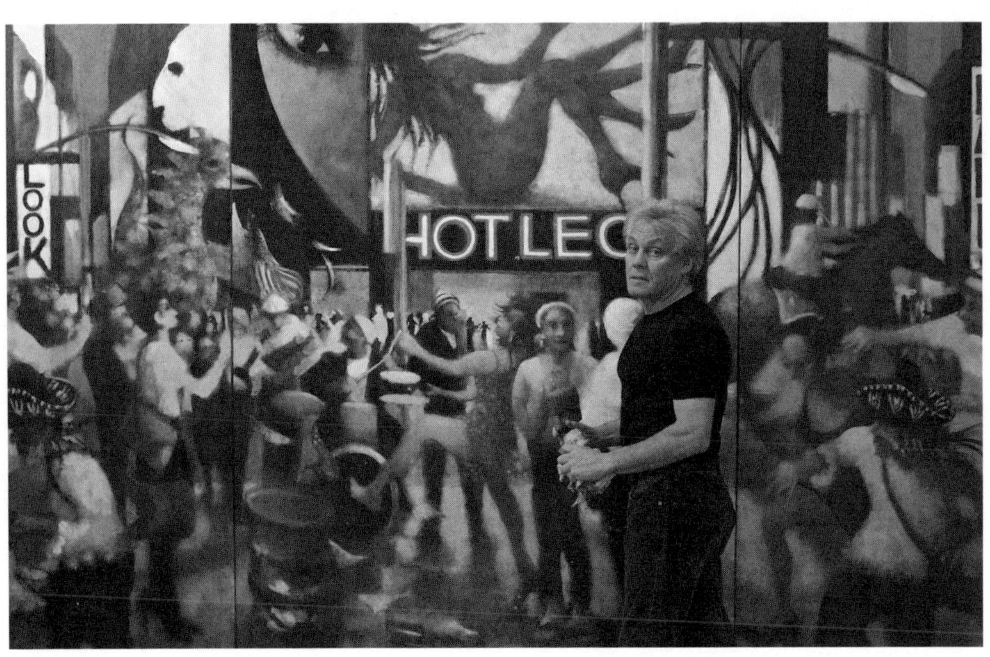
LOOK
HOT LE

BILL JACKLIN

NEW YORK / LONDON 2011–12

Bill Jacklin and I have talked so often over the past thirty years, usually during long congenial evenings in London or New York, that we were both convinced we had already done an interview together. When we realized that we'd never recorded any of our conversations, we decided to try to get something on tape. In the end we snatched a moment to meet for drinks while I was in New York in November 2011. The interview could not have got off to a worse start. It was raining hard and I arrived late, having lost my briefcase and having retraced my sodden steps in a vain effort to recover it. Jacklin listened to my tale of woe with polite equanimity, then told me of the number of wallets, credit cards and mobile phones he had managed to lose at critical moments in recent months. He had treated his last mobile phone with infinite precaution, he added, checking for it at night on his bedside table – only to wake up to find he had carefully settled it into a glass of water. Jacklin's stories, like his paintings, teeter regularly on the edge of chaos when they don't actually plunge headlong into it. Suddenly, in this vista of accidents waiting to happen, the briefcase incident receded. I began to relax and, without any plan or questions in mind, I turned the voice recorder on.

MP You told me once that there's always an incident behind what you paint.

BJ There's always something that triggers a painting off, although the way I actually paint it comes afterwards. There has to be a force or something there in the beginning.

MP An experience of some sort.

BJ An experience that excites me. So to go back, as I was telling you, I was sitting in a bar with a friend in 1985, about a week

Bill Jacklin (1943–). Unpublished interview, 2011–12.

after I'd arrived in New York. And there was a crash and a bang and it was obvious that someone had shot somebody outside the restaurant that I was sitting in. I was sitting at the bar and a bullet came across and ricocheted and hit down at the end of the bar and there was a silence and then I heard a voice say, 'Oh my God, he's coming in.' Whoever it was then hit the deck, so there was another silence and then everyone appeared to hit the deck. And what I got, as I started to hit the deck, was the impression that the wine bottles and the glasses moved this way and everything was on diagonals. So I fell to the floor from my stool at the bar. And then there was another silence, and suddenly everyone sort of collectively decided they better get the hell out of there. So everyone started running out towards the kitchens at the back. And it was mayhem in so far as there was one moment of silence and the next moment it was chaos. The result was that I don't think the man ever did actually come in. But there was someone who was shot in the eye and he was taken to hospital and the police came and we were all kind of huddled in the kitchen, then everyone started to leave, and being the only Englishman there, I was the only one actually saying, 'Well, can I pay my bill?' Then I realized that this was a different place and that the cashier was looking at me like I was just crazy and I'd just said the craziest thing. And that was my first impression of Manhattan.

MP And is the memory of the various things that have happened to you in New York still coming through in the paintings you're doing now? Are they recollections or reflections of events?

BJ Well, yes, I think everything is a reflection of itself. I think it's all about how you receive things. Maybe we want to recapture the dramas that we've had. You know, I was thinking as I was walking over to talk to you this evening that I was born in 1943 when the Doodlebugs were dropping on London, and I was trying to work out what it is that gives you the sense of actually being alive, and I think certainly in those early years I had a heightened sense of being alive through those bombs, that were like an external force.

I think you're a product of your time, and I was a war baby. As a result, certainly in artistic terms, I was brought up with a whole kind of existential group of people that had a particular attitude to how they perceived the world. And I guess I became part of that. But I was sufficiently younger not to be philosophically in tune with a pessimistic way of viewing the world. I basically viewed the world as post-war, and I'm still caught up by the idea of drama and the drama of life.

MP That we can be extinguished from one second to another?

BJ Well, the idea that you go very quickly from a structure to a sort of chaotic situation. My early artistic career had a kind of parallel of non-figurative equivalence, of drawing structural things that were systematic and held in abeyance what I perceived to be chaos, a chaotic situation. I thought that if you put together all these ramifications you could hold chaos.

MP But are the more recent paintings about chaos, because some of them are apparently quite jolly, almost Renoir-like scenes, with people enjoying themselves at the beach or in restaurants?

BJ That's what I aspire to but there's always a kind of dark shadow moving over and the sense of people wanting to escape. I don't have any a priori principles or beliefs. I don't have a position. I have a kind of anxiety, if you like. But I have an aspiration beyond that anxiety.

MP Which is what?

BJ Well, it comes from being a post-war baby. I mean, like I was part of that sixties moment in the way you rejected a certain position about how everything was dire, everything was black and the black cloud hovered over everybody and every day you could wake up and have …

MP So are you saying your paintings are either about a fragile stability, a fragile order, or about chaos to a large extent? Is it order on the edge of chaos or is chaos always lurking under the surface?

BJ Well, yes, I think chaos always is lurking; I think we're all aware of that. And we're well aware of what's going on in the world right now. I've always been interested in what's going on around me and for quite a while now I've felt much more like a reporter of my time than someone who's involved in artistic pursuits. I'm not part of an artistic culture. I'm way beyond that, I'm too old for it. Like at the moment I've been down at Zuccotti Park to paint, I go down there to paint like a reporter.

MP To look at the people in protest against Wall Street...

BJ And I want to be involved in what's going on right now. I don't have a philosophy about it. I just have an instinctive position.

MP Did you know you were going to start painting those kinds of scenes, or did you just go and look and then suddenly you thought, this is something I'd like to get down on canvas?

BJ I think it's to affirm a sense of life. As I said, I don't have a particular ideological position but I do believe in being at the centre of energy. I mean, my paintings are above all about energy. I'm a closet abstractionist and I've always been that way. I find ways of swirling things out of focus, so they become something else. Maybe in another lifetime I'd have made a movie. I don't have an adherence to style. I don't have a stylistic position within the art world because that for me is a kind of death sentence.

MP But you actually came out of abstraction?

BJ I came in and out of abstraction. My early work was very much a reflection of what I was looking at. After that as I got more involved in the art world and had some degree of success, I got more involved in systems of painting which ultimately I determined were less interesting.

MP You mean in the 1970s, when the art world was very given to theory?

BJ Yes, and I thought that was fine in its way but that it was better for me to kind of walk away from it.

MP And come back to life?

BJ Come back to waking up every morning and having a sense of energy, a kind of 'how do I see the world?' I think in the end every artist is based on that very simple principle. You wake up in the morning and you say, how do I see the world, how do I feel, and what do I want to say? And even if it's in a contradiction of what you did yesterday, there's a life to it. And that seems to me to be the most wonderful thing to be able to do.

MP But this isn't a political consciousness, is it? It's a consciousness of what you see around you, what strikes you and what you want to try and record.

BJ It's an affirmation of life. You know, for quite a few years I taught. Most artists didn't have any money in those days and they taught in order to kind of sustain what they did, and you saw young students going into the library to try and find a language that would allow them to feel that they were on the road to being an artist. And they were often starting with manifestation. They weren't starting with impressions.

MP By manifestation you mean?

BJ What to do about it, what to paint. And in my view it always was, I always felt, what am I receiving as an artist? What food am I getting, what am I getting from this street light that I'm looking at, what am I getting from the people I'm talking to? Impressions that you can say something about. You start from stage one, you don't start from stage two. You never say how am I talking, you say, and what am I talking about…

MP The subject.

BJ The subject, and that seems to be even more important now because as the art world becomes more and more about money and it becomes stultified and becomes all about business. The real question is how do you cut through that and say: what am I looking at, how am I receiving this? And that's not just artistic, that's life.

MP From these impressions that you receive, whether it's the incident in the bar, where a bullet comes whistling through, or a feast that you've seen and appreciated in a restaurant in Little Italy – do you think very closely how am I going to relay this on the canvas? Do you start doing drawings or compositions? Do you say, oh I should get that fat waiter in or the dog snapping around at the end of the table? Or do you just go in and reinvent as you go along?

BJ Well, I think it's about a sense of place. I think a lot of artists, a lot of painters speak about space and the relationship that you have with it. And I think a lot of the best work is all about that relationship. It's not about the image. The image is important, but it's the relationship you have with something, it's the relationship you have with anybody, at any moment. Like when I'm speaking to you: I have a sense of being with you and there is that moment of space between us. If you look at a wonderful Rembrandt self-portrait, what you're actually aware of is the space between you and him. That's what the emotional content of your relationship is and that is the relationship, not just the image. So in anything, if I'm really serious, I'm aware of being in a place at a certain time and it becomes a memory for me ultimately, that has a resonance for me. And it's real. It wasn't concocted. And if it was concocted and if I'm critical enough, then I'll say that wasn't so good, it was a concoction. But if it was real, I know it.

MP Do you have a very clear idea about what you want to paint, or at least an overall impression, before you start a canvas? Or is it very spontaneous?

BJ Usually in terms of the process of how I work, because of the life in the particular areas I'm working in, I have a kind of figurative base. I know for example that if I'm working on a group of people in Times Square everything will move and change, often quite dramatically. So much of my work is about movement, you know, that I don't hold to a rigid structure at all.

MP But does this come from a drawing to begin with or do you go straight into the canvas?

BJ I use whatever I can. I'll work from drawings, and I'll work from a sense of being in a place. For me it's very important that I was there.

MP But not from photos?

BJ Well, I'll take whatever I can. I think that any artist will steal and make it their own.

MP Sure. But you might have taken the photos yourself?

BJ I might have, or I might not. If I fail in the image that I make it's because I didn't make it my own. And that's all.

MP And do you know when you've made it your own?

BJ I serve myself into it, so that it's coloured by my feelings because it's a subjective process that we're involved in here. I don't pretend to think it goes beyond that.

MP Do you judge one of your paintings according to how successful you were in imparting your own feelings to it?

BJ I'm always totally in conflict about that. I'm confident enough to know that I'm engaged in the dialogue. I'm not confident enough to believe that what I saw was real and every day I wake up and feel that there is another opportunity to see the world. At the end of the day, Michael, I just want to say that as I get older I'm hitting a certain point. I want to be able to say to myself that I kind of saw something and I had the presence of mind to record it in a way that has a resonance. So when I paint, if I'm talking in formal terms, I've always said to myself, well the painting is a residue of what happened. I don't just put it down, because it seems to me everything is always shifting and changing and moving, and if I try consciously to find a way for painting something, it won't work. I don't know in advance how a picture is going to come out. That's why I still believe in painting. I still believe it has a relevance because the very simple old-fashioned process of hand to canvas allows an immediacy, you know, it's not technically rigid.

MP It's straight down the nerve ends.

BJ There is still a kind of touch, a feel, by which I can say something. I think the less interesting work for me is where someone's identity is attached totally to their stylistic content.

MP Yes, because it becomes empty.

BJ I think the most interesting artists are the people who have a handwriting and their stylistic content maybe can shift and change accordingly. Once it goes into that place, and every artist knows that, where you try to hold on to something that's already been done or seen in some way, it always has its downside. You have to cut through that. So it's not easy.

MP So how would you describe your average day in the studio?

BJ You know, Michael, I basically spend my time sitting alone in a room, viewing the world through the reflections on a doorknob – or on water or whatever – reflections of something I've seen or experienced, but at one remove.

MP You want the distance or a different angle on a moment that you've lived through?

BJ I think of the artist as a voyeur, the person who's watching. There's the observer and the observed, right? You're watching the world go by, and you're watching your own life go by. Time is ticking.

MP So you're snatching a moment?

BJ You're waking up to the moment. Because I think a lot of the time you go through your life when you're not aware of the moment. You're caught up in things and not very aware. Then this very particular moment comes along, and a very particular feeling – of being removed. Some people might call it loneliness.

MP Is that what Joyce called an epiphany – an unusual awareness of existence? And is that when you think you've got a picture, an image, when you have this moment of heightened reality?

BJ The image is another stage. What you do about it is another whole issue. You might or might not make something of that feeling. You know, in New York, you're always out on location, the whole city is a location. I paint about an energy mass, it gets figurized in various ways, if you like, but it's actually about a flowing, pulsating energy. That's what Manhattan is – it shifts and changes, people love it or hate it, but it's always pulsating.

MP This is what attracted you to New York in the first place, isn't it?

BJ Yes, I found my subject. It was a conduit for me to experience all those things that excite me. When I first arrived, every street corner I went round I found something. New York, for want of a better word, is my muse. Suddenly all these images were given to me that I could transform. And what really transforms them for me – I should have mentioned it earlier – is light. Light, or the absence of it, holds everything together. I look at certain scenes, certain situations, and I see either light or darkness and that to a large extent decides how I paint. Light is spirituality and emotion. Light for me is everything.

MP Yes, that comes across very strongly in your pictures. And it's often as though one doesn't know how long the light will last before darkness descends ... To change focus for a moment, who are the artists you look at with most pleasure? I believe Seurat is one.

BJ Did I tell you the story of buying a little Seurat when I was quite young? Well, I had a show in the West End and there was a gallery in Davies Street and I went in and I saw a little Seurat drawing. I didn't know it was a Seurat drawing at the time and I didn't have any substantial money, but I had £1200 to spend and there were certain contemporary artists that I could buy, but only a graphic. And I went into this little gallery in Davies Street run by a man called Christian Neffe, and there was an artist called Josef Herman who had bought a little Seurat drawing and I admired it. There were Bonnards there and Vuillards, and I always had an affinity to that kind of attachment to urban life they had towards the end of the last century. I've sometimes felt I was out of my own time in a funny kind of way. Anyway, the drawing had been bought, but about a month later Christian called me and said, that drawing of Seurat is available again if you'd like it. I said I don't have that kind of money, I've only got £1200.

MP So what did he say?

BJ Well, he said you can have it for £1200, so I bought it and I've had it ever since. It's always been a kind of little spiritual supplement.

MP What's the scene?

BJ It's a man sitting on a little donkey, an art school donkey. It's not one of his big expensive charcoals; it's just a very minimal little pencil drawing. But it was the idea that there was someone viewing urban life in another century that drew me to it.

MP You are an urban person, you like big cities and you like going around and watching people carry on and…

BJ Yes, I'm basically a street kid. And I'm an observer, a voyeur, as I said. And the relationship between the observer and the observed is a very interesting one. You know, it's always in flux. I mean why I like Manhattan is because it's contradictory, it's not what it seems, nothing is what it seems. You know there is always a moment where things will happen, that you're taken unawares, you have your wallet stolen or you lose your briefcase and you're always on one foot. What interests me is that sense of waking up in the morning and being alive and feeling that you can go out and see something and from that perspective I really am an old-fashioned artist. I have a sketchbook and I sit in a corner and I draw things and I make notations of things that I've seen. And they are notations and they are dots and splushes and blibs and blobs and they are actually the subjective equivalent of something seen. It's not a record.

MP It's your notes.

BJ It's a subjective equivalent.

MP But to finish, so it would be Seurat, Vuillard, Bonnard and?

BJ And then I wrote my thesis as a student at the Royal College of Art on Rauschenberg and Jasper Johns. So if you like you make a sandwich and you make a BLT, it's really what you show, it's like the top of it can be the bacon or the lettuce or whatever, and although a lot of people will only see what's on top, the sandwich is compressed of…

MP Different layers?

BJ That's right. You could say Seurat was a very important influence on my life but so was Rauschenberg and so was Jasper Johns. When I was student I did a philosophy class at the Royal College and Iris Murdoch was my tutor for three years. So I had all that English sandwich compressed into me as well.

MP I hadn't thought of you as a sandwich before, but I'll look anew to see what level I'm at.

BJ I think we're all a bit of a sandwich really.

MP In one of the interviews I did with a painter friend called Miguel Condé, I tried to pin him down about something and, you know, he clearly wasn't going to be pinned down and he wriggled out by saying: 'I'm just a salad of comings and goings.'

BJ There you are. I think we all are.

THREE PHOTOGRAPHERS

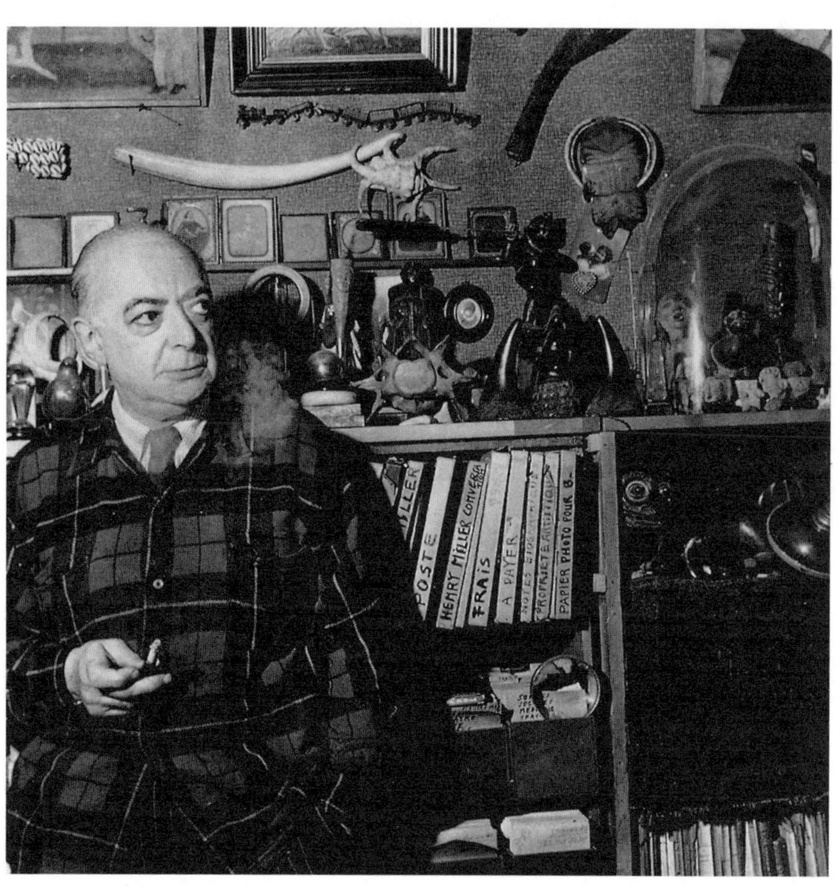
ILLER
POSTE
HENRY MILLER CONVERSA
FRAIS
A PAYER
PAPIER PHOTO POUR B.

BRASSAÏ

MONTPARNASSE PARIS 1976

Within an hour spent in his exuberant, talkative company, Brassaï made you feel like an old friend. Once we had finished a lively late supper in Montparnasse, he seemed as eager to explore Paris by night as he had been when he made his most famous photographs before the War. But if Brassaï had not changed, Paris had grown visibly less 'saucy', with Montparnasse looking quite tame compared to his marvellously gritty evocations of its low life in the 1920s. And although we roamed the area's well-known 'hot' streets conscientiously, both the girls, their clients, their 'protectors' and other night-time personages turned out to be disappointingly well behaved. Knowing this, Brassaï had not even bothered to bring his camera, but his darting eye regularly found some anomaly in a dark doorway or fugged-up, neon-lit café. As we parted, I felt that this quick-witted Hungarian could have created a dramatic, black-and-white world, full of veiled threat and leering innuendo, wherever he was, in any period.

Brassaï has just turned seventy-seven, but a stroll with him around his beloved Montparnasse quickly reveals that his visual sense is as sharp as ever. He frequently urges you to savour some chance composition – such as a hand (dark, male and hairy) abandoned on a female bottom – with the obsessive glee of a man whose eyes have not stopped photographing the streets of Paris for half a century. His sense of fun and evident enjoyment of life make him appear astonishingly young, even though he has lived through and recorded an epoch that already belongs to history.

Brassaï arrived in Paris in 1924, when he himself was twenty-four years old. He had left his native Transylvania (then Hungarian, now part of Rumania) with little more than a romantically artistic mien and a desire to become a painter in the great centre of the arts. He

Brassaï (1899–1984). *New York Times*, New York, 19 September 1976.

plumped right away for Montparnasse and was quickly caught up in its effervescence of new ideas and attitudes. He was also lured away from painting. 'With so many fascinating people around, from all over the world, how could I stay shut up alone in a studio with a canvas?' he puts it, with his gregarious smile.

So he went out, and generally stayed out, moving from one café to the next and meeting everyone – the new writers and painters, their girlfriends and such legendary Montparnasse ladies as Kiki and Lily, the artists' models and opium addicts. 'I used to end up around four of five in the morning with coffee and croissants and the new day's paper,' Brassaï recalls with relish. 'Then I'd go back to my little hotel, and when I woke up and it was dark outside I never knew whether it was the same night or the next one.'

Although Brassaï had actively disliked the idea of photography, he came to see it as the ideal medium for recording the spectacle of Paris, picturesque and poignant by turns, which riveted him each night. 'I wanted to record the life in the streets around me, as Rembrandt and Goya, Daumier and Degas – I'm not making comparisons! – had done. And I realized that photography was truly an art of our time and the best way of capturing all the fleeting impressions which excited me.' From an observant *noctambule*, he turned into an eye, the 'eye of Paris', as his friend Henry Miller was to call him. He seems, what's more, to have made himself invisible, so as to creep up on the seamier side of Paris and catch it unawares. Pimps, prostitutes, drug addicts, thieves, homosexuals, lesbians, tramps – every kind of social outcast – became his camera's favourite prey.

Brassaï's natural affability plus whatever he could give in tips helped him get near these frequently thin-skinned and dangerous birds of the night. 'In some of the bars where the pimps and gangsters hung out, you could never be sure when someone might turn nasty,' he explains. Several times he had his camera smashed, and once one of his subjects came at him with a knife swearing he would kill him (fortunately, he was persuaded to settle for cash). 'I was very lucky to have got away with some of those shots. The only thing I regret, in fact, is not having photographed the really classy brothels of the day. You wouldn't believe how lavish and kinky they were!

'I loved that whole side of Paris at night – it was part of the reality of the city. I never went after subjects just because they were extraordinary. What interested me was their reality – even, in a way, their banality. That's why I never fully agreed with the Surrealists, who adored everything exotic and strange. I've always loved the ordinary, the everyday – because I think that, if you really look at them, they are so often the most astonishing things of all.'

When he was not prowling around the red-light districts or recording an effect of mist and street lamps over the Seine, Brassaï was photographing his writer and artist friends. Looking at them today, one realizes with a start that one's mental picture of people like Picasso and Miller, Genet and Giacometti is often based on a Brassaï portrait. As with his less well-known subjects, Brassaï has caught their most naked, everyday and undisguised selves.

Friendship has undoubtedly been one of Brassaï's talents in life. Of the thousands of volumes that line the apartment behind Montparnasse where he has lived since 1935, he visibly values above all the couple that contain scores of notes and letters to him from virtually all the major artistic figures of the time. He himself still bubbles with enthusiasm and laughter when he comes on a quip from Dalí or a polished apology from Malraux.

Brassaï's other talents, which include drawing, sculpture and writing, are no less evident. 'When Picasso saw my drawings, he said to me, 'You should draw rather than photograph. You've got a gold mine in your drawings and yet you go on working a salt mine!" More recently, Brassaï turned his hand to carving, and he has transformed large pebbles picked up on the beach into voluptuous female forms. 'I hate specialization,' he says, handing you one of the well-rounded stones to feel. 'It seems ridiculous to me to do just this or just that if you feel you can do several things. What interests me most of all at the moment is writing. I've written several books over the years – the last two were *Picasso and Co* and *Henry Miller Lifesize* – and I feel I have several more to write.

'I still adore photography, and I've got masses of unpublished photos. Some of them aren't even developed! I do my own developing still, you see, and at the moment, with this new show in New York and the very latest book, *The Secret Paris of the Thirties*, that's coming out with it, there's just too much else to do. But I'll get around to it. I can wait. I think photographers don't wait long enough nowadays. They publish too much too soon, and their bad photos spoil the good ones. Time makes a selection for you. The nice thing about having lived as long as I have is that you can see much more clearly what's good – which photos you can show and which ones you'd do better to throw away.'

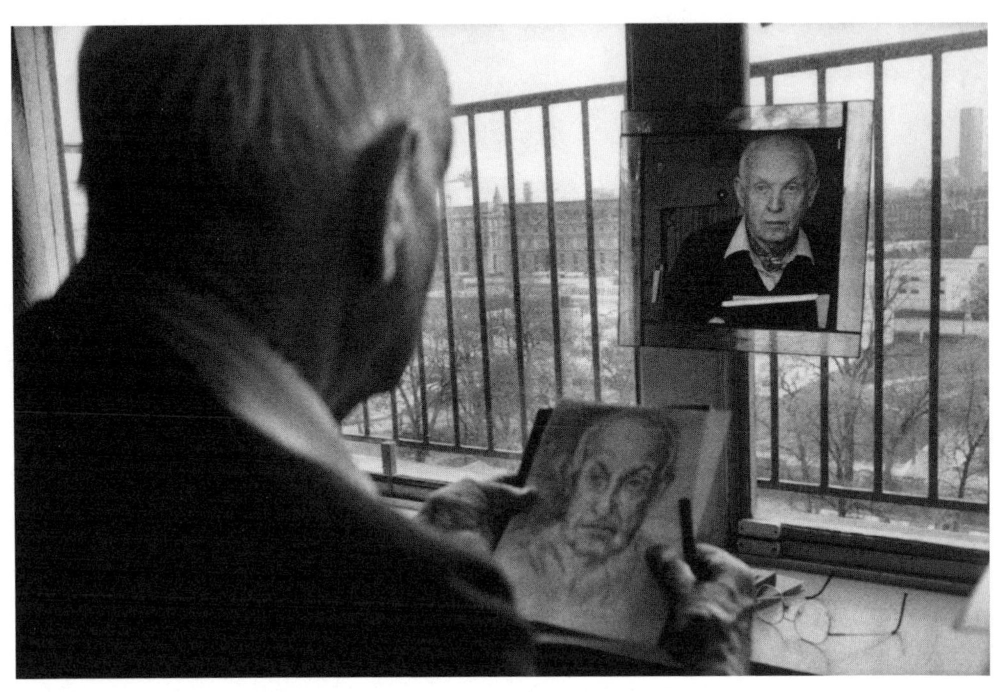

HENRI CARTIER-BRESSON

RUE DE RIVOLI PARIS 1987

Having interviewed Henri Cartier-Bresson for Architectural Digest *(see page 179), I took the opportunity to do a parallel interview with him for my own fledgling magazine. By this time Cartier-Bresson – who was a great admirer, like me, of Giacometti and Bacon – had become a good friend, and he immediately gave* Art International *his support, recommending certain artists and writers and suggesting ideas for articles. He and his wife, the photographer Martine Franck, lived in a comfortable, bookish apartment high up over the Tuileries Gardens; its magnificent view, leading over the parterres and fountains to the Seine and the Left Bank. The flat had once been lived in, Cartier-Bresson explained, by Cézanne's great collector, Victor Choquet, and it was there that Cézanne had painted his famous portrait of Choquet. Cartier-Bresson continued to be totally obsessed by art, to the virtual exclusion of photography, and his conversation here extends and amplifies what he said during my first interview with him. For this interview, as for several others that appear subsequently in this book (notably with Sicilia and Tàpies), I tried a new technique by abbreviating a fairly discursive question-and-answer session into a monologue that, I hoped, would allow the reader to feel in direct contact with the artist being interviewed.*

'One thing that drives me really mad,' Henri Cartier-Bresson says, 'is when people want to bury me alive – 'So you're the well-known photographer', they say. It's as if they're talking to me about a woman I lived with for fifty years, with joy and passion, but whom I haven't seen for the last fifteen. It's not that we've completely fallen out, we're still on speaking terms. But I have another love now – for drawing, photography's elder sister – and I'm monogamous. You can't give

Henri Cartier-Bresson (1908–2004). *Art International*, Paris, Autumn 1987.

yourself to two activities at once. I still do a few portraits and the occasional landscape: they're the two opposite ends of photography. But reportage – what I call working on the *trottoir* – is completely over for me. It was wonderful for a time, but it's over now.

'Do you know who put me back on the right track? The art publisher, Tériade, who brought out my book, *The Decisive Moment*. He was a kind of guru for me, and one day, back in 1972, he said to me, 'That's enough photography now, Henri. You've said all you have to say.' I knew he was right. I'd been wanting to go back to drawing for years, because that had been my original passion. I'd studied painting at André Lhote's atelier, and I'd always wanted to paint. It had never even occurred to me that I would go in for photography until the War was over. I'd been very influenced by the Surrealists, but doing forced labour in German POW camps does tend to change your view of aesthetics. When I got back to France, I realized I wanted to wander round the world and see more of life at first hand. That's to be expected of a Norman like me, all Normans are basically adventurers ... And I found that through photography I could have that kind of life.

'Everything was so different then. For one thing, there was a whole mass of reportage crying out to be done. Nowadays people take up photography for all kinds of reasons. That's their affair. But for some reason or other photographers get annoyed with me for having taken up drawing. They didn't say anything when I was making films. But the idea that I'm drawing seems to infuriate them – they say I've turned my back on photography. It's not that at all. Painting and drawing have always been my first loves, they've been at the source of everything I've done. My eye, my visual sense – whatever you want to call it – was formed by them.

'I stopped drawing because I got very discouraged after I'd tried time and again to draw my own hand – and failed. Of course, it's a difficult thing to do. Drawing is an introvert activity, and taking photographs is quite extrovert. I think the eye behind both of them is the same, but the tools you're using – your Leica or your pencil – are totally different and require a totally different approach. After all, a photo lasts a second, then you lose it and it becomes something else. Photography is a kind of intuitive drawing. You don't have time to go over it when you're back in your room. It's instant drawing really – but it's a constant struggle with time. Whereas with a drawing you've got all the time in the world. You can go over it as much as you want.

'Nowadays I draw all the time. I never stop. Wherever I am – in Paris or in the South of France or travelling – I just draw. I never know whether what I've done is any good, so when I've done something that seems a bit better than the rest I show it to a few artist friends for them to criticize. That kind of criticism is very useful. The French painter Sam Szafran has helped me enormously in that way. And when Saul Steinberg wrote to me saying that photography has only been 'calisthenics, decoy, alibi' for my real thing, I was terrifically encouraged. I never stop doubting myself. Drawing is a kind of constant self-questioning. And when you have an exhibition, the only important thing about it is that it allows you to see where you are. Even after all this time, I feel like a beginner who's still got everything to learn.'

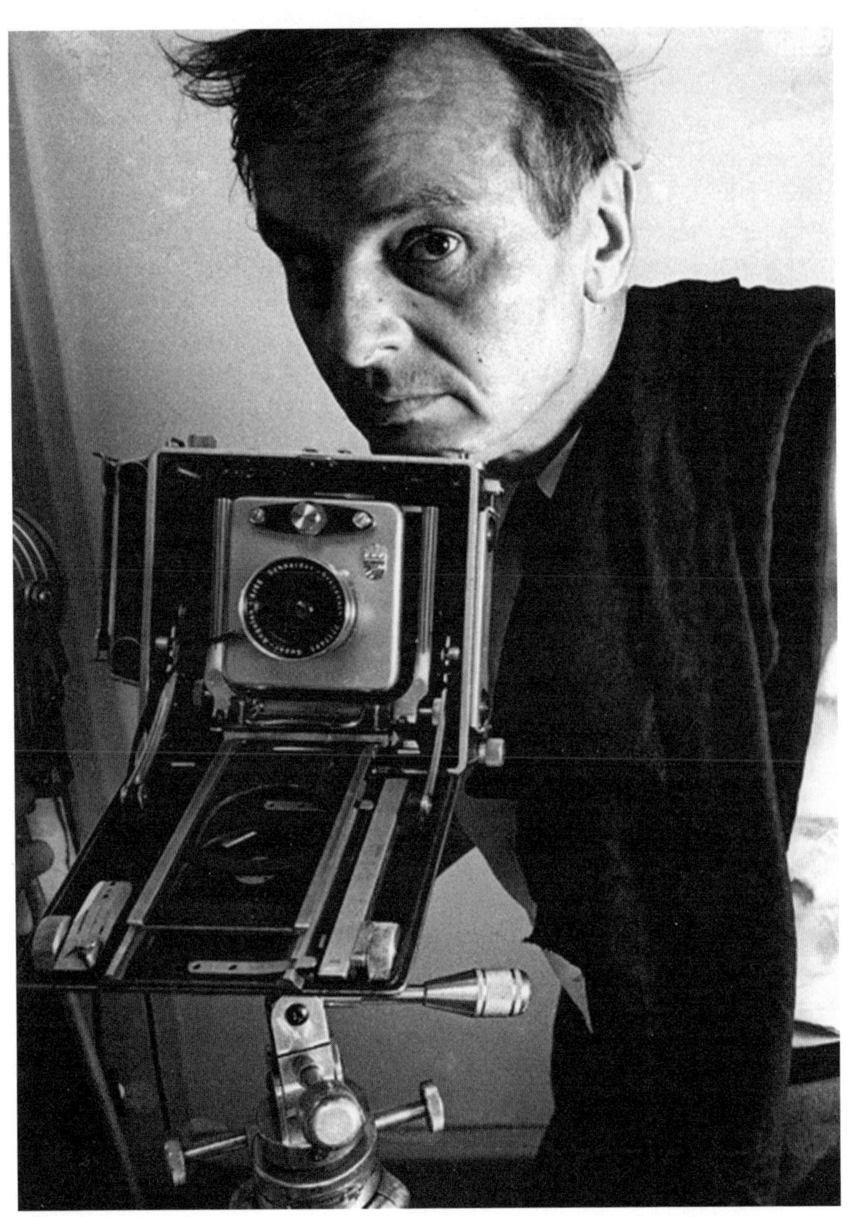

HANS NAMUTH

CHELSEA NEW YORK 1989

Anyone interested in the American Abstract Expressionists will know Hans Namuth's portraits well. In a sense he became their official photographer, and although he is best remembered (somewhat controversially) for photographing and filming Jackson Pollock at work in his studio on Long Island, Namuth took pictures not only of the other leading American artists but many younger, lesser-known ones as well.

*My first contact with Namuth came about in the early 1980s when I was writing a history of the artist's studio (*Imagination's Chamber: Artists and their Studios*) and wanted to reproduce some of his evocative images of the New York school. We saw each other regularly thereafter, and Namuth was very generous in making his work available when I relaunched* Art International *in Paris in 1987. We also worked together on a film about Balthus. Because of his commitment to the magazine and our growing friendship, it seemed natural to publish a selection of Namuth's best photographs with his own comments on them. At several points before his untimely death in a car accident, Namuth and I had discussed working together on a book devoted to his portraits of artists.*

HN I became a photographer in 1935, and soon after World War II I started taking pictures of artists. Artists have always fascinated me. I grew up with the German Expressionists. That was in Essen, and from an early age I looked at their paintings in the Folkwang Museum there. I left Germany in 1933, when I was seventeen, and went to Paris. I had been gaoled for political reasons – I was a communist – and had to get out of Germany. Otherwise I would have been destroyed. My father became a Nazi – out of disillusionment. He had been a liberal, and he

Hans Namuth (1915–1990). *Art International*, Paris, spring 1989.

had many Jewish friends. The Depression destroyed him. I was drawn towards the Nazis when I was fifteen, and I actually became a member of the Nationaler Schülerbund for three months and read *Mein Kampf*. The more I learnt about the Nazis the more horrified and disgusted I became. After Paris I got caught up in the Spanish Civil War, and later I joined the Foreign Legion. I didn't realize it when I got there in 1941, but New York was to be my home. In 1944 I returned to Germany – but then as a master sergeant in the American army …

MP How have you managed to photograph so many different artists?

HN Mostly on assignment, except right at the beginning. Back in 1949, when I was a student of Alexey Brodovitch at the New School, he brought up Pollock's name in class, and I felt that I simply had to meet the man. The following year my family and I took a summer house in the Hamptons and the opportunity cropped up. I saw Pollock at an opening at Guild Hall in East Hampton. We talked. It was somewhat comical – one shy man talking to another shy man. He said 'yes' to my request to let me come to his house during a painting session, but when I arrived he said, 'Sorry, I've just finished the painting', and that was that. He had obviously changed his mind – or perhaps Lee, his wife, had decided against it. I was absolutely crestfallen and asked if I could go inside and photograph him with the new work. He agreed reluctantly, and as he was looking at the enormous canvas at his feet he suddenly started the whole thing all over again – and he feverishly covered the original image, replacing it with a new one, while I clicked away.

MP What kind of man was he?

HN He was at his best at that time, back in 1950, after a period of almost two years on the wagon – very ascetic, lean and good looking. I instantly liked him. I met Helen Frankenthaler in 1953 at the Pollocks', and in short order thereafter Ad Reinhardt, Barnett Newman, Clyfford Still and others. I took pictures of all of them, just for my own files, so to speak, without an assignment. I still do the same today. As a rule, artists trust me. They know I will never betray their confidence.

MP How did you take de Kooning next to your picture of him as a much younger man?

HN That was set up beforehand. De Kooning loved the idea and let me do it. Then I gave him the print. Nowadays he's still painting furiously, but he's not 'there' any more. He lives in order to paint. He's a grandfather now and his daughter Lisa suggested I do all three generations. So that's my next project.

MP Do people feel intimidated at the idea of being photographed?

HN Some don't trust you. They think you may distort them.

MP What about when you go back to photograph Jasper Johns? Is he a very shy man?

HN Yes, but we had our difficulties twenty-five years ago – when the picture where he is kneeling was taken at Tanya Grosman's workshop where he made prints. Tanya taught him printmaking and gave him complete freedom. Now when I see Jasper, we're old friends. He goes about his business and he is himself, and that's the secret. He doesn't pose.

MP What about the Calder picture?

HN It's in his studio at Saché in the Loire valley in France. I visited him for four days and we became good friends. After my visit I sent him one of the pictures and he asked me to come back and take a photograph of a particular stabile, one of the first ones he ever did. So I took the photo and about six months later he called me and said, 'Hans, go to the Perls Gallery and pick any mobile of mine you want.' He had sold the stabile to the museum in Caracas. So I went to see Klaus Perls, his dealer. He had a little package there and said 'This is for you.' And I said, 'Klaus, Sandy told me I could pick anything I wanted.' Klaus was surprised and phoned Sandy, who confirmed I could have whatever I wanted. So I went downstairs where all the Calders were and picked the biggest one I could find.

MP Where was the Motherwell picture taken?

HN That was in East Hampton, in a Nissen hut built during the War. A French architect, Pierre Chareau, had transformed the hut into a marvellous studio, but it was basically a Nissen hut.

MP And the Cornell photo?

HN That was in a studio in Flushing, on Utopia Parkway. It was in what he called his 'music room'. I tried to get to him but I couldn't. He had been through a terrible experience with a *Life* magazine photographer. He never explained what happened, but he wanted to call off photography forever. He finally called me and we had a long conversation but he still didn't ask me to come. He used to call in the middle of the night and we had long conversations. He lived with his mother and his brother and, by the time I met him, both had just died and he was in a deep depression. He lived alone then. I discovered he liked the company of attractive women, so I used to try and find one to come up and see him with me. When it came to taking pictures of him, he made most of the suggestions. Artists don't need any directing. They know.

EUROPEAN ARTISTS

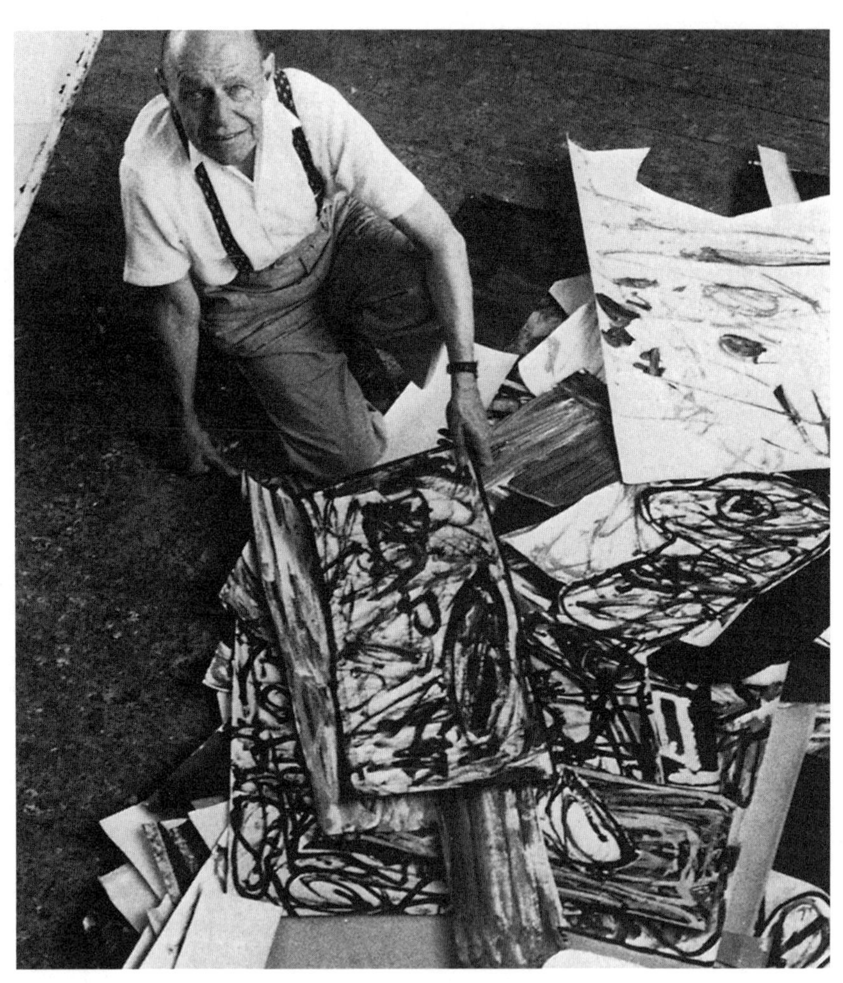

JEAN DUBUFFET

RUE DE VAUGIRARD PARIS 1977

Dubuffet was a force to be reckoned with – famous, unpredictable, controversial – so I was suitably apprehensive when I trooped over to his studio, notebook in hand, to meet him. As with several of the interviews published here, this one was brought out a few years ago as a small book by the French publisher, L'Echoppe, and to put the article into some kind of context I wrote the preface below. This was an attempt on my part to recall what it felt like to be a minor art critic visiting a major artist – which hopefully explains what now comes across, to me at least, as the preamble's rather strange, not to say strained, tone.

A conversation you had more or less forgotten comes back to you thirty years later. It took place between a much younger man and a man now dead. You realize as you read it that although it had since slipped your mind it was very important to you at the time. You were a young art critic, making your way precariously enough by writing freelance journalism from Paris. Interviewing Dubuffet was no small affair. You had already done a few things of the kind, but nevertheless this was an artist of the first importance whose work you had been following for years – and whose reputation as a formidably intelligent man who did not suffer fools gladly was very clearly etched on your mind.

So when it was time for the interview (it had been organized rather formally through a secretary), you were suitably apprehensive. How dismissive would Dubuffet be of an obscure young man who didn't know much about anything – and who, at that very moment, felt he also knew very little about Dubuffet? You had no tape-recorder with you, only a good ear and the conviction that you would get the gist

---

Jean Dubuffet (1901–1985). *Art News*, New York, May 1977.

and tone of the interview better if you wrote it down later from notes and from memory.

That Dubuffet received you so cordially came as a surprise. That he made you and your questions sound intelligent was even more unexpected; you were too naïve to realize that this was his intelligence at work, and that he was pleased, for reasons you could not have grasped, to be speaking from his relative isolation in Paris to a large American audience. It didn't matter. You were charmed and he gave you a good interview – so much so that you would have liked to have gone back and spoken to him again; he seemed so ready to talk and glad to have someone there in that austere little room. But you were too shy to ask, and once the interview was over you continued to follow his work while regretting you would never see Dubuffet himself again.

*

As recent exhibitions at Le Havre (at the Musée des Beaux-Arts André Malraux) and the Pace Gallery in New York indicate, Jean Dubuffet at seventy-five is no less prodigiously active and turned towards the future than ever. For anyone fortunate enough to be admitted into the cloistered privacy of Dubuffet's studio in Paris, this impression of vigour is amply borne out.

The studio is one of several that line a mews-like passage off the rue de Vaugirard. Dubuffet himself opened the door and ushered his visitor in with a mixture of the courteous simplicity and firmness that characterized his manner throughout the interview. What strikes one instantly about the artist is the speed with which he appears to sum up a situation. His slight, ascetic silhouette and the luminous shrewdness of his pale blue eyes suggest a total concentration on whatever happens to be the matter in hand.

The interview took place in a ground-floor room which serves Dubuffet as an office. It is sparsely furnished and very orderly. One senses that, as with the artist himself, anything that does not have a direct bearing on his work has been excluded. On the tiny courtyard at the back of the house the light was fading quite tangibly, and conversation happened easily in the office's comfortable gloom. Dubuffet stressed a point right away.

'I don't usually give interviews because I think an artist is necessarily a solitary person. After all, real artists are antisocial people – they go against received ideas and mental habits. If they invent, it's because they're not content with what's already there. And it's just that discontent – being angry and dissatisfied with what other people have made – that forms the lifeblood of creativity.

'The trouble is that nowadays, and nowhere more so than in the United States, artists have become more concerned with presenting their work than creating it. They've got two quite separate functions muddled up. Creating is antisocial, swimming against the tide of what is already accepted and admired, but the whole business of presenting one's work to the public is a highly social activity. And when you mix the two, you get something inferior, like a wine that's been cut with a bit of this and a bit of that. Some artists get so completely caught up in the business of presenting their work that they become like stars – the very opposite of inventors.

'I've set up a secretariat to deal with all the problems arising from my work once it's left the studio. In that way I'm freer to concentrate. Of course, I'm in a very curious position. When I decided to drop commerce altogether – I had a wine wholesaling business – and become a full-time artist back in 1942, I didn't want to exhibit or to sell my paintings. At that time I painted entirely for myself. And one other person. Just one. Then two or three friends became interested. It was an ideal moment, but it didn't last for long and I regret it now. You see, the success my work has had is quite contrary to the beliefs I hold. I've always thought that the most powerful and vital art – like Art Brut – is the one that society has the most trouble in accepting. Well, my success has put me in an uncomfortable position. In fact, ever since my work started to get known, I've lived in contradiction with my own beliefs.'

Dubuffet says this with the calmness of a man who has accepted his contradictions. Even so, one cannot help reflecting that a success as solid as his requires at least some active assent from its beneficiary. One is fascinated, here and at several points later, by the often warring complexities that underlie the 'spontaneous' simplicity which this artist has always so openly sought to achieve.

'What I tried to do, you know, was to make paintings that were really unsellable. Little by little they sold, even when I said to myself "Ah, now that one no one will want to buy." But someone did. In spite of all that and even though I know it doesn't correspond to reality, I go on working as if no one was interested in what I'm doing. I avoid social contacts, I don't go round the galleries or to exhibitions, not even mine. To tell the truth, I simply am not interested in what other artists are doing. It's unhealthy to keep looking at other people's work, it can interfere with your own. It's much better to stay alone, forget everything else and create one's own particular universe. The only things I have time for are completely unknown works – books that authors can't get published and paintings no one will exhibit. The things the system rejects because it can't absorb them. That's where the real innovations lie.

'I've always wanted to take the opposite course to everyone else,' Dubuffet pursues with a serene smile. 'To go against the grain, challenge mental habits and be generally subversive. That's my temperament. My work has always been better accepted in America than France, you know. Of course, Americans welcome new things more eagerly, they're much more open to innovation. They're not stifled by a sense of what's ridiculous and what isn't as we are in France. That's a terribly destructive thing here, don't you think? It means that people can never act spontaneously. So there's always been much more opposition to me in France. What support I've had here tends to come from a fairly obscure, anonymous section of the public. Paris's clan of gallery people and intellectuals are to a large extent against me, oh yes they are, I've got quite a few enemies here you know. Well, I can't say I'm sorry. I like to feel my work creates opposition. That's the way it should be.'

The evening light has faded completely now. Dubuffet gets up to turn on the switch, and the room springs back into focus, bare and white. The artist has been talking with the unhurried clarity of a man who knows exactly what he wants to say and how he wants to say it. When he finds a phrase that seems particularly apposite, he repeats it, as if to underline its importance to the interview. His fluency cannot help but recall the apparent paradox that the champion of an instinctual art unencumbered by 'knowledge' impresses by his highly disciplined and thoroughly cultivated mind.

'Obviously,' he explains, 'we are all conditioned by culture from childhood onwards. I've always hoped to de-condition myself through art, because I want above all to make myself completely free and receptive to new ideas. That's the real function of art: to change mental patterns by making new thought possible. *Only* new things are interesting. But they're difficult fish to catch. You have to take them by surprise – by luck or accident. That's why I'm always after the easiest, quickest techniques, because they enable you to catch things more quickly, before they lose their inventiveness. But it's enormously difficult to de-condition oneself completely. At times I've said to myself "Now I've really managed to get rid of accepted ideas" and then I've looked back on the work of that period later and seen that I've still not succeeded.

'When I begin on a new phase in my work, I literally feel as if I'm diving down, going underground. And after a time I need to resurface, see the sky again, as it were, and start looking round for something new. I deliberately imposed an end on my *Hourloupe* suite. I'd been doing it for twelve years, and even though there were still things I wanted to take further, I thought it was time to come up for air.

'A lot of people who'd liked my earlier work didn't like the *Hourloupe*. It's true that it was more difficult – there's a schizophrenic quality to the whole suite that makes it less easy to grasp. But, just as now, I wanted to get away from what I'd been doing before. It's curious, I've noticed two quite opposed tendencies going right through my work. I start by giving very personal – *outrageously* personal – and human interpretations of things. All my early trees and cows and people had a kind of carnival air to them. Then they slowly became more impersonal and dehumanized. And I think on one side I have this love for the sap and savour of life, with all its oddities, whereas on the other I see the world in a more oriental way, as an undifferentiated continuum, and gradually the individuation in my work fades away. I make figures, you could say, and then I 'de-figure' them.

'Other painters have been talking a great deal about 'reality' recently,' Dubuffet continues with a faintly withering smile. 'But there is no such thing. They say they paint 'reality' or, on the contrary, 'irreality', but we live in mental fictions – in the conventions that have been imposed on us. 'Reality' is basically a question of habit. Most people are afraid of breaking it because they sense they might lose contact with other people and find how alone they are.

'Since the *Hourloupe*, I've done several different series of paintings. Most recently I've been doing assemblages of quite different images put together so as to create a purposefully discordant whole. I'm calling them *Theaters of Memory*, and what I'm hoping to make is a group of images that are each in its own key. A while ago I did some experiments with a huge number of musical instruments, and I'd like to get a similar mixture of discordant elements in these new paintings. I think the result should be much closer to the way things go on inside one the whole time. I mean, when you're going down the street, for instance, and you're aware of several unconnected things going on simultaneously – the person who's coming towards you and the shop window you've just passed and what you were doing a week before. Now that I'm into this new series, with its separate keys, I must say I find any painting done in only one key flat and boring. Including my own.'

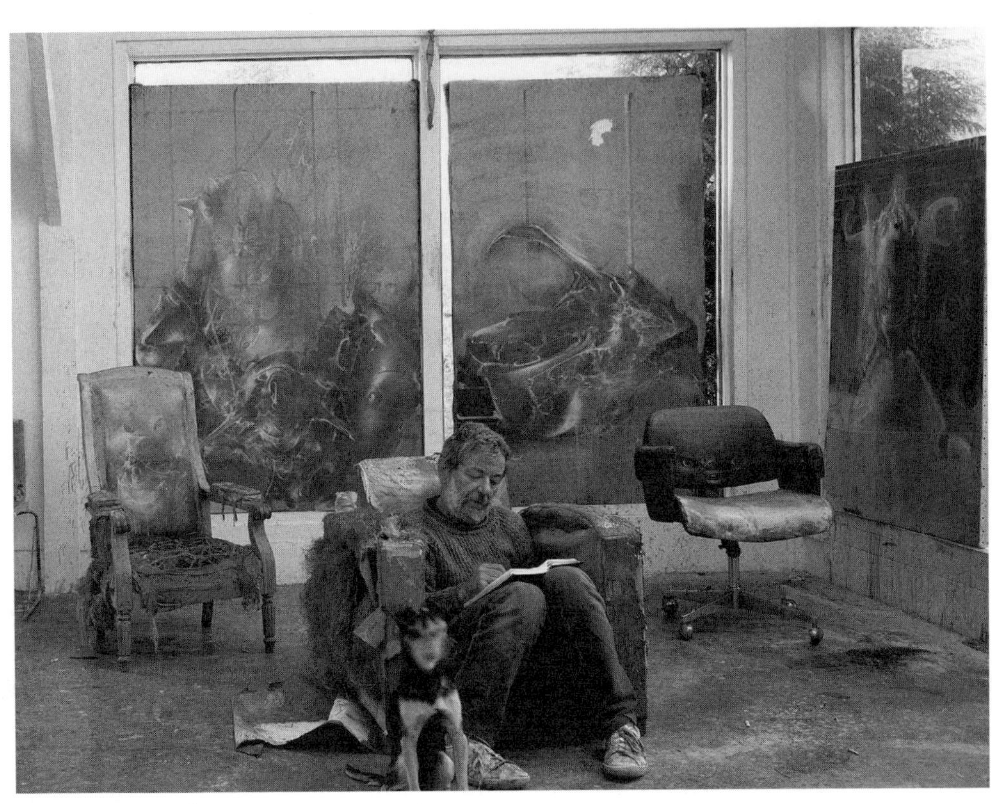

DADO

RUE DES ARCHIVES PARIS 1978

For the last couple of days I have been walking round Dado trying to come up with a verbal sketch that would show how unusual he was and how he captivated the people around him. With his unkempt beard, matted hair and crumpled old clothes, he looked more like a tramp than a successful artist who had been first discovered by Dubuffet in Paris in the late 1950s and who, by the time of his death in 2010, had been given a retrospective at the Venice Biennale and become a hero, as famous as any footballer, in his native Montenegro.

What first entranced me about Dado was his conversation, a kind of non-stop, stream-of-consciousness gabble that sounded preposterous at first, like the outpouring of a minor, demented surrealist, until I noticed how brilliantly his imagination worked, forever spotting the canker in the rose and forever pursuing the signs of decay he saw everywhere around him, and not least in himself. Dado was possessed by the vision of death and disease as the one essential reality of existence. He had first witnessed it as a child in Cetinje exposed to the horrors of war (corpses left by the roadside, bodies strung up in the trees), then found that it offered his prodigious graphic gifts an endless subject. Even as a young boy, he had impressed everyone around him with his facility as a draughtsman, making caricatures of his schoolmates for a penny a time ('you will be the Walt Disney of your generation,' his mother had prophesied).

It was Dado's extraordinary fluency in conjuring up every form of disaster and degradation that impressed Dubuffet and everybody else who saw his work. Like a man possessed by demons (which is exactly what he was), Dado could never stop. Even while he was talking or eating his hand went on drawing on whatever surface he could find – a cigarette pack, a paper napkin, a nearby wall (and no surface in or outside his ramshackle farm in Normandy had escaped his obsessive image-making). He made entire buildings – caves, deconsecrated

Dado (1933–2010). *Dado dessins*, exhibition catalogue, Galerie Isy Brachot, Paris, November 1978.

chapels – his own by covering them with frescoes of monstrous figures, mutilated bodies and severed limbs. Old cars, doors and abandoned bath tubs were similarly bedaubed with his unending nightmare of man's inhumanity to the world at large (a nightmare that became all too real again in the Yugoslavia he had left).

For all the horror he portrayed, Dado was the liveliest, funniest companion to be found, never more at ease than when trawling through the bars and cafés of Saint-Germain picking up old and new friends as he went. If the imagery was tortured and frightening, the man himself was warm, generous and always up for a laugh. Small, wiry and immensely resilient, he could fool around all night, then put in a whole day at his studio, moving from one huge canvas to another. His life was chaotic. He often slept rough, and his idea of comfort, when the winter in his unheated farmhouse became unbearable, was to take a couple of sheep in and sleep with them for warmth.

Dado drew me into his world by his talent, his sense of fun and his charm. I met him in the early 1970s and began writing about his work not long thereafter; gradually I began to appear in various grotesque guises in his pictures. He was the first artist I wrote about directly in French, perhaps because we were both seasoned foreigners in Paris and in each other's company neither of us was afraid of massacring the language to get a particular point across. In the following interview, which was translated from the original French for inclusion here, one senses how difficult it was to pin Dado down. Like many artists, he had a secret at the heart of his work that he was unwilling to discuss or disclose – for fear that, once named, it might disappear, or that it would cast too literal and banal a light on the reasons behind his manic creativity. The following exchange has something of a cat-and-mouse chase to it, with me trying to get Dado to admit the horrific nature of his imagery and he sidestepping so deftly that the cat I started out as was soon turned into a mouse.

D For the last two and a half years I've been doing drawings almost every day, especially towards evening when the light has gone or during the winter. After the heavy slog of painting big pictures in oil, these pen and ink drawings were meant to be a kind of relaxation – or at least an escape from oil painting and a way of eventually coming back to it with fresh eyes. But the thing is that it's quite as difficult to do a good drawing as a good painting, so in fact there is nothing relaxing about it ... you have to be tense, keyed up, to do anything worthwhile. I've noticed there's a distinct complicity between my paintings and my drawings. They follow a different rhythm, but they turn out to be equally demanding and difficult. Sometimes, when a drawing gets too rounded and liquid, I can feel it's going over into painting. So I break off when that happens and start all over again.

MP And are you chasing the same themes in drawing as in painting?

D I'm not chasing the themes, the themes are chasing me!

MP Whatever ...

D What I love about drawing, you see, is its austere side. It's terribly austere and unappealing and as hard as a block of salt. The actual process of drawing with a pen is, let's say, about sixty times more difficult than pencil drawing. A pen is always putting on the brakes, and you almost have to gouge the paper, as though you're doing a tattoo – because the paper itself has the vulnerability of skin. Every time I get into it, I want the sheet of paper to absorb a kind of rain of venom and yet be beautiful.

MP Do you elide or draw over images as you do when you paint?

D No. That's what's so unforgiving about pen and ink drawing. Everything leaves its mark, everything is recorded. It's like an electrocardiogram. And what excites me most, of course, is when the images take on shapes and forms I could never have imagined.

MP Is there any kind of image in your mind as you start drawing?

D No. None whatsoever. I'm quite incapable of imagining or 'feeling' a drawing in advance. I wouldn't even know what it would be like to think in those terms. When I'm working, I'm looking for a way out of life – of plunging into a different sphere. And whenever I manage to achieve something, on the rare occasions I do, it comes about suddenly, like an accident, like a brick falling – *bam!* – on your head.

MP Is art a means of escape for you?

D It seems to me that all art, not just mine, is bound to be the search for another life. It is a means of escape, if you like, but what's more important and what's really interesting in art is that it leads to self-betrayal. You might try to give yourself the slip, you might try to avoid saying the things that really get to you, but they always come through.

MP Art always ends up telling the truth …

D Exactly. It's like being in a kind of delirium. Or a confession. And since I don't see myself engaging with the priests, the analysts and all those other little assholes … For me, the work I do is parallel to reality. I think of it as another reality – that's a very pretentious thing to say, I know. It's not the reality we live in, it's not even my own reality, since the reality of my work becomes greater than my reality, which is miserable, like everyone else's. Having said that, I don't think that the drama I experience with my work is in any way more interesting than the drama of someone who finds it difficult to walk.

MP Why is this 'parallel reality' filled with decaying corpses?

D Decaying corpses? People often talk about decay in my work, but I don't think that's what it is really about. That's just the obvious, superficial side. What really fascinates me is the extraordinary, unfathomable complexity of a human body. When you look at a face or a body, you only see the epidermis, although you see everything, even if you can't see it or touch it. I can easily imagine someone in love wanting to touch the nerves and the inner organs of the loved one. I see the human body as a whole, unique world – a complete universe.

MP But all the strange creatures in your work – where do they come from?

D I don't really know.

MP You don't know, or you don't want to say?

D I can't ...

MP Are you superstitious, in the sense that you once told me that if you talked about these things they might disappear?

D Let's say it's not my paintings or my drawings that frighten me but the void they come from. I don't know what that void is. I deliberately don't know what it is because I don't want to know. In any case the void is all around us. Every creature, every object is floating in the void.

MP Do you avoid analysing those kinds of things?

D I loathe analysis. It always leads to some fancy theorizing or other that's fashionable for five minutes. Analysis seems absurd, inconceivable, to me. I only know the few things I know when I bump into them.

MP There are so many body parts, so much rotting flesh in your work that the interest cannot be simply anatomical. Are you obsessed with death?

D Yes. I think the whole horror comes from the fact that there's life and death, good and evil. All the fuck-ups come from that. I think right at the source there's a universal and ineradicable stupidity, even if there are a few prodigiously intelligent people from time to time ...

MP But are you particularly aware of death? Looking at your pictures makes people feel ill at ease. They often feel a shock, not to say a feeling of repulsion.

D Repulsion? Great. I'm having a good one this morning.

MP You know it yourself.

D I don't. Not really. How should I know what people feel in front of my work? But you know what? As time goes by I wonder if physical mutilations are really worse than more subtle wounds like humiliation. Physical wounds are simply more spectacular. I pour everything into my drawings, unrestrainedly, and that allows me to discover all kinds of things.

MP Yet you are open above all to vulnerability and destruction.

D That's all I am: vulnerability and destruction. It would be stupid to try and hide it. Artists are like their work.

MP Do the people you create sometimes grow out of other images, such as photos, or people that you've noticed somewhere, like all those bald-headed men we saw the other evening when we were at the Coupole?

D No. I don't know if it's comic or tragic, but when I've done a drawing the person I've brought to life will then walk past the window.

MP So it's life imitating art.

D Exactly. If I've done a good drawing, everything starts to pose for me.

*

MP At the outset, I think you began by doing portraits.

D Yes. When I was growing up in Montenegro, I did drawings of my father and my friends, and told them to pull faces. That's how I got into this whole thing of distorted faces. Even then I was into weird stuff. Then, early on, when I was about seventeen or eighteen, I started doing things that had nothing to do with conventional appearances. That got me into quite a bit of trouble at the art school I was going to.

MP It was already a fantasy world.

D Yes. You might call it the beginning of a bad dream. A bad dream that continues thirty years later.

MP How was it connected to your life?

D Let's say my work is a bad dream and my life is another bad dream. And that every now and then a few things, a few luminous moments, emerge from this confusion. But I've never really been able to differentiate dream from reality. That's one reason why I go on painting desperately. Why is dreaming not a reality, and when the cops come and take you away it is a reality?

MP How would you say your drawing has developed?

D It's a kind of writing that has been freed and become more probing. That's what I'd say if I were playing at being an art critic. But it's the same problem of being alive – '*la difficulté d'être*' – that's in play. It might sound a bit grandiose, but there's clearly something that's not quite right with me.

MP And you accept that?

D If I negate that, I negate everything in one go. You can't change your life, whatever current fashionable theory tells you to the contrary.

MP Is there a theme running through the drawings? I get the feeling that some of them have prompted others.

D That's true. Everything is connected. There's just one drawing that is never finished and which stretches to the horizon. That's what keeps me going, do you see? But there's no real theme.

MP Perhaps you're more interested in compositional space and formal relationships – to the exclusion of everything else, perhaps?

D Well, of course. There's no point even asking the question. When I'm thinking in terms of pure plasticity, I know I'm on the right track and I'm not simply copying things I've seen in 'Paris Match' or some bald head from La Coupole. OK?

MP When do you feel that you should stop working on a drawing?

D When I need the fucking money! All right, I never feel I've finished whatever I'm working on. But there's always something that crops up which makes me turn them to the wall and start on something else . . . In the end I think what you called my 'fantasy' is a kind of reality. I think my drawings contain what Victor Brauner called 'premonitory signs' – hints of what is to come.

MP As we get older?

D Since things tend to get worse in time – all right, we won't start a litany of despair, but people say things get better with time and that's totally untrue. It's to comfort children, and by the time you're eight years old you know time isn't going to make anything better. On the contrary, time gobbles and destroys everything!

MP And that is what comes through in your work.

D Sure. My work is a kind of private diary, a travel journal of someone who stays put. It's hopefully not too boring, it's what's called 'art', I think. That's to say: having to talk about things without knowing why. And the only way that can be good, I think, is if it's difficult. I can produce all kinds of images very easily, but they would be worthless. It would be like ready-to-wear clothes. Your drawing or your picture has to come about like some disease erupting, out of your control. That's how it is.

That's why I can't analyse it and you can't subject it to some set of aesthetic or philosophical rules. Or whatever. You can only give into it – if you want to!

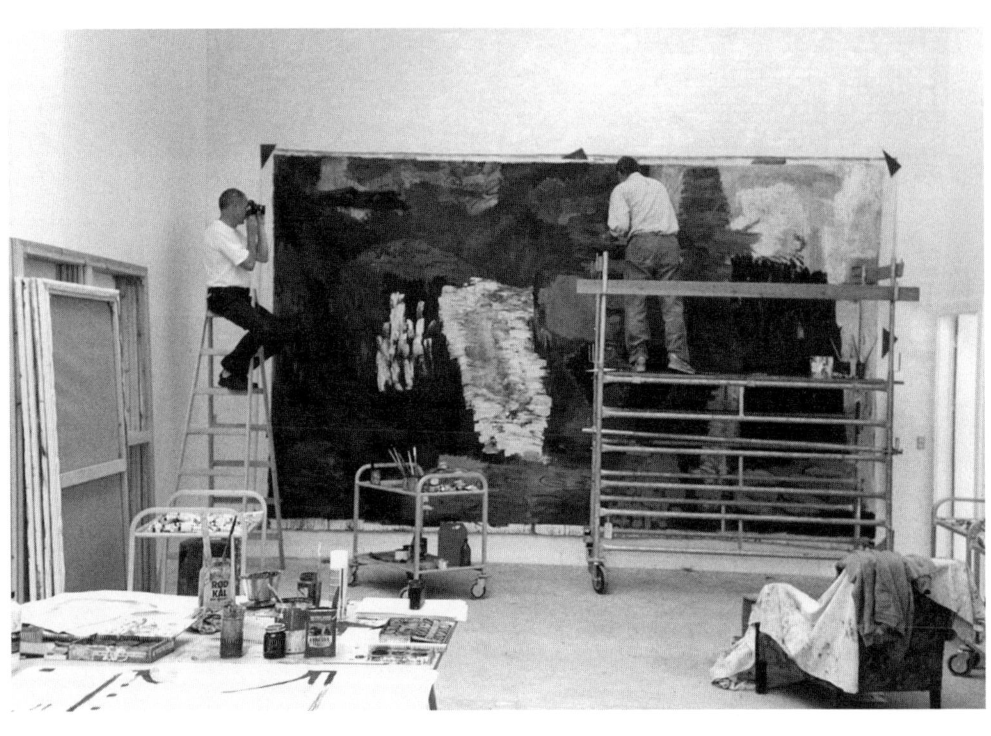

PER KIRKEBY

COPENHAGEN 1991

As running an independent art magazine like Art International *became increasingly hazardous, I looked for ways of increasing its income without making overt concessions to the commercial galleries. One traditional route lay in print publishing. It had proved a mainstay for many of the magazines I admired most, such as Albert Skira's* Minotaure *and Christian Zervos's* Cahiers d'art. *We were lucky in finding support for this venture from Francis Bacon, Antoni Tàpies and Per Kirkeby. As part of the issue in which our edition of an engraving by Kirkeby was made available to the readers of the magazine, we included an interview with the artist which took place in his studio in Copenhagen.*

MP You approach life in a very open spirit. It's unusual today to find an artist with such a wide range of activities, not just as a painter and sculptor but as a film maker, a poet, a writer on art…

PK I like to have an entertaining life, so I don't want to get caught up in useless repetition. Most of all, though, it has to do with being born and raised in Denmark. You can see the same range and restlessness in an artist like Asger Jorn. In the 1960s, Copenhagen became one of the centres of the Fluxus movement and this was where I began. Because we were a small group, everybody tried everything out. In those days an artist was nothing special – music was more important and everyone carried around a guitar, whether they could play it or not. Now it's better to go to the hip places with some paint splashed on your trousers.

Per Kirkeby (1938–). *Art International*, Paris, Spring/Summer 1991.

MP There seems to be a dialogue between order and chaos in your paintings.

PK That's probably what it's all about – both on a private, immediate level and in a broader art historical sense. My first big push into Modernism coincided with seeing Jackson Pollock's all-over paintings. I remember being very moved when I saw his handprint in the corner of one of his huge canvases – like that of a man who has been thrown into the cosmos and who makes his mark to ensure he is still there. When I was young, Minimal art was the hot issue, and this was also an attempt to bring order into chaos. By making art into nothing more than an object, the Americans tried to eliminate the chaos that was connected to the process of trying to handle spatial problems on canvas. Donald Judd was like an art policeman – it was almost as if you weren't allowed to do a painting. I had a very naïve and direct way of coping with this because I couldn't stop myself painting. I worked on squares of hardboard, which I always exhibited in a row, like a series of Minimalist objects. Then I could have all the fun I liked, and I could be absolutely chaotic because I had a framework which controlled the chaos. It's been like that ever since, in a way. There are periods when my painting is very open and a lot of people have trouble in defining what's there. Then I have periods – often of stress – when I force my paintings to be more explicit.

MP Are you ordering a chaotic vision when you paint?

PK I take a long time to paint. When I begin a painting I always have a very clear idea of how it should be. I come home after periods of travelling with my sketchbooks, and immediately it seems as if ten paintings have been dammed up, waiting to be done. I have a clear image, but then I realize, in the process of painting, that my idea was worth nothing, apparently. So I keep on working, trying out different solutions, knowing all the time that it's not really going to help. Then one day things start to fit, and even though I know it will still take a long time, I begin to feel less worried. I eliminate my alternatives and finally, when I look at the painting, I say 'That's what I had in mind all along'. I had the wrong image for what I wanted and the search for the right image is a chaotic process, but there is always some kind of resolution in the end.

By this time the colours are all mixed up and strange and sometimes very brutal – sharp yellows and acid greens. But they are still beautiful. I'm so bored of hearing that I'm a romantic landscape painter, because I don't see it that way at all. I'm doing what I call a pornographic landscape, and this is the only way you can make landscape paintings nowadays. I like to draw from nature for my own pleasure and as a form of discipline. But for the paintings I steal things from everywhere – trees from Dick Tracy comic books, for example – using all sorts of unfair tricks, breaking all the rules. I don't like to be too obvious about this and I try to bring the paintings to a point where all the pieces of the puzzle fit. But it is a puzzle made up of very strange components.

MP What does the image you say you start with consist of?

PK It's always something very banal: something I see and the emotions it provokes. The sunset, let's say, on the evening when your first wife kicked you out. That's a different kind of sunset and the colours are not orange and green but very special colours with no names. When I'm trying to find an exact nuance of colour, it's always connected to an emotion or psychological state.

MP Do you come back to specific landscapes that have meant a lot to you, in Denmark, for example?

PK Not at all. They are not landscapes in that sense. I think I'm marked by a certain light that is Danish or Nordic. You can't escape this, it's like the nose you happen to have on your face. You know we have an inferiority complex here in Scandinavia and we try to compensate by talking about Nordic landscapes and Nordic light. People in other countries love to make exhibitions about all this. I think it's very silly – every place has its own light. Most of my ideas come from just looking out of the window but, like most people I guess, I have memories of strange moments. Sitting in a train at a certain time of day in Germany, for example – there are a handful of these things.

MP You mean moments when some kind of truth dawns ... what James Joyce called epiphanies?

PK I don't know about truth, but they are moments when you are particularly open and sensitive. I don't try to illustrate these things. I'm a professional painter and I work every day – sometimes, in the process, these memories come to mind. I'm aiming for a landscape like those Turner or Delacroix painted. Both are artists who were always on the brink of doing something unacceptable and even today you feel uneasy in front of their paintings. In Delacroix's wall painting of *Jacob Wrestling with the Angel* at Saint-Sulpice in Paris, for example, the main figure is the big tree in the middle, and the caravan of people apparently moving into the distance are really running rings around that tree. I think it's very important to use trivial elements in art. All good painting is more kitschy than tasteful.

Landscapes are about beauty and death. The only way you can define beauty – in a tree, for instance – is to know that death is hiding behind it. This is what haunts you when you're doing a so-called landscape painting.

MP Is this because human life is transient and the landscape continues?

PK You know, I worked as a geologist in the northernmost part of Greenland, where the country's extremely rough – also very beautiful and deserted. You're about as alone as you can be on this earth up there – with no company but the moon. You feel that you can somehow be swallowed up or disappear in the landscape. I've always been very fascinated by the polar expeditions. It always seemed as if the British Navy sent all those explorers simply in order for them to disappear – they were surely never meant to come back.

I tried to get money for a time to make a big movie in which the main characters were to become smaller and smaller. In the end you'd just see them as small spots moving around the landscape and finally they'd disappear in the grain of the film. But nobody thought it was a good idea to make a film in which the stars disappeared.

MP Do you think that there is a strong element of charade in life itself? The way we strut around in the face of death does have something deeply comic about it.

PK If you listen to people who are up against the wall, dying of cancer or AIDS, they repeat a lot of clichés about the value of life and living for the moment. But all this kitsch is also true and authentic. When it comes to the big questions of life we have nothing to offer but kitsch, and a painting that doesn't take this into account isn't very interesting – it's just a nice, tasteful decoration. There should always be some very strong weak spots in a good painting. Turner is very good at this.

MP But both Turner and Delacroix are Romantic painters.

PK I'd call them pornographic. They are tougher than the rest of the bunch because they go beyond the boundaries of good taste. That's what makes some of their paintings so painful. Take Delacroix's paintings of scenes from *Ivanhoe*, for example. Can grown-ups take this seriously? No – but I can. I like their strange quality. Delacroix took a lot from English painting – from Turner and Constable – but he turned what they did into a strange kind of classicism that isn't classicism at all.

MP Perhaps there is a crossover between romanticism and classicism in your work, too. Your brick sculptures in particular display a sense of order and harmony.

PK Are they really so orderly? After all, they are buildings with no function and the proportions and disposition of light are not so orderly, although I use classical means. I think my brick sculptures are very explicit demonstrations of the structures in my paintings. If you look at the real classicists, like Antonio Canova and the Danish sculptor Berthel Thorvaldsen, they are much more problematic than people usually think – their proportions are all wrong, they make one arm longer than the other, for example. For a few years at the turn of the eighteenth century something really interesting was going on, and you see this again in the 1760s in the architecture of Boullée and Ledoux. I see classicism as a big traffic accident with a lot of people lying around injured.

This continues up until Rodin, whose most moving works have only one arm, maybe one leg. Then there are Giacometti's tiny sculptures. Every time he tried to make a big representational figure it turned out to be just a leg. He had all this trouble because he realized that questions of proportion are not simply an aesthetic issue. In my brick sculptures I always make sure that the entrances are never too high, maybe they are even a little too low ... That way you have to stoop slightly and measure yourself against the sculpture.

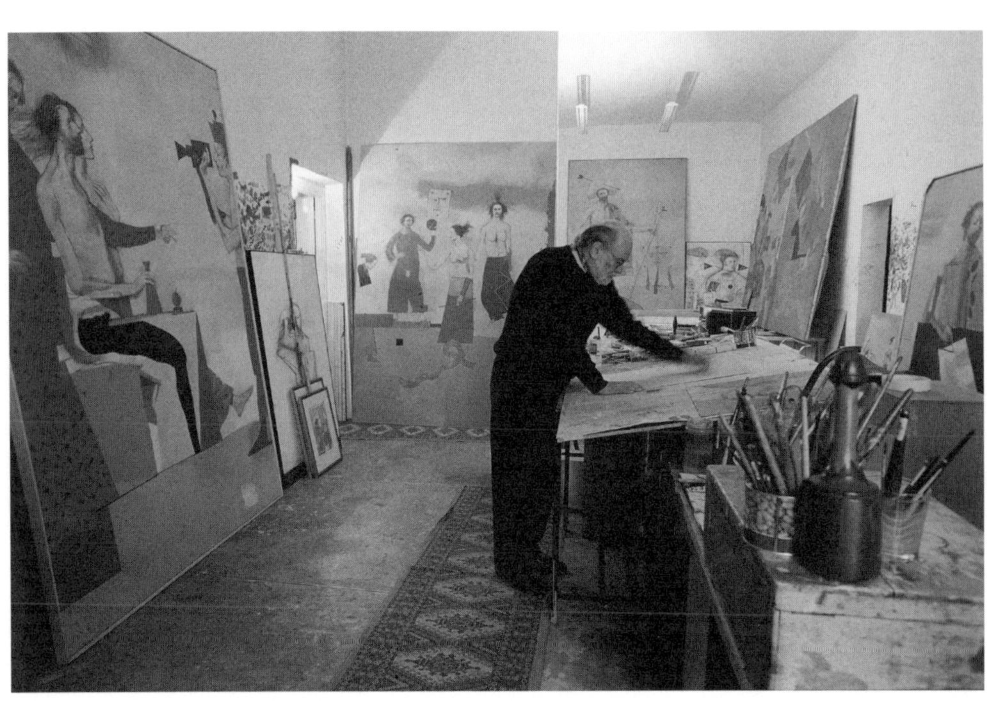

MIGUEL CONDÉ

RUE DES ARCHIVES PARIS 1992

Miguel Condé talks almost too well, both about anything and anybody, and also about his own work. There is a mellifluousness, an aptness of phrasing and ease of verbal jousting, that outwits the interviewer from the start. As with many artists that I have met, Condé appears to welcome interviews but reveals himself as past master of evading the dull, plodding questions that seek to go to the heart of his art. The heart of his art is just what Miguel, and most other dedicated painters, refuse to reveal. The interviewer blunders forward, intent on pinning down source and influence, practice and technique, and Miguel gracefully sidesteps, like a experienced matador. In this he lays bare the futility of much talk about art – and the even greater futility, perhaps, of the art interview. For what artist really seeks to disclose the real secrets of his studio, or take the outside word into what Cézanne called his 'petite sensation'. Preserving his 'petite sensation' is what keeps Condé at his easel, producing one enigmatic scene (in which we nevertheless see ourselves impishly reflected) after another without betraying the inner drama that impels them on.

MC I'm not sure that I am the best person to put my painting into words. It's the same old song, the painting is really what it's all about. I guess it's what I'm all about. Although one of the things that does come up often about me is that I'm a Mexican who grew up partly in the States.

MP What do you feel – half and half?

MC I have no idea. I'm just a salad of comings and goings, things I've seen and places I've been. I lived my early years in Mexico. But even then, at the very beginning, we travelled constantly. My father was a painter, and I grew up in the ambience of

Miguel Condé (1939–). *Miguel Condé*, exhibition catalogue, Galerias Ignacio de Lasaletta, Barcelona, November 1992.

his studio. In today's jargon, you'd say I had an unstructured home life. That's the best way of putting it. So I grew up in that atmosphere, and we moved back and forth between Mexico and the States from the very beginning.

MP And of course all of this goes into the comings and goings in your paintings. People seem to be in a kind of a procession, almost a flight from Egypt.

MC Well, yes. There is a process. A processional mood. There's another thing that's a constant – a kind of dialogue. People talking to each other, looking at each other.

MP There's a lot of quizzing, and what looks like charade playing with people in disguise.

MC Yes. I like ceremony. I like circumstance. I like the word 'circumstance'. When people try to pin me down, that's one of the key words I use. I say I like circumstance. I don't bother to explain it. Don't ask me to explain it. You know what I mean.

MP I actually don't.

MC Well, I like artifice. I'm not a realist. I like theatricality, and I rely on it for effect. I have no qualms about deliberately creating effect in my work and using it to cause a reaction, as Caravaggio does. When I was growing up, Caravaggio represented what I thought would be marvellous about European painting. When I finally got to Europe, I discovered I was right. I am crazy about Caravaggio.

MP What are the things that really preoccupy you, that you paint about, that come through?

MC Except for a brief period, I've always painted the figure, always dealt with people. It probably sounds presumptuous to say that I'm interested in the *condition humaine* because it's such a vast phrase. But I think that's really it. Now I can hardly conceive of myself painting something abstract.

MP What do you mean when you say the *condition humaine*? What it is like 'to be a human being'?

MC Yes. Sometimes there must be a confusion between what it's like and what it looks like to be a human being. I think there are painters who painted people, painted figures, painted portraits without somehow going beyond, looking at the *condition humaine*.

MP The overall atmosphere in your work, I would say, is one of people who have fallen from some greater station in life. They often look disinherited, as if they've been expulsed from better circumstances.

MC Well, I hadn't thought of that, but it's true. One of my personages is the wanderer – someone who doesn't have a home.

MP Is that what you yourself feel like?

MC Oh yes. I feel at home in many places, but I don't have the ultimate *foyer*. I guess that would be my father's pueblo in Mexico, if I went back. But I have never tried. I'm not attracted to going back. So I guess I am a wanderer.

MP You mentioned the word 'theatricality'. Is there a cast of characters in your painting?

MC Yes, there is the wanderer. There's an Icarus figure. Yes, yes. I do have figures who go in and out of my paintings and etchings. I think a lot of my *dramatis personae* are just borrowed from paintings – or stolen from them.

MP Is your painting about painting? I know you are a painter who has looked a great deal, read a great deal and thought a great deal.

MC I'm an observer. I've always been observant. It's one of my pastimes. I used to read a lot about painting. I used to look at painting. But I haven't for a long time. I didn't want to become too knowledgeable, quite frankly. I didn't want art 'historicism' to become part of my makeup. At some point a number of years ago, I thought to myself, 'Well, I've read enough about painting really.' That doesn't mean I stopped looking at painting, but I virtually stopped reading about it.

MP Would you say that one could trace things in your paintings more clearly to art than to your biography?

MC Probably. There's a vicariousness about the whole act of painting for me, living in my pictures or through my pictures. Because I have been drawing as long as I can remember. As a child I always drew.

MP And you always knew you wanted to be a painter?

MC Well, it was confirmed for me when I was nineteen because I was a dreadful student, and I was thrown out of school so many times that I rented an atelier and started painting. Not very seriously at first, but that's what I did and that's all I've done since.

MP When you say you live vicariously, you mean you create situations in which you yourself are represented?

MC I don't always see what I do clearly. But I've been told I myself am in a lot of my paintings. They're not conscious self-portraits, but people will say 'Oh this show is full of you. It's full of self-portraits. They're everywhere.' I don't see that or do it consciously, but it must be so because people see my work probably more clearly than I do. I think that vicariousness is part of art.

MP It's another way of living.

MC It is in a way.

MP What would you say that you live through, vicariously, when you do them?

MC When I do them? Even though I don't work in a very physical way – I don't splash or trowel things – it's a very physical thing for me. I feel tired when I'm through with a large canvas or a drawing which is *chargé*. I don't think when I work. It's a physical sort of thing that takes over, and I'm completely absorbed in it.

MP Does one painting trigger off another?

MC I think there are cycles. I wouldn't say that all my work is cyclic. But there are cycles, and sometimes, I only become aware of them from a distance, the distance of time and physical distance. That's one reason I like to see my own exhibitions.

MP To go back to the history of art, can you pick out the artists who are evoked most clearly? Would it be Caravaggio?

MC He's always there. There's always an Italianate, Baroque thing – a sort of opera with big spaces that have since become historical. Yes, very much Caravaggio. And on the other hand, I see Vuillard – the dense little bourgeois apartments, the patterns on the wall, the patterns on the lampshades, the curtains, the flock, the wallpaper. I know it's in there somewhere.

MP Your spaces don't actually look like interiors at all. They look like exteriors, even though they're lit in a strange way.

MC I think to come right down to it, space is the least important thing. It's the personages, the way they're dressed up.

MP What is the dress-up?

MC The dress-up is fantasy. *Un Ballo in Maschera*.

MP People carrying on about themselves with their own sort of pretensions and fantasies about themselves, their vanity. It seems to me as though sometimes you are satirizing.

MC I love satire. I'd love to think I'm capable of it. I don't like the feeling of too much finesse. We need satire. It's a vehicle for truth.

MP Would you say there is an element of satire?

MC Yes.

MP Your characters look a little out of kilter, and they seem to be playing games either among themselves or with the spectator, and doing something with a sort of sly expression. What is going on? Are they cheating at cards?

MC Well, sometimes. Sometimes they're doing very specific things. Yes, sometimes it is specific and anecdotal. There are the card players, the tumblers, the jugglers that are very specific. But sometimes there are people or personages who really aren't doing very much of anything – they're just there. I have to mention that among the painters and sculptors whom I love, that I respond to, who work in a way that is very difficult to describe, is Giacometti. His personages are there but they're disappearing before your eyes in a way.

MP What about this feeling that I got from your figures that they are kind of disinherited? The wandering I can see. But what about the raggedness? There's a sort of disjointedness. The limbs that don't quite fit. They're people who are literally out of joint.

MC I think there is a tradition of beggars and misfits in Spanish painting that I became aware of in Mexico through museums and books. Also, when I was a kid growing up in Mexico, it was a culture with very poor people and beggars. I used to buy Chiclets from a lady who was obviously a leper. She had a black veil hanging over her face, but you could see that part of it was gone. I think we all are, and I know I am, a filter for experiences. I don't mind that allusion at all because I think it is absolutely true.

MP But when you actually paint, there are technical problems that you're trying to solve – how to compose and so on?

MC Yes.

MP You don't think of the actual story?

MC No, I don't, and the story changes a lot too during the life of the canvas. I have lots of canvases that have six or eight layers on them. It's just a composite of things. The paint also takes you places. Just the stroke takes you somewhere. If it doesn't quite work, you change it. You alter it. The face changes. The personage changes. The body changes. There's not that much control. At least not for me. I never pretend to be in control of my painting.

MP One of the principal things that I wanted to suggest was that while these people seem out of joint with their times, you might feel out of joint with your times in the sense that you're interested in a tradition that has dwindled dramatically. You mentioned Giacometti, and I think perhaps there might be only a handful of people in this century who have been obsessed with the human figure. And I don't know if to any extent you would relate to them as being driven out of a tradition, being disinherited from a tradition?

MC There are times when, as a figurative painter, I am told I'm in the wilderness, although I don't feel as though I am. I don't feel like a pioneer or a campaigner. Bacon is obviously one of the great painters of our times, and he's always been anchored to the figure, what happens to it, what it does to itself.

MP I also feel there's a lot of melancholy floating through. These are people that seem to exude a kind of sadness. Nostalgia. Melancholy.

MC Nostalgia. Yes. Yes.

MP For what?

MC Perhaps other times. Perhaps other times.

MP The times celebrated in great paintings of the past?

MC Could be. I think the modern condition of mankind is often so dangerous. It could just be a nostalgia for quieter times, more private times. It's hard to put a label on it. No. No. The words don't come to me. I feel often out of place. But I don't feel uncomfortably out of place.

MP These people seem out of place. It's as if they are disguising themselves for some motive that one can't really grasp.

MC Some of them could be thinkers. If you think enough about anything you are bound to become depressed, if you really go into what happens to you and what happens around you. I've never believed in perfection. I'm not religious. I think it's really probably all chaos. And you seize something in the chaos for a while and you paint it or think about it or ignore it or somehow survive the nine-to-five job in some dreary profession. I think in a way, whoever my people are, they're composites of people, features, characteristics. And also composites of time and costume. Sometimes there is a sort of blending of whatever – a lapel and a hat that are obviously of a different time.

MP Do they amuse you when they appear?

MC Yes.

MP Do they actually make you laugh?

MC Sometimes, yes. I love painting them. I do it because I actually love to do it.

MP When you work up to a new painting, do you draw first, some sort of basic image?

MC I don't do studies. I don't do any kind of preparatory drawings. By now, I've been painting for thirty years. I just go to my atelier, to my studio, and something usually happens. And if I have a very dry, dreary period, I stretch some canvases.

MP You mean you start in the middle and go?

MC Usually more or less in the middle. Sometimes I just stumble around. I love the smell of oil paint, it gets me started. I always paint with oils. I always have. Sometimes I use acrylic gouache for my mixed media on paper, otherwise I work with oils. I love the stickiness, the smell of them.

MP Are the drawings and the paintings done quite separately?

MC I actually do have two separate studios. I don't know why. I think it's just a matter of comfort because my big studio is unheated. So when it's cold and dreary, I tend to draw at home. It's as simple as that. And when the weather warms up, I paint in the big atelier.

MP So drawing is more of a winter activity?

MC It's a little more *intimiste*, and I can roll out of bed, get some coffee and start drawing without going out into the cold. Perhaps if I had a different house, I'd do everything at home. I don't know. It just developed that way. Sometimes the cycles will run parallel. And I also do a lot of printmaking. So sometimes it will run along three tracks.

MP But painting is the main thing?

MC I think of myself as a painter. I think of myself as a painter who prints, and I think of myself as a painter who draws. I hate being called a printmaker in that it has very guild-like craft connotations, like potters and tapestry makers. I have nothing against that, but it's simply not my case.

MP To go back to the painting, what about all the little symbols, the hieroglyphic markings that are stamped sometimes on the hats and things like that?

MC I think that sometimes I simply do them. I think symbols or motifs are sometimes very carefully thought out and very specific and meant to be. But in my case, I don't think they are really. These things just float around. And sometimes I'll see a painting that is more or less finished, and feel it needs a red circle somewhere, so I just put it in. It doesn't mean anything. It's pictorially gratifying. After all, I am the painter.

MP You can do what you like.

MC Of course. Sometimes people feel abused if it becomes that simple. But why not?

MP One thing that I would like to talk to you a little more about is the chaos. That seems to get down to the bedrock. These are paintings about snatches, if you can call them that, snatches of 'significance' in the chaos, or perhaps a reflection of the chaos. A tumble of images of people going through their daily round. Their purposelessness, their futility. There's also in my mind a sense that the characters are well aware of being without great point.

MC That's a good way of putting it. Personally, at least so far, I'm not afraid of chaos. And I don't think I will become so, perhaps because of my being a painter. Painting is a way of dealing with chaos.

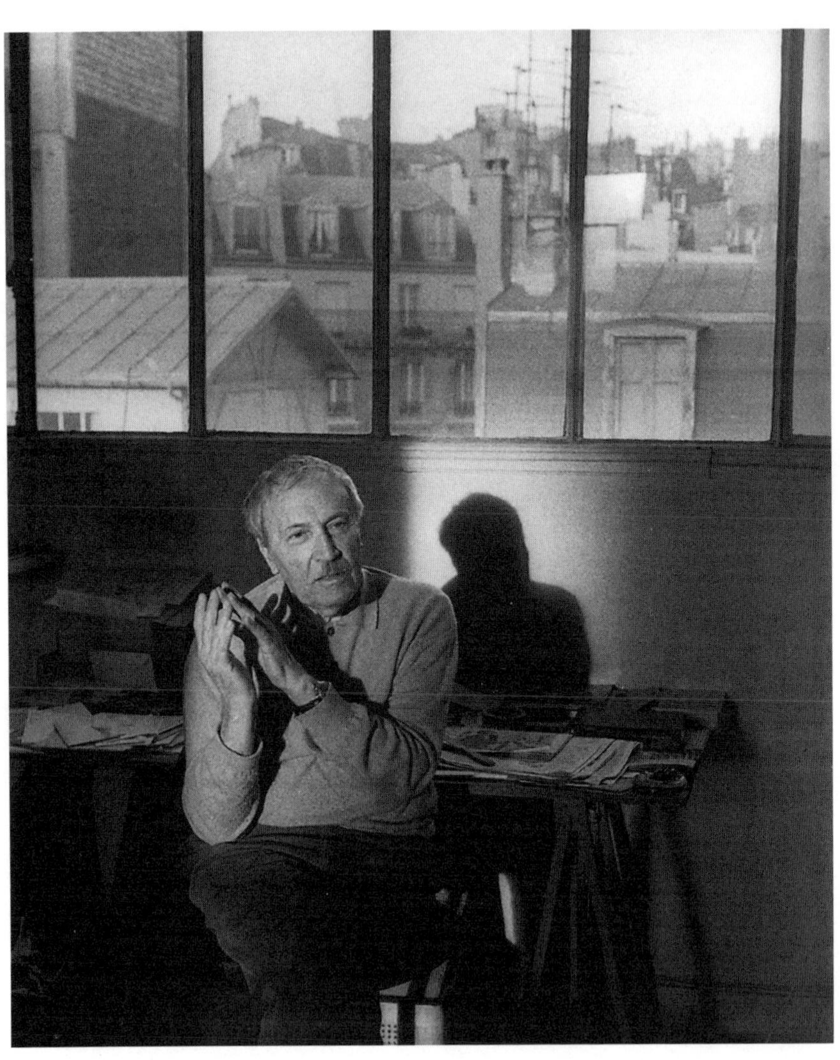

ZORAN MUSIC

RUE DES VIGNES PARIS 1987

For an artist who is not particularly well known in the English-speaking world, Zoran Music no doubt appears to occupy a disproportionately large place in this book. Apart from the fact that I admired and liked Music unreservedly, both as a man and as a painter, the decision to include three interviews with him was taken because they hold together as a single entity and cast light on an artist whose life and work are so revealing of the past century's darkest moments that it seems almost a duty to bring them to a wider audience.

In other parts of the globe, and notably in most European countries, Music is in fact very well known. Numerous museum retrospectives of his work have been organized in Italy, Germany and France (notably at the Grand Palais in Paris in 1995), and whole shelves of books and catalogues attest to the importance many leading art-world writers and intellectuals, from Jean Clair to Peter Handke and Jorge Semprun, have given to his achievement.

In a word, alongside his lyrical evocations of Venice and the Dalmatian landscape, Music is the great poet of the concentration camps ('l'ange à Dachau', as Jean Clair called him). He glimpsed a tragic beauty in the piles of cadavers he saw daily during his long incarceration in Dachau, sketched them in secret (in itself a capital offence) and much later found himself impelled to recall them in a series of unforgettable images entitled We Are Not the Last.

I was lucky enough to become a close friend, seeing him frequently from the late 1970s on, either alone or with his wife, Ida Barbarigo, in Paris and Venice, and also travelling with him for the openings of his shows elsewhere in Italy, Germany and, most memorably, in the far north at Stavanger in Norway. For all the terrible experiences he had been through, or possibly because of them, Music radiated a kind of magnetic calm I have never encountered elsewhere. Simply spending time with him always helped me get the various crises and disorders

Zoran Music (1909–2005). *Art International*, Paris, Spring 1988.

of my life into perspective. Since his death (at the age of ninety-six), I have found the same quality in his pictures, where all the superfluities of existence appear to have been removed and a serene, but by no means necessarily optimistic, light shines through the sparsely applied colour.

A tall, gaunt, silent figure sits opposite you in visible discomfort. You have asked several simple questions. What prompts him to start exploring a new theme in his work? Does he always begin by making drawings? How does he know when a painting is finished? But whatever you ask, the reaction is the same. The figure shifts in his seat, attempts to reply several times, then quickly negates what he has said – as if crossing words out on a page – and relapses into an uneasy silence. The minutes go by, heavy with unvoiced questions and rejected replies. After a long while, the artist takes his large, rather beautiful face, with its astonishingly unmarked skin and deep-set brown eyes, between his hands and begins to groan softly. 'You can't say anything,' he says, with unfeigned despair. 'There it is. There's nothing to say about painting.'

Zoran Music could easily appear to be the interviewer's ultimate nightmare. As if condemned to question and refute the most basic assumptions about himself and his art, he returns endlessly to the refrain that nothing of any truth or importance can be said about the process of painting. To make things worse, he is unfailingly courteous and anxious to help, mocking himself and embarrassed by his seeming inability to come up with answers. The silence in the studio grows quite audible, but curiously enough it never becomes oppressive. On the contrary, the shared silence turns out to be the first, vital stage in the interview. The pencil is put down, the tape-recorder switched off. The interviewer begins to ask himself the questions. What does it mean to be questioning – almost interrogating – an artist about his deepest thoughts and his instinctive ways? What, indeed, is the truth, and would this exchange of imprecise query and faltering response stand any chance of revealing it? And whatever truth there was, would it not be so much part of the painting as to be inextricable, incommunicable in any other form?

Thus, by his constant hesitations and anguished doubts, Music draws us further into his world than any amount of artist's statement would do. Imperceptibly, in his manner of talking as in his painting, he puts us in search of our own truth. What is the essential? What remains of a person or a landscape, an experience or a sensation, when all its superfluities have been stripped away? What is unalterable, and will it really withstand a man's scrutiny, through every season and under every light, unchanged? Can it be caught, over and over again, in charcoal and oil, on paper and canvas, and stand ultimately revealed?

It takes many long silences in Music's company, sitting alone with him in his studio in Paris or in Venice, with all apparent chance of securing an interview fading with the light outside, to understand this unusually demanding dialectic. Yet it underlies every picture, clearly finished or barely sketched out, that stands propped round the studio walls. The artist probes, time after time, the silhouette of an ageing man, hunched over and alone in a room. What has really happened, what remains after a lifetime's search? Instead of a favourite view of Venice, the Sienese hills or even a pile of corpses at Dachau, it is himself that he is questioning. The interview and the interviewer have become superfluous. Music is asking himself all the most exacting questions. And little by little, once this has been implicitly understood, he begins to speak. The ideas and memories form, not unlike the pictures, hesitantly, taking a fugitive shape against a dark, troubled background. Like a leitmotif, references to the concentration camp recur more and more frequently as Music opens up, remembers and reflects. It is against this experience of extremity that everything else is weighed and judged. The sentences form amid all kinds of pauses, the interview is pieced together after infinite hesitation, but there is no thought that has not been subjected to extreme scrutiny, no word that is not freighted with self-doubt.

The following interview was recorded in 1987 in the studio that Zoran Music had for many years in the rue des Vignes, not far from the Seine, in the 16th arrondissement. Music used to say that he felt in exile there, far from his previous haunts on the Left Bank. Yet he was enormously attached to this studio, which was both elegant and functional, with high ceilings and huge windows. Beside the main atelier, there was a smaller drawing studio, and upstairs the artist had his living quarters. To all this light and space, Music brought an extra and almost palpable dimension of calm. It was the calm of a man who had lived through indescribable chaos and who had emerged deeper, darker, yet still whole, and above everyday disquiet. It was this quality in particular which drew me often to the rue des Vignes, when I myself might have been in turmoil over some minor problem (I was editing and publishing *Art International* at the time) and needed simply to absorb a little of this tranquillity. Very generously, Music always made me welcome. We talked a little, but usually, after a while, we sat in silence.

Silence is not easily indicated on the page, beyond a few, tiresome suspension dots. But here, when Music is talking, the silences were long and eloquent. Silence is more important, more revealing, for Music than any conversation. He himself tells the story about a long walk he took at night with Alberto Giacometti. They had met at a bar in Montparnasse and, since their studios were both at that time near Alésia, they decided to walk home together; 'and', Music concludes with some pride, 'we never exchanged a word'. The text below is full of such silences, and the reader is invited to imagine them at will.

ZM I didn't know I'd paint the cadavers again. It's a theme that comes up when everything else has become impossible – when I can't paint the things I love about life. I'd finished a long series inspired by a Venetian cathedral interior. I had no idea what I'd do next. For a while nothing happened. It's as if I'd ground to a halt. And then the corpses came back, just like that, before I had even thought about them.

Not that they're something I forget. In the last couple of months at Dachau, people were dying in droves. All the prisoners had become weak by this time, and disease ran through the camp in epidemics. There were so many dead that they couldn't all be disposed of at once. Their bodies were piled up outside in the yard. These little mountains of corpses fascinated me. It's difficult to explain now. What happened is that little by little you gave in to the nightmare of the camps. You accepted their reality completely, to the extent that you no longer believed in any other possibility. You even grew afraid of the outside world!

Every morning you noticed that this one and that one had died. Death seemed inevitable. I myself had no normal reactions left. I'd grown into a kind of robot, waiting for my turn to come. And yet I became fascinated by these heaps of bodies, built up like bonfires, with their arms and legs sticking out, because they had a kind of beauty, a tragic beauty. Some of them weren't quite dead, their limbs still moved and their eyes followed you round, begging for help. Then during the night, a little snow would fall. The heap wouldn't move again.

I'd begun to draw a little, whenever I had the chance, in secret, on scraps of paper. It was dangerous, but it gave a reason to go on living. Then I fell sick and was put into the camp hospital. The SS kept out of the way because there had been a massive outbreak of typhus, and they were afraid to go near. This meant that for the first time I could draw without hiding constantly, and I went into a kind of frenzy. I could think of nothing else, as if drawing had reawakened me to life. The reality itself was hallucinating. I started drawing one man who was so far gone that he was dead by the time I'd finished my sketch. Outside, the mountains of bodies multiplied.

When I got out, I went back to Venice and slowly I started painting the things I'd painted before: horses, Dalmatian landscapes and Dalmatian women – the subjects I loved. But it wasn't, as people suppose, in reaction to the horror of the camp.

I took up where I'd left off when the Gestapo arrested me in Venice on suspected anti-German activities. I went back to the same themes of life, of joy in living, but my way of seeing had changed completely. My experience of death had transformed my experience of life. I was only interested in images that were stripped down to their essence. In time, as an artist, I became grateful for having been forced to look at the core of things. If I'm attracted to dry, stony, mountainous landscapes, it's because everything's been worn down. In terms of form, the hills around Siena, for instance, are like the cadavers. They've been reduced to essentials.

I don't consciously choose the subject I want to paint. Usually what happens is that I see something that moves me – a landscape or a building, for instance – and forget about it. Then, much later, it might come back to me, transfigured, with its superfluities rubbed away. What I like best is to be so familiar with a subject that I can see it in the dark or with my eyes closed. I never try to will it into existence. The only worthwhile images are those that come about of their own accord. I never think of myself as 'working', in fact. Most of the time I seem to potter around the studio, and then I notice the light fading, and I get this terrible sense of urgency to get something down on the canvas before night comes. I'd been in the studio all day once and I was about to leave on a trip abroad. My bags were packed, and the taxi that was taking me to the airport arrived and the image I'd been waiting for came in a few minutes, unhesitatingly and completely.

Painting itself should be a pleasure. I never understand artists who say how much they suffer when they paint. Why suffer? After all, an artist's life is made up of so many frustrations – getting known, being criticized or misunderstood, trying to make a living – that if he doesn't get pleasure out of the painting part, he should do something else. What matters most to me in a painting is that you shouldn't be conscious of how it's been done. If you're aware of the technique, something's wrong. I like painting that's done with an absolute minimum of means. It's like writing. You try and communicate a maximum with the smallest number of words. Why write an essay about something that can be said in ten lines?

Of course you do suffer when you can't work. It happens to me every time I come to the end of a series. It happened when I'd exhausted my theme of cathedral interiors. But it's a positive suffering. You're renewing yourself. That explains why I've come back to the corpses with enthusiasm. A while ago I dreamt I was in a huge sports stadium and I was fascinated to see the cadavers propped on the tiers, one above the other. I was very moved and excited, the forms had a tragic elegance that made me want to paint them right away. They were like a marvellous landscape. Then, to my horror, they began to slide, they slipped all the way down until they disappeared from sight. And I felt as if I had lost some precious possession!

I'm not trying to make some rhetorical statement when I paint the cadavers. There's no point in protesting. It's something that happened. It would have been much better if it hadn't happened at all. But it did. For me, it's a subject that I need to paint. But whenever I talk about painting, I feel there's very little that one can say to the point. Basically, each person has his or her own truth. The important thing is to be in touch with it. As an artist, I think that experience tends to awaken you to what you are deep down inside. I don't believe in 'influences' in the conventional sense. I mean, I wasn't so much 'influenced' by Byzantine painting as I am 'Byzantine'. It's in my blood, in my ancestry as a Slovene. I'm not a Celt, as far as I know at least. I've probably got more in common with the Mongol hordes, with Attila. Who knows? In the end all you can really do is follow your own nature as closely and deeply as possible.

But how can you be sure of your own nature? Over the past few weeks, as I've got back into the corpse theme, I wonder how true so much of my previous painting has been. Perhaps the views of Venice and the cathedral interiors and so on have been an escape, a refuge, after all. Sometimes I think that the only really true moments of my painting have been the Dachau memories, the cadavers, and the very earliest things I did – the horses, the Dalmatian landscapes and the peasant women. Because both those things keep returning. They're mine, they're my roots, they're my truth. Perhaps the rest has been a lie.

ZORAN MUSIC

DORSODURO VENICE 1995

This interview took place in the artist's studio in Venice in January 1995. Music had just completed a series of oil paintings that he called the Anchorites. *Everything in these large compositions had been reduced to the bare minimum: a tall, ageing male figure loomed up out of a black background or sat, against a surround of raw canvas, as if lost in other-worldly contemplation. The pigment had been applied so thinly that the figures appeared to be on the point of being swallowed by the dark surround or sinking without trace into the canvas's rough weave. Yet they radiated a pale luminosity accentuated by flecks of brilliant white pigment. As the winter light faded and Music began, for the first time in several hours, to talk freely, these ghostly presences came increasingly into their own until they totally dominated the studio's gloom.*

MP The other day you said to me that you had no roots.

ZM I am a person *senza fissa dimore*, as they say in Italian. Without fixed abode. I was born in Gorizia, which was part of the Austro-Hungarian Empire at the time and yet only a few miles from the Italian border. When the War broke out in 1914, my father was sent to the front. The people who lived near the border were evacuated, and we went to the Austrian province of Styria. My father was a schoolmaster and later, because of his job, we moved from place to place. I studied in Zagreb and Vienna. Then I went on a long trip to Spain, and I stayed in Madrid and Toledo. I left Spain when the Civil War broke out, and I spent several years, until 1940, living near the Dalmatian coast. But I never stayed anywhere for very long. In 1943, I left for Venice, where I was arrested by the Gestapo and sent to Dachau …

Zoran Music (1909–2005). *Zoran Music*, exhibition catalogue, Galeries nationales du Grand Palais, Paris, April 1995.

MP Which might have been a very fixed abode.

ZM Yes, a little too fixed. And after Dachau I came back to Venice. Then a few years later, in 1952, I settled in Paris. But I've always been on the move, living here and there. You might say I belong to the Austro-Hungarian kind of civilization, or to 'Mitteleuropa', but those things no longer exist. When I was in Vienna, they put on the first performance of Brecht's *Threepenny Opera*, and one still felt all that extraordinary 'mitteleuropäisch' atmosphere and culture. But the Vienna that existed then has gone completely. When I lived in Dalmatia, I used to go on trips deep into the countryside to half-forgotten places where there were ancient monasteries full of fantastic mosaics. And these mosaics must have made a lasting impression on me, because my painting has always remained flat, without volume or perspective. When I was in Spain, I was terrifically impressed by Goya, although I didn't fully understand him until after Dachau, when I had seen the things he had seen. I've never thought along these lines before, but it's true that I've been influenced by all kinds of civilizations – 'mitteleuropäisch', Byzantine, Venetian, Spanish and French.

MP But you only have one mother tongue: Slovene.

ZM People spoke not only Slovene in Gorizia, but also Italian and German. Some of my relatives were of Italian origin, and so we spoke both Slovene and Italian at home. Then I learnt German, and later French. To some extent I'm linguistically rootless as well.

MP Do you think all these different experiences have had some kind of influence on your painting?

ZM Who can tell? You simply don't know how those things happen. I think the most important experiences are those that awaken something that is already inside you, but you can't say when or how that happens. When I was in Castile, during my time in Spain, I came across the same landscape as the one I'd grown attached to in Dalmatia. I've always liked the most raw, barren landscapes. Switzerland is very pretty, and so are the northern countries that are covered with flowers and trees and grass. But they don't move me. I like landscapes that are almost desert-like, that don't change with the seasons but stay the same forever, like the landscapes in the Bible. I feel drawn by them, I don't know why. It's a need. But that applies to everything. I like things that I can see when I close my eyes, things that have been stripped down, with no masks or coverings or superfluities, things that cannot be reduced any further. That's why I've never used models for my portraits, for instance, because there you are confronted by masks, whereas what you want is the person's inner self.

MP You came to Venice in 1943, having spent several peaceful years painting landscapes in Dalmatia. The Venetians made you welcome, and shortly afterwards you had an exhibition with some of your Dalmatian and a few Venetian scenes. Then, suddenly, your life falls apart. You are arrested by the Gestapo for 'anti-German activities'. Is it true they made you an offer?

ZM First of all, they shut me in a cell, two metres long, one and a half metres wide, underground in a building in Trieste for twenty-six days. I was totally alone, in the dark, with water up to my ankles. I was interrogated, and then tortured, several times. Then, since they did not get anything out of me, they offered me the choice of becoming a local SS officer or being sent as a 'free worker' to Dachau. The idea of suddenly becoming an SS officer seemed so comical to me, in the state I was in, that I laughed outright. So they sent me to Dachau…

One can't really describe what it was like, because it was as if you were living on another planet. It was an unreal, a surreal experience, governed by other laws, by an implacable system of cruelty. One could be annihilated from one minute to the next, for nothing. If you live through that experience, it becomes part of your life. And you remain forever with the corpses you left behind in Dachau. People are often astonished by the fact that when I came out of the camp and went back to Venice, I painted pictures that were full of light and happiness and gaiety.

MP How did that happen, in fact?

ZM I was dazzled by the Venetian light, by the vast sky and the huge horizon around the lagoon. I couldn't believe I was free and that I could work freely without having to cut up my drawings and hide them under my shirt, as I'd had to do in Dachau. I had come out of the dark, out of a nightmare. And when I went into St Mark's, it was like finding something that was deeply buried inside me, something from my childhood: icons and gilded images. I had a feeling of unbelievable freedom and happiness.

MP Yet the corpses were to come back later.

ZM Yes, but in a very strange way. I was on the train one day and I was extraordinarily moved when I looked at the hills around Siena. It was as if I had rediscovered something very important. There is no vegetation on these hills. They're covered by a soil that is almost white, like a skin, with runnel marks on it, that make them look like the ribcages of human bodies. They form a landscape that does not change, that stays the same through all seasons. And later, when I came to paint the hills, I realized that these whitish mounds reminded me of the piles of corpses that had been part of everyday life at the camp.

MP You were reliving your experience of Dachau.

ZM I suppose so, but indirectly. I didn't begin to paint any scenes of Dachau directly until much later. That also happened in an unexpected way. After living in Paris for a number of years, I went through a crisis in my work. Only abstract painting seemed to count for everyone around me. Next to this great movement, to which all the well-known artists and the important critics belonged, I began to feel feeble and useless. In the end I gave in. I tried to do my kind of abstract painting. And as I did I totally lost my sense of being true to myself. That's the worst thing that can happen to an artist, because he ceases to exist without that truth. And it was out of this confusion and frustration that the corpses emerged.

MP It was an involuntary thing?

ZM It's always involuntary. You can't do anything in painting voluntarily. You have to wait for things to come by themselves, and you never know how or when that will be. What I found particularly moving when I remembered the corpses was the terrible beauty of all those bodies stacked like a great pile of logs, with their hands and feet jutting out. I was fascinated by their tragic elegance – the near-transparence of their skin, and their toes, which looked so delicate and so fragile. I looked at them like a sleepwalker, who had accepted the reality of the camp, as if no other reality existed, and who had no normal reactions left. But those are things you cannot describe. It just turns into journalism.

MP You came back to this theme, *We Are Not The Last*, again in 1987. At the time you said that this had also happened because you were frustrated about the way your work was going.

ZM That's roughly true. You could say that I go back to the corpses when I can no longer paint the things I love in life. I had just painted a series of cathedral interiors, a subject that has fascinated me ever since the time, in Toledo during the 1930s, that I went from brilliant sunlight into the near total darkness of the cathedral. The same thing happened to me in Venice, in St Mark's: brilliant sunshine, then darkness. But if you stay for a moment, you gradually begin to make things out in the gloom. I'm very attached to that sensation: little by little, you start to find light in the darkness. It's rather like the way I paint. I wait in darkness for things to happen. Often they are things that have been coming together for a long time, memories that have surfaced from oblivion, images in which only the essential remains. They come to me ready-made, and I paint them directly.

MP Has your way of painting changed much over the years as you go from one theme to another?

ZM No, not at all. I have always painted with a minimum of means. I know that the material aspect of things can be very beautiful, but when the paint is thick, when there are great big layers of it, it becomes – I don't know how to put it – matter without any spirituality. When you are looking at an image, you shouldn't be aware of its material existence. That's very important. There's also this question of always remaining true to yourself, whatever happens. And then there's something else: you must never learn how to do a subject. As soon as you know how to do it, with an ever more perfect technique, it's too late. It will have lost its freshness, its innocence and its real emotion. You have to be very sincere and very tough. If you don't stop, you're just turning things out.

MP How do you know when you are about to begin on a new theme?

ZM I've no idea. How can you explain these things? Sometimes I do nothing for days, even for months. I am empty. I walk aimlessly round the studio. Then for no obvious reason, as I'm going from one room into another, I pick up a sheet of paper and I start drawing. Just like that, without thinking about it. And I begin to work again. Once I spent the whole day doing nothing, and then when evening came, when I was meant to be leaving on a trip, an image came to me and I painted a picture while the taxi was waiting for me down below. It's fantastic when images come. I see them coming out of the canvas, and that's how I paint them, without changing a thing. But you never know if the result is any good, if you've been able to communicate any feeling, especially the day after. In fact, you never know. You always have that doubt, don't you?

ZORAN MUSIC

SAINT-GERMAIN-DES-PRÉS PARIS 1999

This interview was distilled from several conversations with Zoran Music that took place in the apartment high up over the Boulevard Saint-Germain in Paris where he has been living and working for the past few years. There was nothing formal about these sessions. We sat in the studio, often for an hour or two before going on to have dinner together, and talked without any specific purpose in mind. I had noticed that, although his short-term memory was not as good as it had been, Music was able to recall whole episodes and incidents of his earlier life with astonishing clarity. I was very moved that this man, then about to turn ninety, remembered not only the outbreak of the First World War so graphically, but also the fact that he had gone as a boy to buy milk for his family and paid for it in gold coin. I was even more moved when Music broke with his habitual reserve and talked in detail, without anger or self-pity, about the horrors of his imprisonment at Dachau.

MP You have some extraordinarily clear memories of your childhood.

ZM Yes, for some things. But one forgets a great deal. My grandparents were wine-makers, you know. My grandmother owned a vineyard in the Collio, next to the Italian border, on the edge of the Friuli. My grandmother was in fact born in the Friuli, and she spoke an old Friulian dialect with my father. Otherwise my parents spoke Slovene, and in Gorizia, where I was born, you often heard people speaking Italian in the streets. For official business, on the other hand, German was used. Later, when I went to study in Zagreb, I learnt to speak Croatian as well.

My father became headmaster at a village school very near Gorizia. My mother was a school mistress. She could stop you

Zoran Music (1909–2005). *Zoran Music*, exhibition catalogue, Sainsbury Centre for Visual Arts, Norwich, February 2000.

in your tracks with one look. I wandered into her classroom once when I was very little, and when she looked into my eyes I was rooted to the spot, unable to react. My father never dared contradict her, even when they played tarot or other old card games together.

Before the Great War, when I was three or four, we used to spend part of the autumn with my grandparents. The landscape there was magnificent. You could see the Gulf of Trieste on the left, Udine, at the foot of the Alps, on the right, and further on you could make out Venice. My father had two brothers who had a delicatessen in Trieste. When we went to visit them, we would take a little local train which crossed the Karst mountains. In that autumn light the rocks were full of red and ochre. The Karst became a magic word for me. I thought it was paradise.

MP Were you fond of landscapes even then?

ZM I was always fond of nature. When I was older, I used to go on huge rambles in the mountains and the forests, by myself or with a friend, and I used to sleep wherever I could. I knew everything about animals, and sometimes I used to look after them. I kept a hedgehog in my room, for instance, and I knew exactly how it got all the leaves it needed to sleep through the winter. My brother was far worse. He brought every insect in the forest back to his room, with lots of grass and leaves. When you went in, everything seemed to be quivering.

MP Even as a small child, you knew that war had broken out?

ZM Yes. I was with my father in a crowd. It was Sunday. The ladies were wearing huge hats and the men had pointed moustaches and Panamas. Everybody seemed very excited, and I ran around a lot. Suddenly I grabbed a gentleman's legs. Then I looked up: I saw a beard moving up and down, but it wasn't my father's. And all around I could see nothing but beards moving up and down. 'We're at war,' I heard somebody say. 'The Crown Prince has been assassinated.' And for days afterwards, I went around triumphantly chanting: 'We're at war! We're at war!'

MP What happened to you and your family?

ZM Well, my father was sent to the Galician front, and my mother, my brother Ljuban and I were evacuated a long way away to Styria. We got into a cart full of baggage to go to Gorizia, then we took the train to Villach. There were Austrian soldiers everywhere on their way to the War. The station at Villach was chock-a-block with refugees. I went running down on the rails, and when my mother caught up with me, she was totally panicked. Later on, when they took me to Dachau, I went past the same spot. I remember a Slovene girl bringing us prisoners some soup, and when I thanked her in Slovene, she gave me another spoonful.

Eventually we arrived at a little village in Styria where we were taken in by a farmer – but not for long, because my mother was always changing house. I used to go and fetch the post every day, and little by little I delivered the post to the whole village. Sometimes I used to fetch the milk. It was 1917 then, and we still used gold coin. We went to visit my father at his barracks once. He had always refused to become an officer, and he had certainly succeeded because, after having been invalided out for a while, he became the regimental cook. And when we turned up in the great big courtyard in front of the barracks, somebody bellowed out: 'Music! Corporal Music!', and my father came out with his apron on. I remember my grandmother had given me some money, and I used to spend it bribing other boys to play tricks. I got them to set the church bells ringing, for instance, and the priest was absolutely furious. You see, even then, I knew what corruption was. At school, once we had said Our Father, I was always chosen to start everyone off singing the Hapsburg hymn. All the children played war games. One was English, another German, and so on. I always got the role of the German who was losing. That was in 1917–18, and we already knew what was happening. Much later I came across the director of the school – he was called Mr Yankovich – at Dachau.

MP Did you draw a lot when you were a child?

ZM I drew the whole time. I did drawings for other children and showed them to everybody. Drawing came very naturally. When I got older, it was thought I should study architecture. But I couldn't draw a single straight line. On the other hand, I liked painting, so I enrolled at the Academy of Fine Arts in Zagreb. There were lots of gypsies about in those days. They came from everywhere – Austria, Rumania, Bulgaria – accompanied by all their horses, and they spoke an incredible number of languages. They would often come and pose for us in the Academy studios. The women used to wear six or seven skirts, all of them full of dust. It was incredible. I was sometimes invited to gypsy weddings where, at one point in the ceremony, they broke a pot over the bride and bridegroom's heads.

MP Did you travel much at that time?

ZM I went to Vienna and to Prague, and I did some competition skiing here and there with my brother, who became a champion skier. But I didn't really start travelling until I'd finished studying in Zagreb. I went to Spain in 1935 and stayed until the Civil War began. I copied Goya and El Greco a great deal in the museums, and I loved going into the cathedrals, particularly the one in Toledo, where I used to plunge into the dark and wait until one by one all the little lights started glimmering. It's a marvellous feeling to find light in the darkness. Spain was an extraordinary place at that time. The museums were unbelievable, but so was life on the street. There were beggars and mutilated people everywhere. I was particularly struck by the lepers, who were so swathed in bits of cloth that you could only see their mouths. I went from city to city, and you could never tell when you were going to arrive anywhere. The trains used to pull in ahead of time, then simply leave when they had enough passengers on board. You often turned up at the station punctually only to be told: 'The train's left. Come back tomorrow.' After Madrid and Toledo, I went to Barcelona. But as soon as the Falangists moved in, I left.

MP You went to live and paint in Dalmatia. In 1943 you had a show in Trieste.

ZM Yes, but I was still painting in a very illustrative way. I was young and life was easy. I had to live through the horrible experience of Dachau before I went more deeply into things. At that time I had begun making trips to Venice. I had always dreamt of living in Venice, and I found a room in a *pensione* that was run by German nuns.

MP Then one day the Gestapo arrested you for having collaborated with the Resistance.

ZM I was a friend of people in Trieste who reported back to London about everything that was happening in the port there. The local Resistance leader was also a friend of mine, and the Gestapo has seen us together. They had suspicions about me as well because I was always making drawings of the lagoon. The officer who arrested me, I remember, was called Captain Zimmer. I was transported to Trieste on the back of an open lorry. I was standing, with my hands tied behind my back. And suddenly an English fighter came swooping down on the lorry. For a split second the pilot and I looked into each other's eyes, then he pulled away. In Trieste they shut me in an underground cell in an old factory where the Gestapo had set up their headquarters. From time to time they took me out for interrogation and torture. They thought I had been spying for the English. I hadn't, but I did have a friend who worked for the English, and they wanted his name. I told them nothing. I didn't collaborate. There it is. There are some things you can't do. They carried out their work, their torture, on a mattress outside in the corridor. When they took someone out for torture, they came and shut the spy-hole in the other cells. But you heard the screams, of course, and when it was your turn to come out you could see the fresh blood stains on the mattress.

One day they came to tell me I was going to be shot. There were about a hundred of us in the prison, and we were all taken together to the place of execution. When we arrived, they counted up how many prisoners there were. Most of them had been in the Resistance. The Germans had received specific orders as to exactly how many prisoners were to be shot. We were one too many. I was not in the Resistance, and I was attached to another officer in the Gestapo. I was the one they did not shoot. All the others died.

MP And when you got to Dachau?

ZM One can't really talk about these things … There were unbelievable scenes every day. The new prisoners who came by train, for instance, had often had no water or food for two or three weeks. When you opened the doors, dozens of corpses fell out onto the rails. Others had gone out of their minds by the time they arrived. Inside the camp the corpses were piled up one on top of the other wherever you looked. I remember seeing someone eating his bit of bread and putting it down distractedly from time to time on the belly of a corpse. There were corpses beside the latrines, and in the mornings, when we shaved, we used to hang a little mirror from the finger or the toe of the nearest corpse without thinking it at all strange.

Sometimes the corpses were not quite dead. One day in winter, I remember, there was one of these heaps of corpses, with the bodies stacked up like logs, just outside our building. Every now and then an arm or a leg would move, and there were groans and cracking sounds. Then it snowed during the night, and in the morning the heap was quite still. One person would then come to cut off their hair, another to pull out their gold teeth, and a third to note how many gold teeth they had on a numbered tag that was tied to the foot of each corpse. I made a drawing of a corpse like that, with its tag on its foot; it belongs now to the museum in Basel. I drew all the time, as soon as I could. I'd found some bits of paper in the architects' office at Dachau, and I shut myself up in the *Revier*, where they kept everyone who was ill, during a typhus epidemic. The SS was too frightened to come near, so I was able to draw freely for the first time. I was fascinated by the strange beauty of all those corpses. Some very curious things happened. One day, when I was drawing in the midst of the corpses, a man with huge, staring eyes suddenly broke loose from the other bodies that were piled up. He was struggling to get something off his foot; and I saw it as the tag with his number on it. Then he disappeared. And I often wondered what became of that man, dead as far as Dachau's administration was concerned and yet with no place in the camp. There were horrible, absurd things that you came to accept, just as you came to accept your own death. I often passed in front of the ovens, where the corpses were piled four metres high. A Czech friend of mine used to say to me: 'You know, tomorrow or the day after, it'll be our turn to burn. A thing like this will never happen again. We are the last to see a thing like this.'

Later, when I could no longer hold things in, when the memories of the camp surged up inside me, I began to paint them, many years after. Then I realized it was not true. We are not the last.

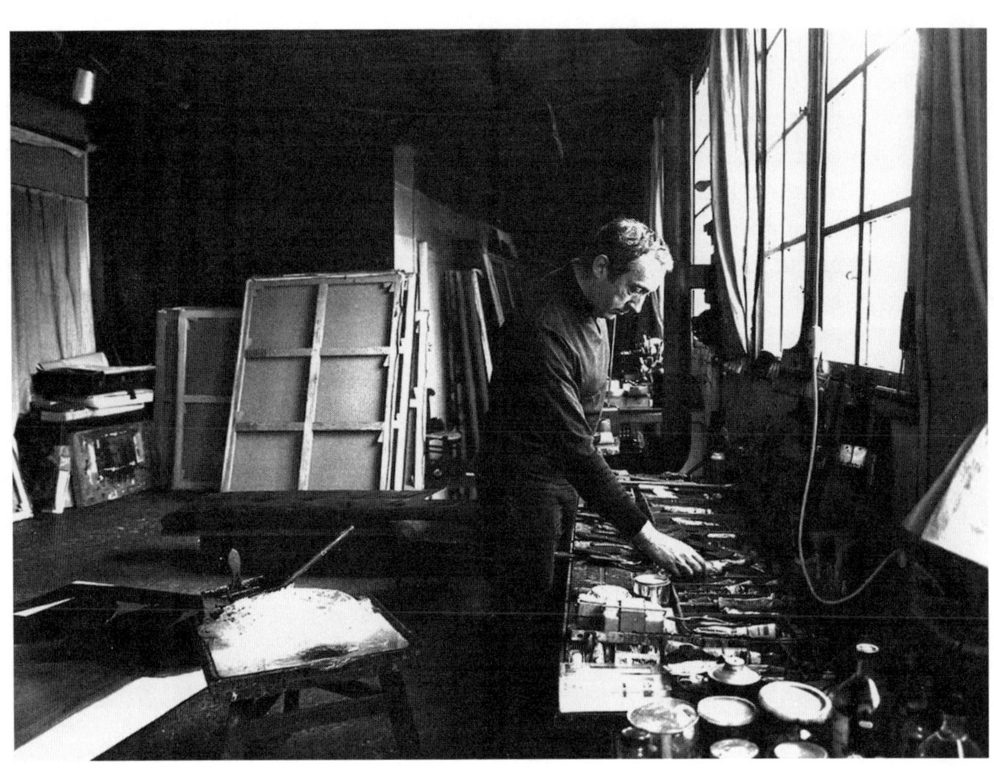

PIERRE SOULAGES

RUE DES TROIS PORTES PARIS 1980

James Fitzsimmons, the founder-editor of *Art International* and a great admirer of Pierre Soulages, asked me to do the following interview with the artist in 1979. Beyond the fact that I was the magazine's Paris correspondent and reviewed art exhibitions of all kinds every month on its behalf in France, I had no obvious qualifications for the job. For although I was quite open to other developments on the contemporary scene, figurative painting had remained my particular interest and area of expertise ever since, as a student in the early 1960s (as previously mentioned), I had got to know Francis Bacon, Lucian Freud, Frank Auerbach and R. B. Kitaj in London and begun to think and write about their work.

But Fitzsimmons, who was an extremely perceptive editor and who had also followed Soulages's career closely, knew that I had been lucky enough to meet the artist not long after I arrived in France. In fact, I had gone to visit him and his wife, Colette, at their summer house overlooking the sea outside Sète in 1967; and I had written an account of my stay there for *Réalités*, the magazine I had come to Paris to work for. I was impressed to learn that the artist and his wife themselves had designed the building, with its transparent, interlocking volumes, and the aromatic garden that surrounded it. I was also struck by Soulages's description of how the house had come about. 'My wife and I couldn't really be called the architects of this place', he had told me at the time. 'The wind decided where the walls should be, the sun pointed out the windows and the landscape gave the whole thing its perspective. We were merely the mediators. That's what nature waits for – someone to put her to new uses.'

Seeing Soulages's paintings for the first time in that environment made a lasting impression on me. The stark contrasts of the Mediterranean light and the rhythms of the sea and sky seemed to have been caught and concentrated in the broad, confident, sometimes

Pierre Soulages (1919–). *Art International*, Lugano, December 1980.

delicate, sometimes brutal sweeps of Soulages's brush. The painter's manifest commitment to his art and his willingness to discuss it in depth were also exhilarating. As a result, over the years, I had gone regularly to Soulages's exhibitions, notably those held at the old Galerie de France on the Faubourg Saint-Honoré. And I had noted with fascination how his work had evolved within its own language until it seemed the vocabulary would no longer suffice and it plunged periodically into areas where no signs pre-existed.

The interview below was begun while walking with Pierre Soulages round his latest exhibition, entitled *Peintures récentes*, at the Centre Pompidou. A few days later, at the Soulages's Left Bank flat, there followed a more formal, tape-recorded session, which developed, once we had moved to the studio nearby, into a very graphic demonstration of the tools and materials the artist prefers.

With its choice of works dating from 1968 to 1979, the Centre Pompidou exhibition consisted in reality of two interrelated shows. On the walls of the extensive 'Salle contemporaine' on the museum's ground floor were works representing the artist's development up until 1978, while across the gallery, suspended between ceiling and floor, hung a totally new series of paintings, executed during 1979.

These all-over black, yet intensely luminous canvases commanded attention: their presence was of steles whose universal significance could be apprehended intuitively but not put into words. One was confronted with the inner eloquence of paint. The genesis and *raison d'être* of this new series inevitably formed the main subject of our talk; and in the studio, amid the great clusters of specially prepared brushes, the more specifically technical details of their execution were explained.

A sensation of space – ample, clear and unconstrained – spread through and eventually characterized this interview. It informed the new paintings' great, free sweeps of glistening jet, the uncluttered perspective of the studio and, not least, the direct, deep-rooted conviction of the artist talking about his work.

MP I should like to begin by asking you two very general questions. What meaning, if any, do the terms 'abstraction' or 'abstract painting' have for you?

PS When I first started painting, I didn't accept them. I used to think: 'Why abstract? Why not concrete?' In the end I did accept them, but as labels, as things that are bound to be torn up.

MP Would you say there is a fundamental difference between what's called 'abstract' and 'figurative' painting?

PS Yes. A fundamental difference. Figurative painting is the area where an image, that is to say a fiction, takes place. It exists and has its effect only through or by what this image represents: it is sign and language. As for abstract painting, I'll confine myself to my own work. It is not an area where an image takes place, not even through the title (I've never given my paintings titles). I don't depict. I don't narrate. I don't represent. I paint, I present. What we call abstract painting has opened up as many possibilities as music – but they are possibilities that belong specifically to painting. In the same way, without taking these kinds of comparisons too far, one can say that figurative painting is relatable to literature. That's why it is easier to talk about it. It's also why, in talking about it, so little is said about painting itself.

MP How did your most recent series of paintings come into being?

PS The whole series is based on a certain approach to colour and values in painting. I began the series early in 1979, but I had already had some experience of this approach – whereby different values are created not by different colour-tones but by different traces in the paint – in 1956. In the paintings I'm talking about, you don't find a black next to a grey, but the same black throughout; but those areas which carry the brush-traces appear to have a different tonal value – a different colour almost – to those that have remained smooth. But back in 1956 that phenomenon was apparent only in certain parts of the paintings.

MP It wasn't something that you particularly wanted to take any further at the time?

PS No. I'm not sure I was aware of its possibilities then. Whereas now I've done these paintings that are entirely based and constructed on this phenomenon.

MP How did the transition to these new paintings come about?

PS While painting, as always! I'd done several paintings that were black on dark grey – sometimes mistakenly called 'black on black' – and I was working on one that was almost black all over. And as I worked on it, I noticed I was giving it different values by means of these traces. So I went one stage further and started doing paintings with nothing but the same black paint. And the result was quite different, because it was the substance, the texture – by means of contrasting reliefs and the brushstrokes – which gave this single black colour its tonal values. Anyone who walks past one of these paintings sees it come into being, sees it built up and transformed, with the light.

MP Would you call these latest paintings the most 'textural' that you have done?

PS No. My yardstick in these paintings is not texture but light. There's something of a paradox here, I suppose, because what these all-over black paintings are really about is light. You might say that was the case in those paintings of mine where you get black on a light background: some of the light-coloured areas seemed lighter – because of the contrasting black – even though the actual colour never changed. But these latest paintings are altogether different, because here the light comes out of the black paint itself, and it vibrates and changes as you look at it and see forms emerge and disappear.

MP One's very struck in these new paintings by the way the black paint is full of light or extremely sombre, according to the angle from which one happens to be looking at them.

PS Exactly. Black is, optically speaking, the colour which reflects the least light; but when it catches the light on a thousand tiny ridges, you get the impression of a colour going from dark grey to quite light grey. And the areas of grey or black produced in this way have a very special quality which appeals to me and fascinates me. It's a very different quality from the one you get in the traditional way, by mixing colours, and it has something unique and irreplaceable about it...

MP Which you can only get with oil paint?

PS No – which you can only get from this way of working, this technique, but it could be done in another medium. The thing about oil is that it keeps the exact trace of the brush. If you use an emulsion paint, such as a resin-based emulsion, the surface contracts once the water has evaporated. Oil, on the other hand, sets, just like cement, and keeps all traces absolutely intact.

MP Are you still using the same brushes as before?

PS I've always preferred house-painters' brushes to those that are specially prepared for artists – from way back, even before my abstract paintings of 1946. I sometimes prepare them myself, that's to say, I alter them – by pruning them, for instance – so that I can get the degree of suppleness or roughness that I need. Some of the new paintings have been done with these wide brushes and also with knives, of the palette-knife type, to smooth the surface. But a number of the paintings have been done entirely with one or the other of these tools. Those that have been painted entirely with a brush draw their tonal variations from three sources: the traces left in the pigment by the brush, the angle at which light falls on them, and the point from which the onlooker is viewing them. For me, that is something new.

MP Wasn't there something of these variations of light on surfaces in the bronze plaques which you made earlier?

PS Yes, the approach is a bit similar. But I didn't notice it until after I'd done the new paintings.

MP How did you get the idea for those plaques?

PS The bronzes – I call them 'bronzes' because I don't want to call them 'sculptures' – came out of my engravings. I used to work, like any other engraver, on rectangular copper sheets. These sheets, as you know, are etched, then dipped into acid. As soon as I began engraving in 1957, I started keeping these plates for their own sake – they had a certain plasticity. But they were lacking something, because they had been worked on solely with a view to the print they were going to produce on paper. They lacked an independent existence. I'd long thought that something could be done with these sheets, and then one day I made an enlarged model of one of them and cast it in bronze. Once the cast had been made, I reworked it, engraving and blackening certain areas over again. The molten metal had made the surface buckle in parts, and I polished these so that they would catch the light and give the whole an impression of movement. What I was after, basically, in those bronzes was not space, as in a sculpture, but light. Light moved over the polished parts as one moved oneself, while the darkened, engraved areas stayed motionless.

MP Do you have some fairly definite idea of what you're going to do when you start on a new work?

PS No. Or if I do, it gets so changed in the process that one would no longer recognize it at the end. For me, there's always been this constant exchange between what's happening on the canvas and the reaction I then have to it. That's what makes me want to go on with it – make it more intense, more precise, take it further in this or that direction. The whole exchange can take place in a short space of time, or a lengthy one. With the texture of the paint I'm using in these latest paintings, everything has to be done within two or three days, otherwise the pigment starts hardening and I'd get technical problems that would prevent me from reconsidering the whole composition.

MP Is there a great deal of reconsidering?

PS Yes, of course. There's a constant need for organization. I organize the light, which is born on and through the paint. And then there are always the unforeseen things which open up new and more interesting possibilities than those I originally had in mind.

MP Do you get to a point where you know a painting is finished and you mustn't do anything more to it?

PS You get to a point where a painting has achieved maximum intensity, where it cannot be taken any further along its own particular direction – or if it is taken further, everything changes and it becomes a different painting. It all depends on one's reaction, on what's going on inside as one paints. And you can't really talk about that, for one thing because you can't find word equivalents for it, and for another because only a small part of it is conscious. It's like an iceberg – there's the part that's submerged. We're individuals, but we belong to a particular culture; and we're not necessarily conscious of the part of ourselves that belongs to our particular epoch and culture, just as we don't recognize some of the myths we thrive on and so many other things that we carry inside us and which go into making us without our realizing it.

MP With this new series of paintings, did you find that one tended to spark off another?

PS Oh yes. But that's not to say that the experience of painting one canvas can help you at all pertinently with another. When you've lived through a painting, the painting changes you. You're not the same afterwards. I think that's the right way of putting it.

MP It's the picture that paints you ...

PS You make paintings, but the paintings make you as well.

MP A number of painters I know talk frequently of the role of chance in their work. Does this concept have any significance for you?

PS Now that's a word that needs to be examined. I think that kind of chance can be defined as the coming together of several causal series. But those causal series are more or less consciously chosen, so that what we're talking about is right away a kind of chosen chance! And the possibilities opened up by those causal series' coming together oblige you to take decisions: for instance, you have to accept or refuse whatever the painting under way offers you. So it comes down to a curious exchange with a very special form of chance!

MP When the word is used in that context, I think it refers to the hope that the work underway will take one by surprise.

PS One's always surprised by the unexpected, of course, but it's a rather elementary reaction. Does one actually know what one's doing? In my case, when I've finished a painting, often I don't know why it's finished. I know that it affects and moves me, that it has a life of its own, that it exists. But I'm not at all sure I know what it is. And so much the better if it eludes me and has all kinds of possibilities that others can see. I don't have to know all the effects that a painting of mine will have on the sensitivity, the imagination or the poetic instinct of the person who's looking at it. He can like it for reasons of his own – for reasons that we have in common, but also for others which I myself will never know. If art were a language that could be reduced to 'what the painter meant', then the 'message' that it got across would be pointless.

MP In that case, one would do as well to read newspapers!

PS Exactly!

MP So you'd say that painting is in part a mystery.

PS If you like, yes. But it has nothing to do with a secret. They're very different things. The secret is known to the person who has made the painting, so that's something that can be found out. But the mystery is precisely what cannot be found out.

MP But when you're painting, do you have the feeling that you're touching on unknown areas, in yourself, for example?

PS It's not a question of that. I might well touch on unknown areas in myself – but that's a psychological way of approaching and thinking about painting. A painting – this object made by one person and perceived by others – is much more than that. It's of another nature . . . First of all, it's a material object made up of stretcher, canvas, forms, colours and so on. But it has a reality that goes way beyond its material existence. There's a relationship that's set up between the painting with all its inherent strength and possibilities; the person who has produced it and allowed it to be shown; and, thirdly, those who look at it, with all that they are, psychologically speaking, but also with all the other things that they – and along with them, their epoch and civilization – are made of. Take a Mesopotamian sculpture. If it touches and moves us, if we call it 'art', the chances are that it's not for the same reasons that prompted the sculptor to carve it or that made it appeal to his contemporaries. No, the life of a work of art is always in this triple relationship between its existence as an object, the person who made it and the people who look at it. That's its reality.

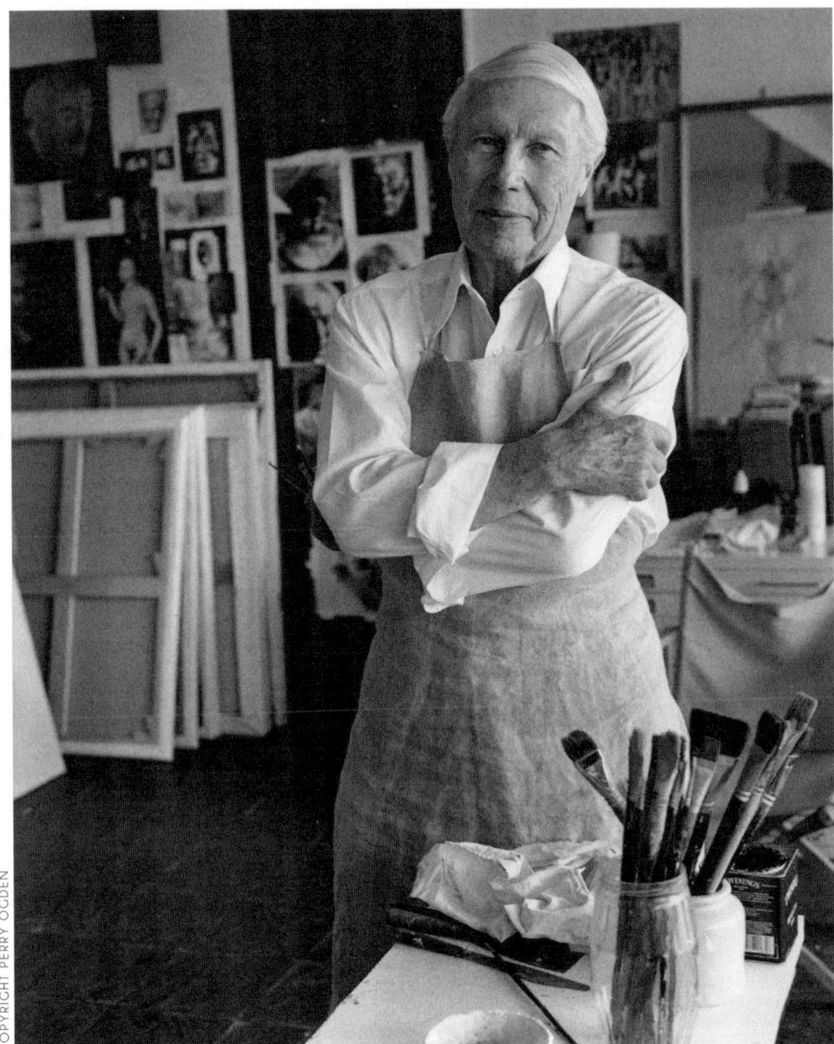

LOUIS LE BROCQUY

CARROS FRANCE 1979

Rereading this interview with Louis le Brocquy took me back immediately to the house with its orange groves in the hills behind Nice where Louis and I talked on several occasions, between visits to his studio and long, sunny lunches outside. Both le Brocquy and his wife Anne Madden were friends of Francis Bacon, and we all met during one of Bacon's frequent stays in Paris in the mid-1970s, when (like the le Brocquys) he found a small studio where he liked to work from time to time in the French capital. Towards the end of that decade le Brocquy began doing portraits – or, more accurately, heads – of Bacon in watercolour and in oil as he had done of Joyce, Yeats and Beckett. I followed the evolution of this series closely and became fascinated by the eeriness with which Bacon, like le Brocquy's other 'heroes', hovered like a ghost on the picture plane, emerging only to recede into the whiteness of the surrounding paper or canvas. In 1979 I wrote a preface to accompany le Brocquy's show of 'Heads', and the following interview was published in an illustrated article in Art International *to coincide with the event.*

Louis le Brocquy was born in 1916 in Dublin, and although his paternal grandfather was Belgian and he himself has lived most of his adult life abroad (or perhaps because of these things), he has remained intensely aware of his Celtic heritage.

In 1958 le Brocquy left London and the considerable early reputation he had gained there to set up house in the South of France with his young wife, the painter Anne Madden. For the past nineteen years they have lived in a village perched in the hills behind Nice, while frequent travel and migratory friends ensure that they are never cut off from less tranquil parts of the world.

Louis le Brocquy (1916–). *Art International*, Lugano, October 1979.

Le Brocquy is tall, slim and white-haired; high cheekbones and very blue eyes combine to give him a look of steadfast absorption. He talks in a mild, yet persuasive fashion, relishing the evocative flexibility of words and touching on subjects as different as geology and mysticism, pipe-smoking and bird-life, with erudite ease. At times his references appear oblique, even unrelated, until the listener becomes aware that they follow the movement of a complex mind more interested in the chance finds of discursiveness (in talk as in painting) than in the linearity of straight question and answer.

The 'interview' below is a distillation, from notes and memory, of several hours' conversation that took place at various times in the studio where both le Brocquy and Anne Madden paint. On one occasion, six new but not fully finished heads of Beckett stared down in a semicircle from their easels; on another, six new heads of Bacon. During the talks their aura of grimness and *terribilità* faded, and something more vulnerable, more human, emerged. Further off, on the wall, James Joyce's death mask, its expression entirely inward-turned under the bronze's faint smile, presided over everything. Under this scrutiny, and in the shifting, probing talk, there came the uneasy sensation that all was appearance, all surface alone – with the painted heads and the living, talking heads two layers of the illusion to be stripped away.

MP Over the past five years you have painted literally hundreds of heads of Yeats, Joyce and Lorca. You're beginning now on Beckett and Bacon. Where does this fascination with heads, heads alone, come from?

LlB Well, you know, it came after I'd gone through a very bad year, a blind year, as it were, when no image emerged and I got completely bogged down. That was in 1963, and for the previous six or seven years I had been working on a series of figures, or what I think of as 'presences', on a white ground. Suddenly nothing of any value seemed to come any more, and at the end of that year I destroyed forty-three bad paintings. By then I was in a bad way myself, of course, and my wife suggested we should go up to Paris as if we were going somewhere quite new where there'd be things to discover. And in fact I made what for me was a vital discovery, by coming into contact with those Melanesian-Polynesian images they have at the Musée de l'homme. They're skulls, you know, partly remodelled with clay, then painted in a typical, decorative way – often with cowrie shells for eyes. They impressed me deeply, and shortly afterwards I started painting heads, disembodied heads, if you like, or rather heads in complete isolation. Then a bit later, in 1965, I came across another head cult near Aix-en-Provence, at Entremont and Roquepertuse – this time of Celtic, or what they call Celto-Ligurian, origin. And it acted as a confirmatory revelation for me of the image of the head as a kind of magic box that holds the spirit prisoner.

MP We're talking now of sculptured heads, I imagine.

LIB Oh yes. You can see what's left of them in the museums in Aix and Marseilles. Very little remains of the Celtic culture there, you know. The Romans systematically obliterated it, destroying both the principal oppidum and the holy place: Entremont and Roquepertuse. Of course, the Celts had some very unpleasant practices themselves, such as cutting off the heads of enemies conquered in battle and wearing them on their belts.

MP Like the Scyths …

LIB Yes. You know, it's struck me that the Celts must in fact be derived in some way from the Scyths. Their arts are distinctly related. The Celtic culture, as I was saying, was destroyed by the Romans: the Druids were driven into the woods and hunted down. But in Ireland this culture – this Celtic way of seeing things – survived. Christianity merely modified it. When Edmund Spenser, the Elizabethan poet, was posted there, he was touched by the poverty – people collapsing from hunger in front of his eyes, and so on – but he didn't understand them; in fact he hardly thought of them as human beings at all. He was a Renaissance man and they were Celts, the ancestors of the mind of Joyce. And this sensitive poet recommended that the Irish be wiped out – quite literally – as they would never become what he called 'civil'. Of course they probably did strike other people as barbarous, just as their Gallic cousins had struck the Romans. The Gauls used to preserve the heads of notable persons in their sanctuaries, you see. Well, you can imagine what Greek and Roman travellers must have felt when the Celto-Ligurians did them the honours, including a good look at one of their precious pickled heads!

MP I was wondering whether you'd thought of your painting as related to them in any way?

LIB I don't exactly feel I'm participating in an Irish head cult! But I do derive from it in a sense. Like the Celts, I tend to regard the head as this magic box containing the spirit. Enter that box, enter behind the billowing curtain of the face, and you have the whole landscape of the spirit. And the face itself, this undeniable outer husk of reality, does express the spirit to a certain extent. That is what fascinates me, because I'm fascinated by appearances and what they reveal, the way expressions change from instant to instant in some people because of the vitality rising within them and transforming them the whole time. So that the head, for me at least, is a paradox, both hiding or masking the spirit and revealing or incarnating it.

MP But what led you to Yeats and Joyce and the others, specifically? Was it admiration for their work?

LIB I'm drawn to their work, yes, certainly, and in each case, before beginning to paint, I have tried to steep myself as deeply as possible in it. On the other hand, I don't think of them so much as famous or brilliant men but as vulnerable, especially poignant human beings who have gone further than the rest of us and for that reason are more isolated and moving. Above all I was drawn to the journey they had made through life and the wide world of their vision.

MP I believe you knew Yeats.

LIB Only in the way a child 'knows' a schoolmaster or some other lofty figure. My mother knew his family, so I was quite familiar with him – and with his very impressive manner! Yeats is a wonderful example of how appearance changes, and in those images – you see, I think of them as traces, images rather than portraits – I allowed very differing aspects of his appearance full rein. I would say that, now photography has shown us how multi-faceted human appearance is, it would be futile and pretentious to try to capture a great man in a single 'portrait'. Anyhow, in those series of flickering images I did of Yeats,[1] I hoped to catch something of the many-sidedness of that extraordinary Irishman, and so, perhaps, touch the landscape behind 'those ancient glittering eyes'. Occasionally I even played a game of conjuring him up, as one might do in a séance of spiritualism!

MP Did a similar sensation ever come when you were working on Joyce?

LIB I often felt it was impertinent on my part to play with the appearances of these men. With Joyce, I confess I felt overawed, even quite literally afraid. His is the most evocative and painful head I have ever attempted. I was extremely conscious of all he must have suffered – the humiliations and neglect, the physical suffering and poverty. And of course I was also thinking constantly of the extraordinary adventure that had taken place in that head. Because he really did push the boat out, didn't he, sailing into realms that very few people dare to enter. I mean, I think these men, Joyce and Yeats, were real heroes, heroes of courage, Promethean. And the tensions became so acute while I was working on Joyce that on one occasion I felt I couldn't go on, I simply couldn't go back and face that head – rather like the Douanier Rousseau who didn't dare go back to his studio to face the fearful lion he had painted!

MP You did something like 120 studies of Joyce.[2]

LIB Yes, if you count all the watercolours and charcoal drawings as well as the oils. And in a sense I could have kept on indefinitely, because I never felt there was anything definite or conclusive about them. I think Joyce's own work was rather like that, cyclic rather than linear, ending as it began, a circle to be entered at any time, at any point. It was the product of a remarkably Celtic mind, a counter-Renaissance mind in a sense and perhaps comparable in its minute patience, in its constant circularity, to the interlacings of the Book of Kells. And then you have the extraordinary plasticity of the head itself, with the great balanced sculptural gestures of the forehead and the chin thrusting forward and the nose taking place in the sweeping hollow between the two. A head like a sickle moon.

MP You steep yourself in the works and lives of the people you paint, but you also collect photographs of them. What importance do the photos have?

LIB They provide, as it were, objective evidence, even when they're considered 'bad' photographs because they don't correspond to the conventional image of whoever it is. I'm interested in making images that are as objective as possible. Naturally, I realize that whatever one does has to be to some degree subjective because it is necessarily reflected from some part of one's mind. In this sense the surface of the canvas becomes a kind of mirror, and in painting others one is, at least partly, painting oneself. Nevertheless, I am interested above all in the other, in the other being. I often think how utterly fascinating it would be to get into somebody else's head, even a cat's head, for a few minutes. I mean, I'm sure we all see each other quite differently. If I were able to get into your head when you were looking at Anne, for instance, I'm certain I'd think 'No, no, that's not Anne, Anne's not like that at all!'

MP How do you actually use the photos when you're painting?

LIB Often I don't refer to them at all, but if I do, I tend to have two or more of them beside me at the same time. These photos tend to give a very differing impression of the person in question, and I make no attempt to relate them. In this way I hope to uncover different sides and layers of the person in the image I am trying to form. And then photos are also useful reminders of how completely changing a face can be, and they help me avoid, or at least be more conscious of, the trap of verisimilitude. I tend to work in series, too, you know – with three images going at the same time, and that also helps to break the merely personal or conventional visual idea one carries around of the other person.

MP You could have gone on doing images of Joyce indefinitely. What made you change to another subject, in fact?

LlB I could have gone on with Joyce alone, you're quite right. But I also welcome the challenge of a new personality, so to speak. I like to think that I might get a leg into another, quite new country, and the change also makes one more aware of the sterile formulas one tends to fall into after a while. You know the way Yeats's nose is broad at the bridge, then suddenly tapers in such a remarkable fashion? Well, once you latch on to such formulas you begin to have a recognizable image of Yeats at your fingertips – and it turns into a trap, an invitation to mere dexterity. The same thing happens with Francis Bacon if you fix on the unusual width of his jaw line. Dexterity is not, as you can imagine, what I'm looking for. I've been reproached for having too much of it, too much technical skill. Well, by a curious mishap, this has now been disproved. About two years ago I injured my right hand; after a bone graft, it had to stay put, in plaster, for several months. For the first time in my life, I began to paint with my left hand, and the images which formed beneath it were indistinguishable from the others: neither better nor worse. And now, although my right hand functions as before, I sometimes still paint with the left to encourage the unexpected or accidental means by which an image may emerge.

MP How would you explain an 'accident' in that context?

LIB Accident is extremely important to me. I believe that my role as an artist, in so far as it exists, lies in the recognition of significant marks as they occur. And these are what I retain and expand, and from which I hope an image will emerge. To me painting is not a means of communication or even self-expression, but rather a process of discovering, or uncovering. I think of the painter as a kind of archaeologist, an archaeologist of the spirit, patiently disturbing the surface of things until he makes a discovery which will enable him to take his search further.

MP How do these significant marks tend to occur? How do you actually begin a new image?

LIB With an oil, I usually make a very rough sketch in charcoal first. Then I take the brush, tip it with a little blue, say, on one side and a little Indian red on the other and I make these free gestures round the area of the eyebrow or the chin or wherever. And sometimes the suggestion of an image – a kind of *objet trouvé*, if you like – begins to emerge. Sometimes not. But those gestures almost always turn out to be significant if one is attentive to their possibilities. They seem to have a queer logic of their own. In my case, all I can say is that there has to be an element of accident, or discovery, or surprise all the way along, so that the emergent image is not so much made by me as imposing itself on me, accident by accident, with its own autonomous life. Otherwise, I don't think it has any value.

MP Can you be more specific about how this process tends to evolve?

LIB Well, what occurs, I think, is this. Successive marks made by a brush dipped in this and that pigment, almost at random, build up a kind of scribbled structure of colour in and out of the features of the image which is gradually forming. Then this free structure usually suggests the areas where white pigment may be heavily brushed on to form the outer planes of the image. But each plane and each coloured mark, whether sharp in contour or melting, has to have its autonomy – its independence, if you like, of any merely descriptive role. And these marks have to coexist independently within the various depths of the landscape of the head-image. They have to be allowed, as it were, to float within it.

MP But with this emphasis on free gesture and accident, don't you ever find yourself in a hopeless mess, having to scrape everything off and start again?

LIB Certainly. But that happens less now than it used to. A great deal of the technical difficulty in these paintings comes from the fact that they are heads in utter isolation – without any particular circumstances, such as a collar and tie, or a recognizable background. Now the difficult thing in my view is to make this isolated head so that it doesn't look like a mere sketch, which it isn't, nor like some kind of decapitation. The image has to emerge from some plausible matrix, beyond habitual circumstance or environment, as if outside time. You may have noticed that these are no circumstantial details in the images – barely even any hair, which I consider circumstantial, since it can be long or short, or indicative of a young or old man, and these are comments which I wish to avoid.

MP I was going to ask you about the origin of the white background. It seems to be almost a traditional feature of your painting.

LIB Yes, well, I first used a white background in 1956 when I was doing a series of torsos or what I called 'presences'. I'd been in Spain that year and was tremendously struck by the way shadow there looked more real than the substance it was cast by. All substance seemed penetrated and eaten up by this brilliance, so I came to see everything as existing in a matrix of pure white light. Then, later, I had the idea of conjuring up images out of nothing, out of light, out of the depths of the blank canvas.

MP Do your reactions change at all when you paint images of living people?

LIB I think the big difference is that with the dead you have the whole life laid out on a plane: youth and age become contemporaneous. The living, on the other hand, are still in time, moving and changing. And then, of course, with the living there's always the potential embarrassment that they'll turn up again and confound all the images one has evolved of them!

MP Has the fact of knowing Beckett and Bacon, of having watched their flesh-and-blood appearance, made any difference?

LIB It's an advantage, but it's also an inhibiting thing. I mean, you may feel it to be an impertinence to be playing with their appearance in this way – and also a distortion to place them outside time, as it were, in the matrix I referred to. Particularly since people believe – it's a reaction I've often come across during exhibitions – that in some way you're making a 'statement' about the person you've painted. I'm not making a statement at all, you know. I'm simply trying to discover, to uncover, aspects of the Beckettness of Beckett, the Baconness of Bacon. But it's also true that once you know people a little in the flesh, those memories of them stay with you. That curiously piercing look that Beckett has comes back to me even from photos where he doesn't have it.

MP Do you ever think of painting people who are constantly close to you, members of the family or old friends?

LIB Oh but I do. At one point I painted a number of portraits of my mother and father. I've painted my children, and I have made more studies of Anne than of any other human being. But essentially all studies of people pose the same problems. What fascinates me is their otherness, and this is what I hope to realize in a painting. With Anne especially, I suppose, it's a kind of fetishism: I attempt to realize her being in paint. I don't want to sound esoteric, but you might say I try to enact a magic process within the limitations of my art and so, hopefully, come up with an image that has a life of its own. Nothing more.

MP You've referred in the past to certain mystical attitudes and also to spiritualism. Does this imply any particular beliefs on your part?

LIB I have no defined religious views. I'm what you might call a good agnostic, who tries to keep his window onto reality as widely open as possible. I was tremendously struck, you know, by something Schrödinger, the physicist, said to me as a student almost forty years ago in Dublin. It was to the effect that matter could not be destroyed – modified beyond all recognition, perhaps, transformed into energy, for example – but never destroyed. Schrödinger also believed that the spirit, or consciousness, was indestructible, too. I must say I remain impressed by that thought … And then, when you think of the universe with its countless galaxies, each with its countless stars, when you think of the infinite possibilities and compare them to our limited perception, it seems impossible to hold any dogmatic belief. I think of us as inhabiting a tiny corner of reality, perceiving what we can, rather like lobsters in a pool, you know, with their sensitive antennae waving this way and that. But what can they really tell, down there in the water, about land or cities or the everlasting night of the stars?

1 Exhibited at the Musée d'Art Moderne de la Ville de Paris, under the title 'A la recherche de W. B. Yeats – Cent portraits imaginaires', in October–November 1976.

2 'Studies towards an Image of James Joyce'. Travelling exhibition (November, 1977–December, 1978) shown in Genoa (S. Marco dei Giustiniani), Zurich (Gimpel & Hanover), London (Gimpel Fils), Belfast (Arts Council), Dublin (Municipal Gallery of Modern Art), New York (Gimpel & Weitzenhoffer), Montreal (Waddington), Toronto (Waddington).

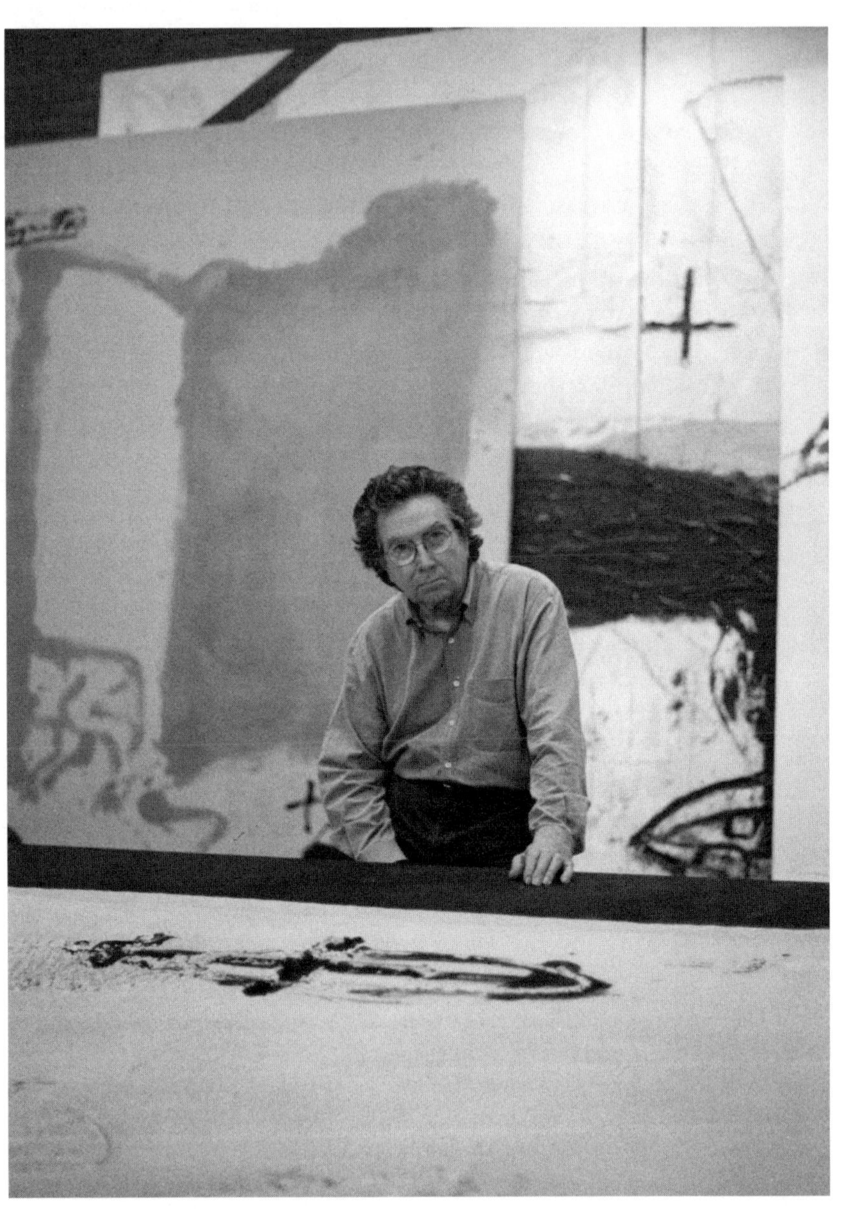

ANTONI TÀPIES

EL PUTXET BARCELONA 1990

When I was editor of the Paris-based magazine *Art International* in the early 1990s, I decided to devote a special issue of the review to the work of Antoni Tàpies. Over the years I had seen many of his exhibitions, notably at the Galerie Maeght, then at the Galerie Lelong, in Paris, and I had met the artist briefly on a couple of those occasions. The originality of his approach, at once deeply serious and light-heartedly serene, fascinated me above all in its duality.

A duality, it seems to me still, runs through Tàpies's entire work, from his small prints and drawings to the most monumental of his paintings and sculptures. At every point of this extraordinarily varied and inventive body of work, Tàpies manages with a rapid hieroglyph or symbol to suggest the highest aspirations of man, while rooting them in the mundane matter – string, straw, socks, earth – of everyday existence. The questing spirit always leads back, as it were, to feet of clay; just as, under Tàpies's inimitable touch, graffiti scrawled like an insult or an obscenity on a rough canvas resound with the fragile secret of existence. It is this profound truth of poets and philosophers down the ages – of the beast bordering the angel, the rose rising fragrant on the dunghill – that Tàpies captures and holds as a talisman against our dark ignorance of ourselves.

Tàpies agreed to the magazine project and invited me to come and see him in Barcelona. We began talking in the studio, in the midst of neatly ranged canvases, new sculptures, paint-clogged brushes and dusty tools. Tàpies was gentle and humorous, glad of the opportunity to talk in very general terms about his work and the techniques he used, but with the wryness and modesty of a sage, shrugging diffidently at certain questions and smiling. After a while, he took me into his library and started to bring out and discuss the books that had a special importance for him. Gradually I began to feel that our inter-

Antoni Tàpies (1923–2012). *Art International*, Paris, Winter 1990. Republished with the above introduction in *Antoni Tàpies*, exhibition catalogue, Centro Cultural Banco do Brasil, São Paulo, October 2004.

view could go in any direction, follow any lead in a discussion that now touched on the history of art and science, eastern philosophy and world culture. After several hours we left the studio and went to dine in a Galician seafood restaurant, where (after a couple of bottles of wine) the bizarre forms of the crustacea seemed to me to recall the strange complexity of Tàpies's own chance-inspired imagery and to underline the ebb and flow of our conversation, which lasted late into the evening.

MP You've said that for you 'the essential value of art is to influence consciousness and to induce a meditative state so that an ultimate reality is revealed'. But you also believe that art has a moral and political role to play.

AT Yes. If you can gain a better understanding of the essential themes in man's life, then everything else falls into place. The real aim of my work has always been to try to change people's ideas so that they are no longer lost in an artificial reality, distracted by advertising or by those advocating an ideology, for example.

MP Is art a religious act in your view?

AT I've always compared the attitude of the artist to that of a mystic. They both follow a path which slowly leads towards an ultimate vision of reality. When you arrive at that point it's difficult to talk about it: what is ultimate reality, or the face of God, as the mystics would say? It's not so much knowledge as inner experience.

MP You're surely not thinking about all this consciously as you paint?

AT When I'm in my studio I am seeking, checking that what I have brought to life succeeds in convincing me, as I am the first spectator of my paintings. I strive to make them speak and offer a clearer vision of reality, and this changes with time as history and human knowledge evolve.

MP Is your interest in oriental art inspired by the cultures that underlie it rather than by purely formal considerations?

AT I think all contemporary art has been influenced by non-western art. But I came to oriental art through my early interest in science, when I was very concerned about the nature of reality, the structure of matter and problems of space, time and causality. I read scientists like Albert Einstein, Niels Bohr, Erwin Schrödinger, Werner Heisenberg, Jacob Oppenheimer – and I noticed all these people, at one time or another, wrote of the Vedanta or Taoism or Buddhism, which encouraged me to read these eastern philosophies.

MP You reached these esoteric teachings and your interest in oriental art through science. That's an unusual path for an artist.

AT Yes, though many artists have been interested in spiritual themes in recent years.

MP But not usually in science.

AT Science has changed a great deal. The new physics has taken a stance which is very close to that of the spiritual traditions. We are more interested in physics now because it has become more human. I had a very strict Christian education and at times I have reacted against this from a philosophical point of view. The Judaeo-Christian tradition with its dualistic conception of reality – spirit/matter, man/God, good/evil – is human, but it is not as true as oriental thought, which comes closer to modern science. Dualities do not really exist, but the orientals talk about non-dualism because the idea of unity can give too simple a picture. Good and evil continue to exist, but they're concepts that must be seen in relative terms.

MP You have always read a great deal. Your painting is well nourished by ideas even when you are not conscious of that fact.

AT I haven't read as much as all that.

MP But you are nevertheless a *peintre savant* – an erudite artist.

AT I know something, but I don't have a deep knowledge. To achieve that, you have to dedicate your whole life to it. I wanted to find out the essential things. We become attached to things of secondary importance these days and we lose sight of essentials. There's even a culture industry whose aim is not to spread knowledge but rather to make money. I think that these are very bad times for art because art has become an object of financial value, completely separated from other fields of knowledge. We must make a real effort to construct these missing connections, which used to be self-evident. Asiatic art, for example, was inseparable from religion and philosophy, so was the art of the European Middle Ages and African art. But now, using the excuse that we have lost our religious faith, we have tried to secularize transcendental values without finding any true equivalent for art's original function. I believe, as Carl Jung did, that the gods have been transformed into philosophical concepts, and I accept that sort of secularization. But modern society hasn't found any new transcendental values.

MP So your ideal spectator is someone who spends time in front of your work and penetrates its essence?

AT I want to provoke him, to arouse his solidarity and altruism and to help him to develop the potential we all have within us but which is stifled by industrial society.

MP Is that responsibility not overwhelming when you are painting?

AT I think that it's very important to achieve a state of transcendental meditation, but it must be in accordance with the demands of studio life. So I often place everyday objects next to transcendental things in my pictures, in order to provoke a contrast and make people more aware.

MP Images like the foot? How did the foot come about?

AT I'm told that there are a lot of parallels between my work and the writing of Georges Bataille. Apparently Bataille often writes about the foot as a rather dirty part of the human body. But I still haven't read any of Bataille's books.

MP But you were inspired by the Surrealists?

AT Early on I was very influenced by Surrealism – although little was known about it in Spain at the time. I was friendly with the group around Miró. They were ready to fight for the modernization of culture and they helped me a great deal. When I first arrived in Paris in 1950, the French Surrealists were already quite old, but I met André Masson. I missed Max Ernst, but I feel as if I knew him because our mutual friend Roland Penrose often told us about each other.

MP Calligraphy is very important to you, isn't it? Is that because it mediates between letters and images?

AT Calligraphy allows me to suggest fine shades of meaning without having to be too precise. The orientals don't like making things too obvious, they prefer to leave space for the spectator's imagination. Calligraphy is also intimately linked to our physiology, it is an expression of the soul revealed by the hand, a movement which expresses our interior life.

MP Has sculpture come to occupy a more important place in your work lately?

AT Not really. My sculpture was not so well known but, from the start, I've worked with something of a sculptor's mentality. I've always conceived of the picture as an object quite unlike an academic picture with perspectival illusion and chiaroscuro. I think of paintings as magical objects, like something you could use to cure an illness. I made a few small assemblages in the early years, and once I made a sculpture out of a ball of newspaper.

MP Were the materials you used considered very shocking at first?

AT Yes. Even my father thought I was completely mad.

MP So it took a lot of courage to keep on using these materials?

AT Courage, or recklessness. Viewed in terms of art history, my materials are not all that remarkable. There were already newspaper collages and the like. I just used such materials a bit more systematically. I was very influenced by my master, Miró, who used all sorts of bizarre materials in his work.

MP But very early on you created an original vocabulary, and you have evolved a truly personal technique over the years.

AT Little by little. But there's nothing really new in what I do. It always involves rediscoveries from some other time or place. I thought I had invented a mixture of powdered marble, but I've since found out that it was used by Roman and Catalan artists. I was told this by a traditional church artist when he came to see me in my studio in the mountains. He used the technique himself, and he told me that medieval muralists used it as a base to prepare their grounds ... There is always a good reason underlying all the old techniques. Sometimes I employ materials which seem incompatible and which repel each other. For example, the black paint I often use is plastic-based, and I mix it with water, whereas the varnish is usually mixed with oil.

MP Do you have a different approach to small- and large-scale works?

AT I work with the same intensity on both. When I'm working on a large-scale painting, I like to get right into it and sometimes I leave the marks I make walking over it. The size of my works depends on my mood and my ideas. The small works tend to be more subjective, and the large ones are made in a more collective spirit.

MP There's the same interest in rough surfaces ...

AT After searching a great deal for a personal vocabulary, I made a discovery. I had been attacking pictures with lots of scratchings and I even made holes in them. But finally, after all that stylistic excess, I realized that I had arrived at a new unity. I made a picture with a smooth surface which reminded me of a wall, marked by traces of time and weather. To another artist, it may not have been very important, but my name means 'wall' in Catalan, so it seemed a mark of identity to me. I was very influenced by Brassaï's photographs of graffiti on walls, which I discovered in an issue of the Surrealist magazine *Minotaure* ... Some time ago, I received a letter from a Swiss-German who was in prison because he had been caught doing graffiti. He said that he had been influenced by my work, and after he was released he began to collect my paintings. This touched me deeply.

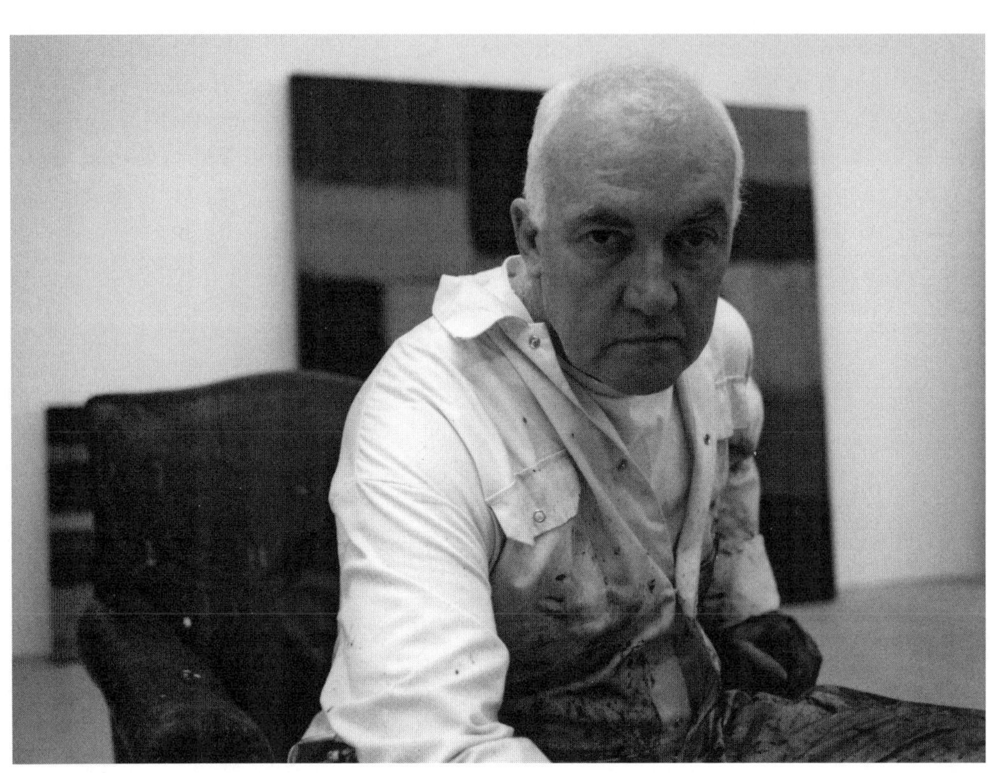

SEAN SCULLY

BAVARIA 2004

The interview took place in the studio Sean Scully has built for himself on the upper floor of a farmhouse about an hour's drive outside Munich. Recently completed, the big loft-like space looks out onto a yard with outbuildings on one side and onto rolling fields and agricultural land leading to mountains on the other. It is comfortably but sparsely furnished, and from Scully's paintings on the walls of the living area to the studio itself, the entire focus of the space is clearly concentrated on work.

Inside the studio, Scully has numerous paintings stacked against the walls, some completed, others at every stage from a preliminary underdrawing to awaiting the last, decisive touch of the artist's brush. A small island of ladders, paint pots, brushes and rags occupies the centre of the large, functional space, along with a pair of paint-splashed chairs. The interview begins here, breaking off occasionally as Scully goes over in search of a canvas he wants to illustrate a particular point.

MP So you feel as at home out here in the Bavarian countryside as you would do anywhere else? It's a good atmosphere to work in?

SS Yes. Above all, the thing about being here is that it's very private.

MP It's quite cut off. It could be anywhere. In that sense, it's very different from your studios in New York and Barcelona. I have a notion that since you travel constantly and have different studios in different countries, the only place you really live is in your canvases.

Sean Scully (1945–). *Sean Scully*, exhibition catalogue, Galerie Lelong, Paris, May 2004.

SS Well, I do have an attachment to places. I'm not an artist who's cut off from the world. I'm connected to people and places. So I wouldn't say that I really live in the canvases.

MP I was thinking that, as a rather rootless person, you made yourself a kind of permanent place in the canvases.

SS It's true to say that my identification with my paintings is tremendous. I'm sure one could say that about any artist, but in my case it's exceptionally true. There's something in the paintings that I'm constantly building out of a kind of emotional precariousness. That's how I would describe my emotional state: precarious.

MP And painting is the arena where you play this precariousness out – for some kind of balance or reassurance?

SS I'm not playing it out. I know what it is. I'm trying to make something that is bigger than I am. Something that is universal and not just driven by my neurosis. I think that makes me fundamentally no different from an artist like Francis Bacon. And my work is a lot more driven by a desire to build a kind of emotional classicism – if you can put it that way.

MP ... an emotional order?

SS I wouldn't say that is was an order that I'm trying to build, because I allow the poetry in the painting to be the ultimately dominant force.

MP So that you give yourself up to something that you hope will be bigger than you and take *you* in.

SS I'm not really painting for myself. So that statement is perfect, until you get to the last sentence. I would say: that would 'take you in', rather than take me in, would be right! My paintings are meant to communicate, they're meant to move people.

MP When you're painting, are you conscious of wanting to communicate with others or to find some firm ground, some structure, for your emotional precariousness?

SS Well, I'm doing both. When I'm painting, my feelings are extremely strong, and the actual making of the paintings, with this insistent brushstroke, is a very obsessive thing. And I'm trying to pull everything together and make some kind of pact between my emotional world and the world of bigger things, of ideas, so I'm constantly moving big structures, big forms, around and I'm also making rhythms to give the whole thing a sense of balance.

MP So it's a lyrical thing too. And an Irish thing, perhaps?

SS A friend of mine in Dublin who's been in the art world for a long time said that my work was more Irish than anyone else's she could think of. She also talked in the same vein about Jackson Pollock, who was Irish of course. She talked about this endless, swirling line. In my work you have the endless line coming back at itself. My line is a kind of geometric version of Pollock.

MP ... always beginning again.

SS ... always beginning like Irish music, like Irish speaking, a whole process of carrying forward and coming back and continuing. And of course the Irish, when they're talking, are never really interested in arriving anywhere or coming to any kind of a stop. I mean they'll put in a stop from time to time, but only to take a breath or a drink of whiskey. Basically the full-stop in Irish talking does not have a big place. Their talk is a stream, a continuous, flowing thing, and that's what's so charming about it of course.

MP Yes, it can go anywhere and of course it does go anywhere, so that you're not quite sure after a moment in Irish conversation whether your feet are still touching the ground or whether you're floating a hundred feet up! But that's part of the magic.

SS My paintings nevertheless are far more worldly, far more intellectual...

MP Because you are. You're not a tinker telling a tale ...

SS No, no. I'm not a painter down in Cork with only his lyricism. In many ways I feel I'm taking on the whole history of painting. And I know the history of painting. I mean, I pretty much understand it like an art historian. So I've made myself into a universal painter, rather than a local painter, or even a notional painter.

MP But there is a source there that is Irish.

SS Yes. There is an emotion in the paintings that drives them. What I have done is that I've added knowledge to that emotion to try to make the paintings more humanistic and more universal.

MP You are very open and communicative about what you feel. Is that ease you have in talking about your emotions at all Irish?

SS I don't know. I'm completely relaxed and confessional about what I'm thinking or feeling – I see no reason not to be.

MP Perhaps you have no fear in that regard?

SS I don't have any. In fact, I don't understand the fear. I can't identify with it at all.

MP In that sense, your painting is like an open book about yourself.

SS That's a nice expression – an open book. The other nice thing you came up with when we were talking a moment ago is that I give myself to people. And that is what I do. I really give myself, body and soul. And when it happens, it's sublime. It's a moment I experience over and over again as I paint, and when it happens I feel that my life has been taken to a different, universal level.

MP And that's the moment that you aspire to, that you work towards …

SS I see a painting, particularly my painting, as a bridge. And I use those kinds of titles – 'Bridge', 'Window' – all the time. In a way they mean the same thing, since both of them take you out of yourself. And that's what I want. I'm always trying to make paintings that help to take you to another place in your life. In other words, I'm not making paintings that are just to be looked at, as phenomena to be appreciated – which is what a lot of painters, particularly abstract painters, do. My painting isn't really meant to work like that. It's meant to work like a bridge.

MP It's metaphysical, taking you beyond…

SS Well, it is metaphysical on some level. It's certainly religious and spiritual. I think it has a very strong spiritual dimension. And I pull a lot of other threads into my work. Obviously there's simple geometry, simple drawing, all the way through it. And there's the rhythm, the kind of rhythm you find in weaving and folk arts all over the world – in Morocco and other parts of Africa, in Ireland, in Lapland. Those rhythms are very strong in Japan as well. I once went to a restaurant in Tokyo, when I had a show out there. I think it was the oldest restaurant in the city, and they had this lovely, gnarled old tree outside in the garden. The restaurant was very exclusive, and at some point we were taken to see this great screen they kept there. So they showed us this screen, which was about six metres long with dragons on it. But on the other side of the room they had its poor cousin, which was simply a chequerboard design in cream and brown. And all I could look at was this chequerboard. I wasn't even remotely interested in the dragons. The chequerboard was made of fabric and I suspect that is was printed, although it may have been made out of squares sewn together. In any case, I was at that time considering bringing a chequerboard into my work, and I was fascinated by seeing this quite by chance in Tokyo. It must have been about twelve years ago.

And another time, round about that period, in Madrid, I saw this enormous metal garage door, in a public parking lot. A very rough item it was, and it was painted red and white chequerboard in a huge design – each square bigger than your body. And what was lovely about it was that one side hung off and the hinges were broken. So the junction in the centre had a fault to it.

MP You went for that, didn't you?

SS Big time! Because that is the longing or the heartbreak. Things won't go together properly. There's a fracture. And that is what fascinates me. These relationships and fractures are running through my paintings all the time. These awkward unions.

MP The heartbreak door, or heartbreak garage.

SS Yes, 'Heartbreak Garage' it could be called.

MP So you saw the dividing line running through it and thought, 'Ah, I know about that'.

SS Yes, you want something to fit together – and it doesn't. And my paintings are dealing with all these human problems, of things fitting or not fitting. And I think it's this awkwardness that is the key to the appeal of my paintings.

MP So you have all the degrees of harmony and dissonance that take the eye on a long emotional trip.

SS These paintings are meant to be worked with, to be involved with. I want them to be really connected to your body so that you actually get a sense of your own putting together of things in your life. And of course the whole time there is this constant rhythm running through them.

MP They work on a very subconscious level, don't they?

SS Well, they're simple and not simple. Direct and indirect. Sometimes they have more body or less body, more transparency or less transparency. And I work at pictures until I feel they no longer need me. I think that's part of their durability.

MP There's a dual experience.

SS Yes. I wanted to come to that. And that is why I was so fascinated by that line of Yeats you used at the beginning of your Bacon book: 'No mind can engender until divided into two.' The idea of duality is so strong in my work. My obsession is not with being successful or famous but with leaving something that transcends time and generations. I truly want to leave the world better than I found it, not worse. And so there is a strong sense of loving in my paintings. They can be aggressive – but they also have a lot of love in them. What I should really like is to create a kind of permanent moment of love. You can see that in the way they are painted. They're not pushing you off. They're not saying: 'Here it is, isn't it great, buy it!' The paintings are layered with all kinds of emotions and experience … and they're not saying they're perfect either.

MP These are paintings from a broken home. They embody the duality – the suffering, the need to survive, the feeling of being split, of conflicting emotions.

SS That's a very good reading of my domestic situation, of where I'm coming from. I take all this pain and then try to turn it into something bigger. And that's the reason why that phrase of Yeats's stuck with me as soon as I read it. There are a lot of dual things going on in the paintings that are produced by the pressure of disagreement and the pressure of having split loyalties, which I think a lot of us do. And these relationships in the paintings are constantly trying to show how things can come together. That is what the paintings are about. The body and the light of these forms coming together, and the way they rub up against each other … And there are gaps between them where they are not quite coming together. There is a constant sense of forming and unforming, with areas of paint that have more or less vitality or aggressiveness or lyricism and so on.

MP I suppose what Yeats is getting at is that if you don't have this sense of duality inside you, you have no need to create. The need to create comes because you are split and forced to find some kind of unity. It's not a choice.

SS But the thing that makes my paintings different is that I am actually painting a subject. There are overt subjects, aren't there? You have these cut bits and you have these slightly disembodied or separated elements on a background field. Or column forms that could be read as figures. And I'm very interested in the whole problem of figuration. On the other hand, I'm a good enough painter to paint a field and leave it at that. But that would take out the difficulty, and then the paintings would be about harmony alone. Who knows, I might do that when I'm eighty and paint a moment of total unity. But at the moment the paintings are still battlefields. Luminous battlefields.

MP Luminous because they are nevertheless driven by hope?

SS Well, I'm not sure. To be honest I'm not sure I'm interested in that. I'm not interested in perfection either. I like life with all its problems. I think that is what makes it so rich and fascinating. In a sense, one's difficulties are one's opportunities. Without them you wouldn't have a reason to exist. You would have your energy taken away from you. Because you get that energy from opposition, and from the fact that you are always coming apart.

*

MP What's the actual process? How does the painting begin physically?

SS I work up towards the painting conceptually in my mind. I play with the idea of the painting for a long time before I get to make the painting. When I make the painting it's usually very fast. And suddenly there it is.

MP And you're sure it's finished?

SS Well, I know. As I said, I keep working at a painting until I know it doesn't need me any more.

MP And when you start a new picture, you go directly onto the canvas, without notes as it were?

SS I've never made studies. Sometimes I make watercolours as mementoes, but afterwards, once the painting has been made. And the titles of the watercolours are dedications to the paintings. There's a big difference between them, the difference between public and private. Because I do things all the time for the public, so that there can be exhibitions and people can go and see the paintings. The watercolours are more private.

MP So that's a conscious thing. You want to get the pictures out there so that people can be in contact with them.

SS Yes. I mean, I'm not a careerist in the sense that I am trying to play the market or that I'm trying to show with the most groovy galleries, because I've never had an interest in that. In fact, I often do things that are strategically unproductive. But I am interested in having paintings, a whole body of them, out in the public so people can see them. And people do use them. You know, I think in a lot of situations, particularly now that the museum functions more and more as a fun house, the public is being very underestimated. People are not that stupid. A lot of people now are very knowledgeable and they are able to work with abstract paintings and get tremendous resonance from them. And I know it's really extraordinary what impact art has on people's lives. It's very valuable, and I need to know that it's happening.

So, in my case, it's not a question of art world strategy. It really is a question of communication. I had a show, for example, at the Haus der Kunst and also at the Nordrhein-Westphalen, two of the best exhibition spaces not only here in Germany but in the world. And after that the right strategy might be not to show any more in smaller museums. But I'm showing now in Weimar, and I think it's very important to have these little shows. And I always turn up to them. I wouldn't think of not turning up. There's always a show on somewhere. Over the last five years, I can't think there's been a time when I haven't had a show going on somewhere.

MP And your being present at the shows is all part of the process, your thinking, your vision?

SS I think it's very important to make yourself available. It's part of the communication.

MP To come back to your watercolours, are they done above all as a private record?

SS Well, they're more private. But I don't think any of my work is private anymore. It's just a different degree, and it's something that I can have and put in a drawer and get the sense at least for a while that I made it entirely for myself. But of course it's only a question of time before that little watercolour has to come out of the drawer and go somewhere for an exhibition.

MP Is the watercolour a version of the painting or a response to the painting?

SS One could say it's a version of the same thing in different medium, which produces an entirely distinct reality. Because the watercolour is really only staining the painting. You're only working with the light within the watercolour, and you're trying to articulate that light. Whereas with the painting the metaphor of the skin, the flesh, the body of light, is much more powerful. You're actually taking skin and flesh and making it. You're building the skin, you're building the surface, and that's really potent. And watercolours are the absence of body. The paintings are the compression of light and body and motion. They're big things – you know, the stretchers are big, deliberately big. So they're big, rugged, awkward things on the wall with a real physical presence. Someone recently compared my work with Guston's, which I understand. There are many similarities, you know: we both put paint on in a very direct, very physical way. But where we're very different is in our use and understanding of colour. Guston's colour sense is very simplistic. And, as you know, he gave up on abstraction.

MP Because of that, do you think?

SS I don't know. Human beings are so complicated. If Guston had loved the idea of abstraction more, he might have developed a colour sense in support of it. He may have subverted himself deliberately in some way to get out of abstraction. I'm not developing a colour sense. It's complicated enough to keep it. Guston said he went up the mountain of abstraction and realized when he was near the top he'd forgotten something. I've gone up the mountain of abstraction, and I've realized that I haven't forgotten anything. I'm not going down. This is where I am, and this is abstraction which has body and soul – and there's not much of that around in painting at the moment.

MP When you're conceptualizing a painting in your head, does it come at all ready-made with colour?

SS The concept really comes with a feeling or an impression. But when the colours begin to take form on the canvas, they cannot exist in any other way. It's impossible.

MP Because one tone is suggested by another …

SS Right. The colour in the paintings is so finely balanced that if you're looking at the greys in that horizontal painting over there on the wall opposite, you can see how the vertical grey on the right is a little bit more blue than the vertical grey between the red. They were probably the same colour to begin with, but put on at different times over some other paint, which may have been partly scraped off. The underlying traces have influenced the grey in a way that makes the surface colour extremely complex, because even when colours seem to be repeated, they are not at all: there's always a different nuance.

MP Sometimes you find the colours you've put on is not what you want, so you scrape it off?

SS Well, it's so difficult to know what you want. That begs the question: what is it you want? And mostly I don't even know. I'm stumbling around in the painting looking for my own sense of what moves me most. I have to be moved by the painting to know where I'm going. It's so difficult to understand how these things happen, because the whole enterprise is extremely precarious. Because I've got thick paint, thin paint, a bright colour, a dark colour, this colour over that colour, that colour over this colour, the edge painted this way, the edge painted that way, more space, less space, red coming through, yellow coming through, black coming through, scraped off, not scraped off, et cetera, et cetera. And all this stuff is happening at once. And what I'm doing is dancing with the painting. I'm really just dancing with the painting. And together we are making something which is bigger than I am. And I have to say that when I'm working like that I feel assistance. Some spirit is helping me paint a painting. And that is where my absurd sense of conviction comes from. That's why I simply cannot be deterred. It's not possible.

MP Does it feel like a state of grace?

SS I feel as if I am being contacted by something outside myself, bigger than myself, that is a spiritual force.

MP People say this when they commit murders, too.

SS But I'm not committing murders, that's quite a difference. I know that's what serial killers say: 'I was told to do it'. But I don't hear voices. What I'm saying is that I feel assisted by a spiritual force. And of course my own human intervention is crucial. That is what the painting relies on, and until you get to that state the painting really has not taken off. But in my case, the paintings take off pretty fast.

MP But you can't always reach that state of grace?

SS Well, if I don't, I can't make the painting.

MP Does that happen?

SS Never.

MP You have bad days, though? Bad painting days?

SS No. I don't even know what that is. I have no idea what any of that is. I might have bad days when things in my life are going wrong. But out of the worst days come some of the best paintings. I can be sad and paint something that is full of energy and light. I tell you, I'm really inspired. It's not a contrivance. I don't even talk about this. This is the first time I've talked about this. I don't talk about it because it doesn't really help anybody understand the paintings. When I'm painting I'm so engaged, so inspired, that it never occurs to me that I might paint a bad painting. I really don't think in those terms.

MP You don't have a sort of critical thinking?

SS No, not at all. It doesn't come into it. I don't spend hours trying to get paintings to 'work'. Of course I am trying to make them better, more intense. But some of my best paintings I made in an afternoon. I'm talking about great big pictures, like *No Neo*. I just go nuts. It's like I'm following some music I really like, like Percy Sledge or John Lee Hooker, and I'm following this chord that's both linear and intensely physical – visceral, even – and I don't know what I'm doing.

MP But when you see your work you must feel that not every picture is as good as the other. Do you think: 'Well, I wouldn't mind having that back and working on it again'?

SS No, I never think like that. Well, I might want to get it back – just to have it, not to rework it. I've chased down quite a few of my paintings just so that I can keep them.

MP So you don't feel some pictures could be improved?

SS I'm sure they could be improved. But that is like improving a kiss. Once you've kissed someone, you've kissed them.

MP That's an interesting analogy.

SS I know that the paintings are not all as good as each other. But how could they be?

MP But whatever level of intensity you work on, there must be moments that are more intense than others.

SS Without question, and some paintings are just unbelievably intense and you can't reason with them or even judge them. There's this orange one I painted for my mother, it's called *Holly*, which was her name. It's extraordinarily intense, almost unbearably intense. It's also celebratory, in a way, and very vital. But there are areas in it which are at death's door. There's a white against the orange in this picture that has got an ashen quality. It's ashen with exhaustion, as if it's the last thing you could do. You know, it's just there and not prepared to negotiate. You could call it a dying colour. And it's next to a rising colour, something intensely vital. Now, do those things, those stark contrasts, make it a better painting than a more lyrical painting? I don't know. It's certainly a fiercer painting. Then I've got these others, like one called *Stair Red Yellow*, which has all kinds of different tensions. I mean, my pictures are full of simultaneously competing troops. It's not like Joseph Albers' *Homage to the Square*. My paintings are not actually homages to anything. I am too iconoclastic a person to do homages or to stick with anything like a square. So there are all these slightly discordant or dramatically discordant realities and relationships. That's the beauty of life, that's the rhythm of life. And that's what I want in my paintings. To have life in all its harmonies and discords shining in the light that comes through.

SEAN SCULLY

BAVARIA 2004

This interview followed on from the previous one quite spontaneously the next day, in Sean Scully's studio in the farmhouse outside Munich. We began talking, very informally and with no particular agenda. It was a bright February morning and a fresh layer of snow had fallen over the surrounding countryside. The big, brooding canvases hung round the studio walls glistened in the wintry light, revealing beneath the ridged sweeps of the paintbrush a seething underworld of colour.

MP Is there such a thing for you as an ordinary working day? Do you start in the morning and keep regular hours?

SS Yes, but I never start in the morning. Because in the morning I'm not ready to paint. So I spend the morning getting ready. And I do all the little things I need to do to make that happen. I do letters. I might write something about my work, for instance, if someone asks me a question for a catalogue or something. It gets my mind working. I walk around the place and come in here and look at the paintings and have a coffee, read the paper, make a couple of phone calls I need to make. Go out maybe, look around the place, come back. Kind of getting myself ready. This is all part of the preparation and it's a mysterious thing. Sometimes I even leave working until quite late. But usually I get going sometime in the afternoon, and then I work for five hours. That would be a pretty normal day for me.

MP By that time are you stalking your prey? Are you circling around?

SS You could put it like that.

MP You don't know what you are up to at that point?

Sean Scully (1945–). Unpublished interview, Bavaria, February 2004.

SS No, I have to feel myself into the day. For instance, I might be working wet into wet, which is a wonderful way to work because you get the most beautiful results. Let's say it's Monday and then the next day you know it's not really advisable to go back over the paint. You have to give the paint a day or two to breathe. Let it dry off a bit and start back on it again when it has enough of a surface to allow you to go over it. And I'm making these colours as I work. And this is fundamental to my paintings, that they have in them a light that does not exist outside the paintings. I find that whole notion of paintings having their own unique light very moving.

MP You're creating something that does not exist anywhere else.

SS This is really and truly the power of painting, and this is why painting as an art form can't be replaced. That's why it won't go away. Because what we've done is we've managed to create a surface in which we produce light that can only exist as the light of painting. And the light of painting is a kind of alive and dead thing. And it comes alive very slowly. And this is an extremely profound and beautiful relationship you make with the painting. Of course, you have to have the right painter! It's something that comes to life and it's amazing how slow it is, but then after a couple of minutes the painting is kind of heated up. And then you are engaged with this peculiar light that is distinct from the light you normally live with. And at that moment you enter into the realm of the painting – that special area of painting, the domain of painting. You can't find it in a photograph, in a landscape or in the sky. It belongs to painting alone. It's the mysterious core, if you like, and for me it has an absolute fascination. I find it extraordinarily moving because it's the combination of a hand, a mark, a surface, a form, a relationship, frozen into an expressive place. And it can never then be unfrozen. It can't be changed, you see. Whereas everything else in the world, in the contemporary world we live in now, can be changed.

MP Such as a digital photograph.

SS Exactly. But painting can't be changed. It's a real commitment to leave a painting the way it is. And my strange relationship with painting means I can do that and it's something I agonize about. It's something I work with in a very instinctive, animal kind of way. And the painting is what it is. I give it its life. But it is what it is. Paintings are permanent. They're a frozen gesture. And you know I was talking to the French museum director, Daniel Abadie, and he said that painting is the art of the twenty-first century because it is at once handmade and profound, and yet it can be perceived in a glimpse. I mean, if you know how to look at paintings and you're involved with them, the experience becomes really profound. If I look, let's say, at a Bonnard or a Matisse or whatever for ten seconds, everything's revealed. It's a flash of recognition, and it really suits our developed intelligence, which is greater now than in the past, as we are becoming increasingly perceptive visually. It's the same with my painting, I hope, since it consists of creating a layered compacted experience that opens itself up slowly. I make things you can stare at. I don't want to make something that can get worn out. And I think one of the reasons people are drawn to my paintings is that the colours in them are all kind of 'off'. They're peculiar, aren't they? And this is something that just happens – you can't plan those strange, discordant notes.

MP Do you actually work on different paintings on the same day?

SS Yes. They help each other in the sense that they're not the same. And they keep me alive. I've made a big, big, important painting and I've been ready to stop work and I've been exhausted and then I've made a small painting that is more beautiful than the big painting. But I make the small painting with the ashes of my energy.

MP When you were played out?

SS When I was played out – or almost played out. That's the difference. There was still something there. And I was completely relaxed, and in a sense innocent. And this is something we haven't talked about yet: innocence. When I am painting a painting, I hope to reach innocence, that's to say a point where I really am free of all constraints including envy, ambition, avarice. I think it was Guston who said something about painting being a long preparation for a moment of innocence. I believe that. And when I'm working, I am only interested in this incredible thing I'm working at. As a poet would be, when he is closing in on a poem once he's located its emotional, intellectual resonance. Your self-conscious sense of yourself goes away and your inner innocence is allowed to come out.

MP Like a child?

SS Well, I would hope better than a child. I'm not a great admirer of children. I don't think they know more than a developed adult. People link innocence to childhood but I don't. I think it's a highly evolved state that doesn't have anything to do with childhood. I think childhood is a sort of bumbling state when you are learning and are extraordinarily egocentric.

MP In this innocence, do you think you're getting back to some kind of freedom?

SS Again, I'm not getting back to something. I mean I would have to say that my work, my whole life in art, is an attempt to correct something that can't be corrected. To put right something that can't be put right. In other words, my past.

MP You're talking about your childhood.

SS Yes, which was a nightmare. And of course in that sense it's pathetic, because it can't be put right.

MP What do you mean 'putting it right'? As it might have been?

SS Well, I don't know. I think it's neurotic. I don't think of it as constructive.

MP When you say putting it right, do you mean healing your wounds?

SS I try to heal something that's gone. It's like trying to make your leg comfortable, but your leg has already been amputated. So you might as well forget it. Well, you can't because it's neurotic.

MP But if you didn't have this feeling of loss …

SS I wouldn't be an artist. I've also come to another point in the last few years, where I feel it's not just a futile attempt, trying to put something right. It's not tragic and pointless. But when I talk about innocence – my notion of innocence is not something I try to get back to. It's something I try to go into. So I don't sense innocence as something that is lost. I think it is something I can achieve.

MP Is the desire to arrive at this state of innocence in any way connected to your disastrous childhood?

SS No. Because I never had that notion of innocence. I never experienced it as a child really. So my idea of innocence is something that allows me to make something that's not corrupt, not strategic – something that it is actually an act of love. That's what I mean. If you are capable of doing something for somebody else, and you did it for them because you just love and admire them so much, that is in a sense a kind of innocence.

MP Selflessness?

SS Yes. And that's part of my notion of innocence, when I reach that point in a painting.

MP You are out of yourself?

SS Yes. You are out of yourself and you are entirely unburdened. And that is really an exalting moment.

MP …and that is what you are working towards in your paintings?

SS No, I'm working towards making a painting, and that state is something which is known as a fringe benefit.

MP When you're lucky you get it.

SS Yes, exactly. I'm not working to get that sensation. I'm working on the painting. I'm not really thinking about that. I'm after the painting. I'm serving the painting. And then that comes into it and then I realize how extraordinarily fortunate I am to be making these paintings.

MP You have a very unusual sensibility for colours. You have an emotional range. You can make colour sing or make it bellow. You have a language of colour.

SS Colour to me is automatic. It's an unconscious thing.

MP It's your mother tongue.

SS It's a pure gift. I've never had to work on it or develop it or anything.

MP Like having perfect pitch. It's a rare gift.

SS I can just do it. I don't question it. I never have.

MP Are you particularly conscious of the way other painters use colour?

SS Well, there are moments you're very conscious of the way the painters you admire use colour. You only have to think of Van Gogh. Or Velázquez, say. I mean, the beautiful use of pinks and greys in his *Infanta*, the beautiful greys that make the dress look like a prison for the body that's inside it!

MP Do you ever have to combat your own gift for colour? I mean, I suppose it might lead to paintings that were merely soft and pleasing. Is that something you ever have to fight?

SS The tragedy of life is that things are the way they are to a large degree. And it's true that I couldn't make decorative paintings. I just couldn't. I think what you make is what you are. Especially after making it for thirty years. There's no faking it. You know, you could fake it for a couple of years perhaps. Maybe even ten.

MP No, I wasn't talking about faking. I was wondering whether the gift for colour ever took too dominant a role.

SS I don't really think about it like that. I just think that painting comes out of your character. It's really out of your character, out of what you are. It's a ruthless reflection of what you are, because it's made with the body and it's made with colour and with simple forms. There is almost no mediation, no way of obscuring the truth about you, your nature, because it is such a ruthless reflection of your nature. And I think I can't make decorative paintings because it's not in me. There's too much tragedy, too much feeling in me to be able to do something decorative. Then conversely, if you have the most benign will in the world, if you are not in some way a profound person, you won't be able to make a profound painting. And you could have a fabulous sense of colour, better than me, but you won't be able to do anything, because you are handicapped in fact by your character.

MP You do get people who are simply technically gifted and don't have much to convey.

SS Because people like that are not connected to tragedy – and I am very connected. I'm not saying I make tragic paintings, but I have a very strong sense of the tragic. My paintings are more than just tragic paintings. They're not defeatist at all – they've got a lot of energy in them. They are not resigned in the way that Rothko's are. I think Rothko's paintings don't convey the same energy. They're more like tablets.

MP In your paintings there's often the tension of conflicting forces.

SS Things gets pulled together and pulled apart. There is a lot of dynamic activity.

MP Do you actually go from one big painting to another?

SS Oh yes. Once I start painting I kind of go nuts.

MP So you might work on two big canvases?

SS Yes, I do anything and everything. Walk round them, dance with them. I hoist the canvases on nails in the wall so that I can move them up and down to any height I like. And if they don't come off the wall nice and easy, I just rip them off. I get really upset when they don't come off the wall. But there's no formula. I just do what I do. It's like picking up table-tennis balls off the floor during a game. You don't know how you are going to do it before you do it. You just do what's best at the time.

MP Where do you put your pot of paint?

SS I usually put it on the top of a ladder, in front of the canvas. Then I scrape out a brush and dip it in – but I don't clean the brushes. I just work in a big mess, as you can see. I mean, this whole area is a big mess.

MP Have you been filmed while painting?

SS I have been filmed once or twice.

MP Does it bother you to be watched while you're going nuts?

SS No, because what I say is this. I say: look, I will do my thing and you'll do your thing and I won't mind as long as you let me do my thing. So whenever people film me, I tell them I'm just going to paint and they can do whatever they like. If we make a deal like that it's OK. But I don't allow somebody to choreograph me or give me instructions.

MP I don't imagine that would work.

SS It would be ridiculous. But if somebody is standing there and they want to film, they can film. I remember one time somebody was filming and they got too close. And I don't know what he thought I would do, like just stand still and not turn around and smash into him, which is exactly what I did do. Because when I'm working I'm working. I could feel that he was very close but I didn't take it in because I'd made my deal and my painting was more important than his film. So, I just kind of knocked him out of the way. But he was OK. He recovered.

*

MP Do you have periods when you are not producing? Does that happen?

SS It doesn't happen very often. I really love to paint. It makes me really happy to make my paintings. It's joyous, but it's not just a happy-go-lucky relationship. I don't want to make it sound like it's all easy-peasy. It's not. It's exhausting, because you can't make paintings the way I do without getting exhausted. And they are not what you would call light, decorative paintings. You know they are quite sombre and soulful, so there is a seriousness to the whole activity.

MP Of course! But you don't sit in front of the blank canvas quaking and thinking, 'Oh my God, how am I going to start?'

SS It doesn't occur to me.

MP Right. But you already have an image building in your mind, while you are circling around the studio in the morning?

SS I'm thinking about what I might do and what I can do. I don't know quite how I make these decisions. But I can take something on one day that I can't another day. This painting over here for example is half of a painting. It's going to be a big diptych and I've been waiting for the right moment to do the other half. I've been trying to make that painting for a long time. And I need to make that painting on a day when that day is right for that painting. And it's going to come out of a mixture of will and inspiration. I might, for example, have to start work on a less ambitious painting and have the other painting just sitting there, propped up in the background. And when I get hot, then I just sort of turn on that painting – and bang!, it's finished. When it comes it always comes in a flash of insight.

MP Suddenly you know you've got it.

SS I'm ready for that one and I can do that one that day. Sometimes they kind of kick around for a while because they are more problematic. I'm not recognizing what they need.

MP It's a two-way relationship, of course.

SS It is a two-way relationship. But the whole theatre is made by me. What you're doing is you're giving an animated status to something that is inanimate. You're pretending it's got a personality. And you are suspending all disbelief. You're giving the painting a personality – a living, breathing personality. It's very peculiar. It makes suggestions about what it wants or might want.

MP It's not a mirror image, but it's nevertheless another sort of existence. Whether you make it or not, it's separate from you.

SS Yes. And of course, as you know, the title 'mirror' is very big in my work. It's one of my favourite titles. Because a mirror is also a bridge, a mirror is a bridge to a picture or a view. It's a bridge or a view or a window. And these are all the same. They're all methods of enlarging your view, allowing you to be perceptive. But the basic question of perception is interesting. If somebody says something to you and you paraphrase it, you're really being a mirror. And this can have a positive and a negative consequence, depending on what has been said.

MP Like I often paraphrase you as we're talking?

SS Well, in any kind of conversation, somebody says something and you paraphrase it in some way to demonstrate what it is, so they can see it outside themselves. You turn yourself into a mirror. And in those paintings I've made as diptychs, one side is a reflection of the other side. But the painting of course is also like a mirror. But it's a mirror with a lot of unpredictability, depending on how you make your paintings. I make mine where suggestions and accidents and strange possibilities are built into the process. Because I work without thinking really, when I start a painting.

MP And where do you start?

SS Anywhere. I start with a sketch. The sketches are very beautiful. They look like Matisses.

MP So this gives you your starting-point. They look like very delicate grids.

SS I draw them like this with a loose line and then I pretty much work to the way I've drawn.

MP So the first grid sets the whole thing up. But how do you decide what form the grid will take in the first place? Chance?

SS It's just intuition. In this painting, I made four divisions on the left but I could have made three or six. On the other grid it's five. I could have made seven. There are a lot of different things I could do.

MP This is a complicated picture, with a couple of panels inset. And the panels are disruptions? I mean, how did they come about?

SS Well, they come out of the idea of an inset, or the idea of a window or a passenger. A thing being contained or incarcerated, a thing like cargo being carried in the painting.

MP There are tiny threads of colour at the edges of some of the forms. Is that under-painting showing through? Like that little stitch of green.

SS Yes, and if you look closely, you see the red coming through the black and the yellow through the green. There is a lot of colour working its way to the front of the painting by bleeding through from the back.

MP Do you think your paintings offend sometimes? Does the confrontational side of your character, which you occasionally refer to, come through?

SS I think my paintings are really loved by a lot of people. And I don't just mean they like them. I know that a lot of people love them. I don't know whether people are offended by them.

MP Do you feel on the offensive when you are doing them?

SS Well, I feel that I am fighting for painting.

MP Do you feel that painting-painting is really under threat?

SS I think that many things in society are under threat. Painting is part of that, of humanistic values in general, at least the painting I am interested in. I'm certainly fighting for painting. I'm not in an easy-going coexistence with a lot of other art forms. And I don't pretend to be a liberal when it comes to art. I'm not a liberal. I'm an absolutely, implacably hard-line painter, against what I would describe as ironic, concept-based art. I am the enemy of that art. And there is nothing equivocal, conciliatory or diplomatic about that position at all.

MP Got it! And doesn't this very much tie in with your teaching at the Munich Art Academy?

SS My teaching is utterly connected to this defence of painting and this strong resistance to what I regard as vapid, concept-based art, that's not poetic, not emotional, not deep, but is careerist and opportunistic.

MP You believe in the traditional values of painting?

SS I never think of painting as traditional. It's been around for so long that I don't know whether one can call it traditional. Think about cave paintings! Would you call those traditional? I mean I think I am doing very much the same kind of thing. But it's true that people do sometimes connect me with the idea of tradition. When the German philosopher Juergen Habermass wrote his very beautiful text on me, he talked about how he thought I'd become a strange kind of traditionalist. But I myself don't think of painting as being traditional. I always think of it in terms of how dynamic it is and what its possibilities are.

MP Well, tradition is dynamic. That's the point, and you're continuing it!

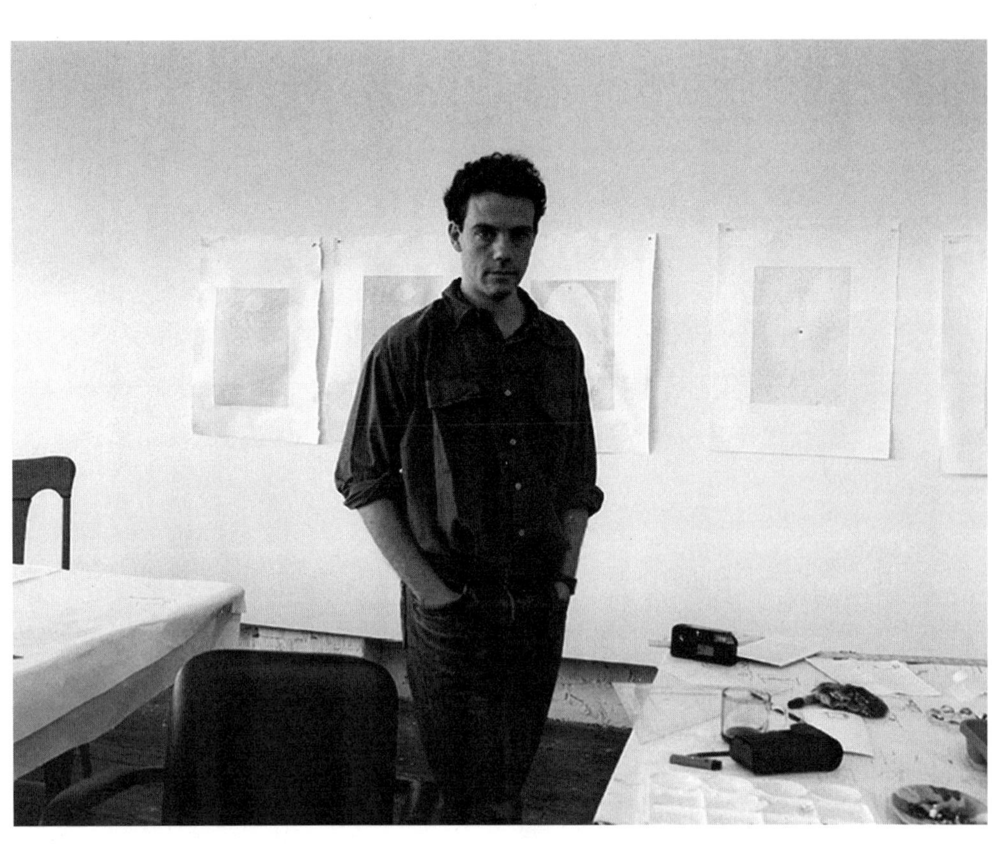

JOSÉ MARÍA SICILIA

BARBÈS PARIS 1989

Born in 1954 in Madrid, José María Sicilia is a leading representative of the group of Spanish artists which includes Miguel Barceló and Miguel Angel Campano and which came to international prominence in the early 1980s. Since 1982, Sicilia has had numerous one-man exhibitions in Europe and America. Paris has been his base for the last eight years, although he frequently spends long periods abroad. His development from a derisive, post-Pop treatment of mundane themes such as a vacuum cleaner to the highly sophisticated and persistently disturbing 'Flower' paintings of the past two years is as rapid as it is impressive. As Sicilia points out, these paintings question not only painting but the way we apprehend and name the outside world.

Equally rapid has been the young artist's success. Though not unhappy with the acclaim, Sicilia has accommodated it with a certain sardonic calm. He lives and works in a raw, colourful area of northern Paris, which at times exactly resembles an overcast Algiers. His studio there is large, light, decrepit and bare. Sicilia's brilliant reds and intense, velvet blacks take on a peculiar vividness against the crumbling grey walls. On first encounter, the artist speaks diffidently about himself and his work. Once a dialogue is under way, however, he becomes less guarded and his staccato way of talking is frequently interrupted by laughter.

'Paris suits me pretty well. I live fairly isolated, not going out much – you know, it's not the Paris where artists get together in cafés any more, and it's not a city where you find friends easily. But that's OK. It helps me to concentrate on my work. I've lived all over this city since I got here from Madrid in 1980. The area around Barbès where I have my studio now is basically made up of immigrants – Arabs, black Africans, Chinese – and it's full of racial tensions. But it's a

José-María Sicilia (1954–). *Art International*, Paris, Spring 1989.

fascinating mix, even if you do get the odd murder. It allows me to feel at home without being tied down. I spent a whole winter in New York working towards an exhibition I had there in December '87, and I really loved it. I loved it so much, I thought, well I'll just find a place and settle down. Then the thought of settling anywhere scared me, so I pulled up stakes and came back to Paris.

'This studio was a real find. It used to be a small factory where they worked leather. I took out half the upper floor, so that now I've got a ground floor and a mezzanine. I think of it a bit like a theatre because parts of it are lit by the skylight and others are in the shadow. The way the light plays on the walls is very important to me. Those crumbly, plastery surfaces have got paintings already in them. They're paintings in themselves.

'You just have to be receptive. Paintings make themselves, in spite of the artist! In the end, the whole space you work in becomes a painting. I keep nothing in the studio, not even a chair. With this kind of space I can have any number of canvases going at the same time. That's important for me, because I've been doing series of big panels, three metres high, that go together – they're not joined, but they're hung side by side with precise intervals separating them.

'I spend most of my time here. You know, after a while, the studio becomes an extension of your painting. It's a space you've created. And nobody comes and disturbs me here beyond the odd alley cat. When I go far away, it's usually to work in a different environment. I spent all last summer in Majorca, painting in a house surrounded by orange groves. I go back to Madrid often, too. I had a show there at the Palacio de Velázquez two years ago, and I realized I've remained quite attached to the place. I was able to develop there as an artist very freely – at least at the beginning. I started going to a drawing school for architects when I was twelve. It was fabulous. They let me do anything I wanted. Later on, I enrolled at San Fernando, the Madrid art school, and things weren't as easy. I didn't want to sit in the classroom – you can imagine, this was the mid-1970s in Spain – and after a while I was asked to leave.

'In painting I've always followed my own course, I think. There are lots of artists I admire. Malevich, Mondrian, de Kooning are obvious examples. Tàpies as well. But I think my *approach* to painting has been specifically different. All my paintings already existed, as far as I'm concerned. They were there before I started them. They're objects that I've recreated and transformed by the *intentions* I've given them. It's a game. It's like looking out of the window and transforming everything you see – but only minimally. You intervene as little as possible.

'But you question what you see. After all, there's the object itself and then there's the name we give it. I mean, if you look at that pot of paint on the floor there, it's a 'pot' – but it's also, perhaps, much more, that intense red colour. I like to work at that level, turning accepted meanings upside down to see what they look like. In one painting, for instance, I have this pure, slender, black shape that to me looks like a distant landscape. But if you take the same shape and hang it vertically it looks exactly like an African mask. There's another shape in one of my paintings that could be read as a doorknob or a huge, stylized comma. What I'm looking for beyond this kind of ambiguity, I think, is to paint something that will have a meaning for everyone – in so far as that can be done. Years ago, when I was in a kind of post-Pop phase, I suppose my images could be seen as making ironical comment. But that sort of painting has a limited lifespan. I wanted to make things that go beyond the moment.

'Tulips have provided me with a fantastic theme. I feel that through them I can say everything about painting, about line and colour – about the way each colour has to have its own space, and that the space you give it decides on its intensity. Obviously, the flowers in my paintings are not flowers. They are taken totally out of context and reinterpreted. I do that instinctively, I think, even with something like a line. A line is usually a frontier, a separation. I see it as a space. A meandering line can be a river, and then the surrounding layers of pigment become a landscape – without ever losing their identity as pigment.

'Everything one does is in relation to something that exists already. I'm extremely interested in matter – in the materiality of things. I'm always trying out new techniques, building up the layers of my paintings with different substances and different ways of applying and treating them. These are studio secrets – *la cuisine*, as the French call it – and I've found it's best to keep one's recipes to oneself, otherwise other artists might pick them up! What I'm looking for in those techniques is ways of creating new depths in the canvases, so that the eye suddenly plunges, or that what seemed to be there in fact isn't when you look closer. With that kind of many-layered paint surface, things appear and disappear the whole time, so that in the end you're left with a kind of mirage. You're not exactly sure what's there at all.

'That mystery is essential. It means that you've escaped from the history of art, and that formal preoccupations are no longer in control of the painting. But I'm usually trying to catch things that can never be caught in painting. Those are the things that tempt me most. Water's a good example. Think of all the layers, the transparent depths, when you look down into the bed of a river. Then think what water becomes when you solidify it into paint, with all its movement and reflections, and hang it vertically on the wall . . . It's impossible. It's a pure paradox.'

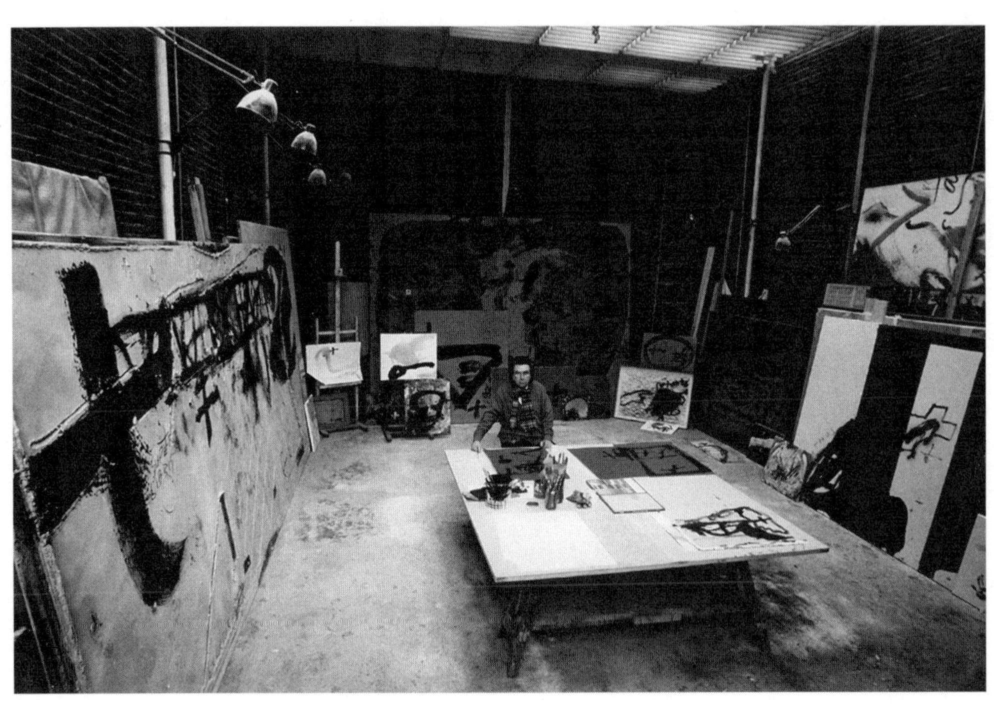

ANTONI TÀPIES

EL PUTXET BARCELONA 1988

In this, as in the previous interview with Sicilia, I used the technique I had recently grown fond of which consisted of removing all my questions and remarks, then editing, eliding and concentrating down everything the artist had said until the interview stood as a kind of essential statement. Pithy though the result may be and a welcome change from the meanderings of many question-and-answer exchanges, I now find that there is a voice missing. That's hardly surprising, since the missing voice is my own. But on these occasions I managed in a brief moment of selflessness to leave the reader entirely in the company of the persons they wanted to hear: the artists, whose work gave rise to their interest and curiosity in the first place and now, years later, to this book.

'Images of all kinds come into my paintings, for every conceivable reason. Recently I've had a good time painting things that are not considered very noble or fit for art. You know, things like feet that swell or are dirty or even smell bad. They're not heroic subject-matter, and that amuses me. But the underlying reason for them, I think, is my belief that you don't need 'important' subjects to communicate something important. It might sound pretentious, but I feel that these pictures communicate a sort of fundamental human solidarity. I like to see them as one way out of the mood of alienation hanging over us today.

'I don't like intellectualized explanations of my work. I try not to make them myself. But I do think a great deal about what I paint and what it means. My whole approach has been deeply influenced by modern science – by reading about the discoveries of great physicists like Heisenberg and Oppenheimer. Take matter, for example. I'm

Antoni Tàpies (1923–2012). *Art International*, Paris, Summer 1988.

fascinated by the way it can be dematerialized: once you break it down and analyse it, it turns into fields of energy, and these can be expressed numerically. I suspect that's why numbers appear in so many of my paintings. The basic concept of material breaking down into energy goes back to Pythagoras, but recent research has made it central to an understanding of our time. In the Middle Ages, matter and spirit were far more distinct, while with us all those distinctions have become much more complex and ambiguous. The old division between the observer and the thing observed, for instance, is not nearly as clear cut.

'What I find particularly exciting is how frequently modern scientific thought and spirituality coincide. Once again, the old divisions have been broken down. The parallels between our scientific discoveries and ancient oriental wisdom are another extraordinary phenomenon. Look how Oppenheimer quotes the Veda, for instance, or the way Niels Bohr refers to Taoism. Eastern philosophy has been the other great influence on my life and my art. I've never travelled in the Far East, but I've been collecting oriental art and studying eastern thought since the 1950s. I enjoy moving between different traditions and disciplines. Raymond Lulle, the great Spanish philosopher of the thirteenth century, has always been a model for me. He was truly encyclopaedic – both a poet and a logician, a scientist and a mystic.

'A tremendous variety of thoughts and memories and emotions goes into the making of a work of art, but art has no *intrinsic* value. As Tristan Tzara said, 'Art is not serious'. It's a game in which the rules have to be constantly reinvented. Art's real importance is to make us see afresh. We're far more conditioned than we realize into seeing things in a certain way. That's why children are so marvellous. They don't see through screens like us. They see the world directly.

'I decided to go against the grain, against convention, when I was very young. It wasn't just to be provocative and to stir things up. I grew up at a time when a very conventional notion of pictorial space was still current. It was still basically in the Renaissance tradition. Renaissance perspective shows man as a little machine in a void, with the finger of God directing everything. It reflects an overwhelming desire to dominate the world.

'That attitude belongs to another age now, I think. After all, there's a current of life that unites people. When I look at someone I'm talking to, I don't see that person in a void. The two of us are joined in a flow of curiosity or sympathy or whatever. Everybody, everything depends on other people, other things. There's no real separation, as I said, between the observer and the observed. We've been accustomed to a kind of dichotomy for centuries – to the supposed duality of mind and body, for instance. But it's a false dichotomy, of course, and it's harmful. It's basically unhealthy.

'You can tell all these things from painting, because painting contains a total vision of the world. There's been a terrific transformation in the way we look at everything. We realize now that instead of wanting to dominate other civilizations, we have to respect them. If we try to destroy them, we destroy ourselves. Pictorial space takes into account all these paradoxes and transformations. At least, in any philosophy it does!

'Things happen somewhat differently in the studio. What I find most difficult is getting started. Like a lot of other artists, I think, I spend a great deal of time wandering about, looking for a way to begin. I like using all kinds of materials – wood, cloth, string, wire, marble dust, earth – and so I usually keep lots of rubble and odds and ends around. At the engraving studio I go to in Barcelona they know the sort of things I'm interested in, and they collect all kinds of flea-market stuff for me. I take as much back with me as I can get past my wife – she tries to keep a little order in the studio – and I love riffling through it. That helps to warm me up. So does humping some of those heavy canvases around. I often have several paintings on the go at the same time. I don't work on them all at once, but just having them around helps suggest what I might do. I like making the various materials I use speak for themselves. After all this time, I know them better and can control them more. There's a painting I did recently that's made of varnish. The varnish was allowed to drip up to a certain point, but not beyond – otherwise it would have dripped right off, and there would have been no picture.

'The great thing about painting once you've begun is that one brushstroke leads to another. You either continue what you've done or amend it. In the end, the work itself takes over, and you don't even know you're working. Once one picture is under way, you see what you need to do on the others – change a colour, make this or that finishing touch. Most of the paintings start off as a series of drawings, but they're only roughed-out ideas. I often mix marble dust into the paint when I start – that makes the paint dry fast, so I have to get the picture quickly. I enjoy that kind of challenge. It means I have to get an image onto the canvas before it gets bogged down in thought.

'When I was a young artist, just starting out, I went to see Miró, whom I admired tremendously. We talked about painting and he said to me: 'Listen, everything's been done in art. What can you come up with that's new?' But I didn't allow that to discourage me. And I've been looking for a new language ever since.

'I'm always experimenting with new ideas and techniques, I'm always trying to surprise myself. If I'm surprised, it's more likely other people will be, too. The Tao says that once everybody agrees something is beautiful, it becomes ugly. The only way to communicate is by renewing everything you do. I'm almost always in a state of tension when I work, and sometimes a picture will come only after I've been at it for so long that I become very tired and my inhibitions break down. What keeps me excited is the thought that I might bring about the ultimate painting, the one I've been trying to do all my life – but never have donc.'

ACKNOWLEDGEMENTS

I feel very privileged to have worked once again with Gillian Malpass as my editor at Yale. This is the fourth book we have seen through the press together, and my admiration for her flair and her commitment increases each time.

I should like to thank Sophie Sheldrake for her unfailingly resourceful picture research and Paul Sloman, once again, for his crisp, stylish design. Frances Spalding and Andrew Lambirth kindly read the initial manuscript and made numerous valuable suggestions.

Among the many people who have helped me with their advice, support and above all their friendship, I should like to record my gratitude to: Jill, Clio and Alex Peppiatt, Alice Bellony, Thérèse Tigretti Berthoud, David and Laurence Blow, Erik Boursier, Kristy Brice, Ben and Louisa Brown, Don Bruckner, Charles and Natasha Campbell, David Clasper, Patrice and Mala Cotensin, Adrian and Jamie Dicks, Christopher Eykyn, Elena Foster, Colin and Sophie Gleadell, Claude Bernard Haïm, the late Philip Herrera, Henry and Alison Meyric Hughes, Natasha Isaacs, Christina, Richard, Ben and Zoe Ives, Janet Russo Jacklin, Glenys Johnson, María Luisa Lax, Jessica Lee, Robert and Mary Looker, Nicholas Maclean, Sandro and Fiamma Manzo, Pierre-Yves Mauguen, Thérèse Meier, Antoine Merlino, Piet Meyer, Serena Morton, Nunzio Massimo Nifosì, Clare O'Donoghue, Tomaso Radaelli, Chris and Carmel Shirley, Neil Sloman, Ian and Mercedes Stoutzker, Derick Thomas, Jorge Virgili, Ortrud Westheider and Thomas Williams.

ILLUSTRATIONS

Designed by Paul Sloman

Printed in China

Library of Congress Cataloging-in-Publication Data

Peppiatt, Michael.
Interviews with artists 1966-2012 / Michael Peppiatt.
p. cm.
Includes bibliographical references.
ISBN 978-0-300-17662-9 (cl : alk. paper)
1. Art, Modern–20th century. 2. Art, Modern–21st century. 3. Artists–Interviews. I. Title.
N6490.P386 2012
709.2'2–dc23

2011047461

A catalogue record for this book is available from
The British Library